Silver from Early Byzantium

The Kaper Koraon and Related Treasures

A WALTERS ART GALLERY
PUBLICATION IN THE HISTORY OF ART

Edited by Gary Vikan

Published in conjunction with the exhibition *Silver Treasure from Early Byzantium,* The Walters Art Gallery, April 18–August 17, 1986, and on the occasion of the *17th International Byzantine Congress,* Dumbarton Oaks/Georgetown University, August 3–8, 1986.

This publication was made possible by a grant from the National Endowment for the Humanities, a federal agency.

Designed by Shub, Dirksen, Yates and McAllister, Inc., Baltimore

Typeset by BG Composition, Inc., Baltimore

Printed by Collins Lithography, Baltimore

Produced by the Publications Department of The Walters Art Gallery

LIBRARY OF CONGRESS CATALOGING-IN-PUBLICATION DATA

Mango, Marlia Mundell.
Silver from early Byzantium.
(The Walters Art Gallery publications in art history)
"Published in conjunction with the exhibition Silver Treasure from early Byzantium, The Walters Art Gallery, April 18–August 17, 1986, and on the occasion of the Seventeenth International Byzantine Congress, Dumbarton Oaks/Georgetown University, August 3–8, 1986"—P.
Bibliography: p.
Includes index.
1. Silverwork, Byzantine—Exhibitions. 2. Orthodox Eastern Church—Byzantine Empire—Liturgical objects—Exhibitions. 3. Christian antiquities—Byzantine Empire—Exhibitions. I. Snow, Carol E. II. Weisser, Terry Drayman. III. Walters Art Gallery. IV. Title. V. Series.
NK7108.8.M36 1986 739.2′37495′07401526 86-50138
ISBN 0-911886-32-X (pbk.)

Library of Congress card number 86-50138
ISBN 0-911886-32-X

SILVER FROM EARLY BYZANTIUM

The Kaper Koraon and Related Treasures

Marlia Mundell Mango

With technical contributions by Carol E. Snow and Terry Drayman Weisser
Department of Conservation and Technical Research

PUBLISHED BY THE TRUSTEES
OF THE WALTERS ART GALLERY
BALTIMORE, MARYLAND 1986

CONTENTS

FOREWORD

Henry Walters would have been proud of this book and of the exhibition that inspired it. The Byzantine silver project highlights several aspects of importance to him as a collector/philanthropist: acquisition and preservation of an important artistic treasure; first-rate, innovative scholarship; and public presentation of a vital part of the permanent collection, enhanced by related material from other museums and private collections around the world.

Mr. Walters' reputation as one of the outstanding art collectors in our nation's history depends on both the extraordinary catholicity of his taste and the enviable perspicacity of his eye. Walters, collecting during the roughly three decades from 1897 to 1931, acquired numerous representative examples of the most sought-after styles and artists, such as Raphael, Manet, and Monet, but perhaps his greatest accomplishments as a collector were in fields in which interest had not yet peaked. Among these, his acquisitions of Byzantine and western European medieval art were particularly outstanding. For this reason, among American museums The Walters Art Gallery's holdings in these areas are second only to those of New York's Metropolitan Museum of Art. This is not simply a coincidence: Walters' only true rival as a collector in the Byzantine and medieval fields was J. Pierpont Morgan, most of whose great collection of medieval antiquities was given to the Metropolitan. Morgan and Walters also shared a passionate interest in the illuminated manuscripts of the Middle Ages and Renaissance. Here, too, it is worth noting that The Walters collection of illuminated manuscripts ranks second in the nation—after that of the Pierpont Morgan Library. The two great collectors seem to have been more rivals than friends. But this did not stop Morgan from having Henry Walters elected to The Metropolitan Museum's board, over which he presided for many years. Whether or not Morgan assumed that this election would ensure the future gift to the Metropolitan of Henry's collection we shall never know for sure. In fact, at his death in 1931 Henry Walters bequeathed his entire collection to the city of Baltimore, his birthplace, "for the benefit of the people." This was the origin of The Walters Art Gallery.

The Hama silver treasure, which is the central focus of this book and exhibition, was acquired by Henry Walters in 1929 and remains to this day the centerpiece of The Walters' Byzantine collection. In reuniting these silver objects with others from around the world we hope to have reconstructed a small but significant aspect of our collective artistic and cultural history. In publishing The Walters silver and a considerable amount of related material in a volume whose scholarly merit is of the very highest order we honor both Mr. Walters' legacy and the great scholarly tradition of The Walters Art Gallery that derives from its founding curators. In fostering an effective collaboration between scholar and conservator the Byzantine silver project pays homage to yet another important aspect of Walters' tradition, most significantly represented by Federico Zeri's catalogue of our Italian paintings, in which conservator Elisabeth Packard's contribution is so essential and conspicuous.

A precious aesthetic and spiritual heritage is transmitted by these silver liturgical vessels. Henry Walters was not the only collector to have been entranced by such objects. Important collections at Dumbarton Oaks in Washington, D. C., and at The Metropolitan Museum of Art testify to a shared fascination on the part of Mr. and Mrs. Robert Woods Bliss, J. Pierpont Morgan, and other distinguished collectors. The inherent attraction of these silver implements only increases with the passage of time.

Many individuals and institutions who contributed to this scholarly enterprise are acknowledged at appropriate points in this publication. Gary Vikan, The Walters' Assistant Director for Curatorial Affairs/Curator of Medieval Art, who first conceived the project, organized the exhibition, and edited this volume was indeed the mastermind behind the whole operation. Not the least of his accomplishments was securing the collaboration of Dr. Marlia Mundell Mango as Guest Curator and author. Dr. Mango, a leading authority in the field of Byzantine liturgical silver, had over the course of some years made startling discoveries concerning the Hama treasure and related works. These are published here for the first time. Her authorship of this catalogue provides The Walters with the most authoritative treatment of its Byzantine silver and, at the same time, offers to the world of scholarship a truly ground-breaking study. We are deeply grateful to her for this accomplishment.

To Walters conservators Terry Weisser and Carol Snow we extend thanks and congratulations for their vital contributions to this volume and to the exhibition. Their technical analysis described in Chapter III provides data essential to our understanding of the silver's fineness and means of manufacture that materially affects art historical conclusions. They are also responsible for the thorough cleaning and treatment of the Hama treasure prior to the exhibition.

The exhibition would never have been possible without the gracious collaboration of individuals and institutional lenders, to whom The Walters extends great appreciation: The Baltimore Museum of Art, Arnold Lehman, Brenda Richardson; the Museum of Fine Arts, Boston, Jan Fontein, Cornelius Vermeule; The Cleveland Museum of Art, Evan Turner, Patrick de Winter; the Menil Foundation Collection, Houston, Mrs. John de Menil, Bertrand Davezac, Mary Jane Victor; the Museum of the Church of St. Anne, Jerusalem, Pierre Bonnet, W.F.; the British Library, D. P. Waley, Yasin Safadi; the British Museum, David Wilson, I. H. Longworth; the Pierpont Morgan Library, Charles A. Ryskamp; The Metropolitan Museum of Art, Phillipe de Montebello, Margaret Frazer; Musée du Louvre, Hubert Landais, Catherine Metzger; the Virginia Museum of Fine Arts, Paul Perrot; the Pinacoteca, Siena, Professor P. Torriti, Dr. A. Bagnoli; The St. Louis Museum of Art, James D. Burke; The Toledo Museum of Art, Roger Mandle; the Honorable W. L. Eagleton, U. S. Ambassador to Syria; Dumbarton Oaks, Robert W. Thomson, Susan A. Boyd; the Textile Museum, Washington, D. C., Patricia L. Fiske; the Worcester Art Museum, James A. Welu, Tom L. Freudenheim; a private collection in Switzerland; and a private collection in New York.

I extend our gratitude to the National Endowment for the Humanities, which has provided generous grants in support of the Byzantine silver project: the exhibition, this publication, and an international scholarly symposium held at The Walters and Dumbarton Oaks in May, 1986. Indeed, it may fairly be said that all three components of the enterprise—exhibition, publication, and symposium (and, in addition, the public educational programs)—would not have been possible without the enlightened patronage of the National Endowment for the Humanities.

Robert P. Bergman
Director

PREFACE

It was in 1983, during the initial planning phase of the first-ever meeting in America of the *International Byzantine Congress*—cohosted by Dumbarton Oaks and Georgetown University, August 3–8, 1986—that the idea for this exhibition and accompanying catalogue began to take shape. Every host nation, since the first congress in Bucharest in 1924, had mounted a special exhibition of Byzantine or related art as a complement to the scholarly meetings. We in America were not about to become the first exception. But where would the exhibition take place? Dumbarton Oaks was clearly too small for such a show, and Georgetown had no appropriate site. The solution, of course, was The Walters Art Gallery. For not only is it close to Washington, D. C., it is a major museum in its own right, and has long enjoyed an international reputation for its superb Byzantine collection. As for the theme of the exhibition, this, too, seemed obvious: it would be Early Byzantine liturgical silver, that one very important category of Byzantine art wherein The Walters, and American museums generally—Dumbarton Oaks, The Metropolitan Museum, The Cleveland Museum—far surpass those of Europe. The stage was set. We would assemble these American collections around the Walters own silver for a special exhibition that would coincide with the congress and we would publish an accompanying scholarly catalogue. Though at that time, initiating the project as a member of the Administrative Committee of the congress and Senior Associate for Art at Dumbarton Oaks, I could not have guessed that I would oversee its culmination here at The Walters, as Assistant Director.

This catalogue was conceived with the goal of significantly advancing understanding and appreciation for The Walters' famous Hama treasure of Early Byzantine church silver specifically, and of Byzantine liturgical silver more generally. Thus from the outset, the highest standards were set both for its scholarship and for its physical appearance; each object would be illustrated at original size and in multiple views, each would be scientifically analysed to reveal its structure and metallurgical content, and the hallmarks, inscription, and profile of each would be rendered graphically by a professional draftsman. The goal was to make these important pieces of silver visually (in a sense almost physically) "available" to scholars, students, and the public in America and abroad who might otherwise never have the opportunity to visit Baltimore and to study the Hama treasure at first hand.

But much more than illustrations, tables, and drawings would be required for a first-rate publication. It was clear that the scholarship of Marlia Mundell Mango would be an essential ingredient as well, for just as plans for this publication were taking shape, she was completing a doctoral dissertation at Oxford University in which Walters and related Byzantine/Syrian church silver played a central role. Indeed, news was quickly spreading in the scholarly community of her startling discoveries, which seemed to confirm what some had long suspected—namely, that the four famous north Syrian silver treasures associated with Hama (at The Walters), Stuma (in the Archaeological Museum, Istanbul), Riha (mostly at Dumbarton Oaks), and Antioch (mostly in The Metropolitan Museum of Art) in fact comprised a single great hoard clandestinely excavated at or near Stuma, Syria, in the winter of 1908. She further discovered that the Byzantine village named in the inscriptions on some objects among this four-part treasure, *Kaper Koraon,* could be identified with a modern Syrian village, named Kurin, just a few kilometers from Stuma.

Dr. Mango's scholarship was clearly an ingredient essential to the success of this project, and one which could not have come at a more opportune moment. For on one hand, her discoveries gave shape to both exhibition and catalogue, and on the other, she was herself able to begin work as this book's author literally from the week of her dissertation defense in January 1985. The goal was to assemble from around America—and the world—as much as possible of the four-part "Kaper Koraon treasure," to publish an account of its ancient and modern history (Chapters I and II, respectively), to subject it to scientific analysis (Chapter III), and to catalogue its fifty-six individual pieces with the same comprehensiveness which otherwise would only have applied to the two dozen Hama objects at The Walters. But more than that, the exhibition (and catalogue) would include related Byzantine/Syrian church treasures (e.g., those associated with Beth Misona, Ma'aret en-Noman, *etc.*), representative domestic treasures of the region (e.g., the Daphne treasure), and contrasting treasures from elsewhere (e.g., that from Gallunianu, in northern Italy), all in order that the Koraon material might be presented in its fullest artistic and historical context. Thus, while Entries 1 to 56 are devoted to thorough publication of the reconstructed, four-part treasure, Entries 57 to 106 are assigned to more summary treatments of those related hoards and comparative pieces. Indeed, this even extends to objects in other media such as the Ibion papyrus inventory (Entry no. 91) which, although too fragile to travel from Oxford to Baltimore for the exhibition, nevertheless warranted publication in the catalogue because of its central importance to the question of Byzantine church treasures, and because of the frequency with which it is cited in other parts of the text.

By virtue of its broad scope and high scholarly standards, this volume transcends the bounds of a traditional exhibition catalogue; yet, it was produced on the schedule of an exhibition catalogue, in just one year. For this we are indebted to Marlia Mundell Mango, guest curator and author, whose tireless dedication to quality, seemingly boundless creative insights, and good humor under pressure never diminished over the last twelve months. This was a substantial achievement, and we are all deeply grateful to her for it.

But there were others as well upon whom the high quality and timely publication of this volume came to depend heavily over the last several months. Foremost among them are Joyce Duncan, Troy Moss, and Pam White of The Walters' Publication Department, Dianne Schuster and Carla Brenner of the Curatorial Division, and Librarian Muriel Toppan whose passion for accuracy is reflected on every page of this book, and whose truly amazing ability to "process words" (and images) kept author and editor from falling hopelessly behind schedule. The appearance of this volume owes much to the superb photographs of the newly cleaned Hama silver by Walters photographer, Susan Tobin, and to the many excellent graphic renderings of inscriptions, stamps, profiles, and maps by Michael Ingraham and Carol Snow. But especially, it is the work of designer Sherry McAllister who, though outside The Walters, became an integral member of a publication team working under considerable pressure. Also outside the Gallery are three other individuals who deserve special mention; they include Susan A. Boyd of Dumbarton Oaks, who played an important role in the formative stages of this project, Margaret Frazer of The Metropolitan Museum, who wrote Entries 85 and 86 and was always available by phone with last-minute photographs and helpful advice, and especially Cyril Mango, the author's husband, whose immense scholarship was brought to bear on many occasions, and who took special care with the Greek inscriptions in this volume, and with several important loans. We thank them all.

Conservation and scientific analysis have been essential components of this project from the beginning, and for both, a very special debt of gratitude is due to Carol Snow and Terry Drayman Weisser of The Walters' highly respected Department of Conservation and Technical Research. Their recent cleaning of the Hama pieces literally shines through in our published photographs, while their technical and scientific analyses are not only integral to each Kaper Koraon treasure catalogue entry, but they have been brought together, with a substantial analytical narrative, to form Chapter III. But most of all, it was the collective professional insight and enthusiasm that Carol and Terry brought to Byzantine silver that has meant so much to the success of this project.

For the exhibition and related events, special acknowlegement is due to Diane Stillman, Director of Education, for the professionalism and imagination she brought to the public programs, and to Leopoldine Arz and Elizabeth Binckley of The Walters' Registrarial Department for the logistical skill with which they arranged the many foreign and domestic loans.

In the installation proper, our goal was to create something of the spiritual power of Byzantium, and something of its physical "reality"—both in order to provide context and meaning for art objects which are more or less unfamiliar to most of our public. We did this primarily in two ways: through a twelve-minute audiovisual presentation based on Byzantium's greatest surviving church, Hagia Sophia, and through the construction, in our gallery space, of an historically accurate replica of a sixth-century Byzantine/Syrian church sanctuary of the sort in which the Kaper Koraon treasure would once have been dedicated. For the former, special thanks are due to Professor Thomas Mathews of New York University, for help with on-site photography in Istanbul, to Professor Miloš Velimirovic of the University of Virginia, who provided us with appropriate Byzantine music, and to Michael Gibbons, who coordinated production on behalf of BGW and Associates of Baltimore.

For all of us, the building of a Byzantine sanctuary was a special adventure, with many challenges—from fiberglass domes, to clay column capitals, to styrofoam arches. Marlia Mango, with substantial advice from French archaeologist Jean-Pierre Sodini, provided the plan; Elroy Quenroe, our exhibition designer, gave it shape and ingeniously fit it into our available space; and John Klink, head of our Installation Department, built it, drawing on the skills and imagination of Eugene Gregorio and Patrick Lears. To this adventurous team of "Byzantine builders" we owe special thanks, as well as to Walters graphic designer Jeff Wyrick, for the skill and creativity he brought to the exhibition graphics and to our poster. Each for a time immersed himself in Byzantium—as, in one way or another, we all have. Thank you. And thank you to the National Endowment for the Humanities, without whose support this all would not have been possible.

Gary Vikan
Assistant Director for Curatorial
Affairs/Curator of Medieval Art

INTRODUCTION

My work on the Kaper Koraon and related treasures started as part of the research for a doctoral thesis (*Artistic Patronage in the Roman Diocese of Oriens, 313–641 AD*) submitted to Oxford University in 1984. This study of the mechanisms of patronage analyzed the types of people and funds responsible for the creation and purchase of buildings, objects, and books within a prosperous part of the Eastern Roman Empire. Within this broad inquiry, silver played an important part in establishing patterns of patronage. Historical sources revealed that while this metal was not coined for commercial purposes in the East in this period, large numbers of manufactured silver objects circulated widely. Recovered objects themselves provided important data: individual prices can be established from weights; dates are provided by imperial stamps; and patrons are identified by inscriptions. To arrange all this information into a coherent scheme, certain questions had to be answered: what was church, as opposed to secular or domestic, silver; what was destined for important urban patrons and what was intended for village use; and what was the original size of each treasure?

With regard to ecclesiastical silver objects, inscriptions and archaeological contexts proved that nearly all the surviving and "documented" (i.e. inscribed) treasures from the Early Byzantine period fell into the category of donations to, or property of, village churches. (Notable exceptions include objects long preserved in the Vatican, such as the cross of Justin II.) Not all these "village" objects are, of course, of equal quality and some treasures are more extensive than others, and weights as an index to prices and value have to be considered. Within this context, the Kaper Koraon, or Hama treasure, mostly now in The Walters Art Gallery, was an important subject of investigation. Although it was said to have been found at, or near, the city of Hama (ancient Epiphaneia), the name of Kaper Koraon inscribed on several of its objects was that of a *kome* (or "village"). Furthermore, while it was known to contain some two dozen objects, its size could have been at least twice that, as it had long, albeit loosely, been associated by scholars with the Stuma, Riha, and Antioch treasures, all found in the same general area and at the same time as the Hama treasure. No truly comprehensive examination of the discoveries of these four treasures and their subsequent dispersals had yet been undertaken. Although much work has now gone into this research, nearly every query made has met with a response which held the promise of further evidence, and the case made here that four treasures are one may one day be further strengthened.

Against such an analytical background, it is highly interesting to see assembled in the exhibition which accompanies the publication of this volume so many Early Christian church treasures that are documented as such—that is, by inscriptions or archaeological contexts. The focus of the exhibition and catalogue is the reconstructed Kaper Koraon treasure, composed of objects from four hoards (Hama, Stuma, Riha, and Antioch), but other silver treasures have been selected, for comparative purposes, for inclusion in the catalogue, although not all could be present in the exhibition. The word "treasure" applied to the objects catalogued here is, literally, the equivalent of the Greek word *keimelion,* engraved on some objects, such as the paten no. 75, which is inscribed "Treasure of the most holy church of the village of Sarabaon." In this case, the "Sarabaon Treasure" is composed of only one object.

Eight other treasures contain objects inscribed with a dedication mentioning a specific church and/or place: those of St. Sergios of Kaper Koraon, St. Sergios of Beth Misona, the Theotokos of Phela, St. Symeon, St. Stephen (twice), St. George of Čaginkom(?), and the church at Gallunianu. In addition to these "named" treasures, there is the Homs Vase, which, like the Ghiné spoon referred to in Entry no. 18, has sacred decoration and was found inside a church. As far as can be ascertained, all these "treasures" are to be associated with villages rather than cities. Eight treasures are Syrian, one Armenian, one Italian, and all are dated between the very late fifth and seventh centuries. It has not been possible to be comprehensive in the coverage, and notable omissions from this list include the fourth-century Durobrivae treasure from Britain, and the sixth-century treasures from Luxor in Egypt and Sion/Pharroa in Lycia—all likewise from villages. Two other important kinds of church "treasures" from both city and village churches—silk textiles and books—are included, as are church inventories of *keimelia.*

Unlike the Ghiné spoon, none of the church silver treasures included here was recovered in a controlled excavation. The *Modern History* of the Kaper Koraon treasure (Chapter II) illustrates the laborious manner in which these treasures must be restored to their original contexts. By way of a contrast, a "proper" treasure, namely one composed of several pieces, discovered in the course of a controlled and recorded archaeological excavation has been included here. This is the fourth-century Daphne treasure which, while contemporary with the oldest extant church treasure from Durobrivae, predates the others discussed here by two centuries. But, as it was uncovered in a house in that affluent suburb of Antioch, it too is literally a "Syrian village treasure." Three other domestic silver treasures are partially represented here, together with a single plate, to illustrate the continuity of certain types of secular silver and the introduction into domestic plate of Christian symbols or themes.

In pursuing the subject of the Kaper Koraon and related silver treasures over the past six years, I have received much help from many individuals who are extended gratitude below. I should like, however, to express special recognition of the substantial contribution made to this catalogue by my husband, Cyril Mango, who took time to accompany me twice to Kurin, Stuma, and Riha, as well as to nearly all the museums whose objects are included here. Only his systematic help in recording inscriptions, stamps, measurements, and descriptions on the spot, and his subsequent advice on many aspects of the text, allowed me to complete my composition of this catalogue in one year.

Marlia Mundell Mango
Guest Curator

Acknowledgments

For their generous response to numerous requests over a long period, I should like to thank in particular Miss Susan A. Boyd of Dumbarton Oaks, Dr. Margaret Frazer of The Metropolitan Museum of Art, and Dr. Catherine Metzger of the Musée du Louvre, as well as those who facilitated the examination and documentation of objects, in the following places: in Baltimore (The Walters Art Gallery), Mr. Richard Randall (1981, 1984); Bern (Abegg Stiftung), Dr. Alain Gruber, Dr. Karel Otavsky; Cleveland (The Cleveland Museum of Art), Dr. Patrick de Winter; Istanbul (Archaeological Museum), Dr. Nuşin Asgari; Jerusalem (St. Anne's), Fr. A. Bouwen (1983); London (British Library), Dr. V. Nersessian; (British Museum), Mr. David Buckton, Mr. Christopher Entwistle; Newcastle-upon-Tyne (The University), Mrs. Lynn Ritchie; New York (The Metropolitan Museum of Art), Mr. Richard Stone, Mr. Edmund Dandridge; Paris (Musée du Louvre), Dr. F. Baratte, Dr. D. Benazeth, Mme Y. Cantarel-Besson; (Musée du Cluny), Dr. J.-P. Caillet, Dr. F. Joubert; (Bibliothèque Nationale), Dr. I. Aghion, Dr. M. C. Hellmann; Princeton (Princeton University), Ms. Shari Taylor; Siena, Professor P. Torriti; (Pinacoteca), Dr. A. Bagnoli; Richmond (Virginia Museum of Fine Arts), Dr. Pinkney Near; Worcester (Worcester Art Museum), Miss Sandra Petrie; Washington, D.C. (Dumbarton Oaks), Miss Carol Moon, Mrs. Charlotte Burk.

I should also like to thank the Director of Antiquities of the Republic of Turkey for granting me a permit to study silver objects in the Archaeological Museum in Istanbul.

In tracing the modern histories of the silver treasures, I profitted from the generosity of the directors and curators of the museums in Baltimore, Bern, Cleveland, Istanbul, Jerusalem, London, New York, Paris, and Washington, D.C., named above, who allowed me access to museum records. I should also like to thank the following individuals for furnishing me with essential information. I am particularly indebted to Dr. Denys Pringle for locating and transcribing for me the important documents concerning the Hama treasure that are preserved at St. Anne's in Jerusalem. For providing me with correspondence of his father, Royall Tyler, concerning the Riha treasure, I am very grateful to the Honorable William Tyler, and for helping to dispel certain claims recently made about the Antioch Chalice, I thank Sir Stephen Runciman, Mrs. Laskarina Bouras, and Mrs. Vasiliki Pennas. In pursuing the treasures to Syria itself, in 1982 and 1985, I, and my husband who accompanied me, received much kind help which I am very pleased to acknowledge here. The Honorable and Mrs. William Eagleton extended generous hospitality in Damascus, as well as information about the "long lost" Bosworth chalice of the Hama treasure. Dr. Kasim Tweir, of the Department of Islamic Arab Antiquities, Damascus Museum, receives special thanks for the help in attempting to trace the Phela and Beth Misona treasures, an inquiry aided likewise by Dr. Bachir Zouhdi, curator of Syrian Antiquities of the Classical Eras, of the same museum. In Aleppo, I wish to thank Mr. Krikor Mazloumian for his help and useful recollections and Père Joseph Kouchakji who spoke informatively of his elder cousins who had owned the Antioch treasure. I am grateful also to Mr. George Antaki for sharing his personal knowledge of the history of the Antioch Chalice and for making certain local inquiries on my behalf. I should also like to thank Mrs. George Antaki and her aunt, Mrs. Missakkel, for their interest and help. We were greatly aided during our trip to Syria in 1985 by Dr. Georges Tate, M. Jean-Luc Biscop, and M. Jean-Pascal Fourdrin, who accompanied us to Kurin and nearby sites and who introduced us to Père Kouchakji and Mr. Guillaume Poche who kindly answered questions about the silver treasures. I am grateful also to Miss Mai Touma who first encouraged me to pursue my subject in Aleppo. For help with our trip to Syria in 1982, and to Italy in 1985, we are thankful to Miss Joanna Sturm and to Professor Mara Bonfioli, respectively. Mr. Robin Symes and Mr. Nicholas Koutoulakis kindly provided information and photographs of silver objects, and Mr. Michel André patiently answered questions about objects restored by the family firm of his grandfather, Léon André. I am also indebted to Professor Robert Thomson for the translation of the inscription on the Divriği cross and for discussing it with me. And, as so often before, Dr. Sebastian Brock generously helped me with Syriac subjects. Dr. Patricia Crone very kindly reviewed the Arabic spellings used here and her recommendations have, with a few exceptions (e.g., Ma'aret en-Noman) been followed. For help with other points I should like to thank Dr. Aslihan Yener, Dr. Denis Feissel, Professor Jean-Pierre Sodini, Mr. Michael Vickers, and Mr. Geoffrey House. For general encouragement and help I am grateful to Professor R. M. Harrison, Professor André Guillou, Professor Philip Grierson, Professor Ihor Ševčenko, and, especially, Professor Erica Dodd.

CHAPTER I:

THE STUMA, RIHA, HAMA, AND ANTIOCH TREASURES: THEIR ANCIENT HISTORY

I. The Stuma, Riha, Hama, and Antioch Silver Treasures: Their Ancient History

Early Byzantine Church Treasures

All evidence suggests that Early Christian churches were, quite literally, treasure houses. Emperor Constantine confiscated the pagan temple treasures in 311,[1] and thereafter much wealth, as Philip Grierson has observed,[2] was deposited in churches throughout the Empire, as if in banks. Constantine gave the Lateran Church in Rome 10,875 pounds of silver (312);[3] Justinian embellished Hagia Sophia in Constantinople with 40,000 pounds of silver (537);[4] and Chosroes II removed from the churches of Edessa 112,000 pounds of silver (622).[5] A "banking" tradition persists in cult buildings from the Roman Temple of Saturn,[6] through the cathedral churches of early Byzantium, to the Great Mosques.[7] In addition to storing large quantities of precious metals, Byzantine cathedral churches were designated by a law of 545 as the places where weights and measures used in imperial taxation were to be kept.[8]

That churches acquired some treasure with institutional church funds is suggested by recorded clerical shopping expeditions from Flaviopolis and Sykeon (in western Asia Minor) to Constantinople;[9] from Palestine to Alexandria;[10] and from villages of the diocese of *Oriens* to Edessa,[11] in order to buy church silver, textiles, and books. Silver objects presented not with personal dedications but with the formula *epi* ("under") a certain clergyman (see Entry no. 65) may have been such acquisitions. But, as their institutional funds derived from a combination of small grants, rents from property, and private donations, churches necessarily relied heavily on the last source for entire church buildings as well as for various furnishings.[12] A law of 321 allowed churches to inherit property, money, buildings, and objects.[13] Some treasures were directly solicited from the public. St. Demetrios himself is said to have issued instructions concerning the replacement to his shrine of silver lost in a fire (582–610).[14] At Antioch, Patriarch Severus spoke to his congregation on behalf of St. Drosis to obtain silver for her ciborium (516),[15] and at Edessa, the archbishop asked the public to contribute towards a silver eucharistic "litter" (*lektikion*).[16] Other treasures, often exceeding the concrete needs of a church, were spontaneously donated by the faithful—to fulfill a vow, to obtain salvation, in thanksgiving for a cure, for a military victory, *et cetera*. Once presented, moveable church property—"gold it may be, and silver and garments and slaves"[17]—remained inalienable. Laws forbade the selling of sacred utensils (*skeue timia;* in 544) and "objects donated by persons in gratitude for their restoration to health" (see Entries nos. 71, 72).[18] Exceptions were the ransom of prisoners of war ("where the souls of men are released from death and chains by the sale of inanimate vessels") and special needs, such as famine and debt.[19]

From texts such as inventories (see Entry no. 91), and extant objects such as those included in this catalogue, one can form an idea of what precious treasures were presented to Early Christian churches. The most complete texts are those in the *Liber Pontificalis* of Rome, which lists donations of property and produce, as well as precious metals and textiles—made mostly by emperors and popes—to Italian churches. The evidence for the Eastern Empire is more scattered but is, on occasion, as detailed. The greatest amounts of precious metal (especially silver) belonging to churches took the form of furniture revetments—for the altar, ciborium, *synthronon,* chancel screen, ambo, and doors. A ciborium four meters square in plan, having four columns five meters high, and a dome, all revetted in silver one millimeter thick, can be reconstructed at a weight of approximately 2000 pounds.[20] (Procopius' cumulative figure of 40,000 pounds of silver in Justinian's Hagia Sophia is easily verified by such calculations.) Silver revetments are attested in other Late Antique cities, including Rome, Ravenna, Thessalonike, Antioch, Edessa, Arabissus, and Jerusalem, and, to judge from the large Antioch cross (no. 42), were to be found in villages as well.

Portable objects in precious metal took four main forms: liturgical vessels (*leitourgika skeue*), *ex-votos* (*psychika* or *charisteria*), lighting equipment, and secular silver, donated for its metal value. Other precious donations included textiles, especially silks, and books (see Entries nos. 87–91). Liturgical and "paraliturgical" objects (i.e., chalices, patens, ewers, strainers, spoons, "processional" crosses, fans, *etc.*) used in the performance of the eucharistic rite and other liturgies, comprise most of the Entries included in this catalogue. The Italian inventories contain four essential liturgical objects—paten, chalice, *ama,* and *scyphus*[21]—with the latter two being replaced in village treasures by ewers and amphorae (see Entries nos. 14, 37, 91). St. Pancratius outlines the fundamental equipment of all Early Byzantine churches as two sets of silver *diskopoteria* (paten and chalice sets), two wooden crosses, and scriptural texts.[22] Justinian, Theodora, and their entourage are seen presenting to St. Vitale at Ravenna a paten, chalice, cross, censer, and book, all in gold and silver, and Chosroes II sent to the Church of St. Sergios at Rusafa a paten, chalice, cross, censer, and curtain, all in gold.[23]

While many of these utilitarian vessels were themselves *ex-votos*—presented to the church "in fulfillment of a vow" or by some other formula—many non-utilitarian inscribed crosslets (*stauria*), plaques, and plaquettes were offered and displayed as personal mementoes (see Entries nos. 9, 10, 71, 72). Lighting equipment accounted for a weighty part of precious (and non-precious) metals donated to churches, as attested by the 174 and 120 lights given, respectively, to the Lateran Basilica and to S. Lorenzo in Lucina in Rome.[24] Even a country church near Tivoli had thirty lights, six of them in silver (see Entry no. 91). Yet, only four lighting devices (nos. 11–13, 33) are preserved among the objects of the reconstructed Kaper Koraon treasure. Silver and gold domestic items were also donated to churches, not just as *ex-votos* (e.g., the "armlets, bracelets, necklaces," *etc.,* left at the Holy Sepulchre in Jerusalem and mentioned *ca.* 570),[25] but also for their monetary value. The treasure of 540 pounds of domestic plate given to two churches by the bishop of Auxerre in the early seventh century was still in their possession in 1297.[26] Similar "hoardings" are suggested by objects in the Numidian inventory (see Entry no. 91) and by the mirror and some spoons in the reconstructed Kaper Koraon treasure (nos. 22, 48–56). Domestic items could also be recycled for church use, as were the silk garments and "many pounds of silver" given to churches of Constantinople by Sosiana in the mid-sixth century.[27]

Inscribed Dedications

Inscribed dedications allow one to put objects in their proper context. While contemporary building, pavement, and book (nos. 88, 89) dedications tend to be lengthy, those on the silver objects catalogued herein are terse, although exceptions elsewhere on gold and bronze offerings are well known.[28] The key elements included the name(s) of the donor, the recipient (occasionally with the location of his church), and the reason(s) for the dedication.

Although a church building (*ekklesia, ecclesia*) is specifically mentioned in a few cases (nos. 75, 79), the object is more often presented directly, for example, to the Theotokos (nos. 62, 64, 65), to St. Sergios (nos. 3, 4, 7, 11, 12, 14, 26, 28, 57, 60), to St. Symeon (no. 71), to St. Stephen (nos. 75, 83) or to St. George (no. 76), while dedications to the Lord Himself are cloaked reverentially in liturgical formulae (nos. 30, 42, 67, 74). This personal rapport with the saint is striking. Indeed, a law of 545 dealing with "Legacies bequeathed to God" personalizes the transaction by making of God or the saint a juridic "person."[29] Thus it is the saint, not the church, who is "appointed heir" to the property donated, which then becomes, for example, "the ewer of St. Sergios" (no. 14). Moreover, a procedure is set out by this law to determine in doubtful cases which of the saint's shrines should inherit. It would seem that the saint or martyr himself "resides" in his original shrine or *martyrion*—Demetrios at Thessalonike, Thekla at Seleucia Isauriae, Sergios at Rusafa, George at Lydda, *et cetera*—where one may visit him or her to pay homage and request favors. But, one may also enjoy the convenience of calling on the saint at a "branch office,"[30] that is, at a church dedicated to the saint in one's own city or village where, through the presence of his relics or by some other agency, the saint also dwelt, literally, "in part." This is implicit in dedications to "St. Sergios of the village of Kaper Koraon" (nos. 3, 28; also nos. 11, 12, 14), to "St. Sergios of the village of Beth Misona" (no. 60), to "the Theotokos of the village of Phela" (nos. 64, 65), and to "St. George of Čaginkom" (no. 76)—just as in an earlier period one made offerings to "Zeus of Beth Mares."[31] One such Christian "branch office," that built to St. Sergios in the Singar Mountains around 565 by the bishop of the Arabs in Persia, was even stated to have been a replica (i.e., architectural copy) of the original church at Rusafa.[32]

A law of 538 observes that "many persons build churches in order to perpetuate their names,"[33] and the same could be said regarding the donations of objects to those churches. Yet the donor would probably protest otherwise, as did Chosroes II on the gold paten he offered to St. Sergios in 592, that "the things that are written on this paten are not for the sight of men."[34]

Although Chosroes proceeded to explain in great detail the "graces and benefits" he had received from the saint, most donors made use of short, standard formulae to state the reasons for their dedications. Bequests made by or for the deceased were given "in (his) memory" (*hyper mnemes;* no. 4) or "for the repose (of his soul)" (*hyper anapauseos;* nos. 15, 33–38, 41, 64, 81); explicitly stated in one case as *hyper anapauseos psyches* (see Entry no. 64), such offerings were perhaps the *psychika* mentioned in the Miracles of St. Thekla. Offerings on behalf of the living were made "for (their) salvation" (*hyper soterias;* nos. 1, 2, 9, 10, 15, 33–38, 41, 61–64), which is explicitly stated elsewhere as *hyper soterias zonton.*[35] An object could also be given in atonement for sins (*hyper apheseos hamartion;* no. 23). Those gifts presented (*prosenegkan*) "in thanksgiving" were inscribed *eucharistion, eucharisterion,* or related phrases (nos. 62, 71, 76) and called, in one source, *charisteria*[36]—acknowledgments of a grace received. According to one interpretation,[37] the "vow" (*euche*) referred to in the frequently used phrases *hyper euches* ("in fulfillment of [or for] a vow") and *euxamenos* ("having vowed") was not a "promise," as one might say today, but a "request"—that is, the gift offered was a "ticket" bought in advance to receive the desired favor, even if the favor was not delivered until later. (If so, such a practice directed toward the Almighty and His saints in a sense paralleled the widespread contemporary "bribery" of state officials in order to obtain favors.) On the cross he sent to Rusafa in 591, Chosroes II explained that "if our knights slay or capture Zadesprain, we will send a golden cross . . . to (St. Sergios') temple."[38] Similarly, on the paten he offered the following year he inscribed ". . . I asked and promised that if Shirin conceives in her womb, I would send to your holy house the cross that is worn by her." The gift, therefore, embodied the vow. One Hama paten (no. 6) is labelled "Vow of the most saintly Archbishop Amphilochios," and a chalice (no. 3), "Vow of Pelagios Basianos. Treasure of St. Sergios . . . "—there is, in other words, an implied equation of "vow" and "treasure" (the object itself).

The Village of Kaper Koraon

The Church of St. Sergios of the village of Kaper Koraon was the recipient of up to fifty-six as yet extant silver objects, presented mostly between 540 and 640 (nos. 1–56).[39] Identified here with the modern village of Kurin, the Early Byzantine village of Kaper Koraon (therefore) stood above the plain of Chalcis to the east, and was surrounded on its other three sides by extensions of the limestone massif of Belus: to the north, the Jabal Barisha; to the west, the Jabal Wastani (behind which flows the Orontes); and to the south, the Jabal Zawiyya (fig. II.1). Located in or near what was known as the *Kynegia chora,* or "hunting country,"[40] the village was encircled by the ancient cities of Antioch, Seleucia ad Belum, Apamea, Chalcis, Beroea, and Cyrrhus. The prosperity of the limestone massif area in the Early Byzantine period, which is attested by the numerous well-constructed villages (the largest being Kaper Barada, Kaper Pera, and Taroutia Emporon; fig. II.1) which still stand there today, has been attributed by Georges Tchalenko to the production of olive oil for export.[41] Although this theory of a "monocultural" economy has recently been challenged,[42] olives and grapes were certainly important crops on the plateau, just as cereals were in the plain. It should be noted also that the cultivation of the silkworm became an important source of wealth in the East in the later sixth century.[43] Mercantile ties between this region and other parts of the Empire have been deduced from the series of epitaphs of Syrians from named villages in the region of Antioch, Apamea, and Chalcis who died in Rome, Aquileia, Salona, Concordia, Trier, Pannonia, Odyssos, Thrace, and Cilicia.[44] Although set among fertile fields, Kaper Koraon may also have been the center of a ceramic, glass or metal industry, as the postulated Syriac version of its name, Kepar Kurin, translates literally "village of kilns."[45] Although geographically closer to both Seleucia ad Belum and Chalcis, Kaper Koraon was apparently under the administrative jurisdiction of Antioch,[46] and its church was therefore directly subject to the archbishop (i.e., patriarch) of Antioch.

No ecclesiastical architecture survives at Kurin today, but the old mosque in the center of the village (fig. II.6) is built of ashlar blocks taken from an Early Byzantine building, judging from its reused fragments of sculpture. Indeed, some of these carved blocks may have formed part of a large volute moulding of the type that flanks many north Syrian church doors and windows.[47] Other buildings in the center of the village incorporate some Early Byzantine walls, as well as much reused masonry, including door lintels and jambs, and at least two ashlar vaulted cisterns remain intact (fig. II.7). The antique limits of the large village are set on the west by a necropolis composed of a number of rock-carved tombs, one of which has an Ionic column at the entrance. There is, unfortunately, little evidence by which to judge whether the domestic architecture of Kaper Koraon was on the more modest scale of that predominating in much of the northern limestone massif,[48] or on the grander scale of that to the south (i.e., the Jabal Zawiyya).[49] But the epigraphically attested presence among its inhabitants of a person of the eminence of the highly-titled Megas (see Entry no. 37) would ensure at least one substantial residence there in the 570s, and a tribune/*argyroprates* (no. 33) and a *magistrianos* (no. 1) may likewise have lived in fairly elaborate houses.

Over the decades when these silver objects were presented to its church, the affluent region of Kaper Koraon produced men of position and influence, such as John Scholastikos, patriarch of Constantinople (565–577), born at Sarmin (fig. II.1),[50] Pantaleon, a *commerciarius* at Kaper Pera (595/6),[51] as well as Megas, curator of an imperial domain. Prominent spiritual forces at the time included Symeon Stylites the Younger, presiding on the nearby Wondrous Mountain (541–591), and Symeon the Fool, active at Emesa/Homs (*ca.* 550).[52] An important relic of the True Cross was venerated at Apamea, where it worked a celebrated miracle in 540, and whence it was removed (in 566 or 574) to Constantinople by command of Justin II (see Entry no. 3). Further to the east, the important pilgrimage site of Rusafa, seat of St. Sergios, patron of the church of Kaper Koraon, was the beneficiary of donations from Anastasius, Justinian, Theodora, and Chosroes II.[53] While the monasteries northeast of Apamea had been noted for their orthodoxy earlier in the century, by the 530s there was apparently an infiltration of Monophysite monks, whose abbots signed documents pertaining to the Tritheist Quarrels in 567–569.[54]

There is nothing among the Hama treasure objects to indicate whether the church at Kaper Koraon was Chalcedonian or Monophysite in the sixth and seventh centuries. Moreover, Downey's suggestion that the inscriptions on the Antioch plain chalice and cross (nos. 41, 42) reflect "Monophysite" and "Chalcedonian" usage, respectively, is unjustified (see their Entries). Among the Riha treasure donors, Chalcedonian Orthodoxy would have been required of Megas, the highly-placed official serving Emperor Maurice, whose cousin Dometios was charged with the persecution of eastern Monophysites.[55]

During this period, *circa* 540–640, Kaper Koraon may have suffered in the military campaigns of 540 and 573—even if not in the Persian and Arab conquests of the 600s and 630s (see below). In 540 the Persian army, led by Chosroes I, marched from Beroea, where it extorted 2,000 pounds of silver, to Antioch, which it sacked and stripped of "enormous wealth." It then proceeded via Daphne to Apamea where, having entered and looted the city of "not just a 1,000 pounds of silver, nor even 10,000 pounds of silver, but all (its) gold and silver," it moved on (possibly skirting Kaper Koraon) to Chalcis, where it obtained an additional 200 pounds of gold (fig. II.1).[56] Thirty-three years later (i.e., in 573) the Persians, under General Adarmanes, returned to Apamea, which they burned, having already seized the city's replenished riches. Kaper Koraon again lay on the general path of the invading army, which committed "all sorts of atrocities" as it withdrew in the direction of Dara, in Mesopotamia.[57] Four years later, the village may have felt the effects of the earthquake which badly damaged Daphne, just south of Antioch,[58] and adding to these disasters were the frequent recurrences of the bubonic plague, which first spread to Syria in 542.[59]

At what precise moment the Kaper Koraon treasure was buried is open to speculation. Although most of its dateable objects fall between about 540 and 640, this interval does not necessarily coincide with the life span of the local church community. After all, this area of Syria was thriving and Christianized by the fifth century and, as postulated above, the church at Kaper Koraon could have been looted in 540 and replenished thereafter (see Entry no. 17). Furthermore, 640 does not necessarily constitute its *terminus ante quem,* since certain objects in the treasure may well have been dedicated after that date—such as patens nos. 6 and 39, which are not directly related epigraphically or formally to other pieces in the group, and chalice no. 41, which has the dedicatory inscription divided between cup and foot, an apparently medieval characteristic. None of the treasure appears to have been in "mint" condition on burial, including those objects dated or attributed by their stamps to the seventh century (nos. 2, 13, 19, 29); indeed, Hama chalice no. 3, which appears to have been donated in the early seventh, is particularly worn.

Although valued for their precious metal, silver objects were not accumulated and used in the way that coins were. That is, once a church had been richly endowed with silver implements, such offerings may well have tapered off in favor of other kinds of donations (e.g., new pavements). And unlike the burial of a coin hoard or of silver belonging to a private individual, the concealment of joint, community property, such as church silver, could indicate the general abandonment of the site, and possibly, in this case, of the entire area, following an attack. Recent scholarship has moved away from the view that the Persian and Arab conquests of Syria in the seventh century brought Late Antique life there to a violent end. Indeed, archaeological evidence from the general area of Kurin—at Apamea, Nikertai, and Dehes—clearly indicates the reverse.[60] The eighth century is increasingly viewed as the pivotal period of change, especially with the removal of the caliphate from Damascus to Bagdad in 750, which was occasioned by civil war, and which resulted in local economic decline.[61] Of course Kaper Koraon may well have suffered, together with other nearby villages, when Chalcis, virtually alone among cities, resisted takeover by the Arabs in 634. But although Sarmin (fig. II.1), for example, is mentioned by al-Baladhuri as "reduced" at the time,[62] both it and Stuma (and, presumably, Kurin) continue to exist today under their ancient names. The ensuing (and unusual) forced conversion of the Christian Arabs, the Tanukh, in the vicinity of Chalcis,[63] may also have affected Kaper Koraon, and church property may have been concealed by those individuals fleeing the area in order to protect their faith. Alternatively, people from Kaper Koraon may have fled eastward, burying their silver at Stuma, during the attack in 694 by troops sent by Justinian II against the Maronite(?) Christians on the Orontes near Apamea.[64]

The Donors

Among the (up to) fifty or so individuals named on the (up to) fifty-six objects in the reconstructed Kaper Koraon treasure (see fig. I.1), just four have titles. The donor of one Hama paten (no. 6) was an archbishop, Amphilochios, who cannot be identified as a patriarch of Antioch (the figure in immediate authority over the Kaper Koraon church), but may instead have been a native of the village, now presiding elsewhere (see also Entry no. 66). Thus, in contrast to the Sion treasure, where a single bishop features as a prominent donor of many essential items,[65] bishops play a very minor role among donors of the objects here catalogued.

Three individuals named among the Stuma, Riha, Hama, and Antioch inscriptions have lay titles, and the most prominent of these is Megas. Erica Dodd noted this unusual, as yet untitled name in the Riha paten (no. 35) inscription of 577(?), and in some of the silver stamps applied to Stuma/Riha objects nos. 33, 34, and 36, which she dated 578–582.[66] She further noted the later accumulation of titles with this name on Riha ewers nos. 37 and 38, of 582–602, and from this reconstructed a plausible career for Megas, in Constantinople as an official stamping silver between 578 and 582, and then as curator of an imperial domain, with the titles "most glorious ex-consul" and "patrician." Moreover, this impressive *cursus honorum* has recently been augmented by Denis Feissel, who identified Megas as one of six principal figures at the court in Constantinople to receive a letter (addressed *ad Megantem curatorem*) from the Merovingian King Childebert in 587–588; in the hierarchical order, Megas ranked third after the Master of Offices and the *quaestor.*[67] And now, a few additional refinements may here be made concerning the chronology of his career. The stamps bearing Megas' name were probably applied between 574 and 578, rather than between 578 and 582 (see Entry no. 33), and there is some evidence, cited below,[68] that this was done at Antioch rather than Constantinople. Moreover, if Megas was stamping silver between 574 and 578, he may have had an official title (e.g., as an *argentarius comitatensis* of the *scrinium ab argento*),[69] omitted, perhaps, for lack of space from the paten (no. 35) he donated in 577(?).

In discussing the career of Megas, Feissel draws attention to its curious parallels with that of his near homonym, Magnus the Syrian, *comes sacrarum largitionum,* imperial curator, and *commerciarius* of Antioch.[70] Occasionally identified with the Megas of the Merovingian letter of 587–588, Magnus was said, in fact, to have died by 585. A further coincidence to be noted between the two is that Magnus built a church in 581 at his native Horin[71] (identified as Hawarin, the Greek city of Evaria; fig. II.1),[72] whose Semitic name phonetically approaches the Greek *Koraon,* where Megas presented his offerings between 577 and 602. Moreover, among the domains administered by Magnus were those of Hormisdas, situated to the north of Koraon.[73] (Those in the care of Megas are not identified.)

Linked with Megas by close similarities between the contemporary patens (Stuma and Riha; nos. 34, 35) they donated, is Sergios, tribune and *argyroprates.* Moreover, the three objects upon which Megas' name appears in stamps (nos. 33, 34, 36) were all dedicated by Sergios, and in the inscriptions on two of these, Sergios is himself associated with the silver industry by virtue of his two

Fig. I.1

Genealogical Tree: Inscribed Objects of the Reconstructed Kaper Koraon Treasure

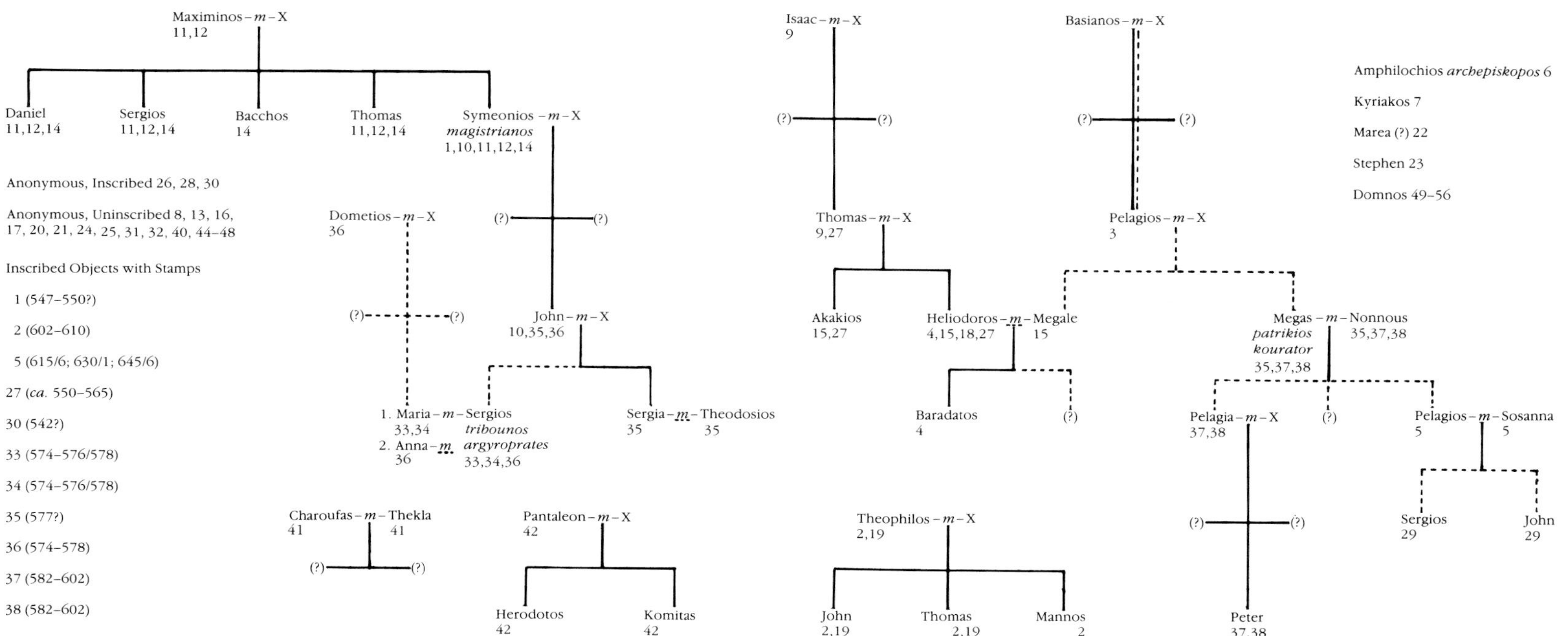

titles—"silver seller," linked both times with *tribounos* (see Entry no. 34). Elsewhere, I have suggested that the two titles combined may indicate a position in a state silver factory.[74] A *tribunus fabricae*[75] may have been attached to one of the metal workshops run by the *largitiones,* such as the ceremonial armor factories of the *barbaricarii,* which the *scrinium ab argento* operated at Antioch.[76]

The third donor with a lay title among the objects of the reconstructed Kaper Koraon treasure is Symeonios, whose abbreviated title on Hama chalice no. 1, *magist,* has been completed as *magistrianos*—rather than as the more important *magister* (as in *magister officiorum, magister militum, etc.*) or the more humble alternatives of *magister vici* or *pagi.*[77] A *magistrianos* (one of "the master's men") worked under the Master of Offices as an *agens in rebus.* By 470, there were 1,248 *agentes in rebus* divided into five ranks.[78] Acting first as couriers, and as postal and port inspectors (*curiosi*) in the provinces, they could also be appointed as deputy assistants (*subadiuvae*) in control of diocesan arms factories or the *barbaricarii.* On retirement, a *magistrianos* could be sent for two years as *princeps* to serve a *dux* or head of a diocese. Their gratuities as couriers could be considerable, and those collected for announcing the consul were in 530 limited by Justinian to six *solidi* a province. Although holding a desirable post leading to enrichment, the *agentes in rebus* have nevertheless been described as "a relatively humble corps . . . none (of whom) rose to eminence in the state."[79]

The other donors of this silver treasure were, presumably, "middle class" property owners, merchants or artisans. However, as already suggested concerning Megas' inscription on the Riha paten, titles may occasionally have been omitted for lack of space. All these donors have been arranged in figure I.1 into groups according to the relationships given in their inscriptions, and the dates indicated by the applied silver stamps. Thus, it has been possible to postulate the existence in Kaper Koraon of four or five important families who for three generations, *circa* 540–640, gave silver implements to their church. While the earliest object, dateable around 540 (no. 30), has an anonymous inscription, the name-bearing dedications begin *circa* 547–550 with the chalice of Symeonios, *magistrianos* (no. 1). Objects mentioning St. Sergios of Kaper Koraon were given anonymously (no. 28), by a family of five(?) brothers (nos. 11, 12, 14), and by Pelagios Basianos (no. 3). St. Sergios is mentioned on another anonymous donation (no. 26), and on objects given by the family of Heliodoros and Akakios (no. 4), and by Kyriakos (no. 7). Following a suggestion by Erica Dodd,[80] and fully consistent with the customs of the period,[81] one can provisionally link as brother and sister certain persons with paired masculine and feminine names: Megas and Megale, Sergios and Sergia, and Pelagios and Pelagia. In the first case, the link would join parts of the Riha (nos. 35, 37, 38) and Hama (nos. 4, 9[?], 15, 18, 27) treasures. One may do likewise by relating Sergios of the Stuma treasure (nos. 33, 34, 36) with Sergia and John of the Riha treasure (no. 35) and then, in turn, with John, son of Symeonios, of the Hama treasure (no. 10, and probably nos. 1, 11, 12, 14). And finally, the two persons named Pelagios on Hama treasure objects (nos. 3, 5) may be related to the Pelagia of the Riha treasure (nos. 37, 38). There are, unfortunately, no such "genealogical" links between the Antioch treasures and the other three. And of course, different combinations of names are possible from those set out here.

There may be some significance in the fact that the earliest dated donations occur just after 540, when nearby cities were systematically stripped of their precious metals by Chosroes I. The concentration of donations made *hyper anapauseos* in the late 570s (nos. 33–36, and perhaps no. 15) may likewise be explained by casualties of the second Persian campaign in the vicinity (573), at which time, however, existing church treasures may have been safely hidden. A third historical observation is implicit in the continued manufacture, stamping, purchase, and presentation of silver during the troubled years of Phocas' reign (nos. 2, 13, 19),[82] and perhaps later in the seventh century as well, at the time of or after the Arab Conquest (nos. 5, 29; also no. 75).

The Economics of Donation

In the Early Byzantine period there were many categories of church donors. At one extreme were those who, like imperial patrons or Flavius Vlalila, a *magister utriusque militiae,* built an entire church and equipped it with furnishings and an income (see Entry no. 91). And at the other extreme were the "subscription" donors, each of whom contributed in a relatively small way towards the construction of a church or its decoration, or who presented it with individual objects, produce or property (fig. I.2; two female donors in a floor mosaic of *ca.* 576–578).[83] Each donated unit—an arch, a pavement panel, a chalice, a book—could be further subdivided by multiple donations, and the size and price of these piecemeal contributions may in certain instances even be calculated. In the case of buildings, there is at one end the well-known figure of 26,000 *solidi* spent by Julianus *argentarius* (or *argyroprates*) on S. Vitale at Ravenna,[84] and at the other, the many very small contributions made to the building of the village churches at Kaper Barada and Nessana, indicated by dedications inscribed on various parts of the structures.[85] While no prices are quoted there, it is known that elsewhere in contemporary synagogues a balustrade and nave pavement could together cost seven *solidi,* and individual pavement panels (called *tabla*) within a nave, from three to five *solidi*—as can be seen in the Gadara synagogue pavement (fig. I.3), whose top panel is inscribed as having cost five *solidi.*[86] The

Fig. I.2

top price known for an Early Byzantine, presumably deluxe scriptural book is forty *solidi* (see Entry no. 87), while books bought by villagers cost from as little as half a *solidus* to four *solidi* (see Entries nos. 88, 89).

Although prices are not inscribed on any church objects, the cost of each may be calculated from its present weight. These calculations are, of course, approximate, for the Roman pound was not an invariable unit (327.45 grams has been used here),[87] and the relative value of gold and silver fluctuated in the Early Byzantine period between four and five *solidi* for a pound of silver. The equivalence used here, four *solidi,* is that recorded in 578,[88] during the period when many of the Kaper Koraon objects were bought. In 516, Patriarch Severus of Antioch had said that each member of his congregation ("even the poorest") could easily afford to donate towards a revetment at least one pound of silver[89]—which is, in fact, the approximate weight of each Beth Misona chalice (nos. 57–59). The cost of four *solidi* for such a chalice, therefore, approximately corresponds to that of a pavement panel or a relatively modest book (see Entries nos. 88, 89). At the bottom of the price scale might be a silver spoon which, weighing about one and a half ounces (no. 19), would cost almost exactly the same (at half a *solidus*) as the least expensive contemporary Syriac book (no. 89).

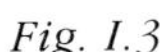

The single most expensive object in the reconstructed Kaper Koraon treasure was, apparently, the Antioch cross revetment (no. 42), whose weight of 18 pounds (72 *solidi*) can be only approximately calculated from its dimensions. It is suggested below (in Entry no. 35) that Megas, the imperial curator, may have donated other revetments, as well as certain objects (e.g., a *cherniboxeston* set) which no longer exist. He may likewise have presented the uninscribed fans

Fig. 1.3

(nos. 31, 32), which have stamps contemporary with those on his paten (no. 35). The total of his potential *surviving* objects (i.e., nos. 31, 32, 35, 37, 38) would have cost around seventy-five *solidi,* which is far less than the approximately 270 *solidi* worth of silver given by Flavius Vlalila to his church at Tivoli in 471 (see Entry no. 91), or the 2,880 *solidi* worth that a consul gave the cathedral at Edessa in 437/8.[90] The other totals spent on Kaper Koraon objects are considerably lower than Megas' amount: the five(?) sons of Maximinos spent less than forty *solidi* (*ca.* eight *solidi* each) for three joint offerings (nos. 11, 12, 14); Sergios, tribune and *argyroprates,* paid less than thirty-five *solidi* for a total of three objects (nos. 33, 34, 36); while Symeonios, the *magistrianos,* bought his chalice for less than three *solidi*—one half the amount he may have collected as an imperial courier announcing the new consul in one province.

Among the largest discrepancies between the weight-value of a Kaper Koraon donation and an equivalent donor and object documented elsewhere is that between Hama paten no. 6, costing about twelve and a half *solidi,* given by an archbishop (whose annual salary could have reached 2,160 *solidi*), and the paten of Bishop Paternus, which was worth about eighty-three *solidi*[91]—or the equivalent of 2,160 *solidi* worth of silver bestowed on two churches by the bishop of Auxerre.[92] Indeed, from the donor's point of view it almost seems as if the *appearance* of the object was as important as its weight. The generic "ministerial chalice" so often cited in papal inventories varied from one to three pounds, a weight spread paralleled on the Byzantine/Syrian chalices here catalogued—which, nevertheless, are surprisingly uniform in dimensions and appearance. Thus, the three Beth Misona chalices (nos. 57–59) weigh between 305 and 332 grams,[93] while the Riha chalice (no. 30), at the same height, weighs 527 grams. Similarly, the Beth Misona paten (no. 60) weighs only 542 grams, while the Durobrivae paten, which is only one centimeter wider, weighs 1,305 grams.[94]

SILVER MANUFACTURE—STAMPS

There is general technical uniformity among the sixth- and seventh-century silver objects found in Syria and included in this catalogue. Most were hammered; cast pieces include just the fans, the mirror, spoons, two strainers, various handles, and the lampstand bases. Nearly half of the ornamented pieces have linear decoration, while the other half are decorated in relief—mainly repoussé, most of which was executed with the same types of tools and techniques. About half the fifty-odd inscriptions were simply engraved, a somewhat smaller number have thick letters keyed for niello inlay, and about a half dozen are in *pointillé* technique. The letter forms are generally consistent among themselves, with one prominent subgroup composed of objects from three treasures (Hama, Beth Misona, and Phela; nos. 7, 14, 28, 60, 61, 64, 65).

Most of these catalogued objects have contemporary counterparts in silver found elsewhere (see individual Entries); moreover, most may individually be traced back to late Hellenistic or Roman prototypes (e.g., ewers, lamps, lampstands, mirror, spoons, and strainers); although the Hama flask (no. 15) and ladle (no. 23) have unusual or unique features. In contrast to the established types, the two fans (nos. 31, 32) are themselves the earliest extant examples of a long series, and the crosses form an important early group of an innovative, distinctly Christian type of object. The chalices and patens—the most essential church vessels—introduce modifications to classical types, which require further examination, and, although of similar shape and decoration to chalices and patens found elsewhere, those from Byzantine Syria are distinctive in points of their construction. For example, Byzantine/Syrian chalices (both our Types A and B; see Entry no. 1) have an external collar joining cup and foot, whereas the western chalices of the Durobrivae and Gallunianu treasures have an internal silver rivet (see Entry no. 77); moreover, except for the Sarabaon plate (no. 75), Byzantine/Syrian patens lack the footring found on the Paternus and Sion patens.[95]

One important distinction noteable among Byzantine silver objects manufactured in the sixth and seventh centuries is between those that are stamped and those that are not. A system of hallmarking with five stamps was introduced under Anastasius (*ca.* 500), and remained in use into the reign of Constans II (*ca.* 670). These stamps contain official insignia, monograms, and names, which have permitted the chronological classification established by Erica Dodd.[96] The purpose of the stamping, however, remains unclear. Although according to written sources, "five-stamp silver" was prized at the time,[97] it is difficult to determine now what set it apart from unstamped silver. Metal analysis has shown the same very pure quality in both categories of silver (mostly 94 percent to 98 percent, as against 92.5 percent for modern sterling; see Chapter III, below), and many pieces of superior craftsmanship, such as the two Hama lampstands, the Antioch Chalice, and the Homs Vase (nos. 11, 12, 40, 84) are unstamped, while many stamped objects are of more modest technical and artistic quality (e.g., nos. 1, 2, 13, 27).

Erica Dodd's interpretation of the stamping system, while not explaining the uniform purity of silver in nearly all Early Byzantine objects, does offer a reason for the variable quality of craftsmanship in stamped pieces. Her theory is that it was partially worked silver which was stamped and released for distribution, to be finished by anyone, anywhere.[98] Recently, I have suggested[99] that silver was stamped *and* finished in state workshops to raise revenue for the government in a period when silver was not coined, but was collected in taxes. This hypothesis would explain—in terms of "mass production"—the long-term standardization of dimensions and weights of certain types of stamped objects (e.g., lamps nos. 13, 33; lampstands and plates). The customer could, of course, ask to have his object personalized with a monogram or a dedication, and there would be several levels of quality available for purchase (e.g., the Paternus paten[100] and the Alouf paten, no. 74). Another feature of this hypothesis is that it presupposes the delegated, centralized control of silver, comparable to that exercised in the system of state mints. That is, the "five-stamp" set would have been applied not just in Constantinople (as Dodd suggests), but in mints or *thesauri* of other diocesan capitals of the Eastern Prefecture, including Antioch. The villagers from Kaper Koraon may, therefore, have traveled no further than Antioch to buy their stamped silver, rather than the 1,300 kilometers to Constantinople. Nor would they have had to bear the inordinately high prices (for mediocre, light-weight objects) which presumably would have been passed along by a Syrian silversmith who had undertaken the expense of importing stamped silver all the way from the imperial capital.

It follows from the above hypothesis that stamped silver articles produced, like *largitio* objects,[101] in state factories, should differ somewhat from unstamped silver fashioned by private artisans. In testing this theory, the number of variables (e.g., of local manufacture) is reduced by comparing objects found in a single area. Of the approximately eighty silver pieces found in Syria and dateable to the sixth and seventh centuries which are included in this catalogue, only seventeen (or 18 [no. 41]) bear stamps. They include five types of objects: seven patens (nos. 5, 34, 35, 36, 63, 74, 75), five chalices (nos. 1, 2, 27, 30, 41[?]), two lamps (nos. 13, 33), two ewers (nos. 37, 38), and two fans (nos. 31, 32). While the last four objects were made as pairs, the two lamps bear stamps dated thirty years apart. Yet, although finished differently, they were nearly identical in their initial stages of manufacture (see Entry no. 33). Uniformity is likewise observed among the five stamped chalices, all of which, by their construction, belong to our Type A (see Entry no. 1). Furthermore, no stamped chalice bears figural decoration. (But predictably, strict uniformity is not observed in their inscriptions, which, as noted above, would have been added to suit personal taste.) Of the seven stamped patens, five are adorned with large engraved crosses (nos. 5, 36, 63, 74, 75), while the other two have figural decoration (nos. 34, 35).

There are, in fact, notable differences between the above stamped objects and the unstamped objects. Seven of the nine unstamped chalices in this catalogue are of our Type B construction (nos. 3, 28, 57–59, 61, 62; see Entry no. 1), and only two of them lack figural decoration (nos. 28, 61). The five unstamped patens all have simple engraved inscriptions, and four of them have a medium-sized cross (nos. 6, 39, 60, 64), whereas only one (no. 4) has the large cross so often found on stamped patens.

Several conclusions may be drawn from these observations. Among objects found in Byzantine Syria, stamped chalices were manufactured by one method and most unstamped chalices by another. Most unstamped patens were decorated with medium-sized crosses, and stamped patens with large crosses. (The two stamped patens with the Communion of the Apostles were apparently made for people directly involved in the silver industry, and thus may have been exceptional.) Interestingly, the unstamped objects which most resemble stamped types in their manufacture or decoration (i.e., chalice no. 29 and paten no. 4) were, in fact, either finished together with a stamped object (no. 29 with no. 5) or were bought by individuals who were also buying stamped objects (no. 4 and no. 27). These and other cases of similarity between stamped and unstamped pieces may thus be attributable to direct imitation. But it would be unwise to draw further conclusions before the appearance of Erica Dodd's supplementary stamp publication, and of a thorough study of the Sion silver treasure.

In conclusion, the donors of Kaper Koraon—and of northern Syria generally—seem to have obtained their silver from a variety of sources. While it has been suggested here that the seventeen catalogued pieces with stamps were made in state workshops at Antioch, the other sixty pieces could have been produced in any number of workshops, in any number of the cities of the region—or even in a village like Kaper Koraon.

NOTES

1. Eusebius, *VC,* III.liv.x.
2. Unpublished lecture given at the Collège de France, Paris, in 1979.
3. *Liber Pontificalis,* 170 ff.
4. Procopius, *Buildings,* I.i.65.
5. *Chronicle of 1234,* II, 180.
6. Platner and Ashby, 1929, 463 ff.
7. LeStrange, 1965, 21; and Creswell, 1958, 80.
8. Justinian, Novel, 128.15.
9. Cyril of Skythopolis, *Life of Abraamios,* ch. 6; and *Life of Theodore of Sykeon,* ch. 42.
10. Cyril of Skythopolis, *Life of Kyriakos,* ch. 6.
11. Mundell-Mango, 1981, 5.
12. Jones, 1960, 84 f., 92 f.
13. *CTh,* XVI, 2.4.
14. *Miracles of St. Demetrios,* mir. 6.
15. Severus, *Homily* 100.
16. Joshua, ch. 28.
17. Severus, *Letters,* 405.
18. Justinian, *Novels,* 37, 120.10.
19. *Ibid.,* 120.10.
20. Mundell-Mango, 1984, 154 ff., 475 ff.; and *idem,* 1986.
21. *Liber Pontificalis,* I, CXLIV.
22. See Mango, 1972, 137 f.
23. Evagrius, *HE,* VI.21.
24. *Liber Pontificalis,* I, CXLIV.
25. By the Piacenza Pilgrim; see Wilkinson, 1977, 123.
26. Adhémar, 1934, 45.
27. John of Ephesos, *Lives,* ch. 55.
28. Evagrius, *HE,* VI.21; and Weitzmann and Ševčenko, 1963.
29. Justinian, *Novel,* 131.9.
30. S. Ronzevalle expressed this idea with regard to Phoenicia in the classical period; see *IGLS,* no. 2909.
31. *Ibid.,* no. 2989.
32. Fiey, 1961; and Oates, 1962, 78 ff.
33. Justinian, *Novel,* 67.
34. Evagrius, *HE,* VI.21.
35. Robert, 1953, 188, no. 218.
36. *Life and Miracles of St. Thekla,* mir. 13.
37. Lassus, 1947, 255.
38. Evagrius, *HE,* VI.21.
39. See Chapter II, below, for a detailed presentation of evidence suggesting that the Stuma, Riha, Hama, and Antioch treasures in fact together constituted a single large silver hoard discovered by chance near Stuma in 1908, and that these objects were originally dedicated to the Church of St. Sergios in the village of Kaper Koraon (modern Kurin, near Stuma).
40. Feissel, 1982, 362 f., notes 56, 59 f.
41. Tchalenko, 1953–1958, vol. 1, 413 ff.
42. Sodini *et al.,* 1980, 294 ff.
43. Stein, 1949–1959, vol. 2, 773.
44. Feissel, 1982, 319 ff.
45. See Chapter II, below.
46. Seyrig, in Tchalenko, 1953–1958, vol. 3, 14; and Feissel, 1982, 326 f., fig. 1.
47. Butler, *AAES,* vol. 2, 30.
48. *Idem, PUAES,* vol. 2, B, 108; and *idem, AAES,* vol. 2, 22.
49. Sodini and Tate, 1984, 392.
50. Feissel, 1982, 327.
51. Seyrig, in Tchalenko, 1953–1958, vol. 3, 28.
52. Van den Ven, 1962/1970; Festugière and Rydén, 1974.
53. Mundell, 1977, 67 ff.
54. Caquot, in Tchalenko, 1953–1958, vol. 3, 63 ff.; and Mundell-Mango, 1983, 407 ff.
55. Michael the Syrian, *Chronicle,* II, 381.
56. Procopius, *Wars,* II.vii–xii.2. For Lakhmid raids in the territory of Chalcis in 529 and 554, see Stein, 1949–1959, vol. 2, 284, 503.
57. John of Ephesos, *HE,* VI.6
58. Evagrius, *HE,* V.10.
59. Stein, 1949–1959, 758 ff.; and Mango, 1984, 27 ff.
60. See, for example, the coin evidence in Morrison, 1972. See also *idem,* in Sodini *et al.,* 1980, 267 ff.; and Balty, 1984.
61. See, for example, the archaeological reports in *Syria,* 1983 (306, 312). See also Sodini *et al.,* 1980, 300 f.; and Mundell-Mango, 1984, *passim.*
62. *Islamic State,* 223, 229.
63. Hitti, 1951, 486.
64. *Ibid.,* 521.
65. Boyd, 1979.
66. Dodd, 1968, 141 ff.; and *idem,* 1973, 45 f.
67. Feissel, 1985, 469 ff.

68. See also, Mundell-Mango, 1986.

69. See Kent, in Dodd, 1961, 44.

70. Feissel, 1985, 471 f.

71. John of Ephesos, *HE,* III.40 (Brooks, 174 [text], 130 [trans.]).

72. Mouterde, 1932, 112, note 4; 115, note 1.

73. Feissel, 1985, 466; and Tchalenko, 1953–1958, vol. 1, 116; vol. 3, 40 ff.

74. Mundell-Mango, 1986 (paper presented in 1983).

75. PW, *Tribunus fabricae.*

76. See Kent, in Dodd, 1961, 44.

77. *IGLS,* no. 2028.

78. Jones, 1973, 578 ff.

79. *Ibid.*

80. Dodd, 1973, 57.

81. *PLRE,* vol. 1, *stemmata* 2–4, vol. 2, *stemma* 10. See also Mundell-Mango, 1986, note 79.

82. Downey, 1961, 572 ff.

83. Cohen, 1979, 21 (Church of St. Elias, Gerara/Orda [Kissufim]?).

84. Agnellus, *Liber pontificalis ecclesiae Ravennatis,* ch. 59.

85. *IGLS,* no. 367; Lassus, 1947, 257 ff.; Alt, 1921, nos. 127–130; Colt, 1950–1962, vol. 1, 141 ff., nos. 17, 20; 162 ff., nos. 64, 73–76.

86. Sukenik, 1935, 129 ff., fig. 11. See also, Frey, 1936–1952, no. 739; and Mundell-Mango, 1984, *passim.*

87. Grierson, 1964, iii, xii; and Johns and Potter, 1983, 36, note 16.

88. Stein, 1949–1959, vol. 2, 462, note 1.

89. Severus, *Homily* 100, p. 247.

90. *Chronicle of Edessa,* 7.

91. Matzulevich, 1929, 105 ff.

92. Adhémar, 1934, 45.

93. Bréhier, 1951, 256.

94. Painter, 1977[I], no. 3.

95. Matzulevich, 1929, no. 6; *DO Handbook,* 1967, nos. 63–65.

96. Dodd, 1961.

97. Cyril of Skythopolis, *Life of Theodore of Sykeon,* ch. 42.

98. Dodd, 1961, 34 f.; *idem,* 1973, 33 ff.; and *idem,* 1980, 3 f.

99. Mundell-Mango, 1986 (paper delivered in 1983).

100. Matzulevich, 1929, no. 6; and Dodd, 1973, 25.

101. Baratte, 1975 [I]; *idem,* 1975 [II].

THE RECONSTRUCTED KAPER KORAON TREASURE

Entries Nos. 1–56

STUMA TREASURE

Istanbul,
Archaeological
Museum

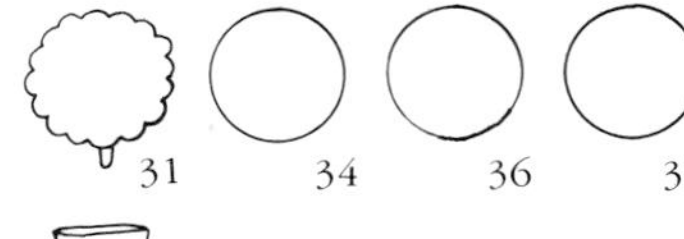

Bern,
Abegg Stiftung

33

RIHA TREASURE

Washington, D.C.,
Dumbarton Oaks

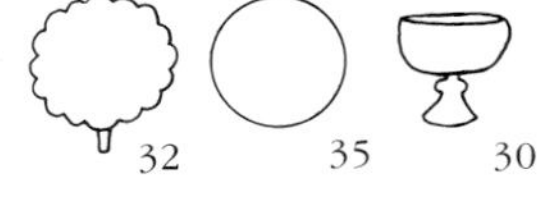

Bern,
Abegg Stiftung

37 38

HAMA TREASURE

Baltimore,
The Walters
Art Gallery

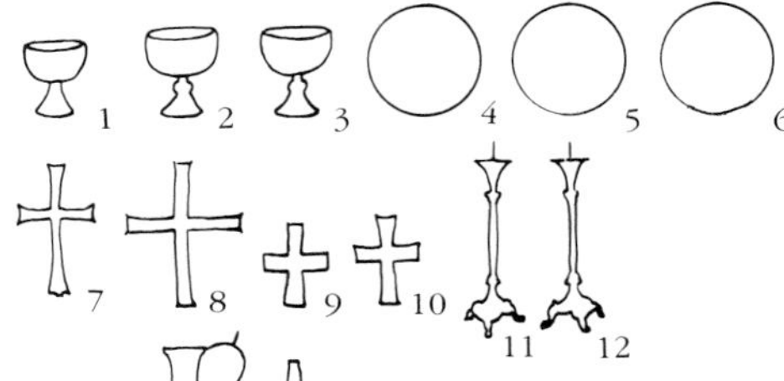

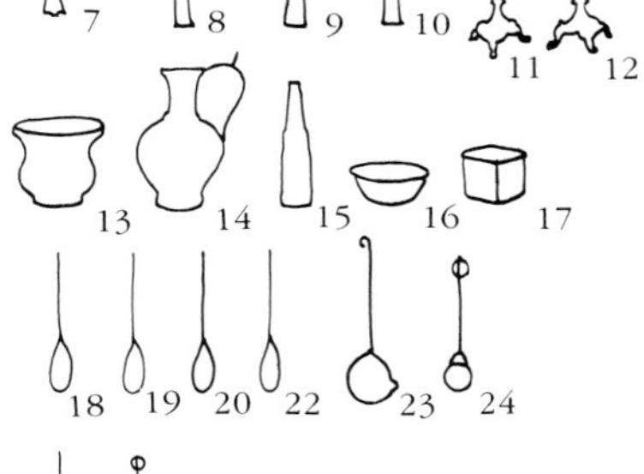

Location
Unknown

21 25

Jerusalem,
Monastery of St. Anne

Washington, D.C.,
Eagleton Collection

28

London,
British Museum

29

ANTIOCH TREASURE

New York,
The Metropolitan
Museum of Art

40 41 42

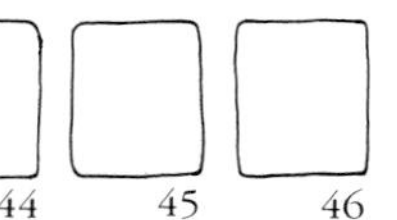

Paris,
Musée du Louvre

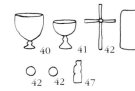

42 42 47

Location
Unknown

43

Washington, D.C.,
Dumbarton Oaks

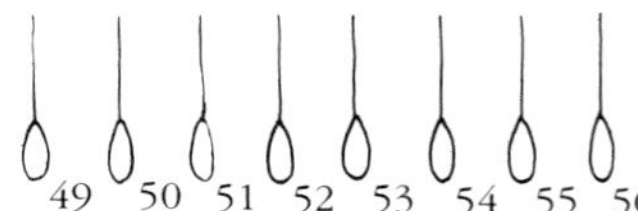

CHAPTER II:

THE STUMA, RIHA, HAMA, AND ANTIOCH TREASURES: THEIR MODERN HISTORY

II. The Stuma, Riha, Hama, and Antioch Silver Treasures: Their Modern History

The Stuma Treasure

The earliest and most secure date concerning the discovery of any of the four famous silver treasures associated with Stuma, Riha, Hama, and Antioch is February 1908, when the Stuma treasure entered the Archaeological Museum in Istanbul. This date, which has recently been confirmed by Dr. Nuşin Asgari, former director of the museum, was first reported in 1911 in an account of the discovery published by Jean Ebersolt in the *Revue archéologique*. This treasure, which was seized by the Ottoman authorities, was composed of four objects: a liturgical fan (no. 31) and three patens (nos. 34, 36, 39). One of the patens (no. 34) is decorated with the Communion of the Apostles; it and a second paten (no. 36) are inscribed with the name of Sergios. These two objects have stamps dateable to 574–576/578, while the fan has stamps of 577.

Ebersolt said that the objects were found "dans un champs à Stuma." The village of Stuma (ancient Aistumak[1]) lies on the ancient road between Aleppo (Beroea) and Latakiya (Laodicea), which links the small modern towns of Idlib and Riha (figs. II.1, II.2). A tell on the north side of Stuma has been the object of recent excavations conducted by Japanese archaeologists (fig. II.3); and in the 1930s, René Mouterde published an Early Byzantine capital seen in the village.[2] In addition to the four objects preserved today in the Istanbul museum, there is a lamp in the Abegg Stiftung, Bern (no. 33), with an inscription and stamps virtually identical with those on one of the Istanbul patens (no. 34). A good case has also been made for linking yet another object (chalice no. 29) to this treasure; both these "additions" will be considered below.

The Riha Treasure

The Riha treasure is directly linked to the Stuma treasure in several respects. In its first known form, it consisted of three objects: an inscribed paten with the Communion of the Apostles (no. 35) very much like that in the Stuma treasure (no. 34), and by its stamps (of 577), almost exactly contemporary; a fan (no. 32) nearly identical to the Stuma fan (no. 31), and having, like it, stamps of 577; and a chalice (no. 30) bearing an anonymous dedication and stamps of 542(?). This treasure was first mentioned exactly a year after the Stuma pieces entered the Istanbul museum. On February 10, 1909, the English archaeologist Gertrude Bell, on a two-week stop in Aleppo, visited George Marcopoli, and that evening recorded in her journal that:

> He has too a very interesting silver repoussé dish, the figures covered with gold. Twice repeated Christ giving the sacrament to the people. Inscription round . . .[3]

This she copied into an album under a contemporary photograph of the paten showing its upper right side covered in corrosion (fig. 35.9). That same evening she also wrote a letter to O. M. Dalton of the British Museum, informing him of the paten and noting that it had been found "in a chapel or *coenobium* near Kalat Seman," together with seven other objects, which were seized by the Ottoman authorities.[4]

Two key points in that letter are incorrect: the number of objects seized (which, in fact, was four) and the place of discovery—although her reference to Qal'at

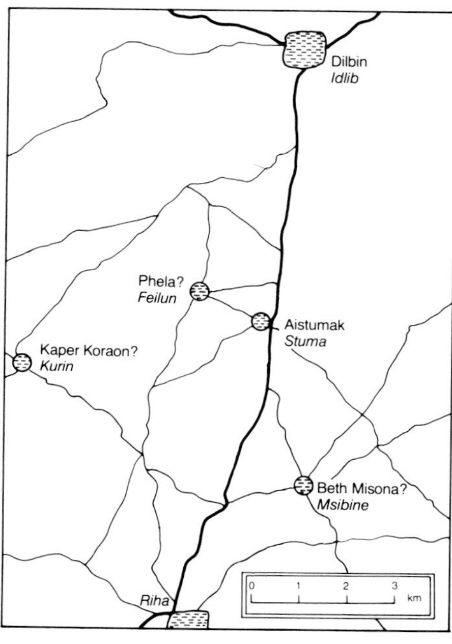

Fig. II.2

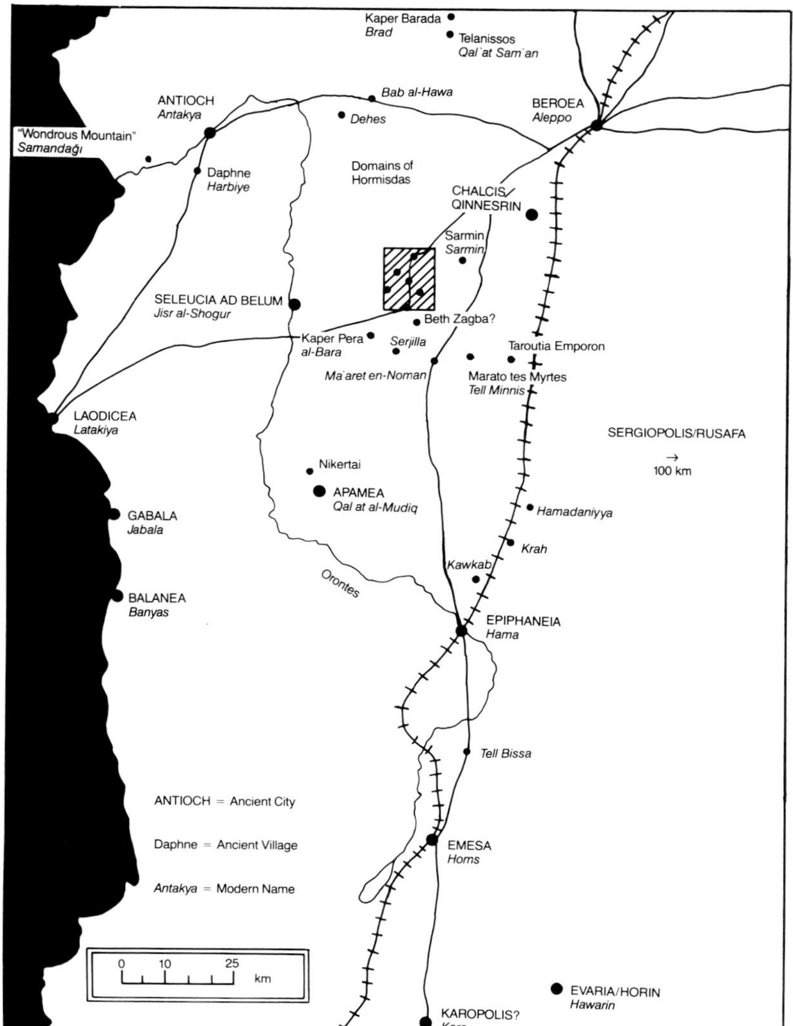

Fig. II.1

Sam'an may simply have been a general allusion to the region west of Aleppo (fig. II.1). The exact wording of the Bell letter is now unknown, but the entry in her journal makes it clear that in early 1909 the Riha paten was owned by George Marcopoli, who was, in fact, a member of a well-known Aleppo family with a large collection of antiquities. Indeed, T. E. Lawrence described them as "the big dealers in Aleppo," and a number of their inscribed objects were included in the *Inscriptions grecques et latines de la Syrie.*[5] Moreover, in addition to this paten, Marcopoli is known to have owned an inscribed bronze votive cross similar to the two small silver crosses in the Hama treasure (nos. 9, 10).[6] On April 19, 1909, he, too, wrote to Dalton at the British Museum, perhaps to correct Bell's information, explaining that the paten had been found "dans une ruine située dans un champs de labour appartenant à un village, situé au sud-ouest d'Alep entre Idlib et Riha."[7] Marvin Ross, in quoting this passage more than fifty years later, concluded that ". . . both the Riha and the Stuma Treasures were apparently found at about the same time and virtually in the same place, that is, in the near vicinity of Aleppo."[8] In referring to the detailed map (fig. II.2), it is possible to go further and say that they were found in precisely the same place, for Stuma is the very village located at mid-point in the approximately fifteen kilometers that separate Idlib and Riha.

After reporting in 1919 to the *Académie des Inscriptions* in Paris that the Riha paten and chalice came from Antioch, Louis Bréhier corrected this provenance the following year in an article on Syrian silverwork in the *Gazette des beaux arts,* where he claimed that the objects were found "au bourg de Riha . . . dans un tombeau."[9] He gave no source for this information, and it seems fairly certain that he had no personal knowledge of the region. One should also take with caution a statement made by T. E. Lawrence that he was present at Riha at the moment of the discovery, and that he bought the Riha chalice (no. 30)—which he says was later stolen from him.[10] A more reliable claim—that he was offered *another* chalice (no. 29)—was made by Lawrence in 1913.[11] Beyond the 1909 allusions to the Riha paten made by Bell and Marcopoli, there is the reference made by the German archaeologist Friedrich Sarre to the Riha fan (no. 32) "im Kunsthandel in Aleppo," where his work with Ernst Herzfeld took him in the years 1907–1910.[12]

In considering the relationship of the Stuma and Riha treasures, one should recognize, as did Marc Rosenberg in the 1920s, that the two fans (nos. 31, 32) bear identical stamps and form a pair:[13] their decoration is linked iconographically, and close examination reveals that they were probably made by the same craftsman. Moreover, their damage—probably from burial—is nearly identical.[14] The Stuma and Riha patens with the Communion of the Apostles (nos. 34, 35) are likewise very similar in composition and iconography, if less so in style. They are even closer, moreover, in their niello inscriptions, which run around the rim of the plate rather than, as is more typical among Syrian patens, around its bottom. It thus appears very likely that the Stuma and Riha fans and patens were made in the same workshop(s),[15] were destined for the same church, and that they were later concealed—together with (at least) the remaining two Stuma objects (nos. 36, 39)—in the same place, that is, in a field at Stuma. This, then, links a total of six objects: the four of the Stuma treasure (nos. 31, 34, 36, 39), and the Riha fan and paten (nos. 32, 35).

The third Riha object, the "Tyler chalice" now at Dumbarton Oaks (no. 30),[16] has an anonymous inscription and what are apparently the earliest stamps among the four treasures. It was bought from the dealer Joseph Brummer in Paris on March 10, 1913, by Royall Tyler who, in a letter written about the object the next day, said nothing about its having been found at Riha.[17] Rather, it was apparently Bréhier, in his second 1919 report, who first related it to the Riha paten. Indeed, four years later—that is, late in 1923—Tyler was offered that paten in Paris by Kalebjian Frères, and the following year he bought it there from Demotte, for Mildred Bliss.[18] Then finally, in 1936 and once again in Paris, the Riha fan was purchased from the dealer Alexander Imbert for the Blisses and Dumbarton Oaks.[19] Thus today, all three pieces traditionally associated as the Riha treasure are part of the Byzantine Collection at Dumbarton Oaks—having arrived by way of different routes which all, however, passed through Paris.

As noted above, Marcopoli, Bell, and Sarre all bore witness to two of the Riha objects' (the paten and the fan) having been at or near Aleppo around 1909 and 1910, but whether these (plus the chalice?) arrived in Paris at the same time and by the same route cannot be determined. The chalice is known to have been there by early 1913, and the paten by at least 1919.[20] That the two may have travelled there together (with the fan?) in 1912 is suggested by a pair of tiny French duty stamps impressed into the rim of the paten (fig. 35.8), which had gone undetected until 1984.[21] Their devices (a weevil and an "M") identify them as having been applied at Marseilles to objects imported from the Ottoman Empire (among other countries). We know that (at least) the paten was in the possession of George Marcopoli in 1909, and that in March 1912, the Marcopoli family, along with all others of Italian extraction, was expelled from the Ottoman Empire with which Italy was then at war.[22] It is therefore quite possible that the Riha paten (fan and chalice?) was taken in that year, by Marcopoli via Marseilles, to Paris.

The lamp (no. 33) mentioned above as having an inscription and stamps identical to those on one of the Stuma patens (no. 34) was bought in 1964 by the Abegg Stiftung, Bern. In her publication of the Abegg silver, Erica Dodd wrote that it had until then belonged for over fifty years to "the same family of landowners in Northern Syria."[23] Moreover, Dodd recognized the lamp as being integral to the Stuma treasure. At the same time, the Abegg Stiftung bought from the same source (i.e., the Paul Mallon family)[24] a pair of ewers (nos. 37, 38) which had belonged to the same Syrian family, and which Dodd identified as being part of the Riha treasure,[25] thanks to their identical inscriptions, which mention the "Megas" and "Nonnous" of the Riha paten inscription (no. 35). Therefore, the three Abegg objects (nos. 33, 37, 38)—one apparently from the Stuma and two apparently from the Riha treasure—must have escaped the Ottoman authorities in 1908 and remained in Syria until the 1960s. Moreover, the family to which they belonged appears to have been the Kouchakjis—a family which, as we shall see below, figures prominently in the histories of the other treasures. On being shown photographs of these three objects in 1985, Père Joseph Kouchakji of Aleppo was "prèsque certain" that they had been among the property sold when the surviving sisters of Constaki (i.e., Constantine), Salim, Georges, and Habib Kouchakji died in Aleppo around 1960.

In sum, then, it is clear that the silver treasure found at Stuma shortly before February 1908 was composed of at least five objects, four of which were seized by the Turks (nos. 31, 34, 36, 39) and one of which (no. 33) remained in a local family, apparently that of Constaki Kouchakji, until the 1960s, when it went to

Fig. II.3

the Abegg Stiftung. The treasure probably also contained at least five other objects, three of which (nos. 30, 32, 35) were transported to dealers in Paris, perhaps by Marcopoli via Marseilles in 1912, later to end up at Dumbarton Oaks, and two of which (nos. 37, 38) stayed with the same family in Syria until the 1960s, when they, too, went to the Abegg Stiftung.

To this point, therefore, ten interrelated objects have been accounted for, and now one can introduce an eleventh—an object first linked to the Stuma treasure more than seventy years ago. According to a letter written from Beirut by Père Sebastien Ronzevalle on April 25, 1912, a certain Naoum Nahas, also of Beirut, had shown him at the end of 1910 or the beginning of 1911 a silver chalice (no. 29) sixteen centimeters high bearing the inscription "In fulfillment of a vow of Sergios and John"; with the letter Ronzevalle enclosed a photograph.[26] Nahas had informed him at the time that the White Fathers of Jerusalem had bought a similar one (no. 27), but "plus joli." He added that "le tout" came "des environs d'Alep." Ronzevalle continued in his letter to say that earlier in that very day he had read the 1911 article by Ebersolt on the Stuma find, where he had noticed that the patens in that treasure were "portant des inscriptions très apparentées à celle du vase de Nahas. . . ." It is not clear from his letter whether this chalice of "Sergios and John" was shown to him at Beirut or, as René Mouterde later said,[27] at Aleppo. But in any event, the object was definitely in Aleppo on February 2, 1913, when it was offered to T. E. Lawrence, who wrote home from the Baron Hotel to describe it as "a high silver chalice like a tureen on a stem of mediaeval Byzantine work (say 800 AD) with Greek dedication to a church of S.S. Sergius and John."[28] Lawrence may also have written about the chalice to the British Museum, which was then financing his excavation work at Carchemish on the Euphrates (1911–1914). At any rate, in 1914 the chalice was in Jerusalem, and the British Museum bought it there in April from F. Vester and Co.[29]

Ronzevalle's letter of April 1912 was addressed to Père Léon Cré, the Superior of the White Fathers Monastery of St. Anne in Jerusalem, which in 1910 had bought the other chalice he had mentioned. This second chalice (no. 27) is still at St. Anne's, together with a previously "unknown" strainer (no. 26) inscribed "Of St. Sergios."[30] The Jerusalem chalice bears stamps dateable to the mid-sixth century and an inscription mentioning a certain Heliodoros and an Akakios. The journal of the monastery notes that on September 26, 1910, Père Cré "se procure" the chalice "trouvé dans un trésor," but from whom and where the sale took place are not indicated. In a letter to Père Cré dated May 13, 1912, the same Nahas who showed the Sergios and John chalice to Ronzevalle mentions the price paid for the monastery's chalice. One has the impression, therefore, that Nahas, an employee of the French Post Office at Beirut, was acting as an agent for St. Anne's (where he had previously been a student), and that it was, in fact, he who in 1910 had bought the monastery's chalice (and strainer?), very likely at Aleppo, and along with it the Sergios and John chalice, which he tried to sell to Ronzevalle (at Aleppo?) later in the same year.

Thus there were two chalices, one inscribed in the names of Sergios and John and the other in the names of Heliodoros and Akakios, seen or sold at Aleppo and at Jerusalem in 1910, 1913, and 1914. According to Nahas, who was selling one or both, "le tout" came "des environs d'Alep." But what was "le tout"? In 1912 Ronzevalle had made the connection between the Sergios and John chalice and the Stuma treasure, but the second (i.e., the Jerusalem) chalice can easily be shown to belong securely to a third treasure, that of Hama, for the names it bears, Heliodoros and Akakios, also appear on three Hama objects (nos. 4, 15, 18).[31] Moreover, the strainer in Jerusalem is dedicated to St. Sergios, as are six objects in the Hama treasure (nos. 3, 4, 7, 11, 12, 14), including the paten naming Heliodoros (no. 4).

The Hama Treasure

By simple coincidence, perhaps, the discovery of the Hama treasure was announced to the same Père Cré less than one month before he obtained his own chalice, on September 26, 1910. For on August 30 of the same year, Père Constantine Bacha of the Basilian Order in Sidon wrote a letter to him with the news of a silver treasure (of which he gave a list) recently found at the bottom of an ancient cistern in the village of Krah (or Karah), near Hama (fig. II.1). It seems that Père Bacha had received his information directly from Hama (where the treasure then was), from the archbishop's nephew, a certain Basil Gebarat, who communicated the details (and list) to him on July 27, 1910.[32]

Fig. II.4

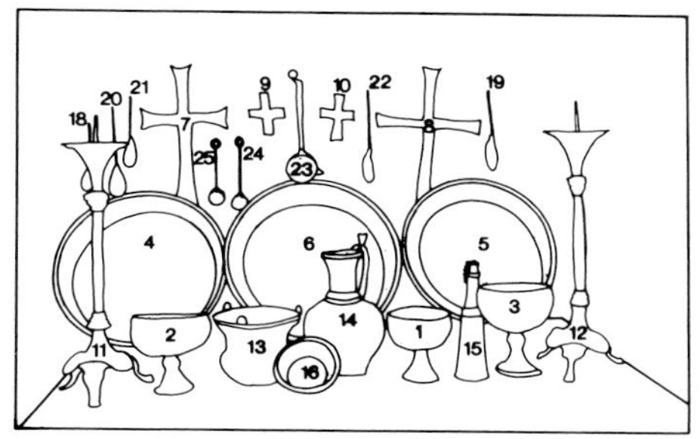

A photograph taken of the Hama treasure at that time (fig. II.4; presumably at the cathedral) shows the twenty-four objects listed by Gebarat. Bacha's "derived" list, in fact, gives only twenty-three pieces (the ladle [no. 23] seemingly having been omitted by accident):

2 grandes croix
2 chandeliers
3 calices
2 petites croix
1 cuvette
1 vase pour l'eau rechauffée
1 vase pour le S. Miron
3 plateaux pour le pain béni
1 lampe
2 petites cuillères
3 grandes cuillères
2 filtres ou couloirs de vin[33]

Fig. II.5

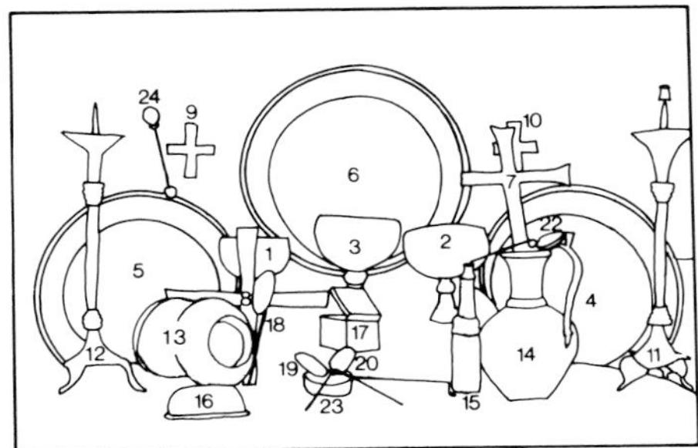

Seventeen of these objects are inscribed, and several form groups given by the same donors. One spoon (no. 18) is dedicated in the name of Heliodoros, who offered a paten (no. 4) to St. Sergios in memory of his son Baradatos. Heliodoros and his brother Akakios had already died when a woman named Megale presented an oil flask (no. 15) in their names. Undoubtedly, the chalice offered by Heliodoros and Akakios (no. 27), which was acquired by St. Anne's in 1910, originally belonged to the treasure gathered at the Hama cathedral that same year.

In autumn of that year, the Prince of Saxony passed through Hama and saw four objects of this treasure: the flask (no. 15) and three chalices (nos. 1–3), and in 1912 he published photographs of two of these chalices in his *Tagebuchblätter aus Nordsyrien.*[34] It was the same nephew of the archbishop, Basil Gebarat, who showed the silver to the Prince and wished to show him "weiterer Kunstschätze," but had misplaced the necessary key. He told the Prince a strange tale about the discovery of the treasure: after having belonged to the cathedral of Hama for several centuries, it had been buried eighty years previously (i.e., *ca.* 1830) and discovered once again in the preceding year (i.e., in 1909).

Despite the fact that this silver treasure was claimed to form an important part of the heritage of the cathedral of Hama, it was sold (soon after?) to Tawfic Abucasem, director of the Ottoman Bank in Hama, who later took it with him when he was transferred by the bank to be its director in Port Said, where a group photograph of the objects was taken and published in 1927 (fig. II.5).[35] Abucasem had bought the treasure some time between 1910 and 1926 (the year when it was published by Diehl), perhaps as early as 1913, when he reported ownership of a seal later associated with the "Second Hama Treasure."[36] Then, at some point between 1927[37] and 1929, the entire Hama treasure passed to the dealer Joseph Brummer of Paris, who sold it in 1929 to Henry Walters of The Walters Art Gallery. (The statement made by Hayford Peirce and Royall Tyler in their publication of 1934 that the Abucasem/Hama treasure was then part of the W. R. Hearst Collection was obviously due to a misunderstanding.[38]) The content of the Hama treasure as owned by Abucasem and Henry Walters was little different from what may be seen in the 1910 Hama photograph (fig. II.4); the later Egyptian photograph (fig. II.5) shows that one spoon and one strainer (nos. 21, 25) had disappeared, and that a small box decorated with *Chrismons* (no. 17) had been added.

There is a final object in the Hama treasure to be considered before reviewing the provenance of the entire group. This is a chalice (no. 28) seen on the antiquities market in Paris in 1911 by A. Héron de Villefosse, *conservateur* at the Louvre, and described by him in a note later published by René Mouterde.[39] In addition to its dimensions (H 21 cm; D 17 cm), Héron de Villefosse copied its inscription, described as being "en lettres grêles," which was rendered by Mouterde as *Tou hagiou Sergiou k(omes) Kapro Koraon*—"(Appartenant à l'église) de S. Serge du village de Kaper Koraon." The name of this village appears on four objects in the Hama treasure (nos. 3, 11, 12, 14), and the church of St. Sergios on six (nos. 3, 4, 7, 11, 12, 14), as well as on the strainer in Jerusalem (no. 26). As Mouterde correctly observed, this chalice clearly belongs with the Hama treasure.

The vessel was sold to an American architect then living in France, Welles Bosworth, who died in 1966 at the age of 97.[40] He in turn left it to his son-in-law, the Honorable William L. Eagleton, currently United States Ambassador to Syria, who believes that it was acquired at the same time and from the same source as the Antioch Chalice (no. 40)—which would mean Kouchakji Frères. As for the date of acquisition, it is clear from a letter written by Bosworth in 1955 to the director of Dumbarton Oaks, that he had bought the chalice before World War II,[41] and it is quite possible that it was considerably earlier, since as early as 1917 Bosworth was personally acquainted with Gustavus Eisen who, the previous year, had published the Antioch Chalice for Kouchakji Frères.[42]

The Hama treasure, then, was seen assembled as twenty-four objects in Hama in 1910 where, apparently, it was photographed (fig. II.4) and an inventory was drawn up, which was communicated to clergy in Sidon and forwarded to those in Jerusalem. In the same year, another chalice (and strainer?) from the same treasure circulated among the clergy of Jerusalem and Beirut, together with a chalice inscribed with names found on objects in the Stuma treasure. Both these chalices (and the strainer) ended up in Jerusalem, where one chalice (no. 27) was bought by St. Anne's in 1910 (with the strainer? [no. 26]), and the other chalice (no. 29) was bought by the British Museum in 1914. A third chalice (no. 28), bearing the name of the village featured on four objects of the Hama treasure, was seen in Paris at the beginning of 1911 and was bought shortly(?) thereafter, perhaps from Kouchakji Frères, by an American whose family still retains it. Before 1926 twenty-two of the twenty-four objects recorded at the church of Hama were bought locally and taken to Egypt, where they were photographed again. Then finally, in 1929, they entered the collection of Henry Walters, by way of Joseph Brummer, in Paris.

Thus far thirty-eight (or thirty-nine) objects have been accounted for: eleven of the Riha/Stuma group (counting, for now, the Sergios and John chalice, no. 29), and twenty-seven (or twenty-eight) of the Hama group (with or without the *Chrismon* box, no. 17). In reviewing the provenance of these latter objects, the first evidence to take note of is the letter of Basil Gebarat of Hama, dated July 27, 1910,[43] which records that the treasure was found in early April 1910, at the bottom of a cistern in the village of Krah, on the railway line between Hama and Aleppo (fig. II.1). Gebarat states that there were twenty-four objects—the number of those in the old photograph (fig. II.4)—and that the government wanted to confiscate them, but that the clergy of Hama refused to relinquish them "en raison qu'ils sont des objets religieux chrétiens dediés à l'église de S. Serge qui est en ruine à Hama; car ils sont réellement dediés à S. Serge." (They would thus be officially exempt from confiscation.) He concluded by saying: "Ma lettre est donc très confidentielle dont la publication nous fait grand tort." A few months later Gebarat had reconciled a troubling fact: how did this hoard found at Krah happen to belong to the cathedral of Hama? When the Prince of Saxony visited that autumn, he recounted the story that after centuries at Hama, the treasure was buried around 1830, and was only rediscovered (at Krah) "in the passed year" (1909?).[44] In 1926, when these objects were published by Diehl for the first time, the provenance was still given as Krah, but according to him, they were found there together with the Antioch treasure.[45] It is therefore necessary to introduce this final group of objects into the account before continuing with the problem of Krah and the provenance of the Hama objects.

The Antioch Treasure

According to an article published by Gustavus Eisen in 1916, Arab workmen digging a well at Antioch (fig. II.1) in 1910 reached, at a depth of several meters, some chambers, where they found seven silver objects and enough folded fragments of silver to fill a sack.[46] The treasure included three plaques (nos. 44–46), two chalices (nos. 40, 41), a large cross (no. 42), and another, smaller cross (no. 43). Eisen said that they were sold directly by the workmen to Constaki and Salim Kouchakji, in Aleppo—that is, two of the several Kouchakji brothers who were dealers operating there, in Paris, and in New York. But in a more extensive publication of 1923, Eisen said it took the Kouchakjis two years (1908–1910 or 1910–1912?) to acquire the whole treasure,[47] while the date of the sale is later (1950) given as "the Feast of the Epiphany" (i.e., January 6 [1910]).[48] According to this version, the Aleppo Kouchakjis melted the fragments for their metal value and soon took or sent the intact objects to their brother Georges, in Paris, where the smaller cross may have been acquired by Wilhelm Froehner, former *conservateur* at the Louvre.[49] With the outbreak of World War I, these pieces were taken to New York to another brother, Habib, and his son Fahim. This account was repeated by Eisen in his successive publications, each time with slight adjustments. Yet two central facts remained constant: that the treasure was found at Antioch and that its discovery took place in 1910.

Although the Froehner cross (no. 43) is mentioned again in Eisen's publication of 1923, it was dropped from that of 1933, and by 1934 a "paten" was introduced into the group, which in 1952 was finally reidentified, correctly, as a mirror (no. 48), following the appearance of its handle.[50] In publishing eight spoons (nos. 49–56) in 1930, Diehl said only that they were "de provenance syrienne, bien qu'on ne puisse preciser l'endroit où elles ont été trouvées."[51] In 1931 they belonged to the Paris dealer J. G. Gejou who, in selling them to the Bliss family in 1937, claimed that they were part of the Antioch treasure.[52]

More convincing is the case made for three silver fragments now in the Louvre (nos. 42b, 42c, 47), which at the time of the exhibition of Byzantine art in Paris in 1931 belonged to the collection of Alphonse Kann of S. Germaine-en-Laye.[53] From there they passed to the Bokanowski Collection, and were eventually presented as a gift to the Louvre, some time before their publication by E. Coche de la Ferté, in 1958.[54] The latter scholar emphasized the resemblance between one of these fragments (no. 47) and one of the Antioch treasure plaques in The Metropolitan Museum (no. 46). The other two fragments (no. 42b, 42c) constitute the two central revetment medallions for a large cross. Significantly, the large (and fragmentary) Antioch cross in The Metropolitan Museum (no. 42a) is also composed of revetment, a form extremely rare among surviving Early Byzantine crosses. Indeed, that the Louvre fragments were once integral to this very cross, and therefore to the Antioch treasure, has been proved by a recent "reconstruction" (see Entry No. 42).

This cross and five other original objects of the Antioch treasure are known to have been restored by the firm of Léon André in Paris, in 1913.[55] Before the restoration at least one object was sent to New York, where in 1912 it was seen by Belle da Costa Greene of the Pierpont Morgan Library.[56] The object in question was the famous Antioch Chalice (no. 40), whose inner cup, set within the shell of an elaborate, inhabited vine scroll, Kouchakji Frères wished to identify as the Holy Grail.[57] The lengthy discussions engendered by this claim are summarized in Entry no. 40, but its bearing on the publicized provenance of the object was succinctly put by René Mouterde in 1926, when he noted that it was:

> . . . hausser la valeur marchande (of the object) en lui donnant une origine illustre, le plus ancien centre chrétien hors de Palestine (i.e., Antioch) . . . (precisely because one wanted to claim it bore) . . . le plus ancien portrait du Christ.[58]

After its restoration in Paris in 1913, the Kouchakjis had wished to show it to J. P. Morgan, who had bought a large part of the second Cyprus treasure in 1905.[59] But Morgan had died earlier that same year (1913), without seeing the chalice, and it was not until 1950 that Fahim Kouchakji (Habib's son) succeeded in selling it to The Metropolitan Museum, together with two of the plaques and the large cross (nos. 40, 42a, 44, 45). The third plaque, the simple chalice, and the mirror (nos. 41, 46, 48) had been sold to Joseph Brummer around 1934, and he in turn sold them to The Metropolitan Museum in 1947.[60] Therefore, of the nineteen objects or fragments associated in one way or another with the Antioch treasure, seven are now in The Metropolitan Museum (nos. 40, 41, 42a, 44–46, 48), three (all fragments) are in the Louvre (nos. 42b, 42c, 47), eight (all spoons) are at Dumbarton Oaks (nos. 49–56), and the small Froehner cross (no. 43) has apparently disappeared.

The attribution of this group of objects to Antioch has long been disputed. Following the publication of Eisen's first book in 1923, a barrage of criticism was launched by L. C. Woolley, René Mouterde, Charles Diehl, and Bayard Dodge. Woolley published information obtained from "the dealers in question" that the treasure, composed of only three objects, was found in 1910 in a mound near Ma'aret en-Noman (fig. II.1), where it was sold for £3 to local people, who then sold it for £70 to dealers in Aleppo; these dealers in turn sold it to Kouchakji Frères for £120.[61] Mouterde repeated, without accepting either, two different accounts learned from two groups of friends of the Kouchakjis: one that the Antioch Chalice was found at Serjilla, and the other that the discovery was made at Tell Bissa, thirty kilometers south of Hama (fig. II.1).[62] This second location was also later indicated by the widow of Frederick Vester of Jerusalem, who sold the British Museum its chalice in 1914.[63]

In 1926 and 1927, Diehl and Bayard Dodge, then president of the American University in Beirut, published their own accounts, presumably relying on information supplied by Tawfic Abucasem, whose source, in turn, was undoubtedly the clergy of Hama; both took the Antioch and Hama objects to be part of a single treasure.[64] Diehl and Dodge each gave the provenance as Krah, on the railway line near Hama (fig. II.1). Diehl, however, mistakenly gave that village's location as thirty-three kilometers west of Hama, while Dodge placed it thirty-three to thirty-four miles north of Hama, on the railroad, between the

Kawkab and Hamadaniyya stations, at a place called Abbariyya, now Quarah (i.e., Krah). (Krah is, in fact, twenty-four kilometers northeast of Hama.) Workmen digging a well were said to have come upon two columns laid in a cross and twenty-seven silver objects (Antioch plus Hama) tied together, at a depth of thirty-three to thirty-four feet—a repetition of numbers that is somewhat suspect. René Mouterde, in 1926, rejected both Krah near Hama and Kara south of Homs (fig. II.1), drawing attention to the fact that the name Krah resembles the Early Byzantine name engraved on objects of the Hama treasure (i.e., Koraon), and suggesting that Krah had been chosen as a provenance solely for that reason. He personally thought instead that the treasure (Antioch plus Hama) was found in a suburb of Hama (he later indicated Hish, "à un quart d'heure de marche au N de Hama") and, like Gebarat, he linked it to a local church of St. Sergios, a reused inscription of which he found in the center of the city.[65]

On reflection, it seems likely that someone knowingly chose as a provenance the site of Krah, both to associate it with the name Koraon, as Mouterde pointed out, and to distance the treasure from the discovery and seizure of silver at Stuma. After all, the fear of confiscation had already been expressed by Gebarat in July 1910, and the stories of discovery were clearly elaborated in the following months in order to justify keeping (or selling) the objects. There is, moreover, nothing about the village—beyond the sound of its name—to favor the association. Krah (or Grah) lies in a region studied in depth by Jean Lassus, who described it in his 1935 publication as a ". . . petit village en cônes, sans ruines, près du chemin de fer."[66] He went on to point out that the railway stations in this region were essentially modern settlements, having no material trace of antiquity. Futhermore, while the Krah provenance for the Hama (plus Antioch) treasure was being promoted in international publications in 1926 and 1927, it was at the same time apparently being dropped by the local clergy in favor of Mouterde's "suburb of Hama" theory. On April 7, 1927, Patriarch Gregory of Antioch wrote that the hoard objects ". . . ont été découverts dans les fouilles organisées au Monastère Sergios à Hama, monastère communément connu là-bas sous le nom de 'Ruines du monastère Sergien'."[67] The chance discovery in a cistern had now become an organized excavation.

But if the Antioch and Hama treasures did not come out of the ground at Krah, where were they found? Just as no one now believes the Antioch Chalice to be the Holy Grail, few scholars today would accept the word of the Kouchakjis that the object was found in Antioch (modern Antakya). After all, that provenance is too integral a part of the sacred relic myth to stand on its own merits. Two of the alternative provenances suggested by others—namely, a place near Ma'aret en-Noman, and Serjilla—bring us very close to the general region of Idlib, Stuma, and Riha (fig. II.1). In 1985, Krikor Mazloumian of the Baron Hotel in Aleppo (from which T. E. Lawrence reported on the British Museum chalice in 1913) recalled a local tradition that the Antioch Chalice had been found "near Idlib." The early testimonies of the Ottoman authorities (cited by Ebersolt and Marcopoli) make clear that the Stuma and Riha hoards can both be accounted for "near Idlib" (i.e., at Stuma) in the years 1908 and 1909. As for the Hama treasure, there is the testimony of Naoum Nahas in 1910 that the two chalices he then had—one clearly belonging with the Hama pieces—came from the region of Aleppo, an idea rejected by Gebarat (presumably) because it threatened the safety of the large hoard photographed at his church in Hama in 1910.

In fact, there is persuasive evidence that the Hama treasure, which bears dedications to a church of St. Sergios in the village of Kaper Koraon, originally came from "near Idlib" (i.e., at Stuma), for five kilometers from Stuma there is a village that still bears a name very similar to that of Koraon: Kurin (fig. II.2).[68] The sixth-century Syriac equivalent of the Greek *Koraon* would be *Kurin,* meaning "kilns," and it is identical to the modern Arabic name. Kaper Koraon (or Kaper Kurin) would therefore be "the village of kilns"—indicating, perhaps, a local industry in ceramics, metal or glass. The Kaper (i.e., "village") would have been dropped, just as in the cases of Kepar d-Birtha/Kaper Pera, which today is el-Bara, and Kaper Barada, which is modern Brad.[69] Unlike Krah, Kurin is a prosperous agricultural village with a palpable historic past. Tombs, cisterns, and vestiges of buildings in ashlar masonry (figs. II.6, II.7), all hitherto unpublished, have survived there from early Byzantium, and medieval occupation is attested by a mosque and Arabic inscriptions.[70]

Fig. II.6

Fig. II.7

Another important element binding all four treasures together is the Kouchakji family. It is well known that the Antioch treasure belonged to the Kouchakjis from 1910 and, although not public knowledge, there is evidence in the files of The Walters Art Gallery to suggest that the Hama treasure likewise belonged to them, presumably before Abucasem bought it (i.e., in the early 1910s), for it was Fahim Kouchakji, who, years later, presented the old photograph of the Hama treasure (fig. II.4) to Marvin Ross at The Walters.[71] Furthermore, the Bosworth chalice (inscribed "Kaper Koraon"), which was seen in Paris in 1911, is believed by its owner to have been acquired from the Kouchakjis. And finally, there is the evidence of the three objects of the Stuma and Riha treasures which were bought by the Abegg Stiftung in 1964, for these, too, had apparently belonged to the Kouchakji family. Confronted by James Rorimer, then director of The Metropolitan Museum, about the persistent attempts to link the Antioch and Hama treasures, Fahim Kouchakji (son of one of the brothers, Habib) answered in a somewhat confusing letter of June 13, 1950, that the Hama pieces were, to his knowledge, found near Hama (and the Antioch pieces, at Antioch).[72] They were bought "by a silversmith," who, having cleaned them, gave them to the cathedral of Hama, and the clergy in turn auctioned them off. The high bidder was Tawfic Abucasem, and the underbidder was Fahim's uncle, Salim Kouchakji, agent of Kouchakji Frères. The story continues that in 1930, the son of the silversmith presented to a nephew of the underbidder (i.e., to Henri Kouchakji, Fahim's cousin) the old group photograph of the hoard which eventually ended up at The Walters Art Gallery. Interestingly, in the letter of Gebarat to Bacha of July 27, 1910, a reverse (indeed, more plausible) transaction is reported: the clergy of Hama turned the hoard over to certain goldsmiths ". . . pour les laver et réparer ce qui en est cassé et faire paraître l'écriture plus évidente."[73]

Undermining Fahim Kouchakji's account of events in 1910 is the fact that at the very moment that the Kouchakjis were said to have been bidding for the Hama treasure, they had mortgaged the Antioch Chalice to the Homsi Bank—this according to George Antaki of Aleppo (in 1985), whose grandfather owned that bank at the time. It is likely, therefore, that the Hama treasure was sold off by the Kouchakjis to an official of the bank at Hama in order to repossess part of the Antioch treasure from the Homsi Bank.

With regard to the evidence of joint burial offered by the objects themselves, several observations may be made, pending a thorough laboratory examination (on The Walters objects, see Chapter III, below). The condition of the objects when found, insofar as it can be determined from their present condition, and early photographs and records, does not contradict the theory that they were all buried together in a field at Stuma (Ebersolt), where they may have been discovered in the process of plowing, as was the Durobrivae treasure,[74] or "in a ruin in a tilled field" (Marcopoli). The dents sustained by many objects (nos. 2–8, 11, 13, 14, 27, 28, 30, 34, 36–39), and the corrosion on some of these and others (nos. 34–36, 39–56), may indicate loose burial in the earth, rather than concealment in a container. Contact with different parts of the soil and varying amounts of moisture (within a ruin?) may account for the varying degrees of corrosion and damage.[75]

Some objects bear signs that they were buried together in groups. As noted above, similar amounts of metal have broken away from the right sides of the two fans (nos. 31, 32), indicating that they were lying (or held) together back to front at the time of their damage. Diagonal dents in the three Hama patens (nos. 4–6), the three Stuma patens (nos. 34, 36, 39), and the Antioch mirror (no. 48) suggest that all these objects could have been stacked together (from the bottom up in this order: nos. 6, 4, 39, 5, 34, 36, and 39). Stuma paten no. 34 has, in addition, the marks of another circular object pressing against its egg and palmette decoration. The Riha paten (no. 35), which has the identical inner diameter as the Stuma paten, may have been lying separately, perhaps half exposed to moisture, which would account for the thick layer of corrosion on its upper right half (fig. 35.9), similar to that documented on the Antioch objects, including the spoons (nos. 40–56). At least three Antioch plaques (nos. 44–46), with equal amounts of corrosion, may have been piled up together. A variation in corrosion can still be seen on four objects obviously buried together—that is, the Stuma pieces in the Istanbul musuem, which apparently have not been thoroughly cleaned since 1908 (although the paten rims have been straightened). The patens (nos. 34, 36, 39), which may have been stacked together, bear corrosion, while the fan (no. 31) does not. It is, of course, also possible that any corrosion on the Hama objects may have been removed by the Syrian silversmiths cited above, before the objects were photographed together as a treasure (fig. II.4; where, however, they are clearly black). The inclusion of baser metals would have retarded the corrosion of those silver objects with which the bronze, iron, *et cetera* came into direct contact. In this context, it is well to recall the bronze seal belonging to Abucasem in 1913, found perhaps with this, rather than with the second Hama treasure.[76]

Conclusions

What, then, may be said in conclusion about the four silver treasures associated with Stuma, Riha, Hama, and Antioch? The story of each, if pursued on its own merits and with its own evidence, leads back to the same short period of time (1908–1910), to the same small geographical area (figs. II.1, II.2), and to the same few individuals (especially, the Kouchakjis). All four are village church treasures of comparable technical quality and monetary value, all are independently dateable to roughly the same decades, and all bear (comparable) inscriptions naming individuals who can be organized into a plausible family tree (see fig. I.1). Can all this be mere coincidence, or does it allow—perhaps require—a single interpretation?

A possible reconstruction of events may run as follows: In January 1908 a large treasure of over fifty silver objects[77] was found in a field at Stuma. The Ottoman authorities, having learned of the discovery, seized four objects but were unaware of the rest. Villagers alerted the Christian goldsmiths in the nearby town of Riha—mentioned by the contemporary American archaeological expedition from Princeton as being a prominent group.[78] One way or another, the Christian antiquities dealers of Aleppo—the Kouchakji and Marcopoli families, as well as Elie Abdini, Salim Djambar, and others[79]—became involved and bought the forty-six or so remaining pieces. In disposing of them, these dealers were quite naturally guided both by a fear of confiscation and by commercial considerations.

In order to buy up the whole treasure from the other dealers, as Eisen stated,[80] the Kouchakjis needed to raise money. Owning perhaps the most outstanding single object, the Antioch Chalice, they mortgaged it to the Homsi Bank. With this money they may have obtained about half the treasure objects, carefully selected on the basis of object type, interrelated inscriptions, and general appearance; these could be organized into a "symmetrical" and seemingly complete altar service comprising three patens, three chalices, two large crosses, two small crosses, two lampstands, *et cetera.* In order to protect this "treasure" from confiscation (so that it could be sold to the director of the Ottoman Bank at Hama), it had to be accepted as religious property in the eyes of the Ottoman authorities. To achieve this, the objects were publically displayed at Hama (in 1910) and described there and abroad as ancient church property, rediscovered at Krah or Hama (both places being conveniently remote from Stuma). Having established its credentials, the Kouchakjis were free to sell the "Hama Treasure," no doubt at a handsome profit, and to regain the Antioch Chalice (which they transported to Paris and New York by 1912).

With the remaining two dozen or so pieces, the Aleppo dealers did several things. Those objects closely related to what had been seized (e.g., the second Communion of the Apostles paten and the second fan) were, in effect, relatively "hot," and so they were offered first to foreigners (to the British Museum by way of Gertrude Bell, and to Sarre), and then taken to France, where they became the "Riha Treasure"—which years later would be reunited at Dumbarton Oaks. Others, bearing related inscriptions (nos. 33, 37, 38), were kept out of the art trade for decades. The two chalices handled by Nahas were probably considered relatively safe and, by the similarities in their design and inscriptions, a natural pair; they were offered for sale together, locally. Finally, what remained—uninscribed pieces and those whose inscriptions mention neither village nor church, pieces in generally poor condition—became the "Antioch Treasure," supporting cast for the Holy Grail, all said to have been unearthed with a large quantity of silver fragments from a sort of ecclesiastical *geniza* on the site of the Constantinian cathedral of that Apostolic city.

Of course, the above reconstruction is, and will always remain, hypothetical. Nevertheless, the convergence of a variety of evidence—some circumstantial and some intrinsic to the objects themselves—renders it (or a variant of it) a distinct possibility. Moreover, several points are by now well established:

1. That all four treasures—Stuma, Riha, Hama, and Antioch—appeared, were owned, and were traded in the same years, in the same area, and by the same few individuals.
2. That the Stuma and Riha treasures were *certainly* found together.
3. That the Bosworth, Jerusalem, and London chalices (and the Jerusalem strainer) are integral to the Hama treasure.[81]
4. That the Antioch, Hama, and Krah find-spots are false, that the Riha find-spot is due to a misunderstanding, and that Stuma is the only one which is justifiable.
5. That there is a distinct possibility that ancient Koraon is one and the same with modern Kurin—which means that the Hama treasure would have been dedicated in a church only five kilometers from Stuma.

In sum, the evidence and arguments that have been presented concerning the four separate treasures strongly suggest that they formed a single large silver treasure—the "Kaper Koraon Treasure"—unearthed in the same place and at the same time: Stuma, 1908.

NOTES

1. Tchalenko, 1953–1958, vol. 3, 100.

2. I owe the information about the excavation to Georges Tate; for the capital, see Mouterde, 1934, 474, 476, fig. 20.

3. Unpublished journal and photograph album of G. Bell, Department of Archaeology, University of Newcastle-upon-Tyne. I would like to thank Mrs. Lynn Ritchie for identifying the relevant pages in the journal, and for supplying a copy of the old photograph of the Riha paten reproduced in Entry no. 35.

4. This letter was for a long time preserved in the British Museum, where in the 1930s, E. Kitzinger excerpted this information, subsequently included in Ross, 1962, 13. Unfortunately, at present the letter cannot be found.

5. See, respectively, Lawrence, 1954, 195 (letter of March 10, 1912); and *IGLS*, nos. 194, 198, 199, 211–213.

6. Giron, 1922, 69; *IGLS*, no. 211 (now in the Cabinet des Médailles, no. S41).

7. Unfortunately, this letter, too, has been misplaced (see note 4, above).

8. Ross, 1962, 13.

9. Bréhier, 1919 [I], 256; *idem*, 1919 [II] 420; *idem*, 1920, 175.

10. Quoted by Royall Tyler in a letter written to Mildred Bliss on February 1, 1924. I would like to thank the Honorable William Tyler for the text of this and other pertinent letters. In fact, Lawrence was nowhere near Riha in 1908. Indeed, his first trip to Syria began in June 1909, several months after both Marcopoli and Bell had announced the discovery of the Riha paten. See Lawrence, 1954, xi, 82 ff.; and *idem*, 1964, 63 ff.

11. See *idem*, 1954, 246.

12. Cited by Rosenberg, 1928, vol. 4, 685, who calls it a "Flabellum von Stuma" and says it is a "Gegenstück" to the fan from Stuma, in Istanbul (no. 31). The journey "von Aleppo bis Balis" (Sarre and Herzfeld, 1911, vol. 1, 113 ff.) was made from October 1907 to March 1908.

13. Rosenberg, 1928, vol. 4, 684 ff., nos. 9862–9869.

14. See Entries nos. 31 and 32.

15. For contrasting views, see Dodd, 1973, 40 ff.; and Kitzinger, 1958, 19, and note 70.

16. It was presented to Dumbarton Oaks in 1955 by Mrs. Royall Tyler and William Tyler in memory of Royall Tyler.

17. The letter was written to Mildred Bliss who, with her husband Robert Woods Bliss, founded Dumbarton Oaks (see note 10, above).

18. This according to a letter of Royall Tyler dated January 1, 1924. See also Ross, 1962, 14; and the Dumbarton Oaks files (DO files), which were kindly made available to me by Miss Susan A. Boyd, Curator of the Byzantine Collection.

19. DO files.

20. Bréhier, 1919, 256.

21. Rosenberg, 1928, vol. 4, 207, no. 5907; Carré, 1930, 190, 192, 208; and Tardy, 1984, 201, 207, 237. These stamps were applied to objects imported from the Ottoman Empire and thirty other countries; "M" designates Marseilles. I thank Mr. Richard Randall, Miss Susan A. Boyd, Mlle. Catherine Metzger, Mr. Derek Content, and, especially, M. Daniel Alcouffe for help with these stamps.

22. Lawrence, 1954, 195.

23. Dodd, 1973, 5; see also *idem*, 1968, 143, 147.

24. DO files.

25. Dodd, 1973, nos. 1, 2.

26. The letter is preserved at St. Anne's Monastery, Jerusalem. I wish to thank Mr. Denys Pringle, who kindly located and copied this and other pertinent documents there. Ronzevalle himself apparently took the photograph of the chalice, which is still on file with his letter in Jerusalem.

27. *IGLS*, nos. 201, 2046.

28. Lawrence, 1954, 246.

29. British Museum files (BM files), which were kindly made available to me by Mr. David Buckton of the Department of Medieval and Later Antiquities.

30. The strainer was kindly brought to my attention by Denys Pringle in a letter of October 18, 1983.

31. Dodd (1961, 20, note 75; 1973, 20, note 71) was the first to make this connection.

32. See note 26, above.

33. See note 26, above.

34. Sachsen, 1912, 10 ff.

35. The information about Abucasem is contained in a letter dated June 13, 1950, from F. Kouchakji to J. Rorimer, in The Metropolitan Museum of Art files (MMA files). These files were kindly made available to me by Dr. Margaret Frazer, Medieval Curator. The Port Said photograph was that published by B. Dodge and presented by him to The Metropolitan Museum.

36. *IGLS*, no. 2049.

37. According to a letter of R. Tyler dated February 3, 1935, the treasure was still in Egypt in early 1927; The Walters Art Gallery files (WAG files).

38. 1934, vol. 2, 124. The misunderstanding apparently arose from a remark made by Brummer, or so indicates a letter of R. Tyler to M. Ross, dated February 9, 1935 (WAG files). See also *Early Christian*, 1947, nos. 394, 408.

39. Mouterde, 1926, 365, note 2; *IGLS*, no. 2045.

40. Letter from W. Eagleton to W. Tyler; see note 10, above.

41. The letter is dated November 15, 1955, and was written to John Thacher; it states that the chalice had been "brought through the war" (DO files).

42. See Eisen, 1923, vii.

43. Translated in a letter of July 6, 1913 from Père Bacha to Père Cré, preserved at St. Anne's, Jerusalem. See note 26, above.

44. Sachsen, 1912, 10 ff. If calculated from the time of the visit, the discovery date would be 1909, and if calculated from the book's publication, it would be 1911. But perhaps this passage was actually written in 1910, in which case the implied date of 1910 would match that of Gebarat's letter.

45. Diehl, 1926, 105. According to Fahim Kouchakji's letter of June 13, 1950 (see note 35, above), Diehl was relying for this information on Abucasem, who wanted to "promote (the) value" of his Hama silver by associating it with the more famous Antioch treasure.

46. Eisen, 1916, 426.

47. *Idem,* 1923, 3. According to this more complicated account, the objects had changed hands until owned by sixteen different people—and two pieces "had been carried off to Mesopotamia."

48. Letter of F. Kouchakji to J. Rorimer, dated June 13, 1950 (MMA files).

49. Eisen, 1916, 426 ff. The Froehner cross was only loosely associated with the hoard: "supposed to be from the same find" (*ibid.,* 426) and "believed found too" (*idem,* 1923, 3). Froehner, however, knew both Eisen and the Kouchakjis for, at Eisen's request, he wrote a letter (9/3/16) saying he considered the Antioch Chalice to be genuine, having been shown it by Kouchakji Frères before it was cleaned byLéon André, in 1913 (MMA files).

50. Eisen, 1934, 6; *Early Christian,* 1947, no. 393; and MMA files.

51. Diehl, 1930, 209.

52. *Exposition,* 1931, no. 375; Ross, 1962, 18; and DO files.

53. *Exposition,* 1931, no. 398.

54. Coche de la Ferté, 1958, nos. 41, 42.

55. Downey, 1954, 277; Rorimer, 1954, 162; and MMA files, which include a statement signed by Léon André and dated August 31, 1916, that the Antioch Chalice was restored by his firm between April 12 and August 21, 1913.

56. Rorimer, 1954, 162.

57. Expressed in Eisen, 1916, 436 f.

58. Mouterde, 1926, 363 f.

59. Rorimer, 1954, 162.

60. *Ibid.; Early Christian,* 1947, nos. 391–393; and MMA files.

61. Woolley, 1924, 281.

62. Mouterde, 1926, 364.

63. In a letter written to J. Rorimer, dated July 16, 1951 (MMA files).

64. Diehl, 1926, 105 (and note 45, above); and Dodge, 1927. (See also, *idem,* 1950.) In a note dated April 10, 1950 (MMA files), Dodge identified the find-spot as a place called "Shiha, the ruined village of Krah," just north of Hama. Shiha is 5.5 kilometers on the road (not railroad) northwest of Hama.

65. Mouterde, 1926, 365 ff. I have not been able to find the suburb of Hish on any map; a village of Hish lies very near Ma'aret en-Noman.

66. Lassus, 1935, 108, 140, 188.

67. A copy of this letter was sent by H. Seyrig to M. Ross on September 29, 1956 (WAG files).

68. Modern Kurin is spelled with an Arabic *kef,* which is equivalent to the Greek *kappa* of Koraon and the Syriac *kaph* of Kurin. The name Koraon is given in three slightly different forms on the silver. "Koraon" is described in *IGLS,* no. 2029, as a Greek neuter genitive plural. As used on the silver, it is unclear whether the genitive was dictated by the immediate syntax (i.e., in ageement with *komes*) or whether it was an integral part of the name.

69. See *IGLS,* nos. 530, 1481.

70. See Sourdel-Thomine, 1954, 192; and *idem,* 1956, 16. See also, Tchalenko, 1953–1958, vol. 3, 122.

71. Letter from F. Kouchakji to J. Rorimer, dated June 13, 1950 (MMA files); letter of M. Ross to J. Rorimer, dated June 8, 1950 (WAG files).

72. See notes 35 and 45, above.

73. See note 26, above.

74. Painter, 1977 [I], 8 f.

75. I thank Richard Stone and Edmund Dandridge, conservators at The Metropolitan Museum of Art, for discussing this and other problems related to the Antioch treasure.

76. See note 36, above.

77. The highest figure, fifty-eight, would count the large cross (no. 42) as three objects. The lowest figure, forty-five, would count the cross as one object, and would exclude those pieces most loosely associated with the treasure: the *Chrismon* box (no. 17), the Riha chalice (no. 30), The Metropolitan Museum mirror (no. 48), and the eight Dumbarton Oaks spoons (nos. 49–56). Of course, various intermediate totals are possible.

78. *Topography,* 1899/1900, 59.

79. I thank Mr. George Antaki for information about these colleagues of the Kouchakji brothers.

80. With regard to the Antioch treasure (Eisen, 1923, 3). See note 47, above.

81. See Entry no. 29 for evidence supporting the London chalice's connection.

CHAPTER III:

A TECHNICAL STUDY OF THE HAMA TREASURE AT THE WALTERS ART GALLERY

III. A Technical Study of the Hama Treasure at the Walters Art Gallery

Carol E. Snow and Terry Drayman Weisser
Department of Conservation and Technical Research
The Walters Art Gallery

The technical study of the twenty-three silver objects that make up The Walters Art Gallery share of the Hama treasure (Entries nos. 1–20, 22–24) was a collaborative effort among conservators, curators, scientists, and silversmiths. In order to answer questions on Byzantine silver technology raised by the curators, the Department of Conservation and Technical Research pursued a series of examination and analytical techniques. An effort was made to provide information on: the composition of the metal; fabrication techniques (i.e., casting, hammering, joining); methods of surface finishing and decoration (i.e., lathe-turning, repoussé, chasing, niello, gilding); alterations to the metal over its history; and the present condition of the objects. In addition to careful viewing of the silver with the naked eye, examination techniques included the use of a binocular stereomicroscope, and x-radiography. Further analysis made use of energy-dispersive x-ray fluorescence and x-ray diffraction. Because of the paucity of published technical information on Byzantine silver, we also examined for comparison objects of the Riha, Phela, and Sion treasures at Dumbarton Oaks, and the Antioch treasure silver at The Metropolitan Museum.[1] The results of our study of the Hama silver have been integrated into the individual catalogue Entries; our technical reports are given in Appendix III.1. Here we will first describe our methods of examination and analysis—why they were chosen and how they were useful for this study—and then we will present a discussion of our general observations.

Methodology

Our study began with a survey of The Walters Hama silver objects using the examination techniques available to us in our own laboratory. Compositional analysis eventually required that we turn to resources outside the Gallery. X-ray fluorescence analysis was provided by Mrs. Janice Carlson, Museum Chemist, Analytical Laboratory, Winterthur Museum, and x-ray diffraction analysis was provided by Mr. Richard Newman, Conservation Scientist and Assistant Conservator for Objects and Sculpture, and Mr. Eugene Farrell, Senior Conservation Scientist, Center for Conservation and Technical Studies, Harvard University Art Museums.

Microscopic examinations were made with the use of a Zeiss OPMI-I Epitechnoscope, a binocular microscope commonly used for eye surgery. Using six to forty times magnification, we examined the general condition of the silver and looked for tool marks, joins, indications of surface finishing, and any other surface information that might bear on fabrication techniques and possible pre- and post-excavation restorations. Photomicrographs were taken of features that might provide information on the tools that were used. Wherever possible, photomicrographs were made of the letters *alpha* and *omega* in the inscriptions so that letter forms and tool marks for creating basically similar shapes could be compared.

The structure of the silver was examined through x-radiography. A Siefert industrial x-ray unit with a maximum kilovoltage of three hundred at a fixed milliamperage of five was used. Exposures for most of the silver were made at 295 Kv, five mA, for one minute at a distance of seventy-five centimeters from the tube. The radiographs provided information on the structure of the metal, fabrication techniques, and modern repairs and restorations. They are presented in the individual entries (nos. 8, 11) only where particularly significant features are evident, but are available through the Department of Conservation and Technical Research for further study.

For the analysis of the metal composition we chose the technique of x-ray fluorescence because it is non-destructive, fast, and readily available. The technical aspects of the instrument and procedures used at the Winterthur Museum are described in Appendix III.2, which also gives the pertinent data. The data obtained gave us information on the absolute purity of the silver alloys used, on the relative compositional differences among the components of each object, on fabrication techniques, and on restorations or replacements.

Questions naturally arise as to the accuracy of the results due to the problems inherent in using a surface technique to analyze ancient metal. These have been discussed thoroughly in the technical literature.[2] One major problem is that silver alloys are not homogeneous; that is, the composition of an object may vary from spot to spot, so that the surface makeup detected by x-ray fluorescence may not be representative of the overall character of the metal. Surface enrichment (i.e., the depletion of the less noble alloying elements, such as copper, leaving a higher percentage of the more noble elements, such as silver, on the surface) may have occurred through the fabrication cycles of hammering, annealing, and pickling, through leaching in a burial environment, or through restoration or conservation treatments after excavation. Surface enrichment may also have resulted from the conversion of silver corrosion products on the surface to pure silver, which can happen under certain burial conditions or during cleaning. Because the corrosion products have been removed from the Hama silver, and undoubtedly a thin layer of metal as well (through cleaning with abrasive polishes in previous treatments), these pieces may well give better surfaces for compositional analysis than untreated objects.

There are other problems inherent in a surface analytical technique such as x-ray fluorescence. The shape of the object may restrict sample site locations and may affect the accuracy of the results of the analysis of any site that is not a flat surface. The half-inch aperture of the instrument limits the sample size, and at the same time, prevents the selective analysis of specific areas or parts of a smaller dimension, such as soldered joins. Difficulty may be encountered in detecting certain elements. With the instrumentation at Winterthur the detection of mercury was difficult due to its close proximity in the spectrum to gold. Therefore, in analyzing the gilded surfaces, the high gold content may have obscured the presence of mercury. The detection of zinc on a gilded surface or in an alloy with gold also has to be treated carefully, since a secondary peak in the spectrum for gold appears at approximately the same peak as zinc. Therefore, an alloy that does not contain a significant amount of zinc may yet appear as if it did. With the above problems associated with x-ray fluorescence analysis in mind, we have presented the results of this technique as relative values that have provided us with some general characteristics and useful information for comparative studies among our group of Hama silver objects.

Neutron activation analysis to detect the trace elements iridium, zinc, tin, arsenic, antimony, and selenium was considered for the Hama pieces. This technique can be more accurate than x-ray fluorescence when a drilled sample rather than a surface area is analysed. However, the destructive sampling techniques required, along with the difficulty in locating an appropriate testing facility, led us to abandon this approach. It should be noted that comparisons have been made between the results of x-ray fluorescence analysis and neutron activation analysis performed on the same Byzantine silver objects in the Dumbarton Oaks Collection, and the results correspond closely (see Appendix III.2, Table III.3, below). In addition, the results of our analysis correspond closely with the neutron activation analysis of a sixth-century silver openwork lamp from the Sion treasure at Dumbarton Oaks.[3]

For our study, x-ray diffraction analysis was used to aid in determining whether the inscriptions and decorative elements on the Hama silver objects had once been inlaid with niello, a compact black silver sulfide or mixture of metallic sulfides. If the Hama objects had been decorated with niello, the exact composition of the material was of interest.

Niello has been the subject of several recent articles.[4] By analyzing niello samples from various contexts and periods the authors of these articles have attempted to establish dates for the use of various recipes for niello and to test the reliability of early written sources on techniques (Pliny, first century; al-Hamdani, tenth century; Theophilos, twelfth century, *etc.*). Even the limited number of analyses carried out over the past ten years has changed our understanding of the history of niello. In the case of the Hama treasure, the large number of objects from one group available for study affords an excellent opportunity to make a significant contribution to the available reference data for comparative studies of niello.

The various metallic sulfides used as niello are crystalline compounds, which each give characteristic patterns on photographic film when analyzed by the powder x-ray diffraction technique. Therefore, this method was chosen to distinguish among the various possible compositions of niello which might be found on the Hama objects. A similar study has been carried out on the Sion silver treasure at Dumbarton Oaks. X-ray diffraction analysis of the niello required the removal of microscopic samples. The small sample size chosen required an x-ray diffraction method that would produce a strong enough crystalline pattern for identification of the compounds (see Appendix III.3, below for a discussion of the instrumentation and the x-ray diffraction data).

The black material from fourteen objects in the Hama treasure was sampled (nos. 1–3, 5, 7, 10–12, 14, 17–19, 23, 24). Several of the objects had large quantities of what appeared to be niello remaining in inscriptions or decorative elements. On other pieces, however, only a black residue was found, which could not be distinguished visually from the common black silver sulfide corrosion product, acanthite. Since acanthite was also used as a niello inlay material during the period of the manufacture of the Hama objects, x-ray diffraction analysis alone could not provide a method for determining whether this black material was true niello, or simply corrosion. Therefore, when acanthite was found, the appearance of the material and evidence of surface preparation to receive niello were also considered. The compounds and their formulae identified through x-ray diffraction analysis can be found in Appendix III.3.

Other potential problems in analyzing niello should be mentioned. Niello is not a homogeneous material; it often consists of more than one phase or distinct part interspersed in another, and our small sample size may have yielded an unrepresentative result. Also, as the composition of the silver alloy substratum may have been altered by leaching during burial or subsequent cleaning, the same fate may have befallen the niello. In fact, an uncleaned object inlaid with niello from the Sion treasure was examined recently, and the black niello was covered with what appeared to be green copper salts. The removal of this green layer during cleaning would probably leave a niello somewhat depleted in copper. Alterations in composition may also occur if silver sulfide niello is heated to around 840° C in the presence of oxygen, since this causes decomposition to metallic silver. This might occur if annealing was not controlled during restoration.

Our study to date has not provided adequate information on possible ore sources for the silver and other alloying elements. Current studies of Byzantine silver mines[5] will add to the existing body of knowledge on ancient mines generally.[6] These studies have included the use of lead isotope analysis to characterize and pinpoint ore sources. Since silver is often derived from a lead sulfide ore, galena, and therefore normally contains at least traces of lead, this method of analysis can be used to identify ore sources for silver. Once lead isotope ratios have been established for Byzantine silver mines, Byzantine silver objects can be analyzed for comparison. A drawback of this technique, beyond the destructive sampling required, is that if silver from different ore sources has been combined, for example through remelting of objects, the results will not be representative of any particular site. This may be a serious problem with the Hama silver, as we believe that at least some of the metal may have come from remelted objects. However, lead isotope analysis is being pursued for a few of the objects, particularly those that were stamped (nos. 1, 2, 5, 13). If the results prove to be significant, consideration will be given to further lead isotope analysis of the Hama silver.

OBSERVATIONS AND DISCUSSION

The emphasis of our technical study was on the identification of fabrication techniques used in the manufacture of the Hama silver. To aid our study, comparisons with Roman and Sasanian techniques were made. Here are defined and described the basic methods used in forming, surface finishing, and decoration by the Byzantine manufacturers of the Hama silver. A compilation of these techniques is illustrated in Appendix III.1, Table III.1. Additionally, we have included a brief statement on the present condition of the Hama silver, which is remarkable for its fine preservation and highly polished surfaces.

Before discussing the fabrication techniques, a few general observations about the composition of the metal should be made. Although the actual sources for the metal cannot be identified at this time, important points can be made about the metallurgical history of Byzantine silver based on the results of our analyses. Overall, the silver alloys used for the Hama objects were of a purity greater than that of modern sterling silver (92.5% silver to 7.5% copper). Compositions with 4–8% copper are known to improve the mechanical properties of the metal; that is, it yields a metal that is strong yet malleable.[7] Some of the Hama silver compositions fall within that range, though some contain less copper. (Surface enrichment, described above, is a factor to consider here.)

Variations in the percentage of copper and other minor alloying elements in the Hama silver reflect an understanding of the above principle, and of the physical characteristics of the alloy. Both the purity and the variations imply that alloying of the silver was controlled. (See Appendix III.2 for an illustration (fig. III.5) of the use of minor alloying elements for cast and hammered objects. A ternary diagram gives the ratios of copper [Cu], gold [Au], and lead [Pb].) For example, the pair of Hama lampstands (nos. 11, 12) both show compositional variations among their components that make metallurgical sense—that is, the spikes and column shafts contain more copper, making them stronger. Another illustration of this point can be found by comparing the composition of the bowl of the Hama ladle (no. 23), which is lower in copper, making it more malleable and easier to hammer, with the composition of its handle, which was cast with more copper in the alloy, which lowers the melting point for easier casting and makes the metal stronger.

Another interesting aspect of Byzantine silver technology is reflected in the compositions of the spoons (nos. 18–20). The spoons were fabricated from two or three parts soldered together, yet compositionally the alloys are very similar to one another. This suggests that multiple parts for each object were cast from one melt of metal.

Four of the Hama objects (nos. 1, 2, 5, 13) bear government control stamps.[8] There is no significant compositional difference between the stamped and unstamped objects. Therefore, based on our results, no correlation can be made between stamps and the purity of the metal. Analyses of the Riha silver at Dumbarton Oaks (nos. 30, 32, 35) seem to corroborate this observation.

Of the twenty-three objects in the Hama treasure, only two crosses (nos. 9, 10) were left in their "as cast" state, with minor surface finishing and decoration added after casting. These crosses contain significantly higher amounts of copper, which lowered the melting point of the alloy; obviously they were not intended to be hammered. Seven other Hama objects (nos. 14, 18–20, 22–24) were made from cast parts and hammered parts joined by soldering, while the remaining objects received their final form through hammering alone. In some cases (e.g., lampstands nos. 11, 12) it is difficult to determine whether a cast form closely approximating the final form was used rather than sheet, but because the final form was achieved by hammering, we have grouped them in that category.

The process of forming metal objects by hammering goes back to Neolithic times[9] and continues to be used by contemporary craftsmen. Generally, for silver objects formed by hammering, the metal is first cast into a billet or ingot which is then hammered into a disc. A centering mark is punched into the bottom of the disc to serve as a guide during the forming stages. The methods of forming by hammering are "sinking" and "raising"—and a combination of the two. Sinking is accomplished by hammer blows to the inside of a concave form, which stretches the metal into shape. Because sinking thins out the metal, thick sheet must be used. On the other hand, raising is accomplished by blows to a convex surface, thereby compressing the metal and making it thicker. For many of the Hama objects both sinking and raising were used. A clear example is the hanging lamp (no. 13). Surface finishing has obliterated the evidence of these forming techniques on many objects, making it difficult to describe accurately which was used where. For this reason we simply use the phrase "formed by hammering." The extensive use of hammering as a forming technique for the Hama silver demonstrates that the metal was used conservatively, and that it was pushed to its limits. Most objects have been hammered very thin. Any excess was no doubt trimmed and saved for other use.

In the process of hammering cold metal, it loses its malleability through the creation of stresses within the structure of the metal. To relieve the stresses and restore its malleability, the metal must be annealed—that is, heated evenly at a fixed temperature for a fixed time. The annealing temperature for sterling silver is 649° C.[10] The proper temperature can be judged by the color of the metal during heating. After annealing the metal is cooled, often in a "pickle" of dilute acid to remove oxides that may have formed. If the metal is not annealed enough, stress cracks will develop from overworking. These can be seen on a number of the Hama objects (e.g., nos. 1, 11–13).

Once the components for an object have been basically formed, they are joined mechanically or with solder. Silver soldering makes use of a silver alloy with a melting point lower than that of the metal being joined. An example of both types of joining is found on the Hama repoussé chalice (no. 3); the foot was attached to the bottom of the cup through the overlapping of a metal ring, creating a mechanical join, and the metal ring itself was attached to the bowl by a soldered join. The other Hama chalices in The Walters (nos. 1, 2) seem to have been joined by soldering alone. (For the joining techniques used on other objects, see individual Entries.)

The surface of the metal can be given a smoother finish by planishing and burnishing. Planishing makes use of a slightly dome-faced hammer that reduces the size of the earlier hammer facets on the surface. Burnishing smooths the surface further by rubbing with a polished tool made of steel, hematite or agate. Files and other abrasives are also used to finish the surface. Further finishing can be accomplished by turning on a lathe. While the object is held firmly on the lathe, metal from the surface is removed with abrasives, or the surface is smoothed with burnishing tools. The Hama chalices (nos. 1–3), patens (nos. 4–6), lamp (no. 13), ewer (no. 14), bowl (no. 16), and strainer (no. 24) all received finishing on the lathe. Of particular interest are the bowl and paten no. 4, both of which have burnished, raised discs in the center measuring 2.3 centimeters in diameter. These discs must have been covered by the clamping device of a lathe, as they do not show the finishing marks from turning. With the possible exception of the lamp, no spinning or forming of the shape was done on the lathe. It is believed that spinning to form objects was a relatively late development. Early examples of silver objects formed by spinning, reported by H. Maryon, were found in the Sutton Hoo ship burial (AD 655).[11]

Some decoration can also be carried out while the object is on the lathe. This technique is especially suitable for creating lines that run around the circumference of a vessel or that make circles on a flat surface (e.g., a plate) centered with the lathe. The lines are made by holding a pointed tool against the surface as the lathe is turned. On several of the Hama objects (nos. 3–6, 14) shallow lines were made while turning on the lathe to define bands, which would later frame inscriptions.

In addition to lines created on the lathe, the types of decoration found on the Hama objects include repoussé work, chasing, engraving, and gilding, each of which will be dealt with individually here.

The repoussé technique creates a three-dimensional, embossed surface by pushing out the metal from the reverse with a small-headed hammer or a hammer and punch, while the metal rests on a soft substance such as pitch. Periodic annealing may be necessary during this process as the metal hardens during working. Once the general shapes have been created, the metal is worked from the front to further define the forms and add detail. This additional working is done with chasing tools which deform the metal but do not remove it. The repoussé technique may be used before or after assembly of the object, depending on the shape of the piece. The three-dimensional quality created by this decorative technique imparts a liveliness to the surface due to the interplay of light and shadow over the forms.

Four objects from the Hama treasure were decorated by the repoussé technique: a chalice (no. 3), a pair of lampstands (nos. 11, 12), and a flask (no. 15). The flask was decorated in its entirety by repoussé and chasing. The figures, inscription, and decorative motifs were worked from the reverse while the metal sheet was still flat—that is, before the vessel was formed and joined. The foot of the chalice was worked in the repoussé technique before assembly, whereas its cup could have been worked either before or after assembly. Only one section of each lampstand, the column capital, was decorated by the repoussé method. The acanthus forms were created by hammering out the thin metal sheet from the reverse and chasing the obverse.

In order to use the repoussé technique the metal must be quite malleable. The compositions of three of the above four objects reflect recognition of this problem on the part of the silversmith: the higher the silver content and lower the copper content, the softer the alloy formed. The body of the flask and the column capitals on the lampstands are higher in silver and lower in copper than other parts of the same objects (their copper content is less than 1.5%). The chalice, on the other hand, does not display the same compositional characteristics, containing from 3% to almost 5% copper. This may at least partially account for the cracks present in the bowl and foot of the object.

Except for the bowl (no. 16), all of the Hama objects were chased and/or engraved. Chasing is used in combination with the repoussé technique as discussed above, while both chasing and engraving are used to create lines, decorative motifs, and inscriptions.

Chasing involves the deformation of the metal from the front by hammering with specially made punches, tracers, and chisels. The shape of the tool determines the effect produced on the metal surface. Chased lines are characterized under low magnification by a series of indentations without sharp edges. No metal is removed from the surface in the chasing process.

Engraving is a process whereby tools such as gravers, burins or scorpers are used to remove metal from the surface of the object in order to create decorative lines or inscriptions. Engraved lines are generally more continuous and sharper than chased lines. The lines may have a shallow, tapering beginning and ending, or they may end abruptly at the point where the tool was forced in and broke off a chip of metal. Engraving may also deform the metal by pushing it out on the reverse if the sheet is very thin and malleable.

Chasing and engraving were used to create purely decorative elements on several objects in the Hama treasure. The repoussé flask (no. 15) demonstrates the use of punchwork to embellish the surface; it shows a cross formed by a series of fine dots on the book held by Christ and groups of three dots ornamenting the *tablia* on the two orant male figures. The ladle (no. 23) and three crosses (nos. 7–9) have simple engraved borders, while the box (no. 17) exhibits elaborately engraved decoration. Three spoons (nos. 18–20) and the three patens (nos. 4–6) are decorated with engraved crosses. Two of the patens (nos. 4, 5) still show evidence of the use of a compass and incised or scratched lines to establish and demarcate the ends of the arms of their crosses prior to engraving.

Inscriptions on the Hama objects were made in most cases by chasing or engraving, although some objects show a combination of the two techniques. (For a visual comparison of the tool marks see the photomicrographs of letters that accompany the individual Entries.) Serifs for the letters may be punched and lines engraved between the serifs to complete the form. This technique is especially apparent on cross no. 10, where a pattern of raised dots can be seen on the reverse which corresponds to the punched serifs of the letters on the obverse. The lines in the inscriptions on two chalices (nos. 1, 2) were alternately chased and engraved. The Hama ewer (no. 14) is decorated with a chased inscription on its shoulder and an engraved inscription on its handle. However, there is some doubt as to whether the extant handle is original to the vessel (see Entry no. 14). Inscriptions made up of a series of dots (i.e., *pointillé*) were created by a form of chasing involving the use of a pointed punch. Examples of this type of inscription may be seen on a chalice (no. 3), the lampstands (nos. 11. 12), and a spoon (no. 22).

The depth and quality of the chased or engraved lines may have depended on whether the inscriptions were to be inlaid with niello. Historically, niello is first referred to in Pliny's *Natural History*,[12] which describes the Egyptian practice of using a mixture of silver, copper, and sulfur to "stain" silver. However, with rare exception,[13] analyses on artifacts from Roman times on show no copper mixed with the silver in niello before the sixth century.[14] The use of lead sulfide in niello is first documented in an eleventh century Byzantine amulet case.[15] It is quite possible that additional analyses will yield other examples of the early use of mixed metallic sulfides.

Analyses of niello on sixth-century Byzantine silver objects, including the Hama pieces, have shown that silver sulphide as well as mixed silver and copper sulphides were used during this period. It has been suggested that small amounts of copper present in niello may not, at this early date, represent an intentional mixture, but may instead be the result of scraps of the silver alloy metal, which would contain copper, being used to make the niello.[16] It was not possible for us to determine whether this is true.

Of the fourteen Hama samples of niello analyzed by x-ray diffraction, nine were found to have silver-copper sulfides (i.e., jalpaite, stromeyerite or mackinstryite) present. Five samples were identified as silver sulfide (i.e., acanthite). Lead was not found in any of the samples and one sample contained no metallic sulfides at all. (See Appendix III.3 for x-ray diffraction data.)

As previously stated, acanthite is a common corrosion product found on silver objects, so other factors must be taken into account in determining whether or not true niello or simply corrosion is present. Visual examination of the decoration identified as acanthite leads us to believe that the chalice (no. 1) may be inlaid with true niello while the cross, lampstands, and spoon (nos. 7, 11, 12, 18) probably are not.

The composition of the niello, and whether or not it is fusible, seems to have determined the method of its application. Acanthite decomposes to metallic silver in the presence of oxygen before it reaches its melting point. Therefore it is not possible to melt a silver sulfide niello and fuse it to the silver substratum. It can be softened by heating, and it is likely that the method of application was to inlay the designated area with pure silver sulfide powder and then heat it to about 600° C, which would render the material soft enough to be compacted and burnished. Since this technique does not create a good bond between the niello and the silver, roughening of the surface by chasing or engraving would have been done to improve the adhesion.

The addition of copper to the niello lowers the melting point of the mixture so that the inlay can be fused to the silver substratum without decomposing the niello or melting the silver. The previously prepared mixture of silver-copper sulfide is ground to a coarse powder, applied to the designated areas of the silver, and heated to the melting point of the niello. The sulfide mixture flows and fuses with the silver substratum. The excess niello can be removed with abrasives and polished.

Gilding is another decoration technique used on the Hama objects to create contrasts on the silver surfaces. Generally, gilding entails the overlaying of the silver surface with a thin layer of gold. Various techniques have been used in the past to make gold adhere to a metal surface. Mechanical gilding, whereby gold foil is simply wrapped around a surface, was used as far back as the beginning of the third millenium B.C.[17] The use of an adhesive under the foil, as well as joining overlapped pieces of gold foil by burnishing, were early advances of this technique.[18] Diffusion bonding—that is, the bonding of gold to a clean metal surface by burnishing and heating—has been found on first millenium B.C., late Hellenistic, and early Roman objects.[19]

Mercury or "fire gilding" was in wide use during the later Roman Empire. Two methods have been proposed for the application of gold to a metal surface using mercury. In one process the substratum is rubbed with mercury and goldleaf is then applied. The other method requires that an amalgam of gold and mercury be made and spread over the metal to be gilded. In both methods the object is heated afterwards to drive off the mercury. This leaves an adherent, continuous film of gold on the surface. If gilding with mercury is suspected on an object, confirmation may be found by visual clues combined with analysis for mercury. Visual evidence of mercury amalgam gilding includes splashes of gilding on areas not intended to be gilded (see no. 30), spreading of the gilding over design borders, and filling up of engraved lines with gold.[20] Qualitative spectrographic analyses of gilding by Lins and Oddy have demonstrated that the absence of mercury indicates that mercury was not used in the gilding process, since detectable traces always remain even after heating and the elapse of time. However, the presence of a trace of mercury does not confirm that it was used, since traces of mercury may be found in ore sources—or, the mercury may simply be a contaminant from the environment.

Fig. III.1

Only five of The Walters Hama objects have gilding remaining on their surfaces. These objects include two chalices (nos. 2, 3), a ewer (no. 14), a flask (no. 15), and a small box (no. 17). Moreover, a paten (no. 4) may have been gilded, since x-ray fluorescence analysis shows a higher quantity of gold in its engraved band containing the inscription.

Selected areas of the chalices, the shoulder of the ewer, and the entire surface of the flask show evidence of gold leaf having been applied (fig. III.1; chalice no.3). Thicker strips of gilding indicate where the ends of each leaf of gold overlapped the next and provide a method for measuring the size of the leaves used, which ranged from 1.8 × 2.0 centimeters to 2.8 × 3.4 centimeters. The gilding on the flask and outer shoulder of the ewer, as well as that on the rim of chalice no. 3, contains traces of mercury (as identified by x-ray fluorescence analysis), while the analysis of chalice no. 2 does not show mercury. (As stated earlier, x-ray fluorescence analysis may not be able to detect mercury in the presence of gold since the peak for gold may mask the peak for mercury). Gilding on the neck of the ewer and on the small box appear from visual analysis to have been through mercury amalgam. Traces of residual mercury were found on the box by x-ray fluorescence analysis. The gilding on the neck of the ewer was not analyzed, therefore we cannot confirm the presence of mercury.

The general condition of the Hama silver is remarkably good. The burial environment for this treasure apparently was not as hostile as the environment of other treasures, and in fact, may have contributed to its preservation. (An examination of the uncleaned Sion silver treasure at Dumbarton Oaks confirms that silver can emerge from a burial environment well preserved, even if somewhat damaged.) The historical records, themselves dubious, give conflicting accounts of the Hama silver's possible archaeological context. One account claims that the hoard was found in 1910 at the bottom of a cistern, while another account states that the silver belonged to the church of Hama for several centuries and that it had been buried in modern times (*ca* 1830) and was discovered in 1910 (see Chapter II, above).

The earliest photograph of the Hama treasure, taken in 1910 (fig. II.4), portrays a group of objects with some structural damage and surface corrosion—but generally, the pieces are in sound condition. At about that time the silver is said to have passed through the hands of a silversmith or a goldsmith (or both). A 1910 letter states that the silver was given to the goldsmith "pour les laver et réparer ce qui en est cassé et faire paraître l'écriture plus évidente" (Basil Gebarat; see Chapter II, above). With this scanty evidence as our first report of the Hama silver's conservation history, we can only hope that the goldsmith did not intervene drastically, and that he respected the integrity of the silver and the craftsmanship of the Byzantine silversmith. The physical evidence suggests that he did.

Some repairs were made between the time the first photograph was taken and 1929, when Henry Walters purchased the silver. From Syria the Hama treasure had traveled to Port Said and Paris, before arriving in Baltimore. We do not know if it passed through any restorer's hands in its travels, though it is certain that the Antioch silver was treated in 1913 by the firm of the Parisian restorer Léon André (see Chapter II, above). Repairs were made at some time to several Hama objects, among them nos. 2, 14, and 15. Repairs to the ewer (no. 14) and the flask (no. 15) were done with modern alloy inserts and solders, which were detected by x-ray fluorescence analysis. Two crosses (nos. 7, 8) are missing their original tangs. One has been repaired by riveting on a copper alloy tang, while the other shows evidence of an unsuccessful repair attempt which has left the metal near the tang rough and misshapen. The riveted repair is visible in the 1910 photograph, but the other cross's base is covered by a paten so its condition then cannot be ascertained. These repairs may have been made during the time of their original use or possibly after excavation of the treasure.

By comparing photographs from 1926 and 1947[21] we see that a crude repair was made to one of the lampstands (no. 12) during that interval. The column was soldered to the base with lead, changing the height and misaligning the facets. This irreversible repair has altered the structural and aesthetic qualities of the lampstand.

The first treatment records at The Walters for the Hama silver date to 1947, when the objects were cleaned and lacquered. The method for cleaning was to use a paste of ammonia and whiting, an abrasive, pure grade of chalk. (Because ammonia dissolves copper, this treatment may have caused some surface enrichment.) In 1959 the lacquer was removed and the silver was polished with a commercial silver polish and relacquered. In preparation for this exhibition, the 1959 lacquer was removed and the pieces were polished with .05 micron alumina to diminish recent superficial tarnish. A commercial polish was used on more persistent tarnish. In most cases the removal of the lacquer, which had turned dull and gray, revealed a bright, highly reflective surface, enhancing the contrasting effects of the niello inscriptions and gilded decorations (compare figs. III.2, III.3).

Microscopic examination of the silver shows that the structure of the metal is very brittle, with numerous stress cracks which in many places appear to have been aggravated by burial and post-excavation treatments. Large stress cracks, such as in cross no. 8, are from straightening the metal without annealing it. (Since it was shown in its bent state in the 1910 photograph, the cross must have been repaired at a later time.) A few objects display evidence of redeposited silver, a result of burial conditions or certain cleaning treatments.

While the removal of the corrosion and a thin layer of the surface may have revealed the inscriptions and more information for study, previous treatments carried out on the Hama silver, especially mechanical cleaning, undoubtedly have caused some loss of detail. Heat treatments, such as modern soldered repairs, may have changed the metallurgical evidence contained in the structure of the metal. It cannot be denied that the silver as we see it today has changed since its fabrication in the sixth and early seventh centuries.

Fig. III.2

Fig. III.3

ACKNOWLEDGMENTS

A collaborative effort such as this technical study is the result of cooperation of individuals from diverse backgrounds. For making possible the study of comparative material, we extend our gratitude to Miss Susan A. Boyd at Dumbarton Oaks and Dr. Margaret Frazer at The Metropolitan Museum. For the compositional analyses of the silver and her contribution to Appendix III.2 we thank Mrs. Janice Carlson, Museum Chemist, Winterthur Museum, and for the analyses of the niello amd their contibution to Appendix III.3 we thank Mr. Richard Newman, Conservation Scientist, Assistant Conservator for Objects and Sculpture, and Mr. Eugene Farrell, Senior Conservation Scientist, at the Fogg Museum's Center for Conservation and Technical Studies. We also owe thanks for a craftsman's perspective to Mr. Edward Collins, the last practicing silversmith at the Kirk Stieff Silver Company, and to Mr. Donald B. Heller, former silversmith and now Objects Conservator at the Winterthur Museum. Without all of these contributions the Hama silver would not have received the comprehensive study it deserves.

NOTES

1. We are grateful to Miss Susan A. Boyd, Dumbarton Oaks, Curator of the Byzantine Collection, and Dr. Margaret Frazer, Curator of Medieval Art, The Metropolitan Museum, for making it possible for us to examine these objects.

2. R. Cesareo, M. Ferretti, and M. Marabelli, "Analysis of Silver Objects by Scattering and by X-ray Fluorescence of Monoenergetic Gamma-rays," *Archaeometry* 24 (1982), 170–180; J. A. Charles and J. A. Leake, "Problems in the Fluorescence Analysis of Cu/Ag Byzantine Trachea and Metallurgical Information from Sections," *Methods of Chemical and Metallurgical Investigation of Ancient Coinage,* ed. by E. T. Hall and D. M. Metcalf, (London, 1972), 211 ff., E. R. D. Elias and Z. A. Stos-Gale, "Classification of Some Silver Coins of Aquitaine on the Basis of the Results of Semi-quantitative XRF Analysis," *Numismatic Circular* 89 (1981), 356 f.

3. On the Sion Treasure in general, see Boyd, 1979, *passim.*

4. S. La Niece, "Niello: an Historical and Technical Survey," *The Antiquaries Journal* 63 (1983), 279 ff. (hereafter, La Niece, "Niello"); *idem* "Roman and Dark Age Niello 200–700 A.D.,"*Symposium on Archaeometry* (Bradford, U.K., 1983), 229 ff. (hereafter, La Niece, "Roman"); M. Lazovic, N. Dürr, H. Durand, C. Houriet and F. Schweizer, "Objets byzantins de la collection du Musée d'Art et d'Histoire," *Genava* 25 (1977), 51 ff. R. Newman, J. R. Dennis, and E. Farrell, "A Technical Note on Niello," *Journal of the American Institute for Conservation* 21 (1982), 80 ff. (hereafter, Newman *et. al.,* "Technical Note"); W. A. Oddy, M. Bimson, and S. La Niece, "The Composition of Niello Decoration on Gold, Silver and Bronze in the Antique and Medieval Periods," *Studies in Conservation* 28 (1983), 29 ff.

5. K. A. Yener and H. Ozbal, "The Production, Exchange, and Utilization of Silver and Lead Metals in Ancient Anatolia: The Bokardağ Mining District Survey," *Symposium on Archaeometry* (Smithsonian Institution, 1984), 162.

6. A. A. M. Bryer, "The Question of Byzantine Mines in the Pontos," *Anatolian Studies* 32 (1982), 133 ff. N. H. Gale and Z. Stos-Gale, "Lead and Silver in the Ancient Aegean," *Scientific American* (June 1981) 176 ff.; E. Pernicka and G. A. Wagner, "Lead, Silver and Gold in Ancient Greece," *PACT* 2 (1982), 419 ff.

7. P. Harper and P. Meyers, *Silver Vessels of the Sasanian Period* (New York 1981), 147.

8. For Byzantine silver stamps in general, see Dodd 1961.

9. R. F. Tylecote, *A History of Metallurgy* (London, 1976), 1.

10. O. Untracht, *Metal Techniques for Craftsmen* (New York, 1968), 246.

11. H. Maryon, *Metalwork and Enamelling* (New York, 1955), 108. However, P. T. Craddock and J. Lang ("Spinning, Turning, Polishing," *Historical Metallurgy* 18 [1981], 35 ff.) disagree with Maryon's observations and believe that the technique of spinning a disc of metal to form an object was not in use before the medieval period and the development of the continuous action cranked lathe.

12. Pliny, *Natural History,* Loeb Classical Library trans. by H. Rackham (Cambridge, Mass., 1952), 99.

13. P. T. Craddock, J. Lang and K. S. Painter, "Roman Horse-trapping from Fremington Hagg, Reeth, Yorkshire, N. R.," *British Museum Quarterly* 37 (1973), 14.

14. La Niece, "Roman," 229; Newman *et. al.,* "A Technical Note," 81.

15. La Niece, "Niello," 287.

16. *Ibid.,* 280, 285–286; La Niece, "Roman," 230.

17. A. Oddy, "Gilding through the Ages: an Outline History of the Process in the Old World," *Gold Bulletin* 14 (1981), 75.

18. *Ibid.,* 75 f.

19. *ibid.,* 77; W. A. Oddy, S. La Niece, J. E. Curtis, and N. D. Meeks, "Diffusion-bonding as a Method of Gilding in Antiquity," *MASCA Journal* 1 (1981), 241.

20. P. A. Lins and W. A. Oddy, "The Origins of Mercury Gilding," *Journal of Archaeological Science* 2 (1975), 370.

21. WAG files.

Working Bibliography

J. W. Allan, *Persian Metal Technology 700–1300 AD* (London, 1979), 13–22.

A. A. M. Bryer, "The Question of Byzantine Mines in the Pontos," *Anatolian Studies* 32 (1982), 133–150.

R. Cesareo, M. Ferretti, and M. Marabelli, "Analysis of Silver Objects by Scattering and by X-ray Fluorescence of Monoenergetic Gamma-rays," *Archaeometry* 24 (1982), 170–180.

J. A. Charles and J. A. Leake, "Problems in the Fluorescence Analysis of Cu/Ag Byzantine Trachea and Metallurgical Information from Sections," *Methods of Chemical and Metallurgical Investigation of Ancient Coinage*, ed. by E. T. Hall and D. M. Metcalf (London, 1972), 211–218.

W. T. Chase, "The Technical Examination of Two Sasanian Silver Plates," *Ars Orientalis* 7 (1968), 75–93.

C. Conophagos, "Silver in Ancient Greece and Byzantium: Production and Art," Gettens Memorial Lecture (Washington, D.C., 1979).

P. T. Craddock, J. Lang, and K. S. Painter, "Roman Horse-trappings from Fremington Hagg, Reeth, Yorkshire, N. R.," *British Museum Quarterly* 37 (1973), 9–17.

P. T. Craddock and J. Lang, "Spinning, Turning, Polishing," *Historical Metallurgy* 18 (1984), 35–41.

C. Crane, "The Examination and Treatment of a 6th c. Silver Openwork Lamp from the Byzantine Church of the Holy Sion," *AIC Preprints* (Washington, D. C., 1980), 9–19.

J. R. Dennis, "Niello: a Technical Study," *Papers Presented at the Art Conservation Training Programs Conference* (Manchester, Mass., 1979), 83–95.

E. R. D. Elias and Z. A. Stos-Gale, "Classification of Some Silver Coins of Aquitaine on the Basis of the Results of Semi-quantitative XRF Analysis," *Numismatic Circular* 89 (1981), 356–357.

E. Foltz, "Zur Herstellungstechnik der byzantinischen Silberschalen aus dem Schatzfund von Lambousa," *Festschrift Jans-Jürgen Hundt zum 65. Geburtstag: Jahrbuch des Römisch-Germanischen Zentral Museums Mainz* 22 (1975), 221–245.

N. H. Gale and Z. Stos-Gale, "Lead and Silver in the Ancient Aegean," *Scientific American* (June, 1981), 176–192.

D. F. Gibbons, K. C. Ruhl, and L. S. Staikoff, "Analysis of Sasanian Silver Objects: A Comparison of Techniques," *Archaeological Chemistry*, ed. by C. W. Beck (Washington, D. C., 1973), 11–21.

P. Harper and P. Meyers, *Silver Vessels of the Sasanian Period* (New York, 1981), 144–163.

M. J. Hughes and J. A. Hall, "X-ray Fluorescence Analysis of Late Roman and Sassanian Silver Plate," *Journal of Archaeological Science* 2 (1975), 365–373.

L. B. Hunt, "The Oldest Metallurgical Handbook," *Gold Bulletin* 9 (1976), 24–31.

H. Jedrzejewska, "Comments on X-ray Fluorescence Quantitative Analysis of Ancient Silver Alloys," *ICOM, 6th Triennial Meeting, Ottawa* (Paris, 1981), 81.23.2.

S. La Niece, "Niello: an Historical and Technical Survey," *The Antiquaries Journal* 63 (1983), 279–297.

idem, "Roman and Dark Age Niello 200–700 A.D.," *Symposium on Archaeometry*, ed. by A. Aspinall and S. E. Warren (Bradford, U.K., 1983), 229–234.

M. Lazovic, N. Durr, H. Durand, C. Houriet, F. Schweizer, "Objets byzantins de la collection du Musée d'Art et d'Histoire," *Genava* 25 (1977), 5–62.

H. Lechtman, "Ancient Methods of Gilding Silver: Examples from the Old and New Worlds," *Science and Archaeology*, ed. by R. Brill (Cambridge, Mass., 1971), 2–30.

D. Leigh, M. Cowell, and S. Turgoose, "The Composition of Some Late 10th-Century Kentish Silver Brooches," *Historical Metallurgy* 18 (1984), 35–41.

P. A. Lins and W. A. Oddy, "The Origins of Mercury Gilding," *Journal of Archaeological Science* 2 (1975), 365–373.

H. Maryon, *Metalwork and Enamelling* (New York, 1955).

P. Meyers, "Technical Studies of Sasanian Silver," *MASCA Journal* 1 (1981).

P. Meyers, L. van Zelst, and E. V. Sayre, "Major and Trace Elements in Sasanian Silver," *Archaeological Chemistry*, ed. by C. W. Beck (Washington, D.C., 1974), 22–33.

A. A. Moss, "Niello," *Studies in Conservation* 1 (1953), 49–61.

R. Newman, J. R. Dennis and E. Farrell, "A Technical Note on Niello," *Journal of the American Institute for Conservation* 21 (1982), 80–85.

W. A. Oddy, "Gilding through the Ages: an Outline History of the Process in the Old World," *Gold Bulletin* 14 (1981), 75.

W. A. Oddy, M. Bimson, and S. La Niece, "The Composition of Niello Decoration on Gold, Silver and Bronze in the Antique and Medieval Periods," *Studies in Conservation* 28 (1983), 29–35.

W. A. Oddy, S. La Niece, J. E. Curtis, and N. D. Meeks, "Diffusion-bonding as a Method of Gilding in Antiquity," *MASCA Journal* 1 (1981), 239–241.

E. Pernicka and G. A. Wagner, "Lead, Silver and Gold in Ancient Greece," *PACT* 2 (1982), 419–425.

Pliny, *Natural History*, Loeb Classical Library, trans. by H. Rackham (Cambridge, Mass., 1952), 99.

D. Strong and D. Brown, eds, *Roman Crafts* (London, 1976), 11–23.

Theophilus, *On Divers Arts*, trans. by J. G. Hawthorne and C. S. Smith (Chicago, 1963).

R. F. Tylecote, *A History of Metallurgy* (London, 1976).

O. Untracht, *Metal Techniques for Craftsmen* (New York, 1968).

idem, *Jewelry Concepts and Technology* (New York, 1982).

K. A. Yener and H. Ozbal, "The Production, Exchange, and Utilization of Silver and Lead Metals in Ancient Anatolia: The Bokardağ Mining District Survey," *Symposium on Archaeometry: Abstracts* (Washington, D.C., 1984), 162.

APPENDIX III.1

Technical Reports for the Hama Treasure Objects in The Walters Art Gallery

1. CHALICE

Silver composition:	Ag	Cu	Au	Pb
Side of cup:	95.71	1.83	.98	1.39
Foot:	95.68	1.69	1.19	1.39

Method of manufacture:

The chalice was made from two sections: the cup and the foot, both of which were formed by hammering. Similarities in the silver composition, analyzed by x-ray fluorescence, suggest that the foot and cup were raised from metal sheet that was fabricated from a single cast billet. Stress cracks, from hammering the metal too thin without enough annealing, are present inside the cup and around the rim. After joining the two sections, probably with a silver solder which is not visible, the chalice was turned on a lathe to finish the exterior surface. While on the lathe, lines were shallowly incised around the rim and the foot. The letters of the inscription were engraved and chased to receive the niello inlay, only traces of which remain. X-ray diffraction analysis of a sample of the black material identified it as acanthite (Ag_2S), a silver corrosion product which may be a component of niello. No gilding is present on this chalice. The stamps inside the foot were applied after fabrication.

2. CHALICE

Silver composition:	Ag	Cu	Au	Pb
Rim of cup:	80.91	1.86	15.71	.54
Side of cup:	96.77	1.36	.96	.80
Inside foot:	97.68	1.41	*	.76

*Au excluded from calculation of alloy composition

Method of manufacture:

The cup and the foot of the chalice were formed by hammering. The upper portion of the foot above the knob is relatively thick; the foot was not hammered out to an even thickness. The similarities in the silver composition, analyzed by x-ray fluorescence, of the foot and the cup suggest the two sections were raised from metal sheet that was fabricated from a single cast billet. The two sections were probably joined with silver solder which is not visible. The chalice was turned on a lathe to finish the exterior surface and to shallowly incise the horizontal lines that run around the vessel. A mark on the bottom of the interior of the bowl was probably made while securing the chalice on the lathe. The letters of the inscription were engraved and chased to receive the niello inlay, only traces of which remain. Analysis by x-ray diffraction of a sample of the niello identified it as jalpaite ($Ag_{1.55}Cu_{0.8}S$), a known component of fusible niello. Parcel gilding was done in two bands around the rim, at the bottom of the cup and top of the foot including the knob, and around the edge of the foot. The gold appears to have been applied in overlapping sections, measuring 2.8 cm to 3.4 cm in length, possibly by burnishing gold sheet onto the surface of the silver forming a metallurgical bond. No mercury was detected. The stamps were applied after fabrication.

3. CHALICE

Silver composition:	Ag	Cu	Au	Pb
Cup:	93.52	4.83	.82	.67
Foot:	95.13	3.03	1.16	.45

Method of manufacture:

The chalice was fabricated from three sheets of silver: one was raised by hammering to form the cup, another sheet was raised to form the foot, and a third flat ring of silver was soldered to the cup and hammered over the flare of the top of the foot to form a mechanical join. Tool marks in the bottom of the cup indicate it was worked from the inside for the attachment of the connecting ring. Microscopic examination reveals green corrosion products under the ring suggesting that a silver/copper solder was used. X-ray fluorescence analysis suggests the silver of the bowl is compositionally different from that of the foot. The repoussé and chasing of the foot was done prior to assembly; no seams are visible in the foot under the microscope or in the radiographs. The repoussé and chasing of the cup could have been done before or after assembly. Horizontal turning marks and vertical burnishing marks on the cup indicate its surface was worked before the repoussé and chasing were done. The presence of stress cracks in the cup and the foot show that the silver was very heavily worked; the stresses in the metal were not completely removed by annealing. The gilding was done after the vessel was assembled. The gold was applied in overlapping sections, measuring approximately 2.7 cm around the rim and 1.8 to 2.0 cm in the arches. The sections of gold on the foot measure 2.8 to 3.0 cm. Traces of gilding are also evident on the rosettes, the capitals of the columns, in places on the figures, possibly on the bases of the columns, and on the knob. The gold may have been applied by mercury gilding as mercury was detected qualitatively by x-ray fluorescence. The inscription between a border of shallow, turned lines was made with a pointed tool to form dots that are now filled with a black material which may be niello or corrosion products. Analysis by x-ray diffraction of a sample of the black material identified it as stromeyerite ($Ag_{1-x}Cu_{1+x}S$; $0 \leq X \leq 0.1$). This is a known component of fusible niello, but may also be a silver corrosion product. The contrasting effect of the black on the silver makes the inscription easy to read.

4. PATEN

Silver composition:	Ag	Cu	Au	Pb
Central field, obverse:	94.13	4.51	.82	.46
Center of cross:	94.51	4.31	.74	.34
Band with inscription:	92.89	5.35	1.08	.61
Center, reverse:	95.10	3.68	.85	.31

Method of manufacture:

The paten was formed by hammering. The radiograph reveals an overall hammered structure. The entire interior and sides of the exterior of the paten were finished with a tool while turning on a lathe, leaving hammer marks still visible on the bottom of the reverse. Two centering marks, probably for the lathe or for determining the center during hammering, are visible on the reverse, one much deeper than the other. A circular area of 2.3 cm diameter which is slightly thicker than the surrounding metal is in the center of the obverse of the paten. There are no turning tool marks within the circle. It is likely that this circular area was masked by a support used on the interior surface to hold the paten during the turning procedure which thins the metal slightly as it removes irregularities. Six lines for the band containing the inscription were engraved while the paten was on the lathe.

Within the central circular area on the obverse a compass centering point can be found. From this point a circle was incised for the ends of the vertical axis of the engraved central cross; 1.5 cm above this compass point another compass point must have once existed for incising arcs, which are still visible, for the ends of the horizontal axis of the cross. The ends of incised perpendicular lines are visible which would have passed through the higher compass centering point, the circle, and the arcs. After the cross was engraved, the silver within the cross was burnished parallel to the axis of each arm to create a contrast with the turned background. The inscription was chased within the engraved band previously prepared for it. The greater amounts of gold and copper in the inscription band as determined by x-ray fluorescence analysis may indicate that it was once gilded and inlaid with niello. The composition of the surface of the cross indicates that it was probably not gilded.

5. PATEN

Silver composition:	Ag	Cu	Au	Pb
Center of cross, obverse:	96.17	2.31	.88	.54
Outside of cross, obverse:	96.43	2.13	.85	.52
Band with inscription, obverse:	96.37	2.15	.80	.56
Reverse:	97.16	1.68	.71	.39

Method of manufacture:

The paten was formed by hammering as is clearly seen by hammer mark patterns on the reverse and in the radiograph. The obverse and sides of the reverse were finished by turning on a lathe, then burnishing. A centering mark, probably for turning and engraving the lines for the band containing the inscription, is visible on the reverse. An indentation from a compass can be seen at the intersection of the arms of the cross from which arcs would have been drawn to indicate the ends of the arms of the cross. Both the cross and the inscription were engraved. The data obtained from x-ray fluorescence analysis shows the overall homogeneous surface composition of the paten and indicates that the cross and inscribed band were not gilded. X-ray diffraction analysis was carried out on a sample from the engraved inscription. No sulfide could be identified in the diffraction pattern; therefore it is difficult to determine whether the inscription had been inlaid with niello. The two stamps on the reverse were applied after fabrication.

6. PATEN

Silver composition:	Ag	Cu	Au	Pb
Center of cross:	95.20	3.56	.73	.48
Band with inscription:	95.38	3.42	.68	.46
Between band and side:	95.13	3.76	.61	.46
Center of reverse:	96.85	2.29	.59	.24

Method of manufacture:

The paten was formed by hammering. A hammer mark pattern is clearly visible on the reverse and in the radiograph. The obverse surface was finished by turning on a lathe. The sides of the reverse as well as a 3 cm band on the outer perimeter of the bottom of the reverse were finished in the same fashion. An indentation for turning can be seen in the center of the obverse. Lines for the rim and the band containing the inscription were engraved on the lathe. The cross was engraved and the inscription was chased. The x-ray fluorescence analysis data shows an overall homogeneous composition of the surface and indicates that the inscribed band and cross were not gilded. If the letters at one time were inlaid with niello, no trace remains.

7. CROSS

Silver composition:	Ag	Cu	Au	Pb
Left arm of cross, obverse:	95.71	2.36	1.35	.42
Left arm of cross, reverse:	96.98	1.20	1.36	.26

Method of manufacture:

The cross was cut from a sheet of hammered silver. After burnishing the surface of the cross, lines were engraved on the obverse and reverse as a border .4–.5 cm from the edges. Two holes approximately 2.8 cm apart were punched through the lower edge of each horizontal arm for suspension of *pendelia*. Inscriptions were chased on the obverse on all four arms of the cross. Traces of a black substance remain in some of the letters. A sample of this substance was analyzed by x-ray diffraction and found to be acanthite (Ag_2S). Although this compound may be a component of niello, it is also a common silver corrosion product. Thus, it cannot be determined with certainty whether the letters were originally inlaid with niello.

Only 1.5 cm of the original tang remains. A copper alloy repair has been added and attached with two copper alloy rivets to the remnant of the original tang.

8. CROSS

Silver composition:	Ag	Cu	Au	Pb
Center, obverse:	94.83	4.03	.64	.46
Center, reverse:	95.76	3.19	.56	.39
Tang, obverse:	96.05	1.78	1.58	.35
Ball:	95.64	3.19	.75	.28

Method of manufacture:

The cross was cut from a piece of hammered silver. The corners of the arms of the cross were originally cut leaving projections, only visible in the radiographs, to receive silver ball serifs. These projections were inserted through holes in the balls, soldered in place, and then the balls were probably hammered and burnished to disguise the joins. X-ray fluorescence data shows that the balls are very similar in composition to the main body of the cross. After burnishing the surface of the cross, lines were engraved on both sides to create a border .3–.4 cm from the edges. Finally, two holes approximately 3.5 cm apart were punched through the lower side of each horizontal arm for suspension of *pendelia*.

The original design included a tang at the bottom of the cross. The end of the tang has been broken off and a repair attempt has left it rough and misshapen. X-ray fluorescence analysis shows that the composition of the remainder of the tang differs from the rest of the cross. The silver and gold content of the tang is significantly higher, while the copper and lead content is lower. This is probably due to an attempt to repair the tang.

9. Cross

Silver composition:	Ag	Cu	Au	Pb	Zn
Upper arm, obverse:	84.88	12.99	.74	.87	.45
Upper arm, reverse:	83.36	14.72	.75	.79	.28
Lower arm, obverse:	89.68	8.19	.90	.79	.35
Lower arm, reverse:	92.67	5.24	.92	.74	.33

Method of manufacture:

The cross appears to have been cast. Neither the surface of the cross nor the radiograph shows any indication of hammering. A hole through the metal on the upper edge of the right horizontal arm and a small vertical crack on the bottom edge of the lower arm are very likely casting flaws. X-ray fluorescence analysis of the cross reveals a significantly higher copper content than that for the hammered crosses. The addition of copper lowers the melting point, which makes casting easier and results in a harder metal. Tool marks on the obverse and reverse indicate that the surface was burnished parallel to the arms of the cross to remove irregularities and improve the reflective quality. A line was engraved .1–.2 cm from the edges to create a border on the obverse. The inscription was engraved, and finally a hole for attachment was punched in the end of each arm. If the inscription was inlaid with niello, no trace of it remains.

10. Cross

Silver composition:	Ag	Cu	Au	Pb	Zn
Lower arm, obverse:	86.30	12.02	.78	.38	.42

Method of manufacture:

The cross appears to have been cast. Neither the surface of the cross nor the radiograph shows any indication of hammering. Small cracks in the corners where the arms of the cross join may be casting flaws. The surface is not highly burnished and appears quite grainy under moderate magnification. X-ray fluorescence analysis of the cross reveals a composition similar to that of no. 9. The high copper content lowers the melting point for casting and creates a harder metal. The pattern of raised dots on the reverse corresponding to the serifs of the inscription on the obverse indicates that the serifs were punched into the surface. Lines were then engraved between the serifs to complete the letters. A hole was punched through the end of each arm of the cross for attachment. On the upper arm a dent next to the hole is probably evidence of an initial attempt at punching the hole that was then determined to be too close to the edge. The letters may have been inlaid with niello. A reddish black fused-looking residue on the right arm was sampled and analyzed by x-ray diffraction. Although a fusible silver-copper sulfide, jalpaite ($Ag_{1.55}Cu_{0.8}S$), was identified, this was considered inconclusive due to a weak diffraction pattern.

11. Lampstand

Silver composition:	Ag	Cu	Au	Pb
Spike:	94.10	4.27	.91	.56
Cup:	95.63	2.31	1.03	.78
Column capital:	96.31	1.49	1.09	.73
Column shaft:	93.26	4.91	.88	.68
Column base:	95.43	3.27	.58	.45
Foot:	95.31	3.39	.65	.53

Method of manufacture:

The lampstand was fabricated from nine silver components:

1) The hollow spike was forged from thick sheet with a vertical seam evident on the surface. The radiograph shows the bottom of the spike flaring out slightly inside the cup. Analysis by x-ray fluorescence indicates the spike contains more copper than other parts of the lampstand, making the metal stronger and less malleable.
2) The flaring cup was formed by hammering from silver sheet. The hammer marks can be seen in the radiograph.
3) A silver insert, hammered from sheet, was attached to the inside of the cup with lead solder. A hole in the center of the insert to accommodate the spike is now sealed with iron corrosion products.
4) The column capital was made by hammering thin sheet. The acanthus appears to have been formed by repoussé and chasing the sheet, possibly with some engraving.
5) The hollow column shaft was forged from thick sheet. A vertical seam was partially closed with silver solder. Like the spike, the column shaft contains relatively more copper, giving it added strength.
6) The column base was raised from thin sheet. It may have been turned on a lathe.
7) The hexagonal base of the lampstand was hammered from sheet.
8) A thin, disc-shaped insert, formed by hammering, was attached to the inside of the base with lead solder.
9) The three feet were rough cast and forged or hammered into shape.

Except where noted, these components were assembled with the use of silver solder. Excess drips of silver solder can be seen on the underside of the cup, on the column shaft, and above the inscription on the base.

Through radiography, interior components of the lampstand can be determined. A partially corroded iron (confirmed with a magnet) rod runs the length of the lampstand from inside the spike to the top of the hexagonal base of the lampstand. This rod most likely served to provide additional structural strength. The inside of the base of the lampstand, from the column base to the top of the hexagonal base, was filled with lead, presumably to act as a counterbalance. At the joins of both ends of the shaft are reinforcing inserts of a material that was not identified.

After assembly, the surface was finished with files and other sharp tools and abrasives, and then by burnishing. The letters of the inscription were made by chasing with a pointed tool. Some of the small dots left by this tool are now filled with a black material. X-ray diffraction analysis of a sample of this material identified it as acanthite (Ag_2S) which can be a component of niello but in this case appears to be a silver corrosion product. The formation of corrosion in the recesses of the letters makes the inscription easier to read through the contrasting effect of the black on the polished silver surface. The black material present in the capital is also probably corrosion. No gilding was detected on the lampstand.

12. LAMPSTAND

Silver composition:	Ag	Cu	Au	Pb
Spike:	92.91	5.20	1.07	.67
Cup:	96.02	2.19	.95	.72
Column capital:	96.45	1.64	.87	.59
Column shaft:	94.33*	4.27*	.74*	.53*
Column base:	94.84	3.75	.61	.55
Foot:	95.18	3.65	.58	.49

*average of two analyses from column shaft

Method of manufacture:

This lampstand was manufactured by the same methods as the other lampstand (no. 11).

When this lampstand was found, the column was merely resting on the base without a proper join. A 1926 photograph shows the lampstand in that condition but, at some time between 1926 and 1947, a crude repair was made using lead solder for the join. The repair changed the height of the base, raising the column 2 cm higher than it is on the other lampstand. Marks from the originally soldered join are exposed at the top of the hexagonal base showing where the column should rest. Also the facets of the cup, column, and base are no longer aligned. The radiograph shows that some of the lead inside the base is missing which accounts for its lighter weight compared to the other lampstand. A modern, threaded iron bolt with a brass nut now extends from the underside of the base through the lead and approximately halfway up into the column shaft. It is unfortunate that this irreversible repair has altered the structural and aesthetic qualities of the lampstand.

13. LAMP

Silver composition:	Ag	Cu	Au	Pb
Bottom:	94.78	2.61	1.30	1.08
Lower side:	95.11	2.38	1.34	1.10
Suspension eyelet:	96.07	1.38	1.52	.91

Method of manufacture:

The lamp was formed by hammering from a single piece of silver. The foot was formed by folding the metal back on itself. The suspension eyelets were formed by cutting away the rim, with the holes punched from the inside out. Many thin areas, caused by excessive hammering, can be seen in the radiographs. The interior of the vessel was left as an unfinished, hammered surface. Under the microscope stress cracks can be seen on the interior surface, further indicating that the silver was heavily worked; the stresses in the metal were not completely removed by annealing. A few holes are present in the side from further working of the metal. After the vessel was basically formed, it was turned on a lathe to further define its final shape and to finish the exterior surface. Shallowly incised turn lines were done at this time: one at the rim, two in the mid-section, one above the foot, and one on the foot. Stamps were applied to the bottom of the lamp after manufacture.

14. EWER

Silver composition:	Ag	Cu	Au	Pb	Zn
Lower body:	96.64	1.96	.89	.39	
Handle:	92.17	5.89	.72	.37	.79
Band with inscription:	93.22	1.90	4.02*	.46	
Rim:	96.56	2.09	.77	.36	
Solder at rim:	81.83	4.68	.66	7.32	5.07

*qualitative indication of presence of gold

Method of manufacture:

The body of the ewer was formed from one piece of silver by hammering. A hammer mark pattern is clearly visible in the radiograph and on the interior of the vessel. The exterior surface was finished by turning on a lathe, then burnishing. There are two centering marks on the base. Both marks may be from turning; however, one mark may be from centering the metal before or during the forming process. While turning on the lathe, lines were engraved above the base, on the shoulder to create a band for the inscription, at the base of the neck, and on the rim. The inscription on the shoulder was chased. The band with the inscription was gilded with gold leaf in sheets approximately 2.5 cm by 3.0 cm. Thicker gilding remains where the sheets overlapped. Curled edges of the gold leaf are visible in the chased lines of the letters indicating that the gold leaf was applied after the inscription was made. Traces of mercury found in this area by x-ray fluorescence analysis indicate that the gold leaf may have been applied over mercury, creating an amalgam and binding the gold leaf to the surface, followed by heating to drive off the mercury. A band at the base of the neck was also gilded; the technique by which the gold was applied seems to be mercury amalgam. This cannot be confirmed since no x-ray fluorescence analysis was done in this area.

The handle was made separately from the vessel and was probably cast. The trapezoidal projection on the handle may have been made separately and attached with what appears to be silver solder. An inscription was engraved on the handle. The handle was attached to the vessel with solder. The original join must have given way and the handle has been sloppily reattached with a solder high in lead and zinc, as determined by x-ray fluorescence analysis. It is possible that the present handle is not original to the vessel, although it appears in the 1910 photograph. Old solder lines indicate an attachment of different dimensions. The composition of the handle differs from that of the body of the ewer. The handle is higher in copper and zinc, which would make the metal melt at a lower temperature for casting, and would also result in a harder, less malleable metal.

A sample of a black residue from a letter on the handle was found to be mackinstryite ($Ag_{1.2}Cu_{0.8}S$) by x-ray diffraction analysis. The presence of this fusible silver-copper-sulfide indicates that the handle inscription was once inlaid with niello. X-ray diffraction was not carried out on the black residue in the inscription on the shoulder of the vessel. Therefore, it is not possible to say whether or not it was inlaid with niello at one time.

15. FLASK

Silver composition:	Ag	Cu	Au	Pb	Zn
Body of flask: **	96.40	1.41	*	.41	
Rim:	95.13	2.82	*	.29	
Bottom:	74.35	19.89	.63	.44	4.52
Strip or patch:	85.30	14.16	*	.35	

*These analyses gave qualitative indications of the presence of gold; gold was excluded from the calculation of alloy composition by the computer.

**average of five analyses

Method of manufacture:

The flask in its present condition consists of four distinct parts: the body, rim, bottom, and a small strip which may be a modern patch. The body was formed from a hammered sheet of silver worked from the reverse in the repoussé technique and chased from the obverse to delineate the figures, decorative elements, and the inscriptions. A small punch was used to add finer decoration to the obverse (e.g., a cross on a book carried by Christ and a three-dot pattern as *tablia* ornament). The silver sheet was then rolled into a tapering cylinder and joined with solder where the edges meet. Thin traces of gilding remain scattered over the body of the flask, indicating that the entire surface was once gilded. Thicker vertical and horizontal stripes of gilding are evident where the leaves of gold overlapped during application creating a double layer. Mercury was found qualitatively during x-ray fluorescence analysis indicating that the mercury gilding technique was probably used.

The rim is a separate ring of hammered silver which was slipped over the top edge of the spout of the flask and soldered in place. Burnishing of the top of the rim has almost disguised the join; however, it is still easily seen from below the rim.

The bottom of the flask was cut to fit from hammered silver sheet. The extant bottom is probably a modern replacement since its composition is markedly different from the rest of the vessel and the solder used to attach it has been carelessly applied, obscuring parts of the lowest band of inscription on the body.

A lid and chain, now lost, are visible in the 1910 photograph. There is a silver strip at the original attachment site for the chain on the neck of the flask located 1.6 cm from the top and lying along the longitudinal soldered join of the body of the flask. The silver strip may be part of the original attachment for the chain, but may also be a modern patch to repair a damage caused when the chain was removed. Green corrosion is evident surrounding the strip and also on the bottom of the flask on the inside, which was examined with a medical cystoscope. This corrosion is probably due to the copper in the less pure silver reacting with solder fluxes or the oil or other liquids once contained in the vessel.

16. BOWL

Silver composition:	Ag	Cu	Au	Pb
Rim:	97.11	1.37	1.08	.32
Bottom:	97.22	1.59	.84	.26

Method of manufacture:

The bowl was formed by hammering from a single sheet of silver. After the general shape was formed, the surface was planished and burnished. The bowl was then placed on a lathe to finish the interior. A 2.3 cm disc in the center, burnished and slightly thicker than the surrounding metal, does not have turn lines indicating it was probably covered by a clamping device while the bowl was on the lathe. Turn lines on both the upper and lower surfaces of the flat rim suggest it may have been formed on the lathe. The exterior of the bowl still shows the facets from hammering.

17. BOX

Silver composition:	Ag	Cu	Au	Pb
Box				
Bottom:	95.52	3.00	.72	.67
Side with hexagons and squares:	95.17	3.18	.75	.85
Side with acanthus:	95.44	3.06	.69	.70
Side with Chrismon (ungilded area):	90.74	3.04	4.73*	.83
Lid				
Top (ungilded area):	95.47	2.96	.84	.55
Edge:	95.07	3.28	.69	.85

*This qualitative indication of the presence of gold in an ungilded area may be due to smearing of the gilding during previous polishing or to gilding in an adjacent area being detected during analysis.

Method of manufacture:

The box was formed by hammering, folding and joining. A hammer mark pattern is visible on the interior of the box and in the radiograph. Join marks on the interior and splits where the metal has separated along the bottom edges of the box indicate that it was most likely constructed from a flat sheet of silver cut as shown in figure 17.1. The sheet was folded as indicated by dotted lines in the diagram and either soldered at the joins with silver solder or joined mechanically by hammer welding. The lid may have been formed by hammering from a flat sheet. The box and lid are of very similar composition according to the x-ray fluorescence data and may be from the same sheet of silver. The exterior surfaces of the box and lid were burnished, then engraved. The *Chrismons* on the box and lid were gilded using the mercury-amalgam technique. Traces of residual mercury were found qualitatively during x-ray fluorescence analysis. A sample of a black substance in the engraved lines was analysed by x-ray diffraction and found to be stromeyerite, ($Ag_{1-x}Cu_{1+x}S$; $0 \leq x \leq .1$), a fusible silver-copper sulfide. Therefore, it is likely that the engraved decoration was at one time inlaid with niello.

18. SPOON

Silver composition:	Ag	Cu	Au	Pb
Bowl:	95.58	2.68	1.13	.49
Handle:	95.85	2.20	1.25	.40

Method of manufacture:

The spoon was cast either in one piece or in two sections, the bowl and the handle with the disc. Analysis by x-ray fluorescence indicates these two sections are compositionally very similar, and so if cast separately, they were probably cast at the same time from a single pour of metal. There may be a soldered join of the bowl to the disc on the handle but this join is not evident under the microscope or in the radiograph. After casting, the bowl was hammered into shape and burnished, and the handle also received further working of the metal to define the facetted knob, possibly shape the handle, and finish the disc. The cross in the spoon's bowl was shallowly engraved. The letters in the inscription on the handle were formed by chasing to receive the niello inlay. X-ray diffraction analysis of a sample of the black material present in the letters identified it as acanthite (Ag_2S), a component of niello or a silver corrosion product.

19. SPOON

Silver composition:	Ag	Cu	Au	Pb
Bowl:	94.88	2.98	.88	1.09
Handle:	94.73	2.48	1.16	1.30
Tip of handle:	95.14	2.39	.99	1.03

Method of manufacture:

The spoon was cast in two sections: the bowl, which was then hammered into shape, and the handle including the knob and the disc. The bowl was soldered to the disc of the handle. X-ray fluorescence analysis suggests the handle and bowl were cast from the same pour of metal since the compositions of the parts are so similar. Alternately, it is possible that the spoon was cast in one piece with the bowl cast as a rough form and hammered into shape. Under the microscope the join of the bowl to the disc appears relatively porous from soldering. After casting, hammering, and joining, the spoon was filed and worked to remove casting flaws and excess solder, and to define the shape of the handle. A cross was shallowly engraved in the bowl. The letters of the inscription were formed by engraving to receive the niello. X-ray diffraction analysis of a sample of the remaining black material in the inscription identified it as jalpaite ($Ag_{1.55}Cu_{0.8}S$) and acanthite (Ag_2S), a fusible niello.

20. SPOON

Silver composition:	Ag	Cu	Au	Pb	Zn
Bowl:	93.17	5.28	.50	.56	.42
Handle:	94.12	3.99	.54	.70	.49
Knob:	93.87	4.41	.45	.62	.49

Method of manufacture:

The spoon was cast in two sections: the bowl, which was then hammered into shape, and the handle including the knob and the disc. The bowl was soldered to the disc of the handle. X-ray fluorescence analysis suggests the handle and bowl were cast from the same pour of metal since the compositions of the parts are so similar. Alternately, it is possible that the spoon was cast in one piece with the bowl cast as a rough form and hammered into shape. However, under the microscope, the metal of the join of the bowl and disc appears porous and has tool marks typical of a soldered join. The alloy for this spoon differs from the alloys of the other spoons in that it contains some zinc. After casting, hammering, and joining, the spoon was filed and worked to remove any casting flaws and excess solder, and to define the shape of the handle. A cross was shallowly engraved in the bowl of the spoon.

22. SPOON

Silver composition:	Ag	Cu	Au	Pb
Bowl:	95.44	2.97	1.04	.34
Handle:	95.07	2.91	1.05	.53
Tip of handle:	95.20	2.65	1.17	.56

Method of manufacture:

The spoon was fabricated from three cast sections: the bowl which was hammered and planished into shape, the disc with a rat-tail, and the handle with an elongated finial. X-ray fluorescence analysis suggests these sections were cast at the same time from the same pour of metal since the compositions are so similar. Alternately, it is possible that the spoon was cast in one piece with the bowl cast as a rough form that was worked into shape. However, porous metal can be seen under the microscope at the joins of the bowl to the rat-tail and of the disc to the handle. This porosity is most likely a result of silver soldering, but may also be from casting. Drips of what look like silver solder can be seen inside the bowl. After casting, hammering, and joining, the spoon was worked and the surface finished. A monogram on the disc was made by chasing with a pointed tool to form dots that are now filled with a black material which may be niello or corrosion products. This black material was not analyzed. The contrasting effect makes the monogram possible to read.

23. LADLE

Silver composition:	Ag	Cu	Au	Pb
Bowl:	96.84	1.17	1.39	.42
Disc on handle:	94.94	3.46	.91	.51
Handle near bowl, obverse:	90.19	7.91	.85	.75

Method of manufacture:

The ladle was fabricated from two parts: the bowl which was formed by hammering and the handle which was formed by casting and working the metal. X-ray fluorescence analysis indicates the composition of the handle is higher in copper making the silver less malleable. The bowl, with less copper, would have been more malleable and therefore easier to hammer. Stress cracks, visible under the microscope inside the bowl where the sides were raised from the bottom and at the bends in the handle, show that the silver was heavily worked; the stresses in the metal were not completely removed by annealing. Pits and porosity in the metal on the underside of the handle at the join to the bowl distinguish that area as a soldered join. After the handle was joined to the bowl, surface finishing was done and shallowly engraved lines were added to the handle. The letters of the inscription were deeply engraved to receive niello inlay. Analysis by x-ray diffraction of a sample of the black material remaining in the letters identified it as jalpaite ($Ag_{1.55}Cu_{0.8}S$) and mackinstyrite ($Ag_{1.2}Cu_{0.8}S$). These minerals are known components of fusible niello.

24. STRAINER

Silver composition:	Ag	Cu	Au	Pb
Bowl:	96.75	2.06	.56	.26
Dolphin ornament:	94.70	3.56	1.02	.44
Handle:	94.07	3.85	1.07	.61
Ring:	91.51	6.66	.57	.68

Method of manufacture:

The strainer was fabricated from three parts: the bowl which was formed by hammering and turning on a lathe, a cast handle with the dolphin ornament cut out after casting, and the ring. X-ray fluorescence analysis shows the compositional variation among these three parts. After the handle was soldered to the bowl, the strainer was worked and finished. The holes in the bowl were punched from the inside out, the lines were engraved in the shaft of the handle, and the hole was made through the knob. Analysis by x-ray diffraction of a sample of the black material, present in traces in the engraved lines in the shaft of the handle, identified it as jalpaite ($Ag_{1.55}Cu_{0.8}S$) and acanthite (Ag_2S). This material is fusible and may have been a niello inlay. It is also possible that it is merely silver corrosion products. The ring was crudely forged, inserted through the hole in the knob, and the ends soldered together.

TABLE III.1

Fabrication Techniques of the Hama Treasure Objects in The Walters Art Gallery

Cat. No.	Object	Cast	Hammered	Turned	Repoussé	Chased	Engraved	Gilded	Niello	Inscription	Stamps
1	Chalice		●	●		●	●		●	●	●
2	Chalice		●	●		●	●	●	●	●	●
3	Chalice		●	●	●	●		●	?	●	
4	Paten		●	●		●	●	?		●	
5	Paten		●	●			●			●	●
6	Paten		●	●		●	●			●	
7	Cross		●			●	●		?	●	
8	Cross		●				●				
9	Cross	●					●			●	
10	Cross	●				●	●		●	●	
11	Lampstand		●		●	●			?	●	
12	Lampstand		●		●	●			?	●	
13	Lamp		●	●			●				●
14	Ewer	●	●	●		●	●	●	●	●	
15	Flask		●		●	●		●		●	
16	Bowl		●	●							
17	Box		●				●	●	●		
18	Spoon	●	●			●	●		?	●	
19	Spoon	●	●				●		●	●	
20	Spoon	●	●				●				
22	Spoon	●	●			●			?	●	
23	Ladle	●	●				●		●	●	
24	Strainer	●	●	●			●		?		

APPENDIX III.2

Energy Dispersive X-ray Fluorescence Analysis for Elemental Composition

Janice H. Carlson
Museum Chemist
Winterthur Museum
Winterthur, Delaware

The use of energy dispersive x-ray fluorescence analysis for the determination of the elemental composition of artistic and historic objects is well established as a tool appropriate to that end.[1] Numerous advantages are inherent to the technique. Since no sample is required, not even a minute rubbing or scraping, the object is not defaced. Complete multi-element quantitative analysis over a wide concentration range of all or most parts of an object, rather than scrapings from a single obscure area, can be achieved in a very short time, usually less than thirty minutes. Alterations or repairs can frequently be detected and the compositional features of objects of certain provenances are now sufficiently established that confirmation or denial of certain attributions is sometimes possible.

Energy dispersive x-ray fluorescence analysis is based on fundamental principles of atomic physics. When an atom is irradiated with x-rays and the energy of the incident x-ray exceeds the excitation level of one of the energy levels of the atom, there is a finite probability that the incident x-ray will be absorbed by an electron in that level. The electron is freed, leaving a vacancy, and an electron from a higher level drops into that vacancy. Simultaneously, an x-ray with an energy equal to the difference between the initial and final atomic energy levels is emitted. The energy released is uniquely characteristic of the particular type of atom involved. Thus, when a sample of silver or other metal is irradiated with x-rays, the various atoms in the alloy emit x-rays with energies characteristic of the elements present. Using appropriate electronic equipment, the emitted x-rays can be detected and counted and the data stored and analyzed by computer to produce both qualitative and quantitative x-ray fluorescence analyses of the sample.

A combination of electronic components made by the Kevex Corporation, Packard Instrument, and the Hewlett-Packard Company[2] was used for the x-ray fluorescence analysis of the silver objects in this study. Briefly, the instrumentation consists of an x-ray emitting radioactive source ($^{109}_{48}Cd$), above which the object to be analyzed is placed. The characteristic fluorescent radiation produced as a result of the source irradiation over a 0–40 keV range is detected by a solid state lithium drifted silicon detector, sorted according to energy, and stored in a 512–channel memory bank. Once a run is complete, the data are transferred from the memory bank to a HP Model 2108A computer, which is programmed to subtract a previously stored baseline of silver, sum the peaks of interest over five contiguous channels, and calculate the weight percent of each of fifteen different elements using factors derived from the analysis of a silver alloy standard of known composition (92.5% silver, 7.0% copper, .5% gold). Factors for other elements of interest (e.g., Pb, Zn) are derived according to the procedure described in the study listed in our footnote 2. Teletype printouts of all standard runs and analyses are recorded, and permanent graphical records of the spectra are recorded on an HP 4004 X-Y plotter. A typical spectrum with peaks appropriately labeled and an accompanying printout are shown in figure III.4.

The analysis of these Byzantine silver objects was accomplished using an isotope of cadmium ($^{109}_{48}Cd$) over an energy range of 0–40 keV. A preset count of 1000 counts on the silver peak was used in order to provide a reasonable run time without sacrificing precision or accuracy.

The precision of the Winterthur x-ray fluorescence analysis system for silver was determined by running two sets of ten replicate analyses of Winterthur silver reference standard 47.4. Averages and standard deviations for the elements of interest are listed in Table III.2. Also included are data from ten replicate analyses of a typical silver object which more nearly approximates the composition of the Byzantine silver, the bottom of a silver tankard in the Winterthur Museum (WM 64.52).

The accuracy of any analytical method is estimated by analyzing a sample or group of samples by an independent analytical method and comparing the data. In the case of the Byzantine silver objects, we were fortunate to have available data obtained several years ago by neutron activation analysis on several of the objects included in the study.[3] A comparison of the data obtained by the two techniques for two different objects shows extremely close agreement (Table III.3).[4]

The close proximity of the energies of primary excitation lines of certain elements in the x-ray fluorescence spectrum occasionally makes detection of some elements in the presence of others difficult. Such is the case with gold and mercury whose most intense lines, the $L_{\alpha1}$ and $L_{\beta2}$, fall at 9.7 and 11.5 keV and 10.0 and 11.9 keV, respectively. Because the entire spectrum is collected over a 0–40 keV range, the gold and mercury lines are frequently not well resolved, particularly when the object contains a high concentration of gold, as from gilding. And, because the Winterthur x-ray fluorescence system is about fifteen years old, it does not have the advantages of spectral manipulation found in newer instrumentation, making resolution and detection of certain elements of interest difficult. Consequently, it was not always possible to determine the presence or absence of mercury in some of the gilded areas analyzed in this study.

A similar problem involved the interference of the gold $L_{\alpha2}$ line at 8.6 keV with the zinc $K_{\alpha2}$ line at 8.7 keV. The presence of a high concentration of gold thus sometimes resulted in a spurious indication of the presence of a significant amount of zinc. These potential errors were corrected by a visual examination of the spectra and estimation of the relative heights of the gold and zinc lines.

Because x-ray fluorescence is a surface analysis technique, the presence of a high concentration of an element on the surface of an object can give a spurious indication of the composition of the underlying alloy. This was the situation in the case of gilded areas. In order to obtain some indication of the composition of the underlying silver alloy, the computer factors for gold were set to zero so that no counts from gold would be included in the summation of counts used to calculate weight percent. Any gold in the alloy itself is, however, also necessarily disregarded by this procedure. However, all other elements of interest are included.

NOTES

1. V. F. Hanson, "Museum Objects" in H. K. Herglotz and L. S. Birks, *X-Ray Spectrometry,* Practical Spectrometry Series 2 (1978), 413 ff; J. H. Carlson, "X-Ray Fluorescence Analysis of Pewter: English and Scottish Measures," *Archaeometry* 19 (1977); G. F. Carter, *et. al.,* "Comparison of Eight Roman Orichalcum Coin Fragments by Seven Methods," *Archaeometry* 25 (1983), 201 ff.

2. V. F. Hanson, "Quantitative Elemental Analysis of Art Objects by X-Ray Fluorescence Spectroscopy," *Applied Spectroscopy* 27 (1973), 309 ff.

3. P. Meyers, L. van Zelst, and E. V. Sayre, "Elemental Composition of Silver Samples" (Byzantine Silver, Dumbarton Oaks Collection), unpublished data, 1977.

4. We extend our thanks to Miss Susan Boyd, Curator of the Byzantine Collection, Dumbarton Oaks, for making the neutron activation data and the objects available for study. The neutron activation analyses were made by Dr. Pieter Meyers at Brookhaven National Laboratory.

Figure III.4

Energy Dispersive X-Ray Fluorescence Spectrum and Printout, Byzantine silver cross (no. 10; The Walters Art Gallery, no. 57.630)

THE WINTERTHUR MUSEUM
ANALYTICAL LABORATORY
SILVER SUMMARY

A.L. #	1732.2.1	1	ANTIMONY	.00000
SEQ. #	#S4938	2	ARSENIC	.00937
TEST DATE	105,1985	3	BISMUTH	.02178
TEST TIME	10:17	4	CADMIUM	.00000
ACCESSION #	57.630	5	COBALT	.01127
OWNER	WAG	6	COPPER	12.01522
OBJECT	CROSS	7	GOLD	.77566
DESC'N		8	IRON	.06146
PART	LOWER FRONT	9	LEAD	.37900
MAKER	'	10	MANGANESE	.00000
DATE	6TH C	11	MERCURY	.01377
PROV'NCE	BYZANTINE	12	NICKEL	.00000
ELEMENT	WEIGHT %	13	SILVER	86.29604
		14	TIN	.00020
		15	ZINC	.41624

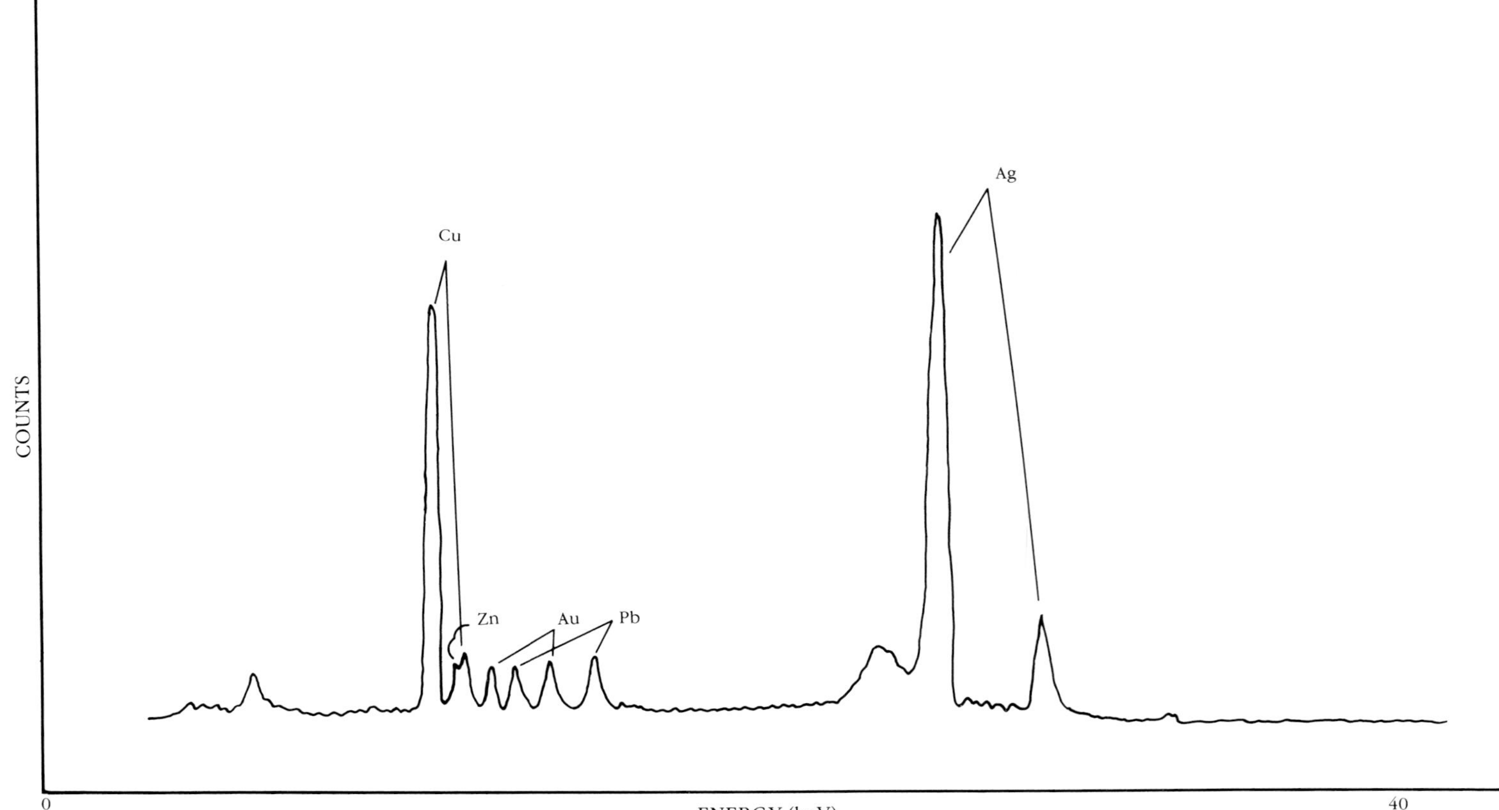

Table III.2

Precision of X-Ray Fluorescence Analysis of Silver

		Ag	Cu	x ± s (wt.%) Au	Pb	Zn
Silver Ref. Std. #47.4	Theoretical Values	92.5	7.0	.5	0	0
(10 replicate analysis)	Experimental Values	92.44 ± .19	7.08 ± .19	.46 ± .03	0	0
Silver Tankard (Bottom)—W.M. 64.53 (10 replicate analyses)		94.58 ± .21	4.75 ± .21	.08 ± .04	.45 ± .04	.04 ± .02

Table III.3

Comparison of Neutron Activation Analyses with X-Ray Fluorescence Analyses of Byzantine Silver from the Dumbarton Oaks Collection

Objects	Technique	No. of Analyses	Ag	Cu	Au	Pb
Riha chalice	XRF	2	96.5 ± .03	1.5 ± .6	.63 ± .13	1.1 ± .01
(no. 30, Dumbarton Oaks no. 36.23)	NAA	1	97.2	2.1	.6	N.D.
Riha fan	XRF	3	96.3 ± .8	1.6 ± .60	.89 ± .04	1.14 ± .25
(no. 32, Dumbarton Oaks no. 55.18)	NAA	1	97.1	2.2	.74	N.D.

N.D. = Not determined

TABLE III.4

Summary of Compositional Analyses of the Hama Treasure with Additional Analyses from the Riba and Antioch Treasures

			Ag	Cu	Au	Pb	Zn
1.	chalice	side of cup:	95.71	1.83	.98	1.39	
		inscription:	96.15	1.49	1.08	1.19	
		foot:	95.68	1.69	1.19	1.39	
2.	chalice	side:	96.77	1.36	.96	.80	
		upper rim:	80.91	1.86	15.71	.54	
		upper rim:	95.99	2.20	*	.64	
		inscription:	94.18	4.60	*	.80	
		inside foot:	97.68	1.41	*	.76	
3.	chalice	upper rim:	85.77	4.44	8.68	.49	
		upper rim:	93.93	4.87	*	.54	
		arch, Peter:	93.18	5.89	*	.43	
		Peter, front:	94.53	4.42	*	.57	
		Peter, background:	94.30	4.87	*	.67	
		Peter, background:	93.52	4.82	.82	.67	
		figure with arm down:	93.80	4.37	.91	.75	
		foot (of vessel) exterior:	93.75	5.01	*	.71	
		foot interior:	95.13	3.03	1.16	.45	
4.	paten	central field, obverse:	94.13	4.51	.82	.46	
		center of cross:	94.51	4.31	.74	.34	
		band with inscription:	92.89	5.35	1.08	.61	
		center, reverse:	95.10	3.68	.85	.31	
5.	paten	center of cross, obverse:	96.17	2.31	.88	.54	
		outside of cross, obverse:	96.43	2.13	.85	.52	
		band with inscription, obverse:	96.37	2.15	.80	.56	
		reverse:	97.16	1.68	.71	.39	
6.	paten	center of cross:	95.20	3.56	.73	.48	
		band with inscription:	95.38	3.42	.68	.46	
		between band and side:	95.13	3.76	.61	.46	
		center, reverse:	96.85	2.29	.56	.24	
7.	cross	left arm of cross, obverse:	95.71	2.36	1.35	.42	
		left arm of cross, reverse:	96.98	1.20	1.36	.26	
8.	cross	center, obverse:	94.83	4.03	.64	.46	
		center, reverse:	95.76	3.19	.56	.39	
		obverse, tang:	96.05	1.78	1.58	.35	
		ball:	95.64	3.19	.75	.28	
9.	cross	upper arm, obverse:	84.88	12.99	.74	.87	.45
		upper arm, reverse:	83.36	14.72	.75	.79	.28
		lower arm, obverse:	89.68	8.19	.90	.79	.35
		lower arm, reverse:	92.67	5.24	.92	.74	.33
10.	cross	lower arm, obverse:	86.30	12.02	.78	.38	.42
11.	lampstand	spike:	94.10	4.27	.91	.56	
		cup:	95.63	2.31	1.03	.78	
		column capital:	96.31	1.49	1.09	.73	
		column shaft:	93.26	4.91	.88	.68	
		column base:	95.43	3.27	.58	.45	
		foot:	95.31	3.39	.65	.53	
		column base—joint:	95.54	4.14	.55	.50	
12.	lampstand	spike:	92.91	5.20	1.07	.67	
		cup:	96.02	2.19	.95	.72	
		column capital:	96.45	1.64	.87	.59	
		column shaft:	93.58	4.80	.86	.57	
		column shaft:	95.07	3.73	.60	.49	
		column base:	94.84	3.75	.61	.55	
		foot:	95.18	3.65	.58	.49	
		repair-column base:	59.24	2.20	1.59	35.68	
13.	lamp	bottom:	94.78	2.61	1.30	1.08	
		lower side:	95.11	2.38	1.34	1.10	
		suspension eyelet:	96.07	1.38	1.52	.91	
14.	ewer	lower body:	96.64	1.96	.89	.39	
		handle:	92.17	5.89	.72	.37	.79
		band with inscription:	93.22	1.90	4.02	.46	
		rim:	96.56	2.09	.77	.36	
		solder at rim:	81.83	4.68	.66	7.32	5.07
15.	flask	body of flask, neck:	97.01	1.32	*	.52	
		body of flask, upper inscribed band:	96.52	1.20	*	.38	
		body of flask, between figures:	96.34	1.37	*	.45	
		body of flask, figure:	96.01	1.63	*	.38	
		body of flask, lower inscribed band:	96.26	1.21	*	.38	
		body of flask, lower inscribed band:	78.04	.98	18.93	.31	
		rim:	95.13	2.82	*	.29	
		bottom:	74.35	19.89	.63	.44	4.52
		strip or patch:	85.30	14.16	*	.35	
		band between neck and rim:	96.23	1.72	*	.37	
16.	bowl	rim:	97.11	1.37	1.08	.32	
		bottom, reverse:	97.22	1.59	.84	.26	
17.	box	box, bottom:	95.52	3.00	.72	.67	
		box, side with hexagons and squares:	95.17	3.18	.75	.85	
		box, side with acanthus:	95.44	3.06	.69	.70	
		box, side with cross (non-gilded area):	90.74	3.04	4.73	.83	
		lid, top (non-gilded area):	95.47	2.96	.84	.55	
		lid, edge:	95.07	3.28	.69	.85	

No.	Object	Location	Ag	Cu	Au	Pb	Zn
18.	spoon	bowl:	95.58	2.68	1.13	.49	
		handle:	95.85	2.20	1.25	.40	
19.	spoon	bowl:	94.88	2.98	.88	1.09	
		handle:	94.73	2.48	1.16	1.30	
		tip of handle:	95.14	2.39	.99	1.03	
20.	spoon	bowl:	93.17	5.28	.50	.56	.42
		handle:	94.12	3.99	.54	.70	.49
		knob:	93.87	4.41	.45	.62	.49
22.	spoon	bowl:	95.44	2.97	1.04	.34	
		handle:	95.07	2.91	1.05	.53	
		tip of handle:	95.20	2.65	1.17	.56	
23.	ladle	bowl:	96.84	1.17	1.39	.42	
		disc on handle:	94.94	3.46	.91	.51	
		handle near bowl, obverse:	90.19	7.91	.85	.75	
24.	strainer	bowl:	96.75	2.06	.56	.26	
		dolphin ornament:	94.70	3.56	1.02	.44	
		handle:	94.07	3.85	1.07	.61	
		ring:	91.51	6.66	.57	.68	
29.	chalice[1]	cup:	95.7	3.45	.62	.21	
		foot:	95.4	3.57	.73	.20	
30.	chalice[2]	foot bottom:	96.44	1.06	.72	1.12	
		side:	96.48	1.87	.53	1.10	
		niello:	90.39	7.36	.68	1.09	
		gilding:	89.38	1.74	6.94	1.01	
		foot:	97.3	2.08	.616		
32.	fan[2]	center, obverse:	96.23	1.65	.86	1.19	
		center, reverse:	95.51	2.20	.88	1.36	
		flange, obverse:	97.10	.98	.93	.87	
		handle:	97.1	2.19	.749		
35.	paten[2]	reverse:	97.15	.94	.85	1.00	
		center, obverse:	96.52	1.59	.71	1.14	
		rim, niello:	95.64	2.17	.82	1.31	
40.	chalice[3]	grapes, 4:00 o'clock (relative to accession number), under foot, 5 cm from top rim:	98.70	.38	.93		
		rim of foot, 4:30 o'clock:	97.8	1.40	.83		
		background, above Christ, 11:00 o'clock, 2.5 cm from top rim:	97.6	.66	1.74		
41.	chalice[3]	edge of foot (corroded):	95.3	2.7	2.03		
		edge of rim:	95.8	3.2	1.02		
42a.	cross sheath[3]	cross bar:	96.0	3.9	.12		
		vertical bar, top:	96.8	3.2	.068		
		vertical bar, bottom:	98.0	1.9	.11		
		drilling, cross bar:	96.9	3.05	.048		
		drilling, nail in cross bar:	94.0	5.96	.051		
42b.	cross medallion[4]	hemisphere at 6:00 o'clock:	96.5	3.4	.11		
42c.	cross medallion[4]	hemisphere at 8:30 o'clock (corroded):	97.2	2.7	.12		
		hemisphere at 9:30 o'clock:	95.9	4.0	.074		
44.	plaque[3]	lower part of cross on top:	96.4	3.0	.57		
		top edge, 0.3 cm from R end of standing base:	96.8	2.3	.91		
45.	plaque[3]	flower, 6.5 cm from top, 1.5 cm from R edge:	97.5	1.7	.82		
		robe, 7 cm from bottom, 10 cm from R edge:	96.2	3.4	.43		
46.	plaque[3]	lower L of cross:	97.6	.80	1.64		
		proper L knee of R side figure (corroded):	97.5	1.9	.62		
48.	mirror[3]	rim at 12:00 (corroded):	93.3	6.0	.70		
		rim at 6:00 (corroded):	95.1	3.8	1.06		
		handle, lower (unbroken) part, R corner edge (corroded):	97.4	.58	1.97		
		handle, upper (broken) part, R edge 2 cm from tip (corroded):	92.4	5.9	1.69		

*Au excluded from calculation of alloy composition

NOTES FOR TABLE III.4

1. Our thanks to Mr. David Buckton of the British Museum for providing this data. The analyses were carried out by the x-ray fluorescence technique by Dr. M. J. Hughes, Principle Scientific Officer, Mrs. J. R. S. Lang, Higher Scientific Officer, and Dr. M. S. Tite, Keeper of the Research of the British Museum.

2. Our thanks to Miss Susan Boyd of Dumbarton Oaks for providing this data. The analyses were carried out by Mrs. Janice Carlson, Museum Chemist, at the Winterthur Museum by the x-ray fluorescence technique except for the foot of chalice no. 30 and the handle of fan no. 32, which were carried out on drilled samples by Dr. Pieter Meyers, Head of Conservation, Los Angeles County Museum of Art, using neutron activation at Brookhaven National Laboratory.

3. These analyses were carried out by Dr. Pieter Meyers using the neutron activation (streak sample) technique. We thank Dr. Margaret Frazer of The Metropolitan Museum of Art for providing the data.

4. These analyses were carried out by Dr. Pieter Meyers using the neutron activation (streak sample) technique. We are grateful to Catherine Metzger of the Louvre Museum for providing the data.

FIGURE III.5

*Ternary Diagram Showing the Relationship between Technique and Composition among Hama Treasure Objects in The Walters Art Gallery**

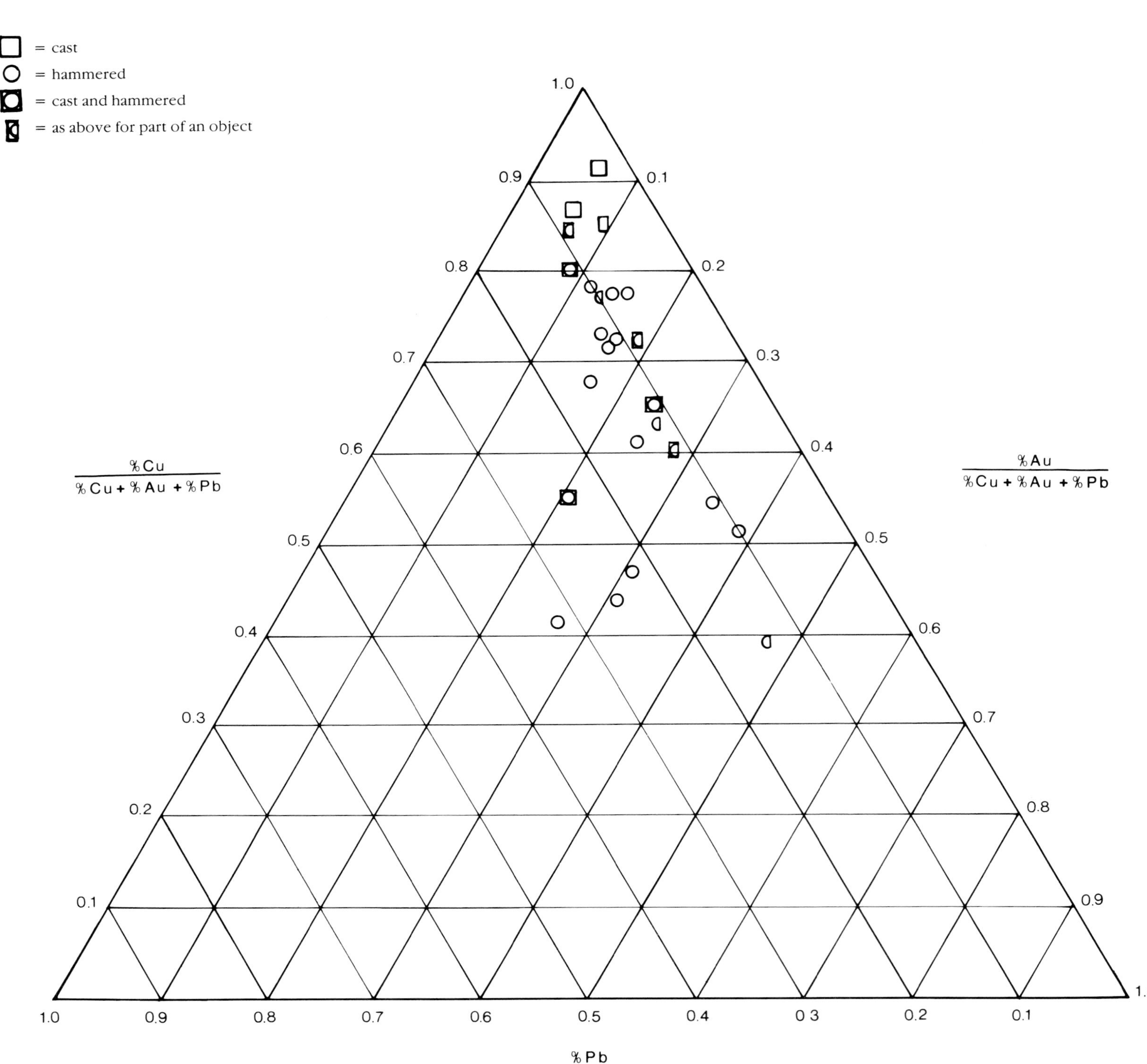

*Specifically, this ternary diagram shows the distribution of cast, hammered, and cast and hammered objects according to their ratios of copper, gold, and lead.

APPENDIX III.3

X-ray Diffraction Analysis of Niello

Richard Newman and Eugene Farrell
Center for Conservation and Technical Studies
Harvard University Art Museums, Harvard University
Cambridge, Massachusetts

Niello consists of one or more crystalline compounds (in the case of these Byzantine niellos, silver or silver-copper sulfides). Given this fact and the small sample sizes required, x-ray diffraction is a particularly useful method to study their compositions. Research on sulfides in the silver-copper system has shown that there are five distinct crystalline phases at room temperature, one or at most two of which will be present in a given sample, depending on the amount of silver and copper used in the manufacturing process. Thus identification of the crystalline phases can also give an appoximate idea of the overall chemical composition of the sample.

For analysis of the niello, very small samples were taken with a sharpened microneedle under a binocular microscope. In most instances these were scrapings of powder. The small samples were dictated by the fragmentary nature of the remaining niello on the objects being studied. The sample sites were photographed through the microscope before and after sampling.

Each of the samples was mixed with a small amount of collodion, attached to the end of a thin glass rod, and exposed in a 114.6 mm-diameter Gandolfi camera on a Diano XRD-8000 for twenty to twenty-two hours. Ni-filtered Cu-K_α radiation was used, at 35 kilovolts and 15 milliamps. Crystalline phases were identified with reference to standard patterns published by the JCPDS International Centre for Diffraction Data.

TABLE III.5

Summary of Analyses of Niello Samples from the Hama Treasure Objects in The Walters Art Gallery

Cat. no.	Object	Phase(s) identified by x-ray diffraction
1	chalice	Ag + acanthite (minor)
2	chalice	jalpaite
3	chalice	Ag + stromeyerite
5	paten	Ag + silicon carbide*
7	cross	Ag + acanthite
10	cross	Ag + jalpaite(?)**
11	lampstand	Ag + acanthite
12	lampstand	acanthite
14	ewer	Ag + mackinstryite
17	box	Ag + stromeyerite
18	spoon	Ag + acanthite
19	spoon	jalpaite + acanthite
23	ladle	jalpaite + mackinstryite
24	strainer	Ag + jalpaite + acanthite

Notes

*No sulfide could be identified in the diffraction pattern.

**This sample gave a weak diffraction pattern; not enough lines were present to positively identify the sulfide phases.

TABLE III.6

Summary of Composition of Niello Samples from the Hama Treasure Objects in The Walters Art Gallery

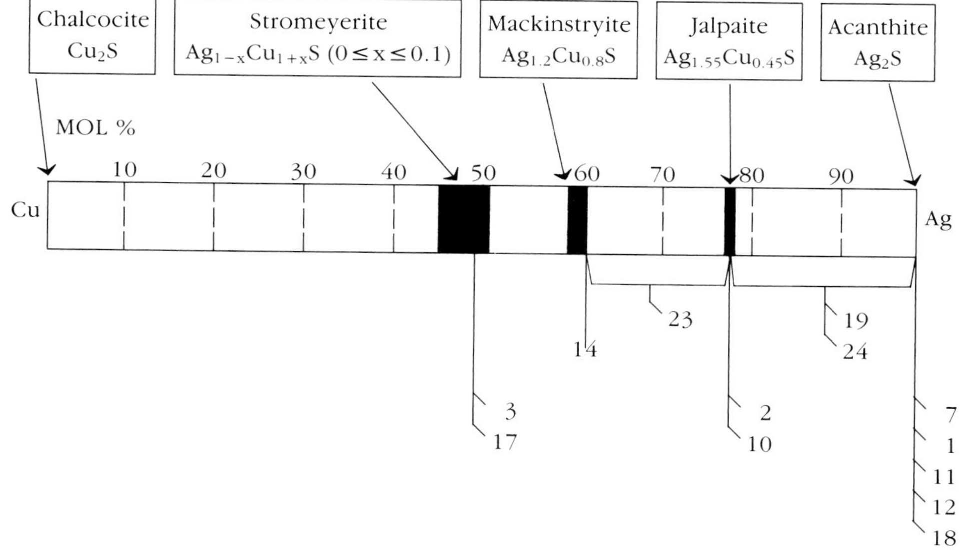

This table shows where the samples fall compositionally in the copper sulfide-silver sulfide system. The phases are identified by their mineral names and their chemical formulae.

The catalogue numbers for the objects are given below the table.

Catalogue: Entries Nos. 1–56

The Reconstructed Kaper Koraon Treasure

A Note on the Illustrations: Where possible, the objects in the reconstructed Kaper Koraon treasure (Entries nos. 1–56) have been illustrated at or very near original size in at least one view. Supplementary views and profiles have been reduced by fixed proportions (e.g., 2 > 1, 3 > 1, 4 > 3). All graphically rendered inscriptions are given at .5 cm or original size, whichever is smaller.

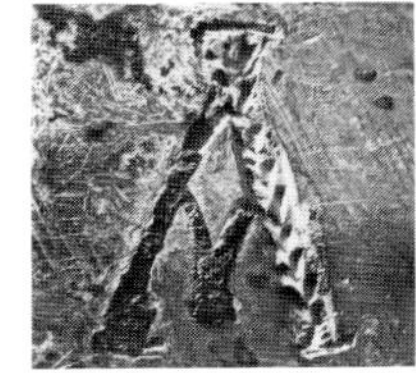
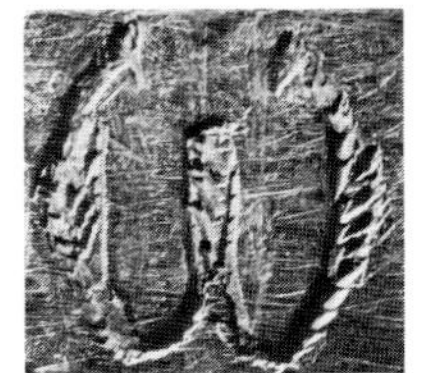

Fig. 1.2

1. CHALICE

POTERION

Figures 1.1–1.6

Baltimore, The Walters Art Gallery, no. 57.633

Hama Treasure, 547–550(?)

For technical and compositional analyses, see Chapter III, Appendices III.1 and III.2.

This chalice has a broad cup supported on a flared foot without knob (figs. 1.3, 1.4). An inscription (figs. 1.2, 1.4) encircles the top of the cup, between a border of double engraved lines; there is another engraved line near the rim of the foot. Five stamps appear inside the foot (figs. 1.1, 1.6).

This chalice was made in two parts, cup and foot, probably from the same melt of metal. Both were formed by hammering, the marks of which remain on their inner surfaces. Stress cracks inside the cup and around its rim were caused by working the metal too thin without sufficient annealing. The cup and foot were joined either by the method described for chalice no. 29, that is, by means of an outer collar secured by silver solder and finished so as to be no longer visible (i.e., by "concealed joint" construction; see below), or else by a simple silver solder join. The vessel was turned on a lathe for finishing (especially at the join), and engraving the decorative lines. The inscription was engraved and possibly deeply chased to receive its niello inlay, the few remaining traces of which were found to be silver sulfide (see Chapter III, Appendix III.3). No trace of gilding was detected. The stamps were applied after manufacture (see Dodd, 1961, no. 13). There is a repair patch in the bottom of the cup, and the rim is torn in four places.

STAMPS

These stamps were dated by Dodd (1961, no. 13) to 547–550, because of the monograms of Justinian (527–565) and Peter, whom she took to be Peter Barsymes, *comes sacrarum largitionum* of 547–550+ (and 539–542?). (See Entry no. 30.) As classified by Dodd, the stamps may be read, with minor emendations (fig. 1.1), as follows:

a. **Round**: nimbed bust; inscribed *DANNOU.*
b. **Hexagonal**: small nimbed bust; monogram of Justinian; inscribed *NILOU.*
c. **Square**: monogram of Justinian (reversed); inscribed *LOUKA.*
d. **Long**: nimbed bust; monogram of Peter; unidentified inscription.
e. **Cross**: monogram of Peter; inscribed *ANDREOU.*

INSCRIPTION

+ *In fulfillment of a vow and (for) the salvation of SYMEONIOS, magistr(ianos), and of THOSE WHO BELONG TO HIM.*

Engraved, chased, nielloed (H of letters = .8 cm). Diehl, 1926, no. 2; *SEG,* vol. 7, no. 90; *IGLS,* no. 2028.

The lettering is lunate, and serifs are used consistently. Letter size is uniform except at the end where the introduction of small letters may have been necessitated by lack of planning. Abbreviations are indicated by *S,* and the genitive *omicron-upsilon* appears in full and in ligature.

On the phrase *hyper euches kai soterias,* see *IGLS,* no. 2027, where it is described as a continuation of pagan dedications on *ex-votos* (e.g., *votum libens anima soluit*). On Downey's association of the formulae used on this and other church objects with those used in the liturgy, see Entry no. 35. *Magistr* is completed (*IGLS,* no. 2028) as

Fig. 1.1

ΔΑΝ||ΝΟV

ΝΙ||ΛΟV

ΛΟV||ΚΑ

..ΡCΟ.||...Ν.

[+Α||ΝΔ]||ΡЄ||ΟV

+ΥΠΕΡΕΥΧΗϹΚ̄ϹΩΤΗΡΙΑϹϹΥΜΕΩΝΙΟΥ
ΜΑΓΙϹΤΡ̄Κ̄ΤΩΝΔΙΑΦΕΡΟΝΤΩΝΑΥΤΩ

+ Ὑπὲρ εὐχῆς κ(αὶ) σωτηρίας Συμεωνίου
μαγιστρ(ιανοῦ) κ(αὶ) τῶν διαφερόντων αὐτῶ.

magistrianos (i.e., *agens in rebus*) rather than the grander *magister* (*officiorum* or *militum*), largely because of the modesty of the object and the village context of the donation. Symeonios (or Symeonis; *ibid.*) may be one and the same as Symeonios, son of Maximinos, who, with his brothers, donated Hama lampstands nos. 11, 12, and Hama ewer no. 14, and as Symeonios, father of John, who dedicated Hama cross no. 10. See figure I.1.

Commentary

This chalice is the only Byzantine example in this catalogue to lack a

H	12.5 cm
D (cup rim)	11.3–11.9 cm
D (foot rim)	7.3 cm
Weight	215.3 gr
Roman Weight	7 oz 21 scr
Original Silver Price	2 *solidi* 15 carats
Volume	*ca.* 600 ml (i.e., *ca.* 1 Roman *xestes*)

Fig. 1.3

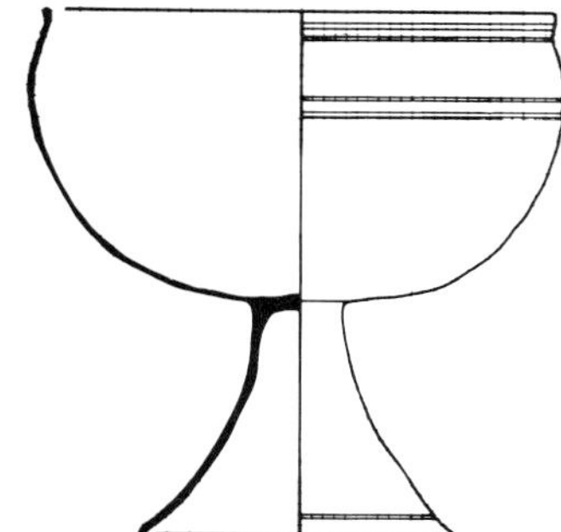

Fig. 1.6

Fig. 1.4

knob at the top of its foot; it bears comparison, therefore, with the four western chalices in the Gallunianu treasure (nos. 77–80) which, however, have taller and narrower cups.

Western chalices of the Early Christian period (e.g., those of the Gallunianu and Durobrivae [Painter, 1977 [I], no. 6] treasures) have a silver rivet join between foot and cup. Byzantine chalices, on the other hand, are assembled in basically two other ways. One category (our "Type A") is comprised of those which are soldered together (nos. 1, 2, 27, 29, 30, 41, 73); this may involve a simple soldered join (as is possible here), or else the more elaborate procedure followed on the London chalice (no. 29). There, a collar was apparently soldered to the base of the cup, and the foot—whose stem was probably slightly cone-shaped—was placed up into it and secured with solder. In either case, all surface evidence of the join is obliterated in the finishing of the vessel (thus, these might be called "concealed joint" chalices). The second category of chalice as defined by assembly (our "Type B") is comprised of those which have a mechanical join (nos. 3, 28, 57–59, 61, 62) between cup and foot. As was discovered upon close examination of Hama chalice no. 3, this involves first soldering a collar to the base of the cup and then placing the flared stem of the foot up into it and joining the two by hammering the collar down. In this case, the collar remains visible (thus, these might be called "ring joint" chalices). Interestingly, all Type A chalices in this catalogue, with the exception of the London and Boston chalices (nos. 29, 73), are stamped, while no Type B chalices are stamped. On the other hand, most of the latter (i.e., nos. 3, 57–59, 62) have figurative decoration. All chalices of both Types, with the exception of this specimen (a Type A chalice), have a knob.

The chalice (Greek = *poterion;* Latin = *calix;* Syriac = *kesa*) and the paten (on which, see Entry no. 4), which together were called a *diskopoterion,* formed the most essential equipment for the liturgical service, and therefore were presented to Byzantine churches in high numbers. The explicit dedications of surviving chalices identify them as liturgical vessels, and many of those in this catalogue correspond in their weights (usually of one to two Roman pounds) to the "ministerial chalice" listed in inventories of the period (see Chapter I, above). For suggested prototypes of the most typical form of chalice in the Early Byzantine period—where the cup rests on a flaring foot with large knob—see Entry no. 2. There is one curious feature of the chalices herein catalogued, namely, that the inner surface of the cup—the surface intended to touch the consecrated wine—was virtually never finished. (One possible exception is no. 41.) This suggests the possible use of glass(?) liners, (e.g., Matheson, 1980, nos. 259, 260; see also Entries nos. 16, 28).

Fig. 1.5

Bibliography

Diehl, 1926, no. 2; Rosenberg, 1928, vol. 4, 728 f.; Braun, 1932, 78 ff.; *SEG,* vol. 7, no. 90; *Dark Ages,* 1937, no. 95; *Early Christian,* 1947, no. 395; Downey, 1951, 350; *IGLS,* no. 2028; Dodd, 1961, no. 13; Ross, 1962, 11; Dodd, 1973, 14, no. 2, 15, 5b; Mundell-Mango, 1986.

2. CHALICE

POTERION

Figures 2.1–2.6

Baltimore, The Walters Art Gallery, no. 57.642

Hama Treasure, 602–610

For technical and compositional analyses, see Chapter III, Appendices III.1 and III.2.

This chalice has a broad, slightly bulbous cup supported on a flaring foot with knob (figs. 2.3, 2.4). An inscription runs between the concave mouldings and engraved lines encircling the cup's rim (figs. 2.2, 2.4). Additional engraved lines (in each case two) surround the join at the bottom of the cup, the top and bottom of the knob, and the rim of the foot. The concave bands, the area around the knob, and the foot rim were gilded. Five stamps appear inside the foot (figs. 2.1, 2.6).

This chalice was made in two parts, cup and foot, probably from the same melt of metal. Both were formed by hammering, the marks of which remain on their inner surfaces. The metal at the top of the foot, above the knob, is relatively thick, and may mark the residual presence of a silver collar like that used to join the cup and foot of the London chalice (no. 29). Here, the silver solder at the join is no longer distinguishable. After assembly, this vessel was turned on a lathe to finish its surface and engrave its decorative lines; the mark in the bottom of the cup may have been made by the lathe's clamping device. The inscription was engraved to receive the niello inlay (see Chapter III, Appendix III.3), and overlapping gold foil was applied to parts of the surface, possibly by burnishing, or more likely, by mercury gilding. The stamps were struck after manufacture (contrast Dodd, 1961, no. 34). In the 1910 Hama photograph (fig. II.4), this chalice is shown with its foot bent and twisted, and its cup severely dented. This damage was repaired by 1926 (Diehl, 1926, pl. XIX.2). Some of the gilding has rubbed off and the niello is missing from most letters.

STAMPS

These stamps were dated by Dodd (1961, no. 34) to 602–610, because of the presence of the monogram of Phocas. There is no round stamp. As classified by Dodd, the stamps may be read, with minor emendations (fig. 2.1), as follows:

a. **Round**: missing.
b. **Hexagonal**: monogram of Phocas; inscribed *IWANNOU.*
c. **Square**: monogram of Phocas; inscribed *THEODORO.*
d. **Long**: nimbed bust; unidentified monogram; inscribed *SYMEONIS.*
e. **Cross**: unidentified monogram; inscribed *PATRIKIOU.*

INSCRIPTION

+ *In fulfillment of a vow and (for) the salvation of JOHN and THOMAS and MANNOS, the (sons) of THEOPHILOS.*

Engraved, nielloed (H of letters = .9 cm). Diehl, 1926, no. 1; *SEG,* vol. 7, no. 88; *IGLS,* no. 2027; Dodd, 1961, no. 34; *Age,* 1979, no. 531.

The lettering is lunate and of consistent size; serifs are used regularly. *Kai* is abbreviated *Ks* once and written out twice.

The umlaut on the *iota* of *Iwannou* is said to be a feature introduced in the sixth century (by Downey, in *Antioch,* III, 83, no. 111). These letter forms resemble, in a general way, the nielloed inscription on Hama spoon no. 19, which was given by two of the same donors, as well as those on nos. 1, 30, 33–36. On the dedicatory formulae used here, see Entry no. 1. Although often called the "chalice of Theophilos" (Dodd, 1961, no. 34; *Age,* 1979, no. 531, where the end of the inscription is mistakenly translated ". . . Mannos and Theophilos"), it is in fact the chalice of his three sons, John, Thomas, and Mannos. See figure I.1.

Fig. 2.2

Fig. 2.1

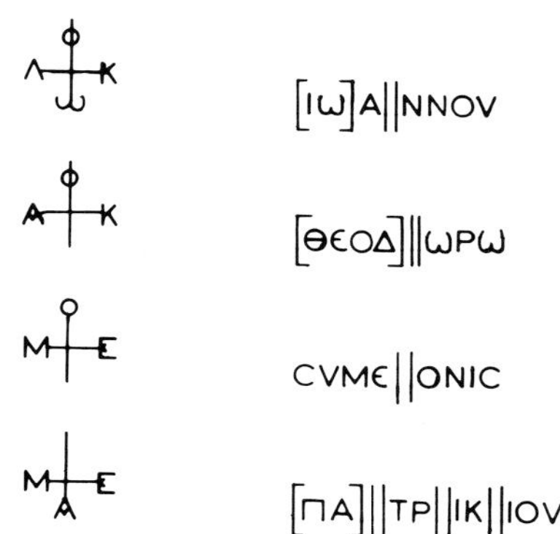

Commentary

By its construction, this vessel belongs to the first of two types of Byzantine chalice included in this catalogue (i.e., our Type A), insofar as it shows no noticeable join between cup and foot (for details, see Entry no. 1, where there is also a general discussion of chalices).

The knob on the foot of this chalice is characteristic of Early Byzantine (nos. 3, 27–30, 41, 57–59, 61, 62, 73), Middle Byzantine (e.g., *Treasury,* 1984, nos. 10, 11, 16, 17) and western Medieval (Elbern, 1963) chalices generally, although it is lacking on Hama chalice no. 1, and on the Gallunianu chalices (nos. 77–80). It is this type of knob-footed chalice that is portrayed on the Riha paten (no. 35; see Ross, 1962, no. 5; Elbern, 1963, 16 ff.; Dodd, 1973, 14 f.). The form appears to have been taken over into the secular realm as well (e.g., Lazović *et al.,* 1977, no. 1; *Age,* 1979, no. 156).

The origin of the knob-footed chalice may be traceable to glass goblets of as early as the first century AD (e.g., Matheson, 1980, no. 11), which apparently translated into grosser form the slender, moulded stem of contemporary silver goblets (e.g., Strong, 1966, 133 f., fig. 27a, b). A glass foot with knob (H 11 cm) found at Qal'at Sam'an may have belonged to a large chalice, but Elbern's (1966) suggested dating places it too late to be considered a prototype for knob-footed silver chalices. It is noteworthy, however, that glass liturgical vessels are attested in Rome by the third century (Braun, 1932), and there are extant examples of the fifth and sixth centuries (Elbern, 1966, 102). Whether the knob also existed on metal vessels of the Roman period, thereby providing a metal prototype for the silver chalices, is uncertain, though by the fourth century it has become a characteristic feature of silver jugs (Strong, 1966, 188 ff., fig. 37, pl. 56A).

Bibliography

Sachsen, 1912, 11, fig. 12; Mouterde, 1926, 366; Diehl, 1926, no. 1; Wilpert, 1926, 136, note 185; Rosenberg, 1928, vol. 4, 726 f.; Braun, 1932, 78 ff.; *SEG,* vol. 7, nos. 88, 89; *Dark Ages,* 1937, no. 102; *Early Christian,* 1947, no. 396; Lassus, 1947, 197 f.; Downey, 1951, 350; *IGLS,* no. 2027; Dodd, 1961, no. 34; Ross, 1962, 4, 11; Dodd, 1973, 15, no. 8; *Age,* 1979, no. 531; Mundell-Mango, 1986.

Fig. 2.5

ϮΥΠƐΡƐΥΧΗϹΚΑΙϹѠΤΗΡΙΑϹΙѠΑΝΝΟΥΚ
ΘѠΜΑΚΑΙΜΑΝΝΟΥΤѠΝΘƐΟΦΙΛΟΥ

+ Ὑπὲρ εὐχῆς καὶ σωτηρίας Ἰωάννου κ(αὶ)

Θωμᾶ καὶ Μάννου τῶν Θεοφίλου

H	14.7–15.2 cm
D (cup rim)	13.2 cm
D (foot rim)	7.7 cm
Weight	284.8 gr
Roman Weight	10 oz 10 scr
Original Silver Price	3 *solidi* 15 1/3 carats
Volume	*ca.* 980 ml

Fig. 2.3

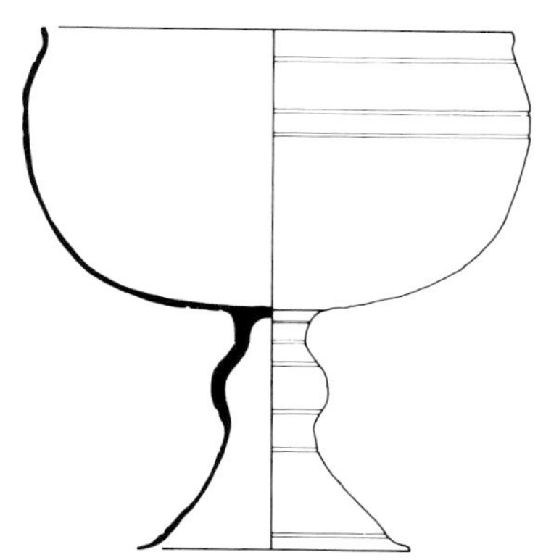

Fig. 2.6

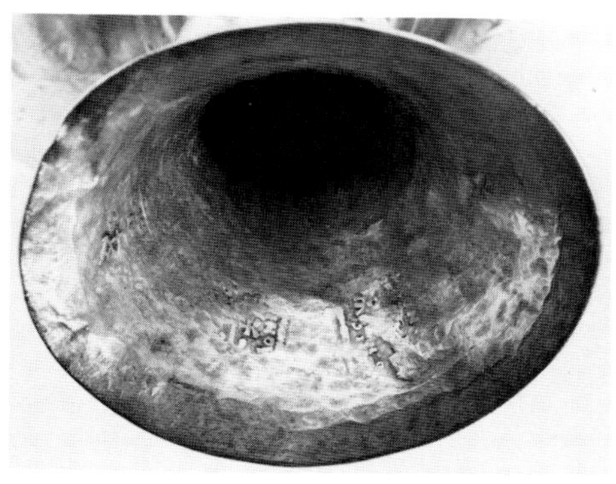

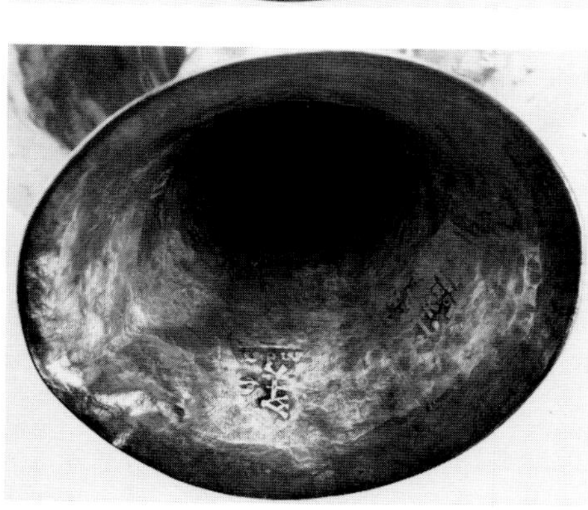

Fig. 2.4

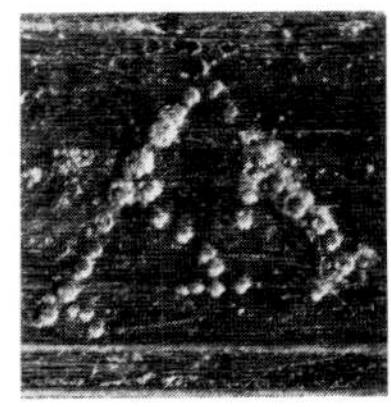
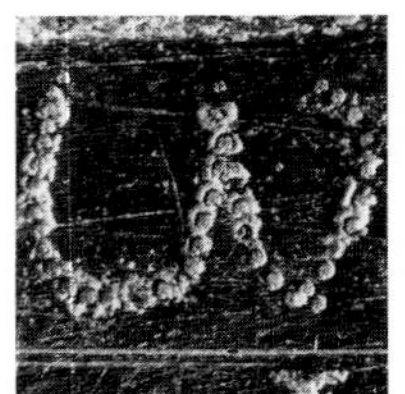

Fig. 3.1

3. CHALICE

POTERION

Figures 3.1–3.11

Baltimore, The Walters Art Gallery, no. 57.636

Hama Treasure, Early Seventh Century(?)

For technical and compositional analyses, see Chapter III, Appendices III.1 and III.2.

This chalice has a broad cup joined by a collar to a flaring foot with knob and flange; its whole surface is decorated in relief (figs. 3.2–3.9). The cup bears an arcade which frames within its six openings two large crosses and four flanking figures of Apostles. Two of the four, Sts. Peter and Paul, are identifiable by their facial characterization, relative location, and attributes. The arcades are composed of spirally fluted columns with profiled bases and Corinthian capitals supporting moulded archivolts, whose spandrels are filled with rosettes. The two crosses have flaring arms with teardrop serifs. Three of the figures (Paul and the two unidentified) hold books with gemmed covers, while the fourth, St. Peter, carries a cross on a staff. The knob is covered with an overlapping leaf pattern, and has a twisted rope *torus* below it; the foot is worked with deep flutes. Around the upper rim of the cup is an inscription between a border of shallow turnings. The black substance in some of the dots may be niello, or else simply a black silver corrosion product (see Chapter III, Appendix III. 3). Gilding highlights the rim, arches, rosettes, column capitals and bases, parts of the figures, the knob, and the lower part of the foot.

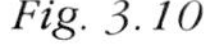

Fig. 3.10

The cup and foot of this chalice were apparently formed from separate melts of metal. Hammer marks remain visible on their inner surfaces. As no vertical seams are detectable on the foot, either under the microscope or by x-radiography, one must conclude that it was decorated by repoussé and chasing before being joined to the cup. The cup was lathe-turned to finish the surface and to engrave the upper linear decoration. It was further burnished in a vertical direction before its repoussé decoration was executed—either before or after assembly. Stress cracks not completely removed by annealing indicate that both cup and foot were heavily worked. The assembly of the chalice was effected by a silver collar attached to the bottom of the cup by a silver/copper solder, which has left green corrosion products detectable under the microscope. The collar was then hammered over a flare on the top of the foot to fix a mechanical join. The gilding on the rim, arches, and foot was in the form of gold leaf applied by mercury gilding or by burnishing.

The dent visible in the foot of the chalice in the 1910 Hama photograph (fig. II.4) was repaired by 1926 (Diehl, 1926, pl. XX.2). The surface of the relief decoration is very worn—perhaps by handling—especially on the faces, the feet and exposed hand of St. Paul, and the corners of the crosses. The design is still sharp inside the cup (fig. 3.10).

INSCRIPTION

+ *Vow of PELAGIOS (son of?) BASIANOS. Treasure of St. Sergios of the village of Kaper Koraon* + .

Pointillé, nielloed(?) (H of letters = .3–.5 cm). Diehl, 1926, no. 3; Mouterde, 1926, 365, note 2; Wilpert, 1927, 336; *SEG,* vol. 7, no. 92; *IGLS,* no. 2029; *Age,* 1979, no. 532.

ΤΕΥΧΕ ΠΕΛΑΓΙΟΥΒΑCΙΑΝΟΥΚΕΜΕΛΙΟΝΤΟΥΑΓΙΟΥCΕΡΓΙΟΥ
ΚΩΜΙCΚΑΠΕΡΚΟΡΑΩΝ +

+ Εὐχὲ Πελαγίου Βασιανου κεμέλιον τοῦ ἁγίου Σεργίου

κώμις Καπερ Κοραων +

The script is lunate, and fairly consistent in form; serifs are used on some letters. There are no ligatures or abbreviations. Spelling: *epsilon* for *eta* in *euche;* dropped *iota,* and *epsilon* for *eta* in *keimelion;* and *iota* for *eta* in *komes.*

These letter forms are fairly close to those of the *pointillé* inscriptions on Hama lampstands nos. 11 and 12, which, however, make greater use of serifs. This inscription starts over an Apostle rather than a cross, as would be expected, and, unusually, does not fill the entire circumference of the vessel. (On the possible equation of "vow" and "treasure" with the chalice itself, see Chapter I, above.) *Basianou* may be interpreted either as "(son) of Basianos" or as a family name (i.e., the *gentilicium* of Emesa current in the time of Heliogabalos [*IGLS*]), in agreement with genitive *Pelagiou.* The latter may be one and the same as the person who dedicated Hama paten no. 5, apparently in the seventh century. (*Komes* [i.e., the genitive of *kome,* "of the village"] was mistranslated in *Age,* 1979, no. 532, as the honorific Latin title *comes.*) See figure I.1.

Commentary

The group of chalices represented by this one, and designated here as Type B, is distinguished from Type A chalices by the use of a clearly-visible silver collar for a mechanical (rather than soldered) join between cup and foot (see Entry no. 1). None

H	16.2–16.8 cm
D (cup rim)	13.7–14.0 cm
D (foot rim)	9.5 cm
Weight	263.1 gr
Roman weight	9 oz 15 scr
Original Silver Price	3 *solidi* 5 carats
Volume	*ca.* 1000 ml

Fig. 3.2

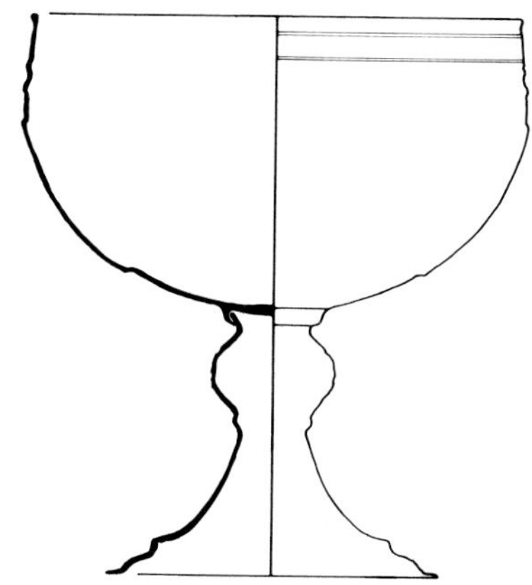

Fig. 3.3

Fig. 3.4

Fig. 3.5

Fig. 3.6

Fig. 3.11

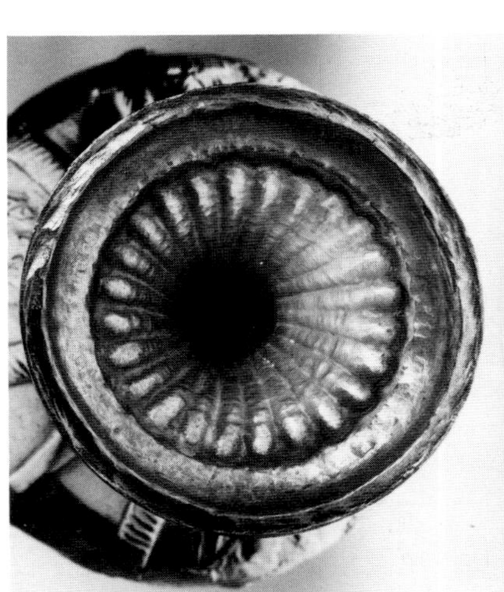

of the known Type B chalices (e.g., nos. 3, 28, 57–59, 61, 62; and the Ardaburius chalice [Ross, 1962, no. 5]) is stamped, but many of them have figural decoration, and a few have ornamental patterns related to those used on this example. The overlapping leaves on its knob, for example, are found also on the Beth Misona chalices nos. 57–59 (as well as on the Antioch Chalice, no. 40). Moreover, below the knobs of nos. 58 and 59 there is the same twisted rope moulding, which also appears under the capitals of the two Hama lampstands (nos. 11, 12), as borders on Antioch plaques nos. 44–46, and on Phela chalice no. 62. The fluted foot of this vessel is, however, unique among Syrian chalices, but may be compared to the fluted cup of an Early Byzantine bronze hanging lamp from Emesa (*Ebla,* 1985, no. 247), and to the fluted cup of an unpublished silver chalice from Lebanon, now in a private Swiss collection. The arcaded composition found here is likewise unique among contemporary chalices; it is commonly found, however, on caskets (e.g., Shelton, 1981, pls. 8 ff.), and appears on the Dağ Pazari censer (Gough, 1965) where there are also columns like these. (For standing figures under single arches, as on the Antioch and Sion plaques, see Entry no. 44.) Such arcaded compositions, enclosing muses and pagan divinities as well as Apostles, may have derived from columnar sarcophagi (see *Age,* 1979, no. 117). The columns and bases on this chalice resemble those on the Riha paten (no. 35), and on two Antioch plaques (see Entry no. 44), while the capitals are closer to those on the two Hama lampstands (nos. 11, 12).

The figures on this vessel suffer distortion on the curved surface of the cup and are worn smooth in several places. They are, nevertheless, among the most successfully executed figures to be found on Syrian silver objects, and may be compared in their proportions and drapery style with those on the Ballana caskets (Emery and Kirwan, 1938, pl. 68) and the Antioch Chalice (no. 40). The bodies are compact and fairly well articulated, and are coordinated with the soft garments draped

Fig. 3.7

Fig. 3.8

Fig. 3.9

over them. Despite their low, broad brows, the heads bear comparison with those on the Homs Vase (no. 84) in their prominent noses, large ears, and "tragic," downward-slanting eyes.

Iconographically, this compositon has been described as "the Apostles Venerating the Cross," as portrayed on two Antioch plaques (see Entry no. 46), contemporary pilgrim stamps, and gems, *et cetera*—a composition which may have originated from a monumental prototype such as that documented at Ravenna and Rome (see *Age,* 1979, no. 532). In view of the fact that three objects among the Stuma, Riha, Hama, and Antioch treasures (nos. 3, 46, 47) are decorated with this subject, it is worth noting that a very important relic of the True Cross was kept at nearby Apamea (fig. II.1), and received great attention in the period when this silver was being made and dedicated. The relic had been purloined from Jerusalem by a Syrian, and it was described at length by both Procopius (*Wars,* II, xi.14 ff.) and Evagrius (*HE,* IV.26), when it performed a miracle at the time of the Persian seige of Apamea in 540; this miracle was subsequently commemorated by a painting in the cathedral there (*ibid.*). In 566 or 574, Justin II forceably secured one half of this relic, which was brought into the capital with great ceremony and housed in a gemmed gold casket in Hagia Sophia (Michael, II, 283 ff., Cedrenus, I, 685; Maraval, 1985, 346, note 132), where it was venerated during his reign on the "Day of the Adoration of the Holy Cross" (John of Ephesos, *HE,* II.29).

Bibliography

Sachsen, 1912, 11, fig. 11; Mouterde, 1926, 366; Diehl, 1926, no. 3; Wilpert, 1926, 136 f.; *idem,* 1927, 335 f.; Braun, 1932, 78 ff.; Peirce and Tyler, 1934, vol. 2, 124; *SEG,* vol. 7, no. 92; *Dark Ages,* 1937, no. 97; *Early Christian,* 1947, no. 394; Lassus, 1947, 197 f.; Downey, 1951, 350, and note 11; *IGLS,* no. 2029; Ross, 1962, 20; Dodd, 1973, 17 ff., 54, 57; *Age,* 1979, no. 532; Zalesskaja, 1982, 109 f.; Mundell-Mango, 1986.

4. PATEN

DISKOS

Figures 4.1–4.4

Baltimore, The Walters Art Gallery, no. 57.644

Hama Treasure, Mid-Sixth Century

For technical and compositional analyses, see Chapter III, Appendices III.1 and III.2.

This paten has high sides, somewhat convex in profile, a flat narrow rim, but no foot (figs. 4.2–4.4). At its center is an engraved Latin cross with flared arms and cusped terminations. Around the central field runs an inscription (figs. 4.1, 4.3) between engraved lines (two inside and two pairs outside), and a pair of lines are engraved on the flat rim. Just below the center of the cross is a raised disc with a compass point at its center, and in the middle of the reverse side are two turning points (fig. 4.4).

This paten was formed by hammering, the marks of which remain visible on its reverse. It was turned on a lathe to finish its inner surface and outer sides, and to engrave the decorative lines. One of the two turning points on the back is deeper than the other, while the raised disc on the front has no turning lines, and was probably masked by the clamping device of the lathe. A compass was used to draw the cross; the vertical arm was inscribed within a lightly traced circle centered on the raised disc, while for the horizontal arm, two arcs were drawn from a (now undetectable) point 1.5 centimeters above the first one. The arms were burnished along their axes, creating a contrast with the circular turning pattern of the surrounding field. Analysis indicates that the cross was not gilded, but that the inscribed band, with its higher concentrations of gold and copper, may have been both gilded and inlaid with niello. There is a slight dent in the lower left quadrant. There are also some scratches there, and on the left and upper right sloping sides. A small bump mars the surface just below the left arm of the cross.

Fig. 4.1

INSCRIPTION

+ *(Treasure) of St. Sergios. For the memory of BARADATOS, son of HELIODOROS.*

Chased, single-stroke (H of letters = .8–1.4 cm). Diehl, 1926, no. 5; *SEG,* vol. 7, no. 94; *IGLS,* no. 2031.

Serifs are used on the usual letters, except *delta.*

This lunate script bears a general resemblance to that of nos. 5, 10, 27, 29, *et cetera,* but its individual letters are less well executed (note the four unconnected strokes for an *omicron*), and it dips noticeably below its border in one place. This reading is completed on analogy with that of Hama chalice no. 3. Except for the Sarabaon paten (no. 75), where the "church" is mentioned ("Treasure of the . . . church of . . . Sarabaon"), it is more often the saint, in the dative case, who is specified as the direct recipient of the gift (e.g., nos. 7, 11, 12, 30, *etc.*). Alternatively, this paten's inscription may be understood as "(Offering to [or Property of] the Church) of St. Sergios . . ." (so *IGLS,* no. 2031). Although the dedicatory formula used here, *hyper mnemes,* does not appear on any other object in this catalogue, it is inscribed on at least three objects in the Sion treasure (*DO Handbook,* 1967, nos. 64, 65, 69). In building and pavement dedications in *Oriens* it is found alone, for example, in 484, 487, and

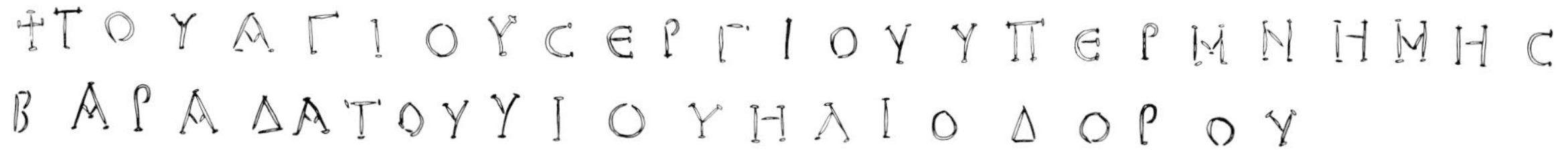

+ΤΟΥΑΓΙΟΥCЄΡΓΙΟΥΥΠЄΡΜΝΗΜΗC
ΒΑΡΑΔΑΤΟΥΥΙΟΥΗΛΙΟΔΟΡΟΥ

+Τοῦ ἁγίου Σεργίου.῾Υπὲρ μνήμης
Βαραδάτου υἱοῦ ῾Ηλιοδόρου.

D	38.6–39.1 cm
H	4.5 cm
Weight	987 gr
Roman Weight	3 lbs 4 scr
Original Silver Price	12 *solidi* 1 1/3 carats

Fig. 4.2

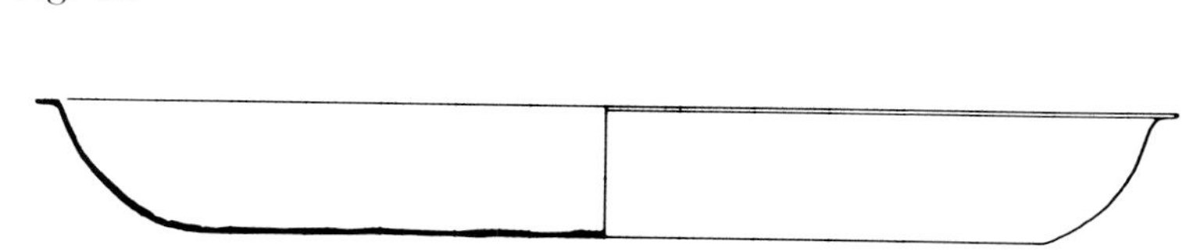

Fig. 4.3

circa 567 (Canivet, 1979, 350–355, 361; Fitzgerald, 1939, ins. 1). Coupled with *hyper anapauseos,* it was used in reference to the Empress Theodora at Mount Sinai (Ševčenko, 1966, no. 4), and elsewhere in 561 (Tsaferis, 1976, 114 f.), in 635 (Mittmann, 1967, 45) and at other, unspecified dates (*IGLS,* no. 1636; Dothan, 1955, 96 ff.; Negev, 1981, no. 74). (For the Semitic version, see Entries nos. 88, 89.) This Heliodoros is undoubtedly the same person of that name (on which, see *IGLS,* no. 2031) who gave Hama spoon no. 18 and, together with his brother Akakios, the Jerusalem chalice (no. 27) stamped around 550–565. Hama flask no. 15 was given "for the repose" of their souls by one Megale. See figure I.1.

Fig. 4.4

Commentary

This plate, and all the others of its type catalogued herein (nos. 5, 6, 34–36, 39, 60, 63, 64, 74, 75), can be securely identified as a paten (Greek = *diskos;* Latin = *patena;* Syriac = *kaphaphtha*); all but one (no. 39) were explicitly dedicated for church use. To this group also belong the fourth-century plate in the Durobrivae treasure (Painter, 1977 [I], no. 3), that of Bishop Paternus of 498–518 (Matzulevich, 1929, no. 6), and those in the Sion treasure, dating 527–565 (*DO Handbook,* 1967, nos. 63–65; Firatlı, 1969, figs. 2, 3). They can all be described as having a broad, flat lower surface and high sloping edges with flat rim. With one exception (the Sarabaon paten, no. 75), the Syrian patens lack footrings, a feature shared with *largitio* plates (see Entry no. 16). Decoration usually consists of a large or medium size cross (or *Chrismon*) engraved in the center, which is sometimes gilded, but not inlaid with niello. Exceptions to this scheme are the plain Gallunianu paten (no. 81), and the Stuma and Riha patens decorated with the Communion of the Apostles (nos. 34, 35). These last two, and paten no. 36 (which are related in other technical and epigraphic respects) have their inscriptions on their upper rims; normally, however, the inscription will appear on the flat inner surface of the plate. This type of plate is easily distinguishable from the group of domestic plates, which have a flatter profile and a very small, niello inlaid cross in the center (e.g., Dodd, 1961, no. 54; see Entry no. 106); no plate of this latter type bears a legend offering it to a church or a saint.

Bibliography

Diehl, 1926, no. 5; Braun, 1932, 202; *SEG,* vol. 7, no. 94; *Dark Ages,* 1937, no. 104; *Early Christian,* 1947, no. 400; *IGLS,* no. 2031; Dodd, 1973, 25 f; Mundell-Mango, 1986.

5. PATEN

DISKOS

Figures 5.1–5.5

Baltimore, The Walters Art Gallery, no. 57.637

Hama Treasure, First Half of the Seventh Century (Indiction 4: 615/6, 630/1, 645/6)

For technical and compositional analyses, see Chapter III, Appendices III.1 and III.2.

This paten has high sloping sides, a flat narrow rim, but no foot (figs. 5.2–5.4). In its center is a large engraved Latin cross with flared arms and cusped terminations; there are four small diagonal strokes at the crossing of the arms. Around the central field runs an inscription (figs. 5.1, 5.3) between a concave moulding set off by engraved lines. Two narrow lines appear on the rim. There are two stamps and a turning point on the reverse (figs. 5.4, 5.5).

This paten was formed by hammering, the marks of which remain visible on the reverse. It was turned on a lathe to finish the inner surface and outer sides, and to engrave the decorative lines. The cross was probably drawn with the aid of a compass, whose point remains visible at the crossing of the arms. There is no evidence of gilding or niello. There is a long diagonal scratch in the lower right quadrant of the paten, and a crack in the flat rim at about 2 o'clock. A large dent crossing the paten from 5 to 9 o'clock, visible in 1926 (Diehl, 1926, pl. XXVII), has been removed.

STAMPS

This paten bears just two stamps, which belong to a sub-series dated by Dodd (1961, no. 98) to the seventh century because of the rectangular stamps, which in three cases contain the names of Heraclius (610–641) and Constans II (641–668; *ibid.*, nos. 94, 96, 97). The hitherto illegible rectangular stamp on this paten is now seen to contain the date "indiction 4" (which fell in 615/6 and 630/1 during the reign of Heraclius, and 645/6 under Constans II). (See *ibid.*, no. 93, for a plate stamped with an indicational date, in Carthage, in 540. Indiction numbers also commonly appear on brick stamps of the period; see Mango, 1950, 22 ff.) As described by Dodd, but with this new interpretation of the rectangular stamp, they may be read as follows:

a. Rectangular: inscription partially identified to include *IND(IKTIONOS) IIII.*

b. Round: eight-pointed star.

INSCRIPTION

+ *In fulfillment of a vow of PELAGIOS and SOSANNA and of THEIR CHILDREN. Amen.*

Engraved, single-stroke (H of letters = 1.1 cm). Diehl, 1926, no. 4; *SEG,* vol. 7, no. 93; Downey, 1948, 21; *IGLS,* no. 2030; *Age,* 1979, no. 533.

This lunate lettering is very well executed. The size is consistent and the serifs are regularly placed. No abbreviations or ligatures are used.

On the dedicatory formula *hyper euches,* see Entry no. 1. This inscription corresponds in every detail so closely to that on London chalice no. 29, that one is justified in concluding that they were done by the same hand.

Fig. 5.1

Commentary

Interesting similarities exist among stamped Syrian patens decorated with crosses. The group includes, in addition to this specimen, the Alouf paten of 498–518 (no. 74), a Phela paten of 577 (no. 63), a Stuma paten of 574–578 (no. 36), and the Sarabaon paten (no. 75), which apparently is of seventh-century date. The nearly contemporary Phela and Stuma plates are, with the exception of their inscriptions, closest in most details of their decoration. This Hama paten, on the other hand, is closer to the early sixth-century Alouf paten than it is to the seventh-century(?) Sarabaon paten, with which, however, it shares the same sub-series of stamps.

The attribution of the inscriptions on this paten and the London chalice (no. 29) to a single hand raises the distinct possibility that the two were part of a joint offering. The paten was given by Pelagios, his wife Sosanna, and their unnamed children. The chalice, also presented *hyper euches,* was given in the names of Sergios and John—who may have been those children. (These two names also appear on the Stuma treasure paten of 574–578 [no. 36], when John is aleady dead; the individuals must therefore be different.) If a joint offering, paten and chalice would constitute a *diskopoterion* set. The Pelagios named on this paten may be Pelagios Basianos, who gave Hama chalice no. 3, to which, however, it bears no stylistic similarity. See figure I.1.

Bibliography

Diehl, 1926, no. 4; Braun, 1932, 202; *SEG,* vol. 7, no. 93; *Dark Ages,* 1937, no. 98; *Early Christian,* 1947, no. 401; Downey, 1948, 21; Downey, 1951, 350, and note 11; *IGLS,* no. 2030; Dodd, 1961, no. 98; Weitzmann and Ševčenko, 1963, 398 ff.; Dodd, 1973, 25 f., 57; *Age,* 1979, no. 533; Mundell-Mango, 1986.

Fig. 5.4

Fig. 5.5

CЄK..COCh
+IИΔsIIII+ ='+ ind(iction) 4 +'
IWANPOS ˥

†ΥΠΕΡΕΥΧΗCΠΕΛΑΓΙΟΥΚΑΙCωCΑΝΝΑC
ΚΑΙΤωΝΤΕΚΝωΝΑΥΤωΝΑΜΗΝ

+ Ὑπὲρ εὐχῆς Πελαγίου καὶ Σωσάννας
καὶ τῶν τέκνων αὐτῶν. Ἀμήν.

D	37.4–37.9 cm
H	2.9–3.2 cm
Weight	1008.1 gr
Roman Weight	3 lbs 23 scr
Original Silver Price	12 *solidi* 7 1/3 carats

Fig. 5.2

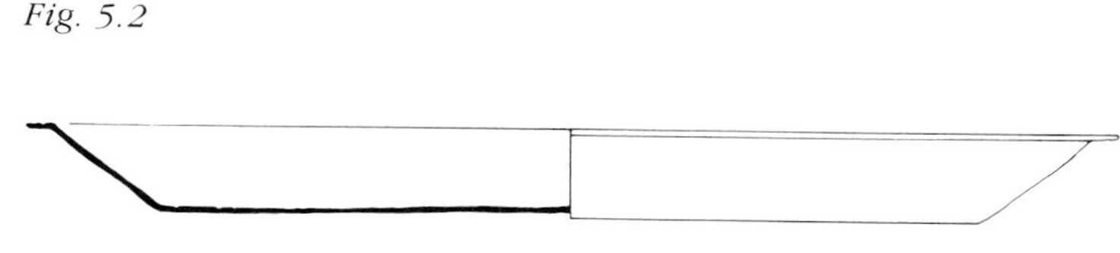

Fig. 5.3

Fig. 6.1

6. PATEN

DISKOS

Figures 6.1–6.4

Baltimore, The Walters Art Gallery, no. 57.643

Hama Treasure, Sixth to Seventh Century

For technical and compositional analyses, see Chapter III, Appendices III.1 and III.2.

This paten has high sloping sides, a flat narrow rim, but no foot (figs. 6.2–6.4). At its center is a small engraved cross with nearly equal, flaring arms, set within a border composed of a chased inscription (figs. 6.1, 6.3) between two single engraved lines. Two narrow engraved lines ornament the rim. Just below the center of the cross is a turning point.

This paten was formed by hammering, the marks of which remain visible on the reverse. It was turned on a lathe to finish the inner surface and outer sides, and a band extending three centimeters onto the bottom of the reverse; its engraved linear decoration was probably also produced on a lathe. There is no evidence of niello or gilding. There is a small tear at the top, where the sloping side meets the bottom. To the right of this tear is a slight bend in the flat rim. In the 1910 Hama photograph (fig. II.4) there is a shadow of a short dent extending from the tear onto the lower surface of the paten.

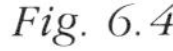

Fig. 6.4

INSCRIPTION

+ *Vow of the most saintly archbishop AMPHILOCHIOS.*

Chased, single-stroke (H of letters = .5–1.0 cm). Diehl, 1926, no. 6; *SEG,* vol. 7, no. 95; *IGLS,* no. 2032.

The lettering, which is partly lunate (*omicron*) and partly square (*epsilon, sigma*), varies in height, some letters being poorly formed (compare Diehl, "fort beau"). There are no serifs and no abbreviations.

This lettering is not particularly similar to that on any other object herein catalogued. The Bosworth chalice (no. 28), one Phela chalice (no. 62), and the Alouf paten (no. 74) have the only other single-stroke inscriptions without serifs. The same mixture of lunate and square characters occurs on the Beth Misona paten (no. 60) and the Phela cross (no. 65). Although the square letters and the form of the *upsilon* led Diehl (1926, 115) to postulate a fifth-century date, these other two objects can on other grounds be safely ascribed to the sixth century.

On the use of *euche,* see Entry no. 3. The title of *archepiskopos* belonged to bishops of metropolitan sees—that is, provincial capitals. The church at Kaper Koraon (see Chapters I, II) was under the jurisdiction of the archbishop (i.e., patriarch) of Antioch—and no patriarch of Antioch was named Amphilochios. Closer geographically to Koraon was the archbishopric of Apamea (fig. II.1), capital of Syria *Secunda* (Balty, 1980), whose lacunose episcopal list (Canivet,

✝ ΕΥΧΗΤΟΥΑΓΙωΤΑΤΟΥΑΡΧΙΕΠΙϹΚΟΠΟΥ
ΑΝΦΙΛΟΧΙΟΥ

+ Εὐχὴ τοῦ ἁγιωτάτου ἀρχιεπισκόπου Ἀνφιλοχίου

D	40.8–41.4 cm
H	3.3–4.0 cm
Weight	1000 gr
Roman Weight	3 lbs 15 scr
Original Silver Price	12 *solidi* 5 carats

Fig. 6.2

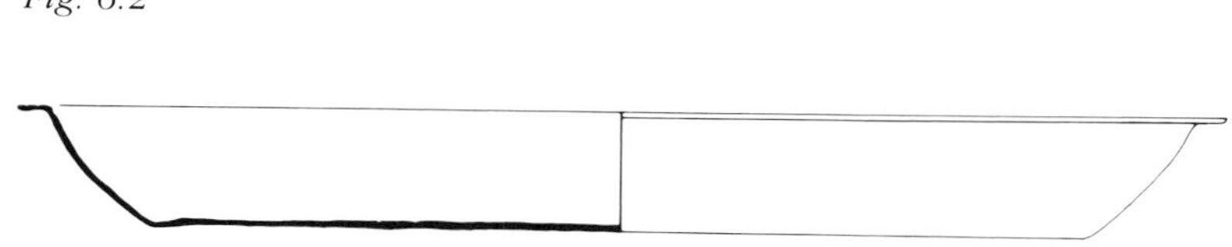

Fig. 6.3

1973) for the sixth century certainly could have contained a native son (i.e., Amphilochios) from a nearby village. As suggested for John, "bishop of Kerania," whose silver seal is part of the Phela church treasure (no. 66), Amphilochios could at once have been an archbishop in any part of the Empire, and a donor to his native church. There is no need to identify him with a well-known Amphilochios, such as the late fourth-century metropolitan bishop of Iconium (*IGLS,* no. 2032) or the fifth-century bishop of Side in Pamphylia (as does Zalesskaja, 1982, 106). See figure I.1.

Commentary

Although as archbishop, Amphilochios enjoyed higher status than Eutychianos, the (mere) bishop who donated much of the opulent Sion treasure (*DO Handbook,* 1967, 18, nos. 63, 66–68), and although he was, among the (presumed) donors at Kaper Koraon, second only to Megas (see no. 37) in social standing, his gift is among the least pretentious—that is, it bears no gilding, no niello, no ornament, a very simple cross, and a somewhat carelessly executed inscription. It is, however, the largest of all the patens in this catalogue and, at one thousand grams, one of the heaviest after the uninscribed and even simpler Stuma paten no. 39 (1090 gr) and the stamped Hama paten no. 5 (1008 gr). For other patens with this type of decoration, see Entry no. 39. Given the paucity of decorative detail, the absence of stamps, and the singular character of its inscription, it is difficult to place Amphilochios' unique gift in a precise chronological relation to the other dedicated objects in this group, although its cross resembles that of the seventh-century Sarabaon paten (no. 75). It should be noted, however, that this paten and Stuma treasure paten no. 39, both of simple design and with small crosses, are the only ones herein catalogued with a burnished band on the bottom of the reverse.

Bibliography

Diehl, 1926, no. 6; Rosenberg, 1928, vol. 4, 732 f.; Braun, 1932, 202; *SEG,* vol. 7, no. 95; *Dark Ages,* 1937, no. 103; *Early Christian,* 1947, no. 399; *IGLS,* no. 2032; Dodd, 1973, 27 f.; Zalesskaja, 1982, 106; Mundel-Mango, 1986.

7. CROSS

STAUROS

Figures 7.1–7.3

Baltimore, The Walters Art Gallery, no. 57.632

Hama Treasure, Sixth to Seventh Century

For technical and compositional analyses, see Chapter III, Appendices III.1 and III.2.

This cross with tang has flaring arms without serifs (figs. 7.2, 7.3). Its obverse bears an inscription (figs. 7.1, 7.2) surrounded by an engraved border, and a similar border runs around the reverse, where the inscription shows through. On the lower edge of each horizontal arm is a pair of punched holes for *pendelia.*

This cross was cut from a sheet of hammered metal, and was burnished front and back along the axes of the arms. The black substance remaining in some letters was found to be silver sulfide (see Chapter III, Appendix III.3). Its silver tang has broken off and been replaced with one of copper alloy secured with two copper alloy rivets. The upper copper rivet can be seen in the 1910 Hama photograph (fig. II.4); the repair is therefore probably ancient. A bend in the lower arm, also visible there, was straightened out before 1926 (Diehl, 1926, pl. XXII). Slight bends still remain in the upper and left arms.

INSCRIPTION

KYRIAKOS, having vowed, presented (this cross) to St. Sergios.

Chased, single-stroke, nielloed(?) (H of letters = .6–1.1cm). Diehl, 1926, no. 14; *SEG,* vol. 7, no. 102; *IGLS,* no. 2039; *Age,* 1979, no. 540.

The letters on the vertical arms are more consistently formed than are those on the horizontal arms, where height varies. Serifs are used regularly. There are no abbreviations or ligatures. Spelling: *epsilon* for *eta* in *prosenegken.*

The chased lettering on this cross is very close to the engraved inscriptions on Hama paten no. 5 and chalice no. 29 (except for *mu* and *nu*), and to the chased inscription on the small Hama cross no. 9 (except for *alpha, mu, nu,* and *upsilon*). The second *upsilon* of this inscription is "barred," as are those on Hama lampstands nos. 11 and 12, and ewer no. 14 (and Phela treasure objects nos. 61, 64, 65). The text is comparable to those of the Beth Misona paten (no. 60), one Phela chalice (no. 62), the Symeon plaque in the Louvre (no. 71), and the smaller Sinai cross (Weitzmann and Ševčenko, 1963, 397, note 48), which reads "Leontios and Sabas, having given thanks, presented (this cross) to the Holy Trinity." Also similar is the Armenian legend on the cross from Divriği (no. 76). In all these cases, thanksgiving or a vow is acknowledged and the object presented to a saint, the Trinity or Theotokos. Kyriakos is not mentioned on any other object in the reconstructed Kaper Koraon Treasure, but Kyriakos, son of Domnos (presumably another individual) presented three (?) chalices to St. Sergios of Beth Misona (nos. 57–59). See figure I.1.

COMMENTARY

This is one of a group of medium-sized crosses, thirty to sixty centimeters high, nearly all of which have a tang (like those on liturgical fans nos. 31, 32) for insertion into a staff by which the cross could be set

Fig. 7.1

ΚΥΡΙΑΚΟϹΕΥΞΑΜΕΝΟϹ
ΠΡΟϹΕΝΕΓΚΕΝΤΩΑΓΙΩϹΕΡΓΙΩ

Κυριακὸς εὐξάμενος
προσένεγκεν τῷ ἁγίῳ Σεργίῳ.

upright or carried. (For larger [i.e., over 1 m] and smaller [i.e., *ca.* 10–15 cm] silver crosses, see respectively, Entries nos. 42 and 9). Like virtually all contemporary crosses, this one has flaring arms, but like nos. 9, 10, 42, 65, and 68, the cross of Justin II, the smaller Sinai cross, and that from Mount Cassius (Mécérian, 1964, 69, pl. XXXIV), it has no serifs on the ends of its arms. Related crosses without serifs are engraved on patens nos. 4–6, 36, 63, 74, and 75. Of all these crosses, those that offer the closest comparisons with this one in proportion, size, level of craftsmanship, and dedicatory text are the smaller Sinai cross and that from Mount Cassius, both of which are in bronze.

Originally this cross had *pendelia* strung through the four holes in its horizontal arms. Two, four or six *pendelia* were common on crosses like this one, where they would be fastened through simple holes (as here) or eyelets (as on the large Sinai cross; Weitzmann and Ševčenko, 1963, fig. 1). That the letters *alpha* and *omega* hung from those with two holes is indicated by the extant cross from Divriği (no. 76) as well as by contemporary pictorial representations (e.g., *ibid.,* fig. 10). "Jewels," crosslets or other letters may have been suspended from crosses with four or six holes (like, respectively, the cross of Justin II and the larger Sinai cross).

Like other medium-sized crosses with a tang, this one could have been carried in procession or affixed in a stand, or both. Among the Stuma, Riha, Hama, and Antioch treasures there are three crosses (in addition to the very small ones, nos. 9, 10, and 43[?]): the tall silver-revetted cross in the Antioch treasure (no. 42; H 150 cm), this one, and another Hama cross (no. 8), whose height without tang is nearly identical to this. The latter two may be seen as a *de facto* pair, although they were probably not offered together, in view of their differences in proportions, serifs, and inscription. Whether two crosses would have stood on an altar together, or whether there may have been an arrangement of three crosses—with two flanking a larger cross—before an altar, as described in Entry no. 42, is a matter of conjecture.

BIBLIOGRAPHY

Diehl, 1926, no. 14; *SEG,* vol. 7, no. 102; *Dark Ages,* 1937, no. 94; *Early Christian,* 1947, no. 404; *IGLS,* no. 2039; Ross, 1962, 20; Weitzmann and Ševčenko, 1963, 397; *Age,* 1979, no. 540.

H	40.2 cm
H (without tang)	33.8 cm
W	20.6 cm
TH	.2 cm
Weight	310.1 gr
Roman Weight	11 oz 9 scr
Original Silver Price	3 *solidi* 19 carats

Fig. 7.3

Fig. 7.2

8. CROSS

STAUROS

Figures 8.1–8.3

Baltimore, The Walters Art Gallery, no. 57.641

Hama Treasure, Sixth to Seventh Century

For technical and compositional analyses, see Chapter III, Appendices III.1 and III.2.

This cross with tang has serifs on the points of its flaring arms (figs. 8.1, 8.2). An engraved linear border outlines obverse and reverse, and there is a pair of punched holes for *pendelia* on the lower edge of each horizontal arm.

This cross was cut from a sheet of hammered metal. Pierced knobs, probably made from the same sheet, were threaded onto pointed projections at the ends of the cross arms (fig. 8.3: radiograph), and soldered. The joins were then disguised, probably by hammering and burnishing, the arms were burnished along their axes, the border line engraved, and the *pendelia* holes punched. The lower arm of the cross is shown bent (as is cross no. 7) in the 1910 Hama photograph (fig. II.4); it has since been straightened out. The tang was broken off; its attempted repair (which caused the surface to bubble) may have been ancient (as may have been that on cross no. 7).

COMMENTARY

This cross is uninscribed, but like most crosses discussed here, it has a linear border near its edge, both front and back. And like several other crosses, it has a tang and (four) *pendelia* holes (for both, see Entry no. 7). This cross also has, at the tips of its arms, small projections called serifs; here they are spherical, like those on the silver crosses from Phela (no. 65) and Luxor (Strzygowski, 1904, no. 7201) and the larger bronze cross on Mount Sinai (Weitzmann and Ševčenko, 1963, fig. 1), while those on the silver Divriği cross (no. 76), and the bronze Madaba (Piccirillo, 1982, pls. 24, 25), Berlin (Wulff, 1909, no. 945), and Louvre (Metzger, 1972) crosses, are circular and flat. (On the function of this cross, see Entry no. 7.)

BIBLIOGRAPHY

Diehl, 1926, no. 15; *Dark Ages,* 1937, no. 101; *Early Christian,* 1947, no. 405; Ross, 1962, 20.

Fig. 8.2

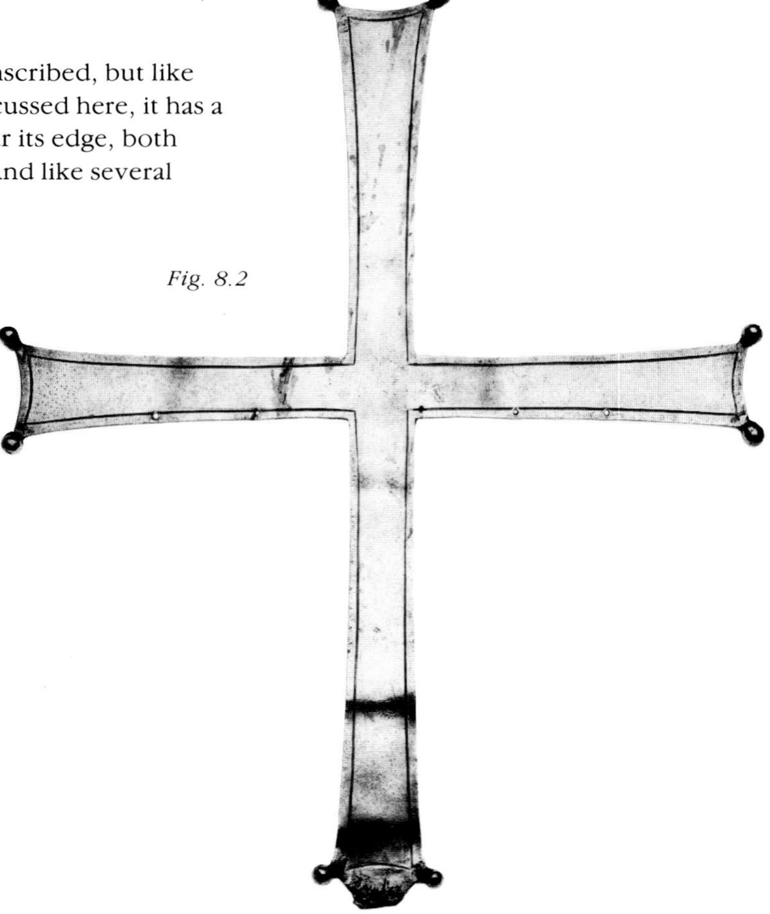

H	34.0 cm
H (without tang)	33.0 cm
W	26.7 cm
TH	.2 cm
Weight	211.2 gr
Roman Weight	7 oz 18 scr
Original Silver Price	2 *solidi* 14 carats

Fig. 8.1

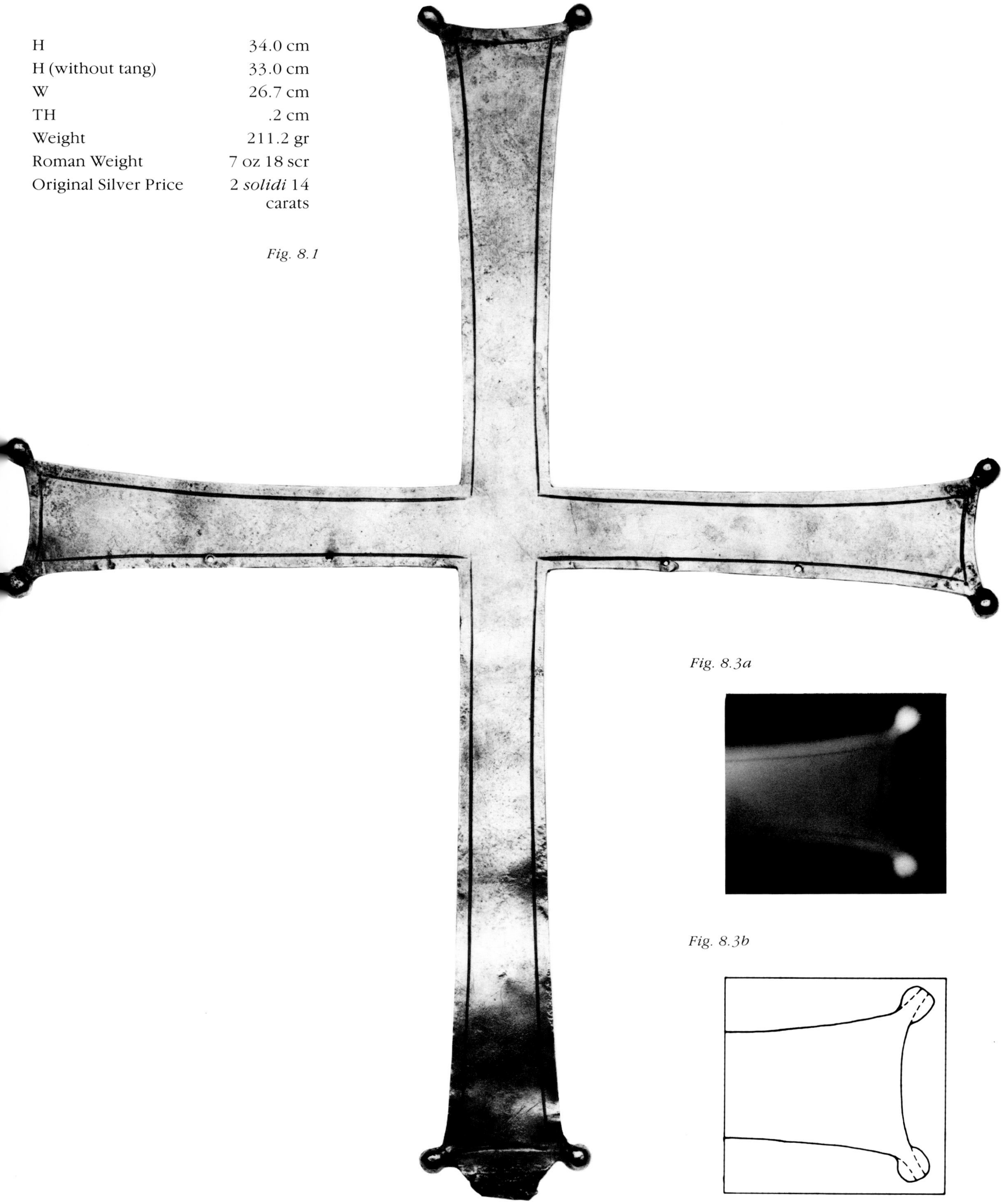

Fig. 8.3a

Fig. 8.3b

Fig. 9.1

9. CROSS

STAURION

Figures 9.1–9.4

Baltimore, The Walters Art Gallery, no. 57.629

Hama Treasure, Mid-Sixth Century(?)

For technical and compositional analyses, see Chapter III, Appendices III.1 and III.2.

This small cross has flaring arms with straight ends and, on its obverse, an inscription surrounded by an engraved border (figs. 9.1–9.3). Its reverse is flat and undecorated, and there are four punched holes, one in the end of each arm, for attachment.

This cross was apparently cast, as radiographs reveal no trace of hammering; a hole in the upper edge of the right arm and a crack in the bottom of the lower arm are probably casting flaws. Its unusually high copper content (5.24–14.72 percent), which is greater than that of hammered crosses nos. 7 and 8, (and of all other objects tested, except cross no. 10), would have lowered its melting point for easier casting. It would also have resulted in a harder metal, which may have been deemed necessary for its intended function. Although this cross was obviously made for attachment, tool marks indicate that both its surfaces were burnished (along the axes of the arms), to remove casting irregularities and to improve the reflective quality. No trace of niello was detected.

INSCRIPTION

In fulfillment of a vow and (for) the salvation of THOMAS, son of ISAAC, and of ALL THOSE WHO BELONG TO HIM. Amen.

Engraved, single-stroke (H of letters = .3 and .4–.6 cm). Diehl, 1926, no. 13; *SEG,* vol. 7, no. 101; *IGLS,* no. 2038.

This inscription reads from top to bottom and then from left to right, twice, and is distributed mostly two letters to the width (contrast cross no. 10). The lettering is lunate and serifs are used regularly. *Kai* is both abbreviated *Ks* and written out in full. Spelling: *omicron* for *omega* in *panton,* in *ton,* and in *diapheronton; omicron-upsilon* for *omega* in *auto.*

For the dedicatory formula *hyper euches kai soterias,* and the phrase signifying "household" (both of which are also used on cross no. 10), see Entry no. 1. Thomas, son of Isaac may be one and the same as Thomas, father of Heliodoros and Akakios, who are mentioned in dedications on objects datable by stamps to *ca.* 550–565 (see Entries nos. 4, 15, 18, 27). See figure I.1.

COMMENTARY

Quite a number of small gold and bronze crosses survive from the Early Byzantine period, most of which were made to be worn around the neck. Extant small silver crosses, on the other hand, are relatively rare—despite the testimony of a text of 449 which describes the donation of many gold and silver *stauria* ("crosslets") as *ex-votos* to the Cathedral of Edessa (Schwartz, I.iii.25/384). This cross and cross no. 10 were not made to be worn around the neck, but rather to be attached by their four holes to some surface, either as *ex-votos* or as dedicatory plaques. Such a cross could have been set into the cruciform sinking of a stone reliquary (Mango, 1985, fig. 3) or slab (fig. 9.4; Mount Sinai, Chapel of the Holy Fathers [latex mold]; Ševčenko, 1966, 258, 263, no. 6); a bronze votive cross to St. Thekla at Dumbarton Oaks (Ross, 1962, no. 67) is still embedded in the lead once used to seat it.

ΥΠЄΡЄΥΧΗϹΚϹѠΤΗΡΙΑϹΘѠΜΑΥΙΟΥΙϹΑΚΙΟΥ
ΚΑΙΠΑΝΤΟΝΤΟΝ ΔΙΑΦЄΡΟΝΤΟΝ ΑΥΤΟΥΑΜΗΝ

Ὑπὲρ εὐχῆς κ(αὶ) σωτηρίας Θωμᾶ υἱοῦ Ἰσακίου
καὶ πάντον τôν διαφερόντον αὐτοῦ. Ἀμήν.

This cross and its close relative, no. 10, may together have been attached to a surface to mark a joint offering of objects or architecture, for, while not identical in craftsmanship, they are very close in their dimensions, weights, dedications, and metallic content.

H	11.0 cm
W	8.6 cm
TH	.1 cm
Weight	38.2 gr
Roman Weight	1 oz 9 scr
Original Silver Price	11 carats

BIBLIOGRAPHY

Diehl, 1926, no. 13; *SEG,* vol. 7, no. 101; *Dark Ages,* 1937, no. 92; *Early Christian,* 1947, no. 406; *IGLS,* no. 2038.

Fig. 9.3

Fig. 9.2

Fig. 9.4

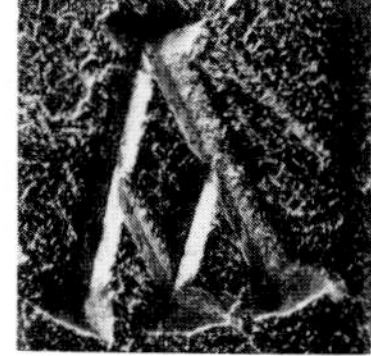
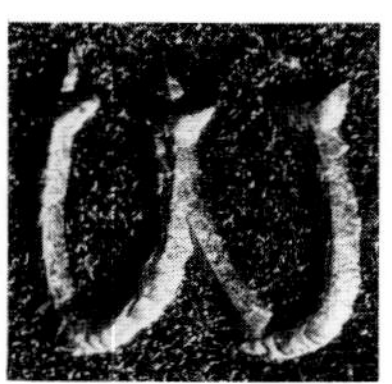

Fig. 10.1

10. CROSS

STAURION

Figures 10.1–10.3

Baltimore, The Walters Art Gallery, no. 57.630

Hama Treasure, Mid-Sixth Century(?)

For technical and compositional analyses, see Chapter III, Appendices III.1 and III.2.

This small cross has flaring arms with bevelled edges and lunate terminations (figs. 10.2, 10.3). It bears an inscription (figs. 10.1, 10.2) and, at the foot of the lower arm, an eight-armed *Chrismon* with serifs. Its reverse is undecorated, although punch marks from the obverse inscription show through. There are four punched holes, one at the end of each arm, for attachment.

The observations made about the casting of cross no. 9 apply here as well; radiographs show no sign of hammering, and small cracks at the crossing of the arms are probably casting flaws. Its unusually high copper content (like that of no. 9) would have lowered its melting point for easier casting. It would also have resulted in a harder metal, which may have been deemed necessary for its intended function. The surface of this cross was not highly burnished, and appears grainy under moderate magnification. The serifs of the inscription were punched and connected by engraved lines. The reddish-black substance in letters on the right arm, when tested by x-ray diffraction, gave inconclusive results (see Chapter III, Appendix III.3). The corners of the lower arm have been bent backward and forward, respectively.

INSCRIPTION

+ *In fulfillment of a vow and (for) the salvation of JOHN, son of SYMEONIOS, and of ALL THOSE WHO BELONG TO HIM.*

Chased, engraved, single-stroke (H of letters = .3–.8 cm). Diehl, 1926, no. 12; *SEG,* vol. 7, no. 100; *IGLS,* no. 2037.

This inscription reads from top to bottom, then two lines left and two lines right (contrast no. 9); its letters are arranged three across on the vertical, two on the horizontal. Letter size is less consistent than on cross no. 9, and many letter lines extend beyond the serifs. *Kai* is abbreviated *Ks* and written out in full; the genitive *omicron-upsilon* is once in ligature and twice not. Spelling: *eta* for *iota* in *hyiou; omicron* for *omega* in *ton,* and in *diapheronton; auton* for *autou.*

Although this inscription is otherwise very similar in phrasing and layout to that on Hama cross no. 9, it starts with a cross, omits *amen,* and adds an ornamental *Chrismon* on the lower arm. (For the pietistic phrases used here, see Entry no. 1.) Symeonios may be one and the same as Symeonios, son of Maximinos, who with his brothers gave three Hama objects (nos. 11, 12, 14), and/or as Symeonios, *magistrianos,* who donated Hama chalice no. 1, around 550. John, son of Symeonios may be the same individual who is named as father of Sergia on the Riha paten (no. 35; 577?), and who is deceased when Sergios (his son?) gives Stuma treasure paten no. 36 (574–578) in his name. See figure I.1.

COMMENTARY

See Entry no. 9.

BIBLIOGRAPHY

Diehl, 1926, no. 12; *SEG,* vol. 7, no. 100; *Dark Ages,* 1937, no. 91; *Early Christian,* 1947, no. 407; Downey, 1951, 351; *IGLS,* no. 2037.

+ ΥΠΕΡΕΥΧΗϹ ϗ ϹΩΤΗΡΙΑϹΙΩ Α ΝΝΟΥΥΗΥϹΥΜΕΟΝ Ι ΟΥ
ΚΑΙΠΑΝΤΩΝΤΟΝ ΔΙΑΦΕΡΟΝΤΟΝΑΥΤΟΝ

+Ὑπὲρ εὐχῆς κ(αὶ) σωτηρίας Ἰωάννου ὑηοῦ Συμεονίου
καὶ πάντων τὸν διαφερόντον αὐτόν.

H	11.9 cm
W	8.6 cm
TH	.1 cm
Weight	30.1 gr
Roman Weight	1 oz 2 scr
Original Silver Price	8 2/3 carats

Fig. 10.3

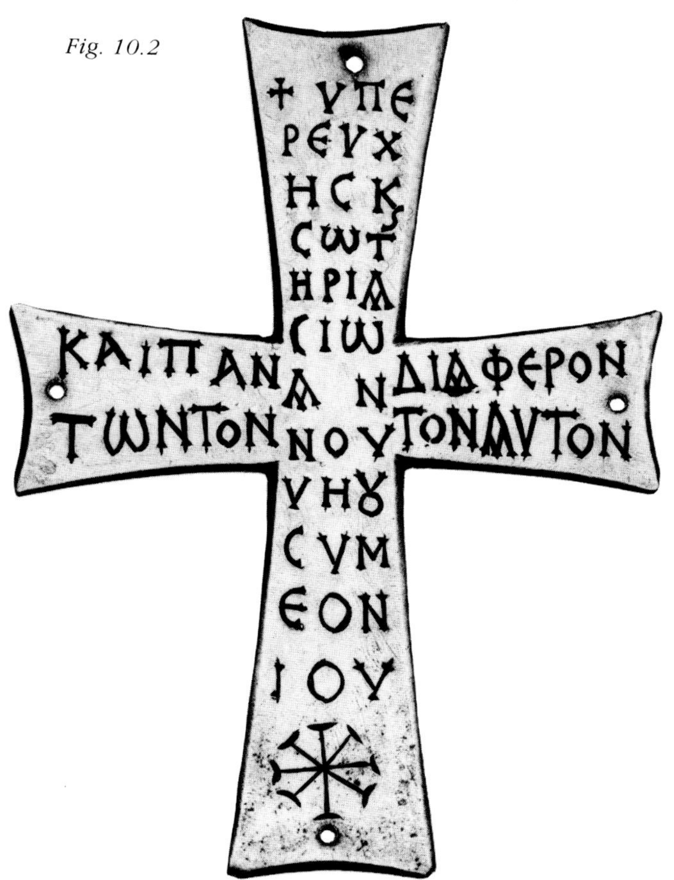

Fig. 10.2

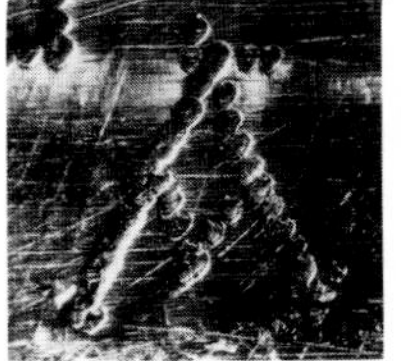
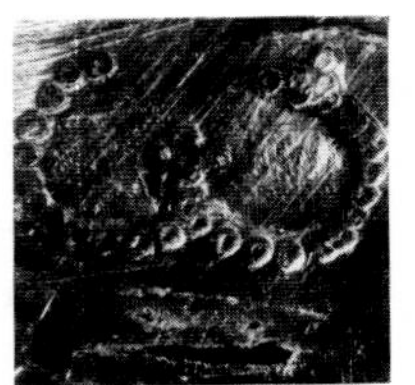

Fig. 11.1

11. LAMPSTAND

Figures 11.1–11.8

Baltimore, The Walters Art Gallery, no. 57.634

Hama Treasure, Mid-Sixth Century(?)

H	52.0 cm
W (across feet)	17.0 cm
W (across cup)	12.5 cm
Weight (including lead and iron)	1305.8 gr
Roman Weight	3 lbs 11 oz 20 scr
Original Silver Price	*ca.* 14(?) *solidi*

For technical and compositional analyses, see Chapter III, Appendices III.1 and III.2.

This lampstand (fig. 11.2) consists of a hollow tripod base (fig. 11.5) with hooflike feet and hexagonal apron, which supports a shaft formed as a hexagonally fluted column. The column in turn supports a hexagonally faceted flaring cup enclosing a stepped plate and a tall spike, square in section (fig. 11.4). The column, which has a marked *entasis,* rises from a profiled base (plinth, *torus,* and three graduated mouldings) and terminates in a Corinthian capital (with twisted rope *torus,* two-zone acanthus, and square abacus with rosette bosses). An inscription (figs. 11.1, 11.3) runs in two lines around the lower edge of the apron of the base; a black substance fills some of the dots. The hexagonal facets of the base, column, and cup are aligned.

This lampstand was made from the following nine silver components which were, except where otherwise noted, assembled with silver solder, excess drips of which remain above the inscription, on the column shaft, and on the underside of the cup: (1) The three feet were cast and then forged or hammered into shape and attached to three upright corners of (2) the hexagonal base, which was formed by hammering from a single sheet. (3) A thin disc of hammered silver was inserted inside the base and held with lead solder. (4) The column base was formed by hammering from a thin sheet and may have been turned on a lathe. (5) The hollow column shaft was forged from a thick sheet of silver containing a higher amount of copper for strength, and then rolled into shape and soldered along the vertical seam. (6) The column capital was formed from a thin sheet by hammering and was decorated by repoussé, chasing, and possibly engraving. The hollow column components were strengthened by the lead added to the column base as a counterbalance, and by an iron rod (now partially corroded; discovered by radiography [fig. 11.6] and confirmed with a magnet) which runs inside the lampstand from the top of the base up into the spike. (7) The hollow spike above the rod was forged from a thick sheet of silver containing a higher amount of copper for strength; it was folded into shape and joined along its vertical seam. (8) The cup was formed by hammering, the marks of which are visible in radiography. (9) A hammered, "stepped" plate with a central hole was slipped over the spike and secured with lead solder; iron corrosion products (from the rod) now seal the edges between the spike and the hole in the plate. After assembly, the surface of the lampstand was finished with files, other sharp tools, and abrasives, and then it was burnished. The black substance (i.e., acanthite) remaining in the crevices of the capitals and in the dots of the inscription is probably a corrosion product rather than

Fig. 11.3

Εὐξάμενοι ‖ τὴν εὐχὴν ἀπέδωκαν τῷ ἁγίου Σεργίου (καὶ) Βάχχου +
+Σέργις (καὶ) Συμεωνις (καὶ) Δανιὴλ (καὶ) Θωμᾶς υἱοὶ Μαξιμίνου κώμη Καπρο Κοραω

niello (see Chapter III, Appendix III.3). There are two tears in the column shaft of the lampstand, and the hexagonal apron of the base is dented in two places. The spike has horizontal scraping marks, possibly caused by a metal lamp.

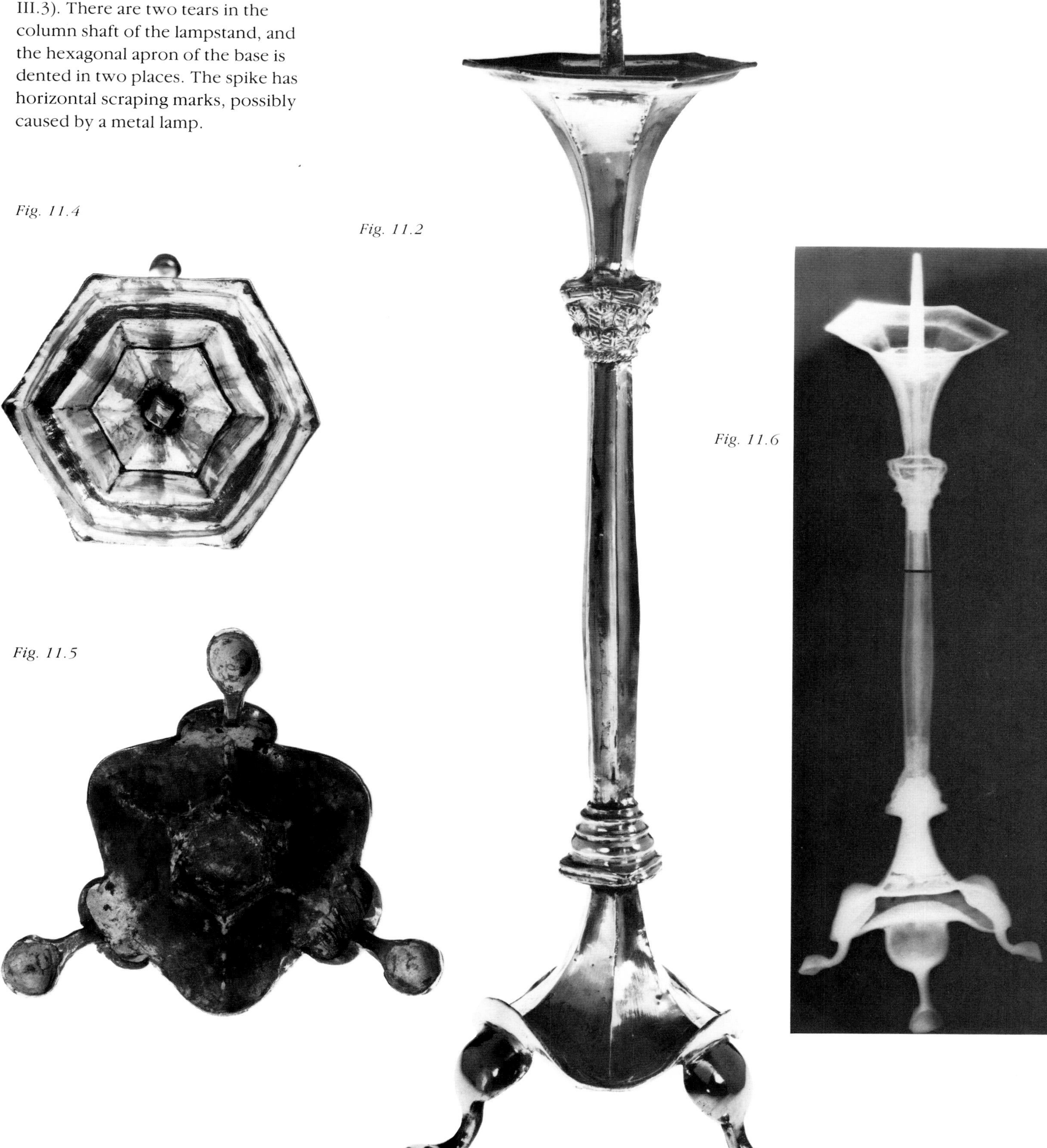

Fig. 11.4

Fig. 11.2

Fig. 11.6

Fig. 11.5

Inscription

+ *Having vowed, they fulfilled their vow to (the Church) of St. Sergios and Bacchos.* + *SERGI(O)S and SYMEONI(O)S and DANIEL and THOMAS, sons of MAXIMINOS, village of Kaper Korao(n).*

Pointillé, nielloed(?) (H of letters = .5 cm). Diehl, 1926, no. 9; *SEG,* vol. 7, no. 97; *IGLS,* no. 2034, II; *Age,* 1979, no. 541.

Diehl incorrectly adds a *kai* above the upper line and a final *nu* below the lower. *Kai* is abbreviated *S'* and the genitive *omicron-upsilon* is twice in ligature. The lettering is lunate and serifs are regularly used. Spelling: *omicron-upsilon* for *omega* in *hagio, Sergio,* and *Baccho.*

This inscription was executed by the same hand that did the inscription on lampstand no. 12; its letter forms also resemble those of some single-stroke inscriptions, such as Hama ewer no. 14 (given by the same donors) and Hama cross no. 7; all have a barred *upsilon.*

This inscription is the same as that on Hama lampstand no. 12, but its distribution on the two objects differs (contrast figs. 11.3 and 12.3); that on no. 12, starting *euxamenoi,* is the "correct" version. The craftsman, who probably did this lampstand first, seems to have begun with the lower line of text and, misunderstanding the desired arrangement, spaced the words closer than necessary; he thus ended by putting *euxamenoi* at the end of that lower line rather than at the beginning of the line above, where it belongs. The cross, which would (as on no. 12) ordinarily mark the juncture between the end and the beginning of the upper line of text, here marks the end only (i.e., *Bacchou*). The formula *euxamenoi, ten euchen apedokan* does not recur on other silver objects found in Syria, but is found several times in building and pavement dedications in Isauria and Cilicia (MAMA, II, 107 f.; MAMA, III, 97; Dagron and Marcillet-Jaubert, 1978, no. 37). The donors of both lampstands are four brothers: Sergios, Symeonios, Daniel, and Thomas. (On Symeonios, and the question of dating, see Entry no. 1.) These four also dedicated Hama ewer no. 14, where a fifth brother, Bacchos, is mentioned as well. Indeed, this ewer may provide a clue to another misunderstanding on the part of the craftsman responsible for the inscriptions on the lampstands. For by coincidence (or simple misunderstanding?) the church named on these objects is called, exceptionally, that of "Sergios and Bacchos." See figure I.1.

Fig. 11.7

Commentary

The design of this type of tripod lampstand, with its shaft worked as a column with capital and base, can be traced back to the lower portion of extending candelabra of the first to fourth centuries (Cahn *et al.,* 1984, 146). Closest to the Hama lampstands in its hexagonally faceted and swelling shaft is a bronze extending candelabrum in Lyons, ascribed to the second century or later (Boucher, 1980, no. 264). However, its four-leaf capital is much simpler than the two-zone Corinthian capital with rosettes and twisted *torus* moulding on the fourth-century silver example from the Kaiseraugst treasure which is itself very similar to these Hama capitals (Cahn *et al.,* 1984, no. 42). An eastern provenance is assured for another, bronze, extending candelabrum, with capital and spirally fluted column, which was bought in Jerusalem and is now in The Royal Ontario Museum (Hayes, 1984, no. 233; attributed to the first to second century).

Other column-shaft lampstands survive from the Early Byzantine period in cast bronze, though not in silver. Lampstands in silver characteristically have baluster shafts, and include a fourth-century(?) example "from Syria" in The Cleveland Museum of Art (Milliken, 1958, 37 f.), as well as three stamped examples dating from the sixth and early seventh centuries (Dodd, 1961, nos. 19, 90; *Byzantine Art,* 1964, no. 507). The fragments of three other silver lampstands with stamps of Justinian, but of uncertain shape, were found in Bulgaria (Gerasimov, 1967). Byzantine bronze lampstands incorporating some form of swelling column with capital or vase on top have been found in Egypt (e.g., Emery and Kirwan, 1938, pls. 99B–E, 101; Louvre, no. E.11916A, B) and Syria (Ross, 1962, no. 39). Others, without provenance and as yet unpublished, are in Richmond (Virginia Museum of Fine Arts, no. 73.26) and Zurich (Galerie H. Vollmoeller).

The trumpet-shaped cup of the Hama lampstands appears in a more rounded form as the upper member of the Lyons candelabrum, and of another candelabrum in the Louvre (Boreux, 1932, 266, pl. XXXV). With hexagonal facetting and cusped edges, the cup appears on the Zurich lampstand and, with knobs on the facet points, on one from Ballana (Emery and Kirwan, 1938, pl. 100: B 121–5). The flaring, trumpet-shaped cup is "flattened" on the bronze lampstands from Syria (Ross, 1962, no. 39), and even more so on the silver baluster stands (Dodd, 1961, nos. 19, 90).

One lampstand that resembles those in the Hama treasure so closely as almost to seem a copy in bronze, is that in the Cluny Museum (fig. 11.7; Caillet, 1985, no. 149). Without provenance (acquired in 1909 from the Victor Gay Collection), it is exactly the same height as Hama lampstand no. 11 (52 cm), although internal proportions vary somewhat in the hexagonal base and shaft. Other differences result mostly from a simplification of details (capital, column base), except for the tripod base feet, which have been more elaborately worked as paws.

Lampstands similar to nos. 11 and 12 are illustrated in the Rabbula Gospels (fig. 11.8; Florence, Laur. Lib., cod. Plut. I, 56, fol. 9v; AD 586). As in that miniature painting, the Hama stands apparently supported not candles but metal lamps (like the silver lamp in The Cleveland Museum of Art [Milliken, 1958, 37 f.]), which have left scratches on the spikes. Undoubtedly, they were intended for use on the altar.

Rightly described as the finest Byzantine lampstands in silver, these two in the Hama treasure were produced by the most complicated manufacturing methods of any object in the reconstructed Kaper Koraon Treasure—with the possible exception of the Antioch Chalice (no. 40). Among Byzantine/Syrian silver objects, they display the same level of accomplishment as the Homs Vase (no. 84), and like that vessel and the Antioch Chalice, they are unstamped. Furthermore, they were produced for the same brothers who bought the much less elegant Hama ewer (no. 14), and all three objects are clearly inscribed as dedications to the Church of St. Sergios in the village of Kaper Koraon. Thus, even within the Hama treasure, there are objects from various sources and of varying quality, including some of the best unstamped work to have survived from the region and period.

BIBLIOGRAPHY

Diehl, 1926, nos. 8, 9; Peirce and Tyler, 1934, vol. 2, 124 f.; *SEG,* vol. 7, no. 97; *Dark Ages,* 1937, no. 96; *Early Christian,* 1947, no. 408; Downey, 1948, 21; *idem,* 1951, 350, note 11; *IGLS,* no. 2034; Ross, 1962, 38; *Age,* 1979, no. 541; Cahn *et al.,* 1984, 146 f., 416.

Fig. 11.8

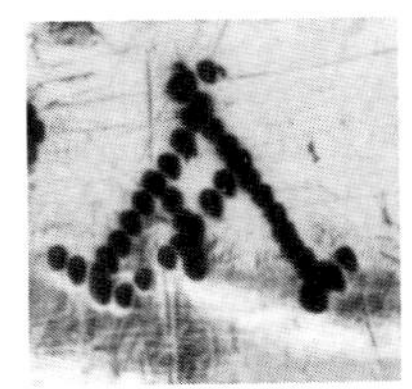

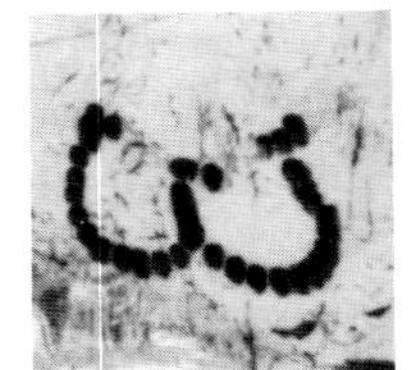

Fig. 12.1

12. LAMPSTAND

Figures 12.1–12.5

Baltimore, The Walters Art Gallery, no. 57.635

Hama Treasure, Mid-Sixth Century(?)

For technical and compositional analyses, see Chapter III, Appendices III.1 and III.2.

This lampstand (figs. 12.2–12.5), and its manufacture, may be described in the same terms used for Hama lampstand no. 11, except that its column base profiles differ slightly. Older photographs (Diehl, 1926, pl. XXIX, right) show the shaft resting on the base, from which it had become separated. Sometime before 1947 (WAG files), the stand was crudely repaired with lead solder, raising the height of the column two centimeters above the original solder join, which is still visible on the hexagonal apron, and upsetting the alignment of the hexagonal facets of base, shaft, and cup. A modern threaded iron bolt with a brass nut was inserted through the bottom, approximately halfway up into the column shaft. The radiograph shows that some of the lead from inside the column base, placed there as counterbalance, was lost, which probably accounts for this object's lighter weight in comparison with lampstand no. 11.

INSCRIPTION

+ Having vowed, they fulfilled their vow to (the Church) of St. Sergios and Bacchos. + SERGI(O)S and SYMEON(IOS) and DANIEL and THOMAS, sons of MAXIMINOS, the village of Kaper Korao(n).

Pointillé, nielloed(?) (H of letters = .5 cm). Diehl, 1926, no. 8; *SEG,* vol. 7, no. 97; *IGLS,* no. 2034, I; *Age,* 1979, no. 541.

S is used as an abbreviation sign, without a stroke (compare no. 11). The gentive *omicron-upsilon* is consistently in ligature. The distribution of the text here differs from that of no. 11 (contrast figs. 11.3 and 12.3; see the text of that Entry).

COMMENTARY

See Entry no. 11.

BIBLIOGRAPHY

See Entry no. 11.

Fig. 12.3

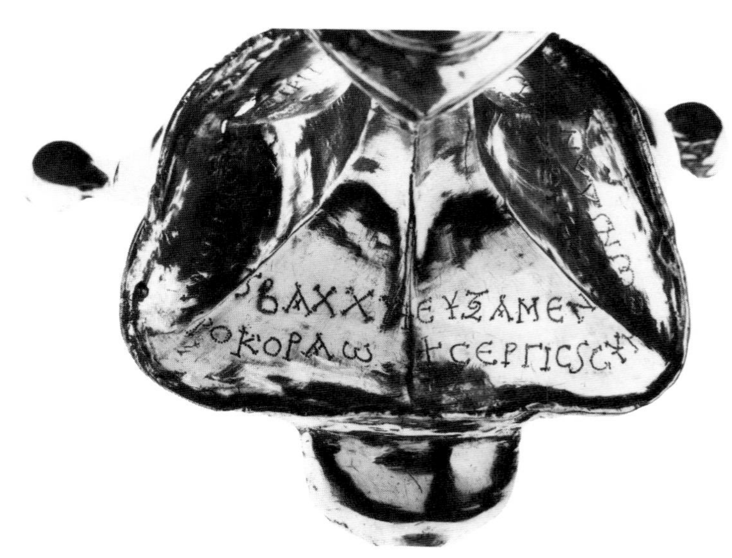

+Εὐξάμενοι τὴν εὐχὴν ἀπέδωκαν τῶ ἁγίου Σεργίου (καὶ) Βάχχου ‖ + Σέργις (καὶ) Συμεὼν (καὶ) Δανιὴλ (καὶ) Θωμᾶς υἱοὶ Μαξιμίνου κώμη Καπρο Κοραω

H	53.1 cm
W (across feet)	16.9 cm
W (across cup)	12.5 cm
Weight (including lead and iron)	1158.3 gr
Roman Weight	3 lbs 6 oz 11 scr
Original Silver Price	*ca.* 14(?) *solidi*

Fig. 12.4

Fig. 12.5

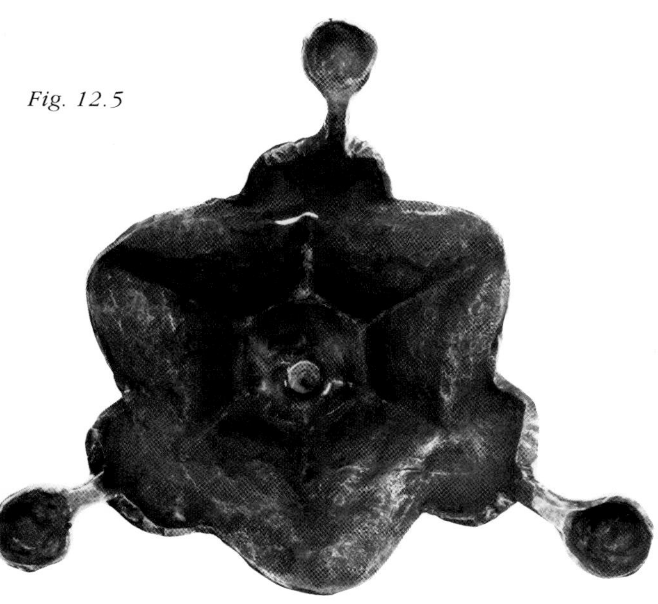

Fig. 12.2

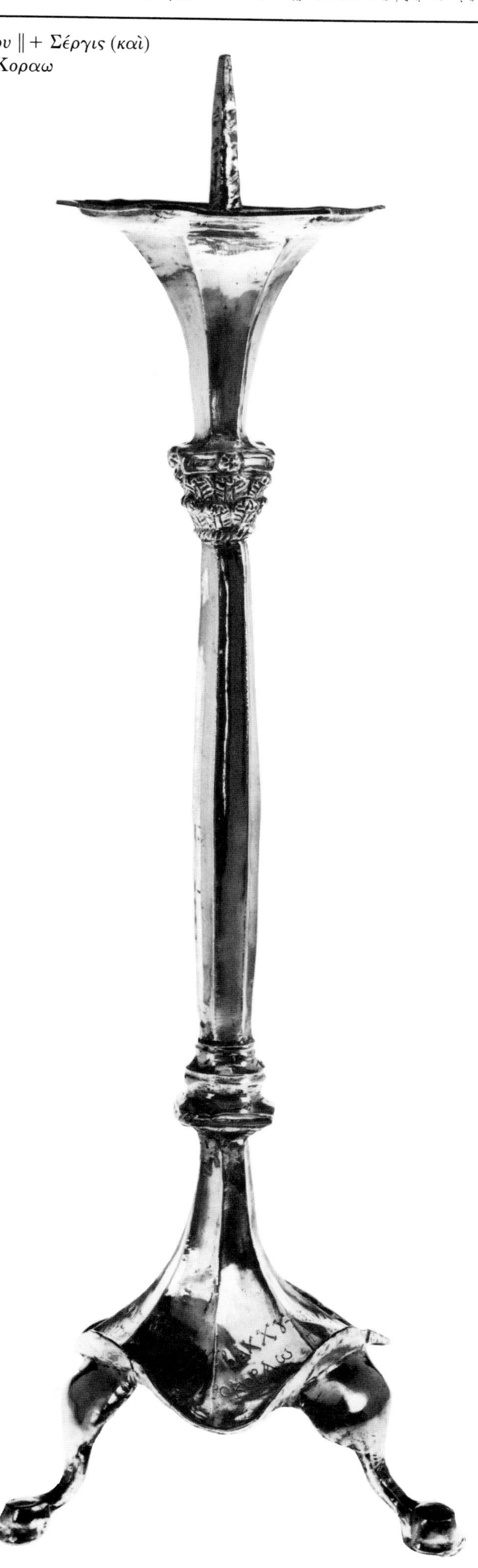

13. LAMP

FARUM CANTHARUM

Figures 13.1–13.4

Baltimore, The Walters Art Gallery, no. 57.640

Hama Treasure, 602–610

For technical and compositional analyses, see Chapter III, Appendices III.1 and III.2.

This hanging lamp with footring has a convex base and flaring sides which terminate in an upright rim with three suspension eyelets (figs. 13.2, 13.3). There is a shallow concave moulding between two engraved lines accentuating the top of the convex base, a single turned line engraved on the rim, and another pair of lines on the foot. Five stamps appear on the bottom of the lamp (figs. 13.1, 13.4).

This lamp was formed by hammering from a single sheet of metal; the foot was formed by being folded back on itself. The eyelets (H 1.4 cm) were made by cutting away the rim, and the holes were punched from the inside out. Hammer marks remain on the inside of the lamp and on the footring. Under the microscope one can detect stress cracks which annealing did not completely remove and, by radiography, thin areas in the metal caused by heavy working. A small hole has developed in the weakened fabric of the concave moulding of the vessel. The final shaping, finishing, and line engraving were done on a lathe, whose turning point marks the center of the bottom; the surrounding stamps were applied after manufacture. Aside from the hole just mentioned, there is a dent in the convex base of the lamp.

STAMPS

These stamps were dated by Dodd (1961, no. 89) to 602–610 because of the presence of the monogram of Phocas. They were apparently applied at Antioch, because the long stamp bears that city's name, *Theoupolis.* Only one other object, a lampstand excavated at Antioch, now at Dumbarton Oaks (*ibid.,* no. 90), is known to bear this stamp. As classified by Dodd, the five stamps may be read, with minor emendations (fig. 13.1), as follows:

a. **Round**: unidentified scene (Acclamation scene?).
b. **Hexagonal**: unidentified monogram; unidentifed inscription.
c. **Square**: monogram of Phocas; unidentified inscription.
d. **Long**: nimbed bust; unidentified monogram; inscribed *THEOUPOLEOS.*
e. **Cross**: inscribed *NIKASIS(?).*

COMMENTARY

In many respects, this hanging lamp is very close to the Stuma standing lamp (no. 33). Their respective heights are nearly identical but because the eyelets of this lamp were cut out from its total height, its sides are slightly shorter, and its proportions correspondingly squatter. Because the top of this lamp was worked downward, its sides have a pronounced outward curve, and an upper diameter equivalent to that of lamp no. 33. Moreover, the elaborate decoration on the latter does not quite disguise the preliminary turned grooves at the top of its convex base, which correspond to the concave moulding on the Hama lamp, which is itself similar to those on the Riha chalice and ewers (nos.

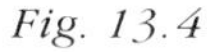

Fig. 13.4

30, 37, 38). In their weights and postulated preliminary forms, therefore, the Hama and Stuma lamps are substantially identical. Elsewhere (Mundell-Mango, 1986) I have argued that these two lamps, which were stamped nearly thirty years apart, together with a series of three lampstands stamped, respectively, in 525–565 and 605–630 at Constantinople, and in 602–610 at Antioch, offer, by virtue of their standardized weights and forms, evidence of a sustained and regulated "mass production" of certain types of silver objects by the state (see Chapter I above).

Because of its *kantharos*-like shape, this type of lamp, whether hanging or standing (no. 33), may be described as a *farum cantharum,* so frequently mentioned in the *Liber Pontificalis.* Plain hanging lamps like this example appear in the Qartamin mosaics (Hawkins and Mundell, 1973, 289, figs. 36, 37; 512).

BIBLIOGRAPHY

Diehl, 1926, no. 11; Rosenberg, 1928, vol. 4, 730 f.; *Dark Ages,* 1937, no. 100; *Early Christian,* 1947, no. 403; Alföldi and Cruikshank, 1957, 243 ff.; Dodd, 1961, no. 89; *idem,* 1973, 11 f., 52.

H	14.6–14.8 cm
D (rim)	16.3 cm
D (foot)	8.3 cm
Weight	485.8 gr
Roman Weight	1 lb 5 oz 19 scr
Original Silver Price	5 *solidi* 22 1/3 carats
Volume	*ca.* 1460 ml

Fig. 13.1

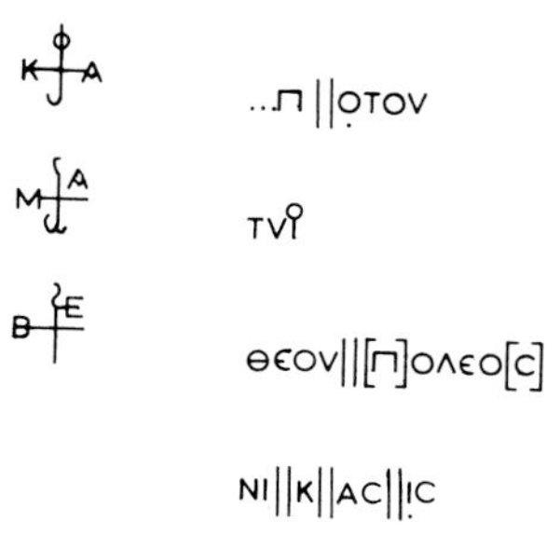

Fig. 13.2

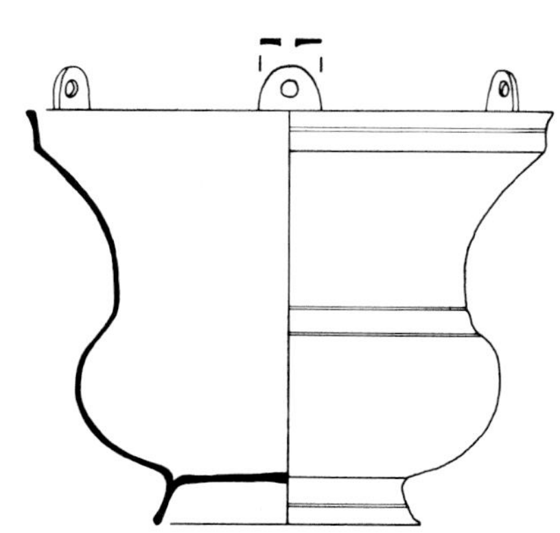

Fig. 13.3

Fig. 14.1

14. EWER

XESTION

Figures 14.1–14.6

Baltimore, The Walters Art Gallery, no. 57.645

Hama Treasure, Mid-Sixth Century(?)

For technical and compositional analyses, see Chapter III, Appendices III.1 and III.2.

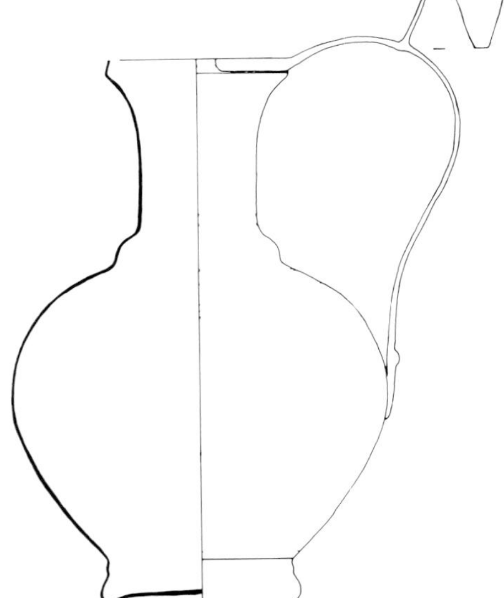

Fig. 14.2

This ewer has a flat, raised foot, bulbous body, narrow neck, and arched handle (figs. 14.2, 14.3). There is a convex profile at the base of its tall, slightly concave neck, and an upright rim at its top. A series of five narrow turnings encircles the base of the neck and two mark the top of the rim. The handle, which is flat in section, has a wedge-shaped tab (H 2.5 cm) on its upper curve and a projecting roll near its base. An inscription runs in two lines over the shoulder of the body and terminates in one line on the handle (figs. 14.1, 14.4, 14.5). An engraved linear border surrounds the inscription on the handle and continues on both sides of the tab. Vertical patches of gilding are visible on the inscribed shoulder and further traces remain on the neck. (Reports of a missing lid [*Age,* 1979, no. 535] are unfounded.)

This vessel was formed by hammering from a single sheet of metal, and then a cast(?) handle was attached. Hammer marks remain inside and on the bottom, and can also be seen in the radiograph. Two points in the middle of the ewer's base may correspond to different stages of manufacture: centering the vessel before or during its formation, and turning on a lathe. While on the lathe, the ewer was engraved with its decorative lines. The inscribed band was gilded with overlapping foil sheets, which were applied after the letters were chased (curled edges of gold leaf are visible inside the letters). The foil was probably bound to the surface with mercury, traces of which were detected by x-ray fluorescence analysis.

The handle, which is higher in copper and zinc content than the body, may have been cast (compare crosses nos. 9, 10), and the tab attached to it by what appears to be silver solder. The solder now attaching the handle to the rim of the vessel is high in lead and zinc; the join is very messy and thus, probably

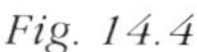

Fig. 14.4

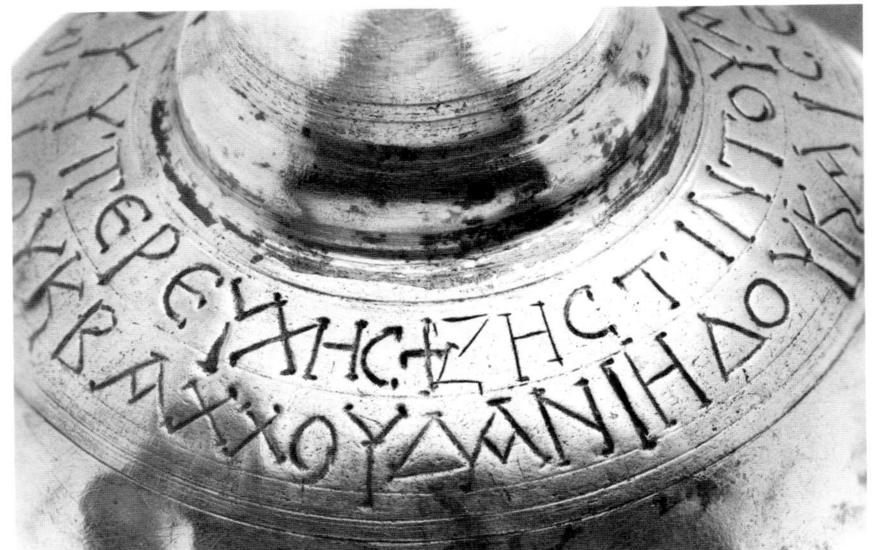

H	27.0 cm
W (body)	15.5 cm
D (mouth)	7.5 cm
D (foot)	8.1 cm
Weight	623.0 gr
Roman Weight	1 lb 10 oz 20 scr
Original Silver Price	7 *solidi* 14 2/3 carats
Volume (to the rim)	2048 ml

+ Ξῆστιν τοῦ Ἁγίου Σεργίου ὑπὲρ εὐχῆς Δανιή(λ)ου καὶ Σεργίου
καὶ Συμεωνίου κ(αὶ) Βάχχου + καὶ ὑπὲρ εὐχῆς Θωμᾶ κόμ(ης) Καπρο Κοραον.

Fig. 14.3

Fig. 14.5

reflects a secondary attachment. The handle itself may be a replacement, as old solder lines indicate an original attachment of different dimensions. This might explain the epigraphic differences between the texts on the body and handle. The black substance remaining in the letters on the handle was found by x-ray diffraction to be a silver-copper sulfide (see Chapter III, Appendix III.3). (There is only a black residue in the inscription on the body, and it was not analyzed.) The upper attachment of the handle to the ewer is weak, and there are three large and several smaller dents in the body. The base is battered and there is a large patch of corrosion above it on the body.

Inscription

Body: + *Ewer of St. Sergios. In fulfillment of a vow of DANIEL and of SERGIOS and of SYMEONIOS and of BACCHOS*

Handle: + *and in fulfillment of a vow of THOMAS, of the village of Kaper Koraon.*

Chased (body); engraved, nielloed(?) (handle) (H of letters, body = .6–1.3 cm; handle = .6–1.3 cm). Diehl, 1926, no. 7; Mouterde, 1926, 367, note 1; *SEG,* vol. 7, no. 96; *IGLS,* no. 2033; *Age,* 1979, no. 535.

This inscription begins at the front of the vessel, on axis with the handle. The height of the letters, which are lunate, varies considerably, yet those on the body are well struck; the mistakes on the handle may be due to the difficult working surface. Serifs are used regularly. *Ks* is used as *kappa* of *kai* and as an abbreviation of the word *kai.* Similar tails appear in *mu* and *pi.* The abbreviation sign *s* is placed over *komes.* Spelling: *delta* for *lamda* in *Danielou; omicron* for *omega* in *komes* and *Koraon.*

The differences in the lettering on the body and the handle of this vessel suggest that the latter may be a replacement (onto which the original inscription was copied?). Nevertheless, the letter forms on the handle appear to be contemporary with those on other objects in this catalogue. The lettering on the body most closely resembles that on Hama cross no. 9 and, not surprisingly, on Hama lampstands nos. 11 and 12, which were given by the same donors. There, however, the inscriptions are in *pointillé,* the *xi* is better formed, and the *upsilon* unbarred. The barred *upsilon* of this inscription is found on Hama cross no. 7 and—together with *rho* rendered like a Latin R—on objects in the Hama (chalice no. 28) and Phela treasures (nos. 61, 64, 65); the Beth Misona paten (no. 60) also has this form of *rho.* In most of these inscriptions there is also a long tail on the *alpha,* and on the Phela cross (no. 65), *kome* is abbreviated exactly as it is here.

Xestin is *xestion,* the diminutive of *xestes* (*IGLS,* no. 2033), and refers here to the ewer itself. The *xestes,* from the Latin *sextarius* (meaning the sixth part of a measure), was used for dry and liquid quantities alike. This word, used in both senses, is found engraved on objects of the fifth and sixth centuries. The definition of the dry "*xestes* of Antioch" as the *xestes stratiotikos* of twenty-four ounces, was engraved by the authority of an officer under a *comes (Adila, PLRE II)* on a bronze measuring goblet from Antioch (*IGLS,* no. 1073). A measure of the liquid *xestes* (1/6 *congius* or 1 pint) is engraved on a marble jar in Berlin (Wulff, 1909, no. 41). That the word *xestes* came to be applied to the ewer (Latin = *urceum*) by the sixth century is attested by its use here, and by the appearance of *xeston* (in the word *cherniboxeston*) in the inscription referring to the ewer paired with a *trulla* in the Hermitage (Matzulevich, 1929, 82 f.; 582–602). The silver *xestes* named in the Ibion church inventory (no. 91) is, therefore, probably a ewer.

On the dedicatory formula *hyper euches,* see Entry no. 1. The donors of this ewer are the same brothers—the sons of Maximinos—who gave Hama lampstands nos. 11 and 12 to the same church. (On Symeonios, and the question of dating, see Entry no. 1.) In this inscription, *Bacchos* appears unequivocally as a donor and not, as on the lampstands, as the saint. See figure I.1.

COMMENTARY

The shape of this vessel may best be compared, as has often been done (e.g., Dodd, 1973, 7; *Age,* 1979, no. 552), with the Homs Vase (no. 84). Other such ewers, with a tall straight neck and broad body, have been excavated in the East: in silver and bronze at Qustul and Ballana (Emery and Kirwan, 1938, pls. 77–80); in bronze from a tomb of 396 at el-Bassa (Iliffe, 1934, 90, fig. 27); and at Scythopolis (Fitzgerald, 1939, pl. XXXVII.11). An earlier ("Roman") bronze pitcher with thicker neck and squatter body was unearthed at Antioch (*Antioch,* I, 74, fig. 9). A bronze amphora from Egypt, now in Berlin, is close to the Hama ewer in contour and size (Wulff, 1909, no. 1033). By comparison with the Hama ewer, the Conçesti amphora has a very slender neck (Matzulevich, 1929, pls. 36 ff.), as does an unpublished ewer in the Beruit Archaeological Museum. The latter and the Homs Vase have at the base of the neck a convex profile decorated with a rope pattern, which corresponds to the plain moulding on this example. The Albanian ewer in The Metropolitan Museum (*Early Christian,* 1947, no. 415) has a similar rope moulding and a handle like that of this ewer, but its shape is closer to that of the Riha ewers (nos. 37, 38).

Despite the diminutive form of its name, the capacity of the Hama *xestion* is 2048 milliliters or about 3.5 *xestai* (one *xestes* equals 604 ml). In addition to the silver *xestes* belonging to the Ibion church, there are apparently two ewers each in the Durobrivae (Painter, 1977 [I], nos. 2, 5) and Sion (Firatlı, 1969, 525, "un vase"; Boyd, 1979, 7) church treasures. To the ewer (the *xestes* or *urceum*) may be ascribed two functions—one involving wine and the other water. As an *oinochoe* (wine pitcher) it may have replaced the large *ama* (amphora?) attested in the *Liber Pontificalis* (p. CXLIV), to function as a wine "reservoir" in smaller churches. As a water vessel, on the other hand, the ewer was teamed with a *trulla* (*chernibon*) to form the *cherniboxeston* (or, in Latin, *urceum-acquamanulis*) pairs, known from attested (Adhémar, 1934, 53 f.) and preserved (Matzulevich, 1929, 82 f.) examples. Both types of jugs (for wine storage and handwashing) are illustrated at the banquet of Dido and Aeneas in the *Vergilius Romanus* (fig. 14.6; Vatican Lib., cod. Lat. 3867, fol. 100v). In the reconstructed Kaper Koraon Treasure, there are three large vessels described as ewers: nos. 14 (Hama), 37, and 38 (Riha). The last two, which form a pair, may have served as wine reservoirs, given their greater combined capacity, while this one may have been a water pitcher used in conjunction with Hama bowl no. 16, as a washing set. On epigraphic grounds (i.e., the donors' names) this ewer seems to have been presented to the Church of St. Sergios some time before the Riha pair, which were given in the period 582–602. This might suggest that originally it had been intended as a wine receptacle to function with the Jerusalem strainer, which would be used to filter its contents (see Entry no. 26). It is possible, of course, that over time this vessel served several purposes.

BIBLIOGRAPHY

Diehl, 1926, no. 7; Mouterde, 1926, 367, note 1; *SEG,* vol. 7, no. 96; *Dark Ages,* 1937, no. 105; *Early Christian,* 1947, no. 398; Lassus, 1947, 197 f.; Downey, 1951, 350, note 11; *IGLS,* no. 2033; Dodd, 1973, 7; *Age,* 1979, no. 535.

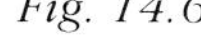

Fig. 14.6

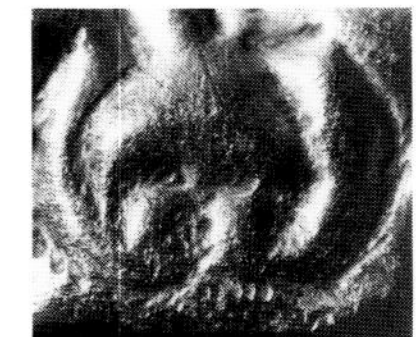

Fig. 15.1

15. FLASK

LEKYTHOS?

Figures 15.1–15.7

Baltimore, The Walters Art Gallery, no. 57.639

Hama Treasure, Mid- to Later Sixth Century

For technical and compositional analyses, see Chapter III, Appendices III.1 and III.2.

This tapering flask has a recessed neck with moulded spout and is covered in repoussé decoration set off with angular profiles (figs. 15.3–15.6). Its lower section is dominated by a panel with four nimbed standing figures: Christ and an orant Virgin Mary on opposite sides, flanked by orant youthful male saints in *chlamys* and *maniakion*. Above is a braided band and above that, an inscription in relief in one line, which is continued in two lines below the panel (figs. 15.1, 15.3–15.6). The neck of the flask is decorated with overlapping leaves with thick outlines (i.e., a debased leaf-and-dart). The vessel seems cut off abruptly beneath the lower inscribed band, and its base is apparently modern. A lid with chain, partly visible in the 1910 Hama photograph (fig. II.4) is missing.

This flask was probably once composed of five parts—body, base, spout rim, lid, and chain—only two of which, body and spout rim, survive in their original form. The body was made from a hammered sheet of metal which was worked from the back in repoussé technique, and then finished by chasing and engraving from the front. Tiny circular punches were used to ornament the saints' *tablia* and the book held by Christ, whose hair was stippled. The sheet was then rolled into a tapering cylinder and soldered where the edges meet, leaving a vertical seam. The original base was presumably a hammered disc soldered to the flask's lower edge; what is there now is apparently a modern replacement, since it has a metal content markedly different from the body of the vessel and is attached by solder so carelessly applied as to obscure portions of the lower inscription. The rim of the flask is a separate hammered ring slipped over the spout and soldered into place; the join, although disguised by burnishing, is still visible from below. In the 1910 Hama photograph (fig. II.4), a flat lid is seen set into the spout, from which hangs a *circa* four-centimeter length of chain. At that time apparently unattached, this chain may once have been secured along the upper seam, where a modern(?) patch now appears. The entire flask apparently once bore gilding, traces of which were detected all over its surface. Overlapping vertical and horizontal strips of gilding indicate the use of foil, applied by mercury which, through x-ray fluorescence, was also found to be generally present.

Inscription

Upper band: + *In fulfillment of a vow and (for) the salvation of MEGALE*

Lower band: + *and of HER CHILDREN and HER NEPHEWS and for the repose (of the soul) of HELIODOROS and AKAKIOS.*

Relief (H of letters = .6–1.2 cm). Diehl, 1926, no. 10; Wilpert, 1927, 338; *SEG*, vol. 7, no. 98; *IGLS*, no. 2035; Downey, 1951, 351; *Age*, 1979, no. 536.

The letters are lunate and flare somewhat at their extremities in imitation of serif letters. Lack of space on the flask probably caused the deformation of the final *nu* in *anepsion* into *upsilon*, and the *rho* in *Heliodorou* into *sigma*, as well as the superscript *lambda* in *Megales* and the *eta-rho* ligature in *soterias*. The genitive *omicron-upsilon* is also in ligature. Spelling: *omicron* for *omega* in *ton*.

+ Ὑπὲρ εὐχῆς καὶ σωτηρίας Μεγάλης καὶ τôν αὐτῆς τέκνων καὶ ἀνεψιῶ(ν) κα(ὶ)
ὑπὲρ ἀναπαύσεως Ἡλιοδώ(ρ)ου καὶ Ἀκακίου

With a few exceptions, such as the *alpha,* the letter forms on this flask correspond to those on the large Antioch cross (no. 42). For raised inscriptions, see that Entry, and for the combination of the dedicatory formulae *hyper euches kai soterias* and *hyper anapauseos,* used here and on the two inscribed Stuma patens (nos. 34, 36) and the Stuma lamp (no. 33), see Entries nos. 1 and 35, and Downey (1951). *Hyper soterias* and *hyper anapauseos* are also

H	21.8–22.1 cm
D (base)	5.8–5.9 cm
D (spout, outer)	2.1–2.2 cm
Weight	173.4 gr
Roman Weight	6 oz 8 scr
Original Silver Price	2 *solidi* 2²/₃ carats
Volume	*ca.* 270 ml

Fig. 15.2

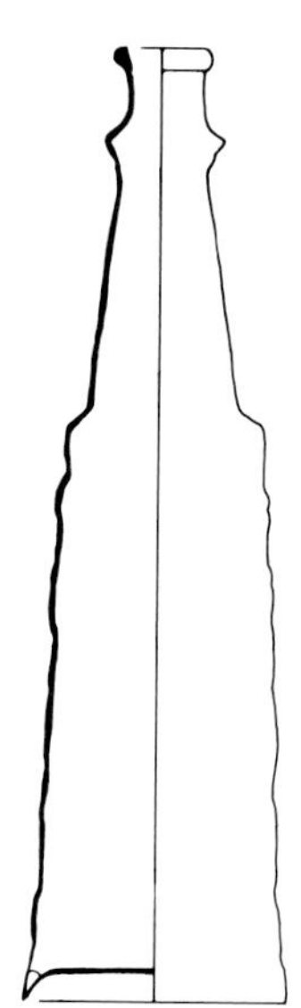

Fig. 15.3

Fig. 15.4

Fig. 15.5

Fig. 15.6

combined (in that order) in Syrian building and pavement dedications of the period (e.g., *IGLS,* no. 1584; Avi-Yonah, 1948, 69, no. 3; Saller and Bagatti, 1949, 171 ff., nos. 2, 5, 6, 12). Because Early Byzantine dedicatory formulae were combined in an almost infinite variety, one must view as unjustified Downey's narrow attribution of the particular combination used on the Hama flask and the Stuma objects to direct influence from the Monophysite Jacobite liturgy (Downey, 1951, 351). The frequency of hope for *anapausis* on these silver objects is explained above (see Chapter I) in terms of particular historical events, rather than a general state of religious persecution (*ibid.,* 353, note 16).

Heliodoros and Akakios, children of Thomas, dedicated the Jerusalem chalice (no. 27) stamped in 550–565, and Heliodoros alone gave a Hama spoon (no. 18) and, in the name of his deceased son, Baradatos, a Hama paten (no. 4). Megale, who may have been related (by marriage?) to one of the two brothers, Heliodoros and Akakios, may also have had family ties with the Megas of the Riha paten (no. 35), as Dodd (1973, 57) has suggested. See figure I.1.

COMMENTARY

The shape of this flask could be described as a cross between the traditional cylindrical *lekythos* (oil flask; Richter, 1959, fig. 466) and a common type of Early Byzantine tall hexagonal flask in glass (e.g., Matheson, 1980, nos. 349 ff.)—both of which, however, have handles. Silver flasks approximately contemporary with this one are, as a group, quite different, having ovoid body, narrow neck, and low foot (Strong, 1966, 191 f.). While the *lekythos* and other classical vessels were decorated with figures in profile (*ibid.*, pls. 32A, B; Richter, 1959, figs. 465–467, 473), comparable Early Byzantine vessels, like this one, show frontal figures (compare also chalice no. 3).

On this flask, Christ is portrayed more or less in His "Syrian" mode, with short, frizzy hair and just the suggestion of a short beard; ordinarily, however, He would have a more triangular face (compare no. 42b, 42c). The Virgin has the full figure she is given in the Rabbula Gospels *Ascension*, where her long and voluminous costume falls in similar folds. The striped cap she wears under her veil also marks her medallion portrait on the Beth Misona chalices (nos. 57–59), and on the Divriği cross (no. 76). The orant saints wear the military *chiton* and *chlamys*, with the latter showing a *tablion* and a *fibula* at the shoulder. Around their necks hang the *maniakion*, the heavy gold pectoral worn by the palace guard (its form here resembles that on the Cyprus bowl in the British Museum; *Age*, 1979, no. 493). It is tempting to identify these military saints as Sergios and Bacchos, at least one of whom (see Entries nos. 11, 12) was patron of the Kaper Koraon church. Their costumes and short curly hair correspond to their portrayal on the contemporary icon in Kiev from Mount Sinai (fig. 15.7; Weitzmann, 1976, 28 ff., pls. XII, LII, LIII).

Although the figure types on this flask have been compared stylistically (e.g., by Buschhausen, in *Age*, 1979, no. 536) with those of the Antioch plaques (nos. 44–47), the two are really not very close, nor are these figures close to any others on objects included in this catalogue. In fact, they are not particularly homogeneous among themselves; the two saints have almost tubular drapery enveloping squat bodies, while the Virgin has an elongated form swathed in sagging and rumpled garments. On the basis of His volume and anatomical coordination, Christ can be placed midway between the full and softly draped Apostles on Hama chalice no. 3, and the flat, angular St. Paul on Antioch plaque no. 44. On the other hand, the disproportionally large heads of the figures on this flask can be compared to the less caricatured and more frontal among the heads on the Riha paten (no. 35), which have similarly rendered hair (a combination of crescent waves and stippling). Moreover, the punched ornament of the Riha altar cloth parallels that of the flask's *tablia*.

The thick, braided band or garland on this flask, related to both twisted rope (e.g., no. 3) and overlapping leaf (e.g., no. 40) mouldings, is found also on two Beth Misona chalices (nos. 58, 59), the Homs Vase (no. 84) and the Louvre Symeon plaque (no. 71). A characteristic Early Byzantine border pattern, it is found as well on objects of western origin (Kent and Painter, 1977, nos. 88–90, 105, 157). The leaf and dart that covers the neck of the flask recalls the ornament placed below the neck of the Syrian ewer with Dionysiac figures in The Cleveland Museum of Art (*Age*, 1979, no. 131), as well as debased classicizing borders such as the variations on egg and dart (or leaf) employed on the Stuma lamp (no. 33) and paten (no. 34), and on two Beth Misona chalices (nos. 58, 59).

This flask was probably used to hold oil, perhaps for the baptismal service. Two silver *vasa* of ten pounds each, one designated *ad oleum crismae* and the other *ad oleum exorcidiatum*, were given as *ornatum baptisimi* to the Titulus Vestinae in Rome (*Liber Pontificalis*, CCXX), and one bronze *lekythos* is included in the Ibion church inventory (no. 91).

BIBLIOGRAPHY

Sachsen, 1912, 11 f.; Diehl, 1926, no. 10; Mouterde, 1926, 366; Wilpert, 1926, 137 f.; *idem*, 1927, 336 ff.; Peirce and Tyler, 1934, vol. 2, 124; *SEG*, vol. 7, no. 98; *Dark Ages*, 1937, no. 99; *Early Christian*, 1947, no. 397; Downey, 1951, 351; *IGLS*, no. 2035; Weitzmann and Ševčenko, 1963, 395; Dodd, 1973, 18 f., 23, 54, 57; Martinelli, 1974, 12; *Age*, 1979, no. 536; Boyd, 1983, 73 f.

Fig. 15.7

16. Bowl

CHERNIBON?

Figures 16.1–16.4

Baltimore, The Walters Art Gallery, no. 57.631

Hama Treasure, Mid- to Later Sixth Century(?)

For technical and compositional analyses, see Chapter III, Appendices III.1 and III.2.

This small, plain bowl has a flat rim and a curved base without foot (figs. 16.1–16.4). Formed by hammering from a single sheet of metal, it was left rough on the outside, while the inside was finished on a lathe, whose clamping device covered the center, leaving a burnished, thick disc. There are many sharp scratches inside the bowl, as well as some hammer marks, which may be due to a repair. A series of tiny oval gouges and short parallel strokes mar the rim.

Commentary

This object, by its design, may be placed in a group of early fourth-century *largitio* bowls and assorted bowls of the seventh century, all of which are distinguished by having neither foot nor footring (Kent and Painter, 1977, nos. 1–5, 150, 241–6; contrast *ibid.* nos. 7–9, 27–29; and Dodd, 1961, nos. 23, 81–83, 85, 88). This feature—or lack thereof—also distinguishes nearly all Syrian patens. That its interior but not exterior surface was finished, suggests that it may have served as a liner to some other vessel (see Entry no. 1). Although its outer diameter corresponds to that of Hama chalice no. 1, the bowl is too shallow for any of the surviving Syrian chalices, whose cups average seven centimeters in depth. Moreover, by the second to third centuries, double-shell repoussé cups with removable liners had been replaced by cast single-shell cups and glass-lined openwork cups (Strong, 1966, 163 ff.). This bowl may, however, have been set into a mount or stand of another material (e.g., marble or ivory). Slightly smaller than the Hermitage *trulla* of 641–651 (Dodd, 1961, no. 77), it may have been used for pouring water, either for hand washing or baptism, in which case it may have functioned together with Hama ewer no. 14 in a *cherniboxeston* set (see Entry no. 14). This object is included in both the Hama inventory ("1 cuvette"; see Chapter II, above) and in the 1910 Hama photograph (fig. II.4).

Bibliography

Diehl, 1926, no. 22; *Dark Ages,* 1937, no. 93; *Early Christian,* 1947, no. 402.

Fig. 16.3

D	11.5 cm
H	4.3 cm
Weight	68.7 gr
Roman Weight	2 oz 12 scr
Original Silver Price	20 carats
Volume	264 ml

Fig. 16.1

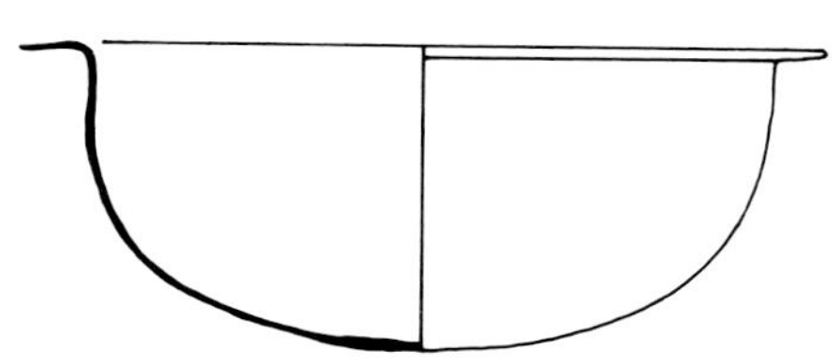

Fig. 16.2

Fig. 16.4

17. BOX

PYXIS

Figures 17.1–17.9

Baltimore, The Walters Art Gallery, no. 57.638

Hama Treasure(?), Early Fifth Century(?)

For technical and compositional analyses, see Chapter III, Appendices III.1 and III.2.

This small square box bears five decorated surfaces, including its lid (figs. 17.3–17.8). The motifs, executed in a combination of sharp and gouged lines, and set inside panels with straight, gouged borders, are distributed as follows:

Lid: *Chrismon* and quatrefoil border (fig. 17.4).
Front (I): *Chrismon* (fig. 17.5).
Right Side (II): Overlapping octagons formed by hexagons and squares (fig. 17.6).
Left Side (III): Radiating acanthus leaves (fig. 17.7).
Back (IV): Quatrefoils (fig. 17.8).
Bottom (V): Undecorated.

The *Chrismons* were gilded and the other decoration inlaid with niello (see Chapter III, Appendix III.3).

This box was formed by hammering, folding, and joining. Hammer marks are visible inside the box, and by radiography. Join marks on the interior, and splits in the metal along the bottom edges of the box suggest that it was constructed from a flat sheet of metal cut as illustrated in figure 17.1. The sheet was folded and either soldered at the joins with silver solder or joined mechanically by hammer welding. The lid was probably formed by raising the edges from another flat sheet, apparently from the same melt of metal. The exterior surfaces of box and lid were burnished, then engraved. Visual indications and traces of mercury indicate that the gilding was applied using the mercury-amalgam technique. There is a tear and hole in the bottom right corner of the front; niello remains only in parts of the quatrefoils and back border.

COMMENTARY

The technique used on this object (i.e., the combination of sharp and gouged lines) has many parallels clustered in the fourth and the sixth centuries (Matzulevich, 1929, 118 ff.; Brett, 1939). Close comparisons both for the technique and for the selection of motifs (i.e., quatrefoils and acanthus leaves) can be found in the West in the later fourth to early fifth century, especially in the Traprain Law, Esquiline, and Mildenhall treasures. (For the treatment of the quartrefoils, see Shelton, 1981, 49, 58 f.; for the gouging technique, see Entry no. 95) An acanthus motif nearly identical to that on the box's left side is coupled with a panel of quatrefoils on a fragment in the Coleraine hoard (Ballinrees, Northern

Fig. 17.2

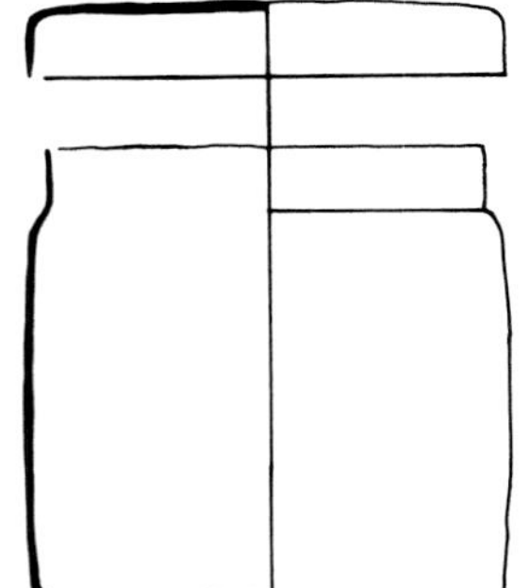

Fig. 17.1

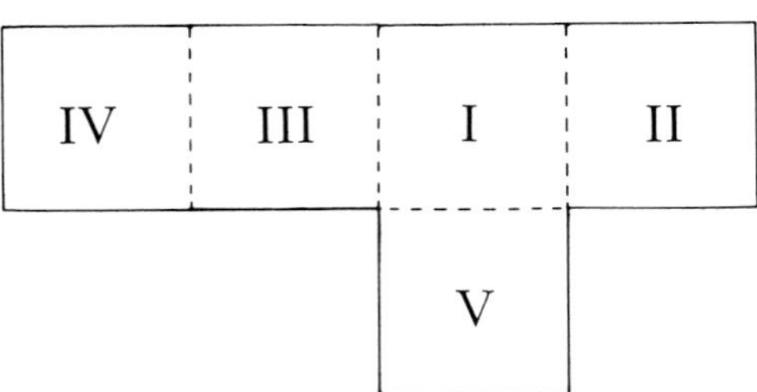

Ireland), which was buried around 420 (fig. 17.9; Mattingly *et al.,* 1937, 43, pl. V; Ross, 1955, 61 f.; and Buschhausen in *Age,* 1979, no. 534). Another such acanthus motif occurs on a fragment in the Traprain Law treasure (Scotland), which also contains a piece bearing overlapping octagons similar to those on the right side of the box (Curle, 1923, nos. 45, 136). The Hama box has also recently been compared with the Soissons plate (Baratte, 1977, 127). Those objects dateable to the

H (with lid)	6.9 cm
W	6.5 cm
Weight	171.7 gr
Roman Weight	6 oz 7 scr
Original Silver Price	2 *solidi* 2 1/3 carats
Volume	*ca.* 300 ml

Fig. 17.3

sixth century which show the gouging technique used on this box include a series of plates with an acanthus frieze (Boyd, 1983, 68 f.), three plates in the Soviet Union (Dodd, 1961, nos. 6, 7, 15), and three plates, two spoons, and a box in this catalogue (nos. 19, 36, 56, 60, 63, 83).

Compared with the fourth-century objects cited above, the geometrical ornament on this box is less uniformly and symmetrically distributed within its panels. Moreover the "quatrefoils" on its lid—which derive from a pattern composed of overlapping circles—have degenerated into loose floral motifs. Nevertheless, the fact that the comparisons for both the gouging technique and the combination of motifs used on the box are to be found in the fourth century supports the earlier dating recently advanced by Baratte (1977, 127) and Buschhausen (*Age,* 1979, no. 534). That this and other fourth- to fifth-century objects discovered (and most likely, made) in Syria find their comparisons exclusively with objects of western provenance (see also Entries nos. 95, 96, 101) may be explained by two facts. First, most fourth-century silver has been recovered in the West—just as most sixth-century silver has been found in the eastern Empire. Second, during the fourth century the multiplication of imperial capitals and the state network of *largitio* production insured a widespread standardization of certain types of silver work. That Antioch was then an imperial residence with a strong Latin presence may have some bearing on the (seemingly "western") style and technique of the silver produced in Syria in that period. Considering the early date proposed for this box, it is important to note that the analysis of its niello inlay has revealed silver-copper sulfide which, despite its discription by Pliny, is rarely found on silver objects before the sixth century (see Chapter III, above).

The question remains of the relationship of this fourth- to fifth-century box with the sixth- to seventh-century Hama treasure. It was disassociated from the Hama group by Peirce and Tyler in 1934 (vol. 2, 109); they, however, had been otherwise misinformed about the treasure's history (see Chapter II, above). Furthermore, given the acknowledged "elasticity" of the treasure (see Entries nos. 21, 25–28), the fact that this object is missing from both the 1910 Hama photograph (fig. II.4) and the 1910 inventory is not conclusive. If not part of the "original" Hama treasure, it was certainly added early, perhaps in Hama, before Abucasem's departure for Egypt, where it was photographed with the other objects (fig. II.5) and published by Diehl (1926). One may speculate that a fourth- to fifth-century box (particularly one used to safeguard something valuable which, in this case, to judge by the *Chrismons,* was of a sacred character) could have been the treasured heirloom of a sixth-century community. Although all the other dateable

Fig. 17.4

Fig. 17.5

pieces among the Stuma, Riha, Hama, and Antioch treasures were donated after the Persian looting campaign of 540 (see Chapter I, above), it is possible that a box such as this, used as a reliquary, may have been sufficiently well concealed (e.g., in a church wall or altar) to escape detection during an attack on the village.

For textual, inscriptional, and iconographic evidence that small containers such as this might have been used (variously) to hold consecrated bread, incense, precious offerings or relics, see Duffy and Vikan (1983, 97 f.). Although boxes like this (especially in ivory) are now often labelled "*pyxides,*" there is no evidence that the Byzantines themselves used this word for them (*ibid.,* 96, note 12).

Bibliography

Diehl, 1926, no. 23; Wilpert, 1926, 136; Rosenberg, 1928, vol. 4, 728 ff.; Peirce and Tyler, 1934, vol. 2, 109; *Dark Ages,* 1937, no. 112; Brett, 1939, 36; *Early Christian,* 1947, 377; Ross, 1955, 61 f.; Volbach, 1963/1964, 76; Buschhausen, 1971, no. C4; Baratte, 1977, 127; *Age,* 1979, nos. 534, 550.

Fig. 17.9

Fig. 17.6

Fig. 17.7

Fig. 17.8

Fig. 18.1

18. SPOON

LIGULA

Figures 18.1–18.5

Baltimore, The Walters Art Gallery, no. 57.651

Hama Treasure, Mid-Sixth Century

For technical and compositional analyses, see Chapter III, Appendices III.1 and III.2.

This spoon has a pear-shaped bowl joined by a solid disc to a handle which is square in section near the bowl and thereafter round, terminating in a facetted knob (figs. 18.2–18.4). There is no rat-tail on the reverse of the bowl, and the spoon lies flat. A flaring-armed cross is engraved slightly off-center in the wide end of the bowl. An inscription runs along the upper and right-hand surfaces of the square section of the handle (figs. 18.1–18.3).

This spoon was cast from a single melt of metal, either as one piece, or as two or three pieces (handle, disc, bowl), to be joined by solder. No solder join is visible between the bowl and the disc, either under the microscope or in radiography (compare spoon no. 19). After casting, the bowl was hammered into shape and burnished, and the handle sections and terminal worked. Niello (see Chapter III, Appendix III.3) is missing from all of the chased letters but the *omega.*

INSCRIPTION

+ *In fulfillment of a vow of HELIODOROS.*

Chased, nielloed (H of letters = .2 cm). Diehl, 1926, no. 17; *SEG,* vol. 7, no. 105; *IGLS,* no. 2041.

The initial cross is misshapen, the last two letters of *euches* are clumsily struck, and the umlaut for the *iota* of *Heliodorou* is misplaced. No serifs are used, and the genitive *omicron-upsilon* is in ligature.

This form of *iota* is said to be sixth-century (by Downey, in *Antioch,* III, 83, no. 111). On the dedicatory formula *hyper euches,* see Entry no. 1. For Heliodoros, whose name also appears on a stamped chalice (no. 27), a paten (no. 4), and a flask (no. 15), see Entry no. 4. See also figure I.1.

COMMENTARY

Traditionally known as a *ligula,* this type of spoon, with a pear-shaped bowl attached to a raised straight handle terminating in a finial, was in use from the first century after Christ (Oliver, 1977, 108). Although its popularity declined in the second and third centuries, it was revived to become the most common type of spoon after the fifth. Until then, the point of attachment between bowl and handle usually took the form of an open scroll, but by the sixth century this was replaced by a solid disc, often inscribed or otherwise decorated (Strong, 1966, 129, 155, 177, 205). Recently, Martin (in Cahn *et al.,* 1984, 78 f.) has described all sixth- to seventh-century spoons, irrespective of shape, as *cochlearia* (see Entry no. 22), on the grounds of their relatively smaller size compared with earlier *ligulae.* The terminal knob on this spoon (and nos. 19–21) was less common at this period than was the baluster finial (compare no. 49); it is known on first-century spoons from Pompeii (Strong, 1966, 156), and on more nearly contemporary spoons in the Esquiline, Carthage, and first Cyprus treasures. This spoon (along with Hama spoons nos. 19, 20) lacks the usual rat-tail extension of the disc attachment on the back.

Fig. 18.5

+ΥΠΕΡΕΥΧΗϹΗΛΙΩΔΟΡΥ

+Ὑπὲρ εὐχῆς Ἡλιωδόρου.

From the fourth century on, ornament of all types, including some with religious overtones, proliferated on spoons (Strong, 1966, 178, 206). And almost without exception, this ornament is so aligned as to be "read" horizontally while the spoon is held in the right hand for eating (see, for example, Milojčić, 1970, figs. 7–9; Sherlock, 1974, fig. 1; and Johns and Potter, 1983, pls. 6–12). While the dedicatory inscription on this spoon, as on spoon no. 19, is positioned horizontally on the handle, the cross engraved in its bowl, and in the bowls of spoons nos. 19, 20, and 21, is not. Instead, all four show crosses that "stand vertically" on the tip of the bowl. Although all four utensils are of basically the same type, with knob finials, they were clearly not made as a set, since their dimensions vary, and two among them were given fifty years apart.

L	17.8 cm
W (bowl)	3.7 cm
Weight	31.1 gr
Roman Weight	1 oz 3 scr
Original Silver Price	9 carats

Fig. 18.2

Fig. 18.3

Fig. 18.4

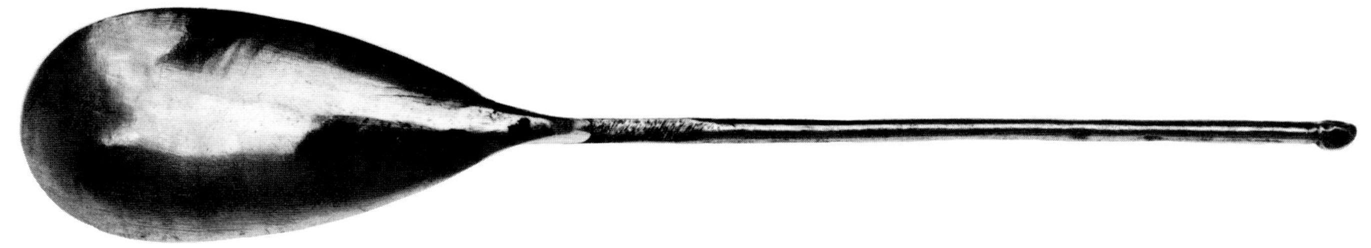

Of the many early church silver treasures discussed in this catalogue, only those of Hama, Antioch, Ma'aret en-Noman, Ghiné, and Gallunianu contain spoons. Other contemporary treasures having spoons (e.g., those of Canoscio, Mytilene, Lampsacus and Cyprus) can be shown to be domestic, and thus may be eliminated from the following discussion. Within the treasures identified as ecclesiastical, the eight Antioch spoons (nos. 49–56) and the fifth Hama spoon (no. 22) appear to constitute domestic silver donated to a church for its monetary value. Among the seven remaining "church spoons," that from Gallunianu (no. 82) has only a *Chrismon* on its disc, but two of the four Hama cross-bearing spoons have inscriptions defining them either explicitly (no. 18) or implicitly (no. 19) as church donations, made for that purpose. The fact that these dedicated spoons, the spoon found inside the Ghiné church (fig. 18.5; Chéhab, 1957, 159 f.), as well as the Ma'aret en-Noman spoon (no. 69) also have unusual—that is, "vertical"—crosses, further sets them apart from contemporary spoons with various horizontally-placed Christian symbols. Perhaps the crosses on the Hama, Ma'aret en-Noman, and Ghiné spoons were so placed and aligned because the implements which bear them were to be lowered vertically into the consecrated wine of the chalice (either to stir or distribute), as shown in later manuscript illustration (Milojčić, 1970, pl. 19.1).

Recent research (*ibid.;* Painter, 1977 [I], 20; and von Hessen *et al.,* 1977, 50 ff.) has shown that early texts do not explicitly define a liturgical use for the spoon. The Syriac text of John of Ephesos (*Lives,* ch. 55), from mid sixth-century Constantinople, states that Sosiana's silver was recycled into "chalices and patens and many dishes and spoons (*tarode*)" for church use, but it offers no further clarification. Contemporary with this text, the six Hama, Ma'aret en-Noman, and Ghiné spoons with vertical crosses suggest an early use for the spoon in the eucharistic service. Indeed, it may be more than coincidence that (at least) two of the Hama spoons were presented by individuals who also gave chalices to their church: Heliodoros, who gave spoon no. 18, also gave chalice no. 27 around 550, while John and Thomas, who gave spoon no. 19, also gave chalice no. 2 (together with their brother Mannos) in the period 602–610. For a suggested joint donation of spoon and paten, see Entries nos. 81, 82.

Bibliography

Diehl, 1926, no. 17; Braun, 1932, 278 f.; *SEG,* vol. 7, no. 105; *Dark Ages,* 1937, no. 111; *Early Christian,* 1947, no. 411; Downey, 1951, 350, note 11; *IGLS,* no. 2041; Milojčić, 1970, 138; Von Hessen *et al.,* 1977, 50 ff.

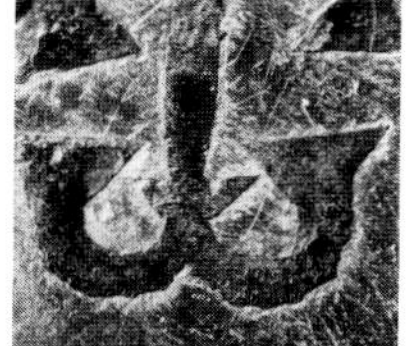

Fig. 19.1

19. SPOON

LIGULA

Figures 19.1–19.5

Baltimore, The Walters Art Gallery, no. 57.649

Hama Treasure, Early Seventh Century

For technical and compositional analyses, see Chapter III, Appendices III.1 and III.2.

This spoon has a pear-shaped bowl joined by a solid disc to a handle which is square in section near the bowl and thereafter facetted, terminating in a knob (figs. 19.2–19.5). There is no rat-tail on the reverse of the bowl. An ornate cross having W-shaped ends and a broad groove gouged in its center is engraved in the wide end of the bowl. The disc bears a monogram on each face, and an inscription runs along the upper surface of the square handle (figs. 19.1–19.4).

This spoon was manufactured in much the same way as spoon no. 18. The similarity of silver composition in its three parts suggests that it, too, was made from a single melt of metal. It may have been cast in one or two pieces (i.e., bowl, and handle with disc). But unlike spoon no. 18, microscopic analysis reveals that the join between bowl and disc is porous, suggesting soldering. The bowl was hammered into shape, and the spoon filed to remove casting flaws and/or excess solder and to define the form of the handle. Niello (see Chapter III, Appendix III.3) inlay has been lost from four of the letters.

INSCRIPTION

Disc: *(Gift) of JOHN (and) of THOMAS,*
Handle: + *the (sons) of THEOPHILOS.*

Engraved, nielloed (H of monograms = 1.2 cm; H of letters on handle = .3 cm). Diehl, 1926, no. 16; *SEG,* vol. 7, no. 103; *IGLS,* no. 2040.

The letters are well executed. No abbreviations are used in the handle inscription, but *omicron-upsilon* appears in ligature in one monogram.

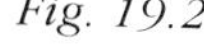
Fig. 19.2

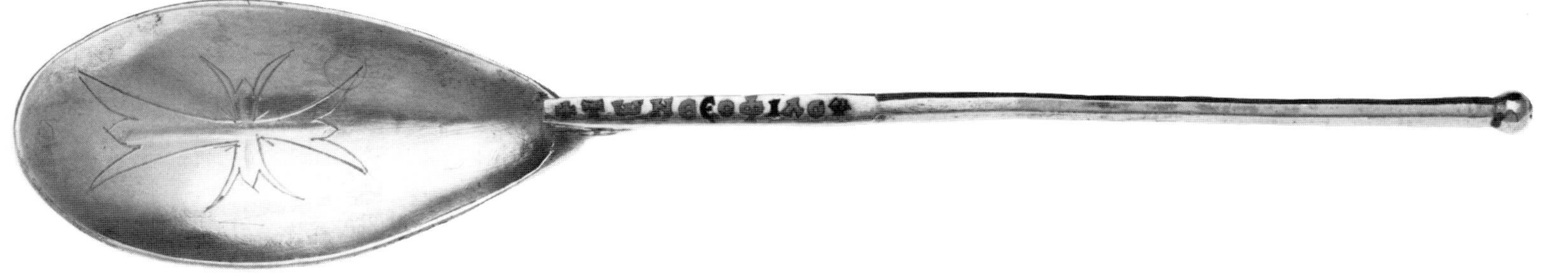

Ἰωάννου Θωμᾶ + τῶν Θεοφίλου.

The fact that two names in the genitive appear together here argues in favor of a donation, rather than a statement of ownership (contrast no. 22). On the brothers John and Thomas who, with their brother Mannos, dedicated a stamped chalice in the period 602–610, see Entry no. 2. See also figure I.1.

Commentary

While the lettering on this spoon's handle is comparable with that of the Hama ladle (no. 23), the broad, shallow groove carved in the center of its cross recalls the technique employed on Hama box no. 17, Antioch spoon no. 56, and Phela paten no. 60. The form of the cross itself, however, is unusual, and is not repeated on other objects in this catalogue, nor are the tiny "rays" at its crossing, which instead turn inwards on the cross on spoon no. 20, as well as those on patens nos. 5, 36, and 63. For a general discussion of church spoons, see Entry no. 18.

Bibliography

Diehl, 1926, no. 16; Braun, 1932, 278 f.; *SEG,* vol. 7, no. 103; *Dark Ages,* 1937, no. 109; *Early Christian,* 1947, no. 411; *IGLS,* no. 2040; Milojčić, 1970, 138; Von Hessen *et al.,* 1977, 50 ff.

L	20.2 cm
W (bowl)	3.8 cm
Weight	40.1 gr
Roman Weight	1 oz 11 scr
Original Silver Price	$11\frac{2}{3}$ carats

Fig. 19.3

Fig. 19.4

Fig. 19.5

20. SPOON

LIGULA

Figures 20.1–20.3

Baltimore, The Walters Art Gallery, no. 57.647

Hama Treasure, Sixth to Seventh Century

For technical and compositional analyses, see Chapter III, Appendices III.1 and III.2.

This spoon has a pear-shaped bowl joined by a solid disc to a handle which is square in section near the bowl, and thereafter facetted, terminating in a knob (figs. 20.1, 20.2). On the back of the bowl there is an indentation above the disc rather than a rat-tail attachment (fig. 20.3). A flaring-armed cross with diagonal strokes at its center is engraved at the wide end of the bowl.

This spoon was manufactured in much the same way as spoons nos. 18 and 19, and like the latter, has a porous (i.e., soldered?) join between bowl and disc, which in this case displays tool marks. For additional observations, see Entries nos. 18 and 19.

COMMENTARY

The cross on this spoon is similar in shape to that on spoon no. 21, which is now lost. Similar crosses, with inwardly pointing diagonal rays at the center, decorate the spoon found in the church at Ghiné (Chéhab, 1957, 159 f.), and patens nos. 5, 36, and 63. For a general discussion of church spoons, see Entry no. 18.

BIBLIOGRAPHY

Diehl, 1926, no. 18; Braun, 1932, 278 f.; *Dark Ages,* 1937, no. 107; *Early Christian,* 1947, no. 411; Lassus, 1947, 197 f.; Milojčić, 1970, 138; *Age,* 1979, no. 539.

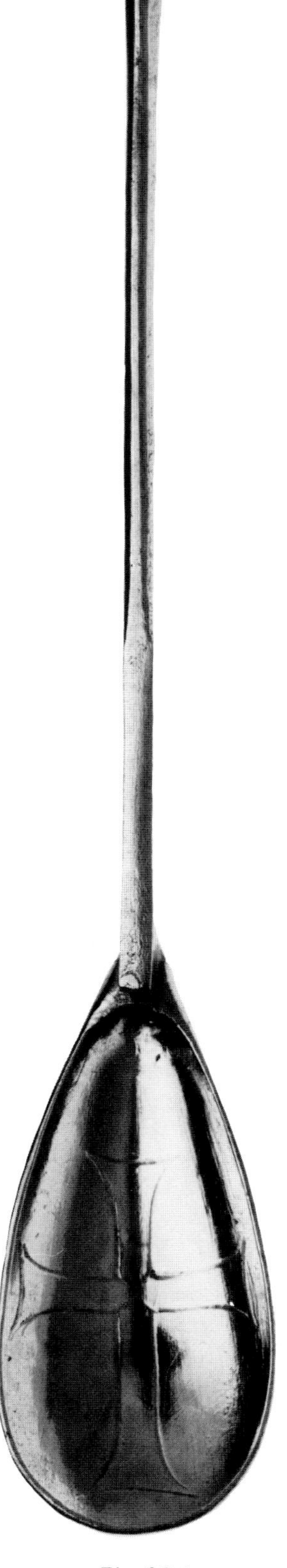

Fig. 20.1

L	22.8 cm
W (bowl)	3.9 cm
Weight	54.0 gr
Roman Weight	2.0 oz
Original Silver Price	16 carats

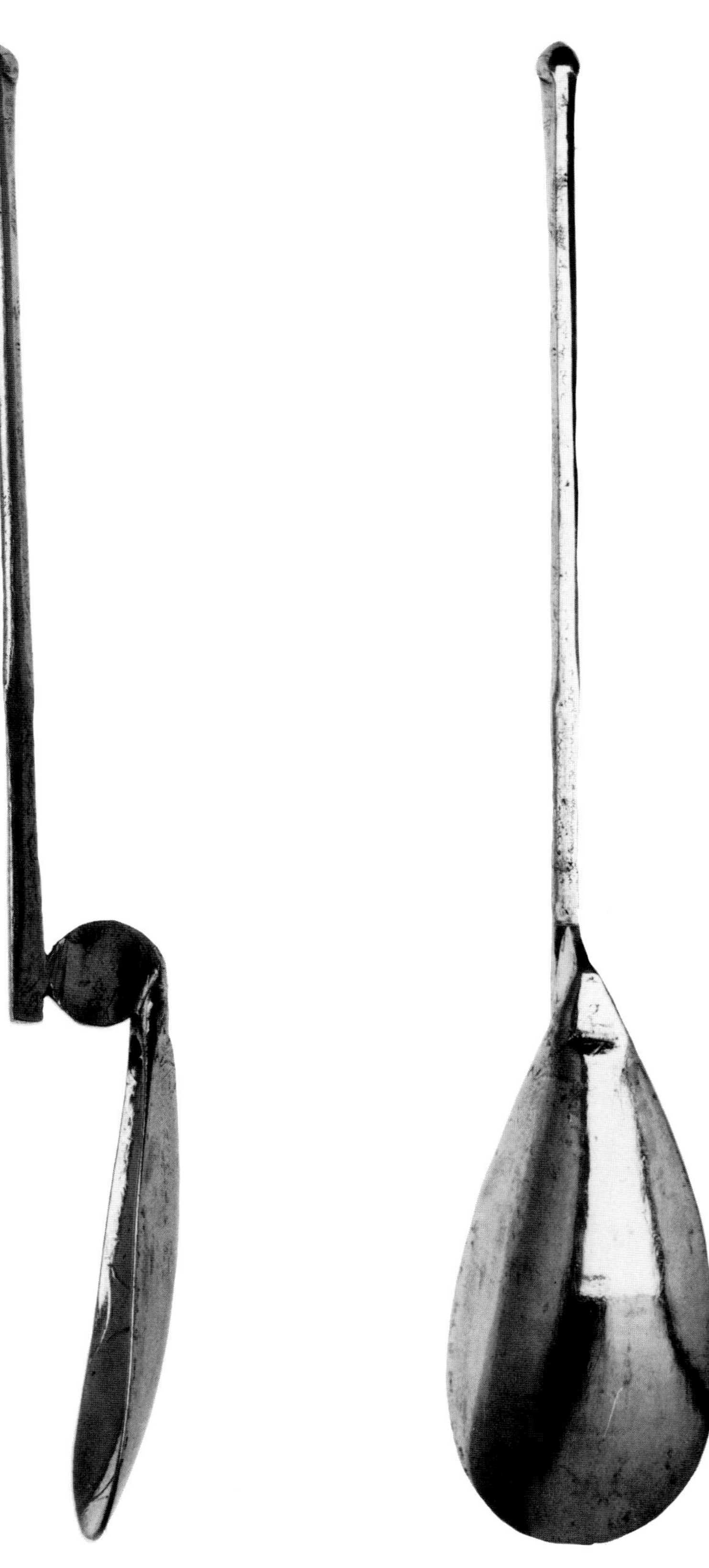

Fig. 20.2 *Fig. 20.3*

21. Spoon

LIGULA

Figure 21.1

Present Location Unknown

Hama Treasure, Sixth to Seventh Century(?)

This spoon has a pear-shaped bowl joined by a solid disc to a handle that terminates in a knob (fig. 21.1). A large cross, very similar to that on spoon no. 20, is engraved in its bowl.

This spoon appears in the 1910 Hama photograph (fig. II.4), and is apparently one of the "2 petites cuillères" mentioned in the 1910 inventory (see Chapter II, above). It and strainer no. 25 disappeared from the Hama treasure before it was first published as a unit by Diehl in 1926. This spoon is likewise missing from the photograph taken some time between 1913 and 1929, while the objects were in the Abucasem Collection, in Egypt (fig. II.5).

Commentary
See Entry no. 18.

Bibliography
Unpublished.

L *ca.* 20 cm

Fig. 21.1

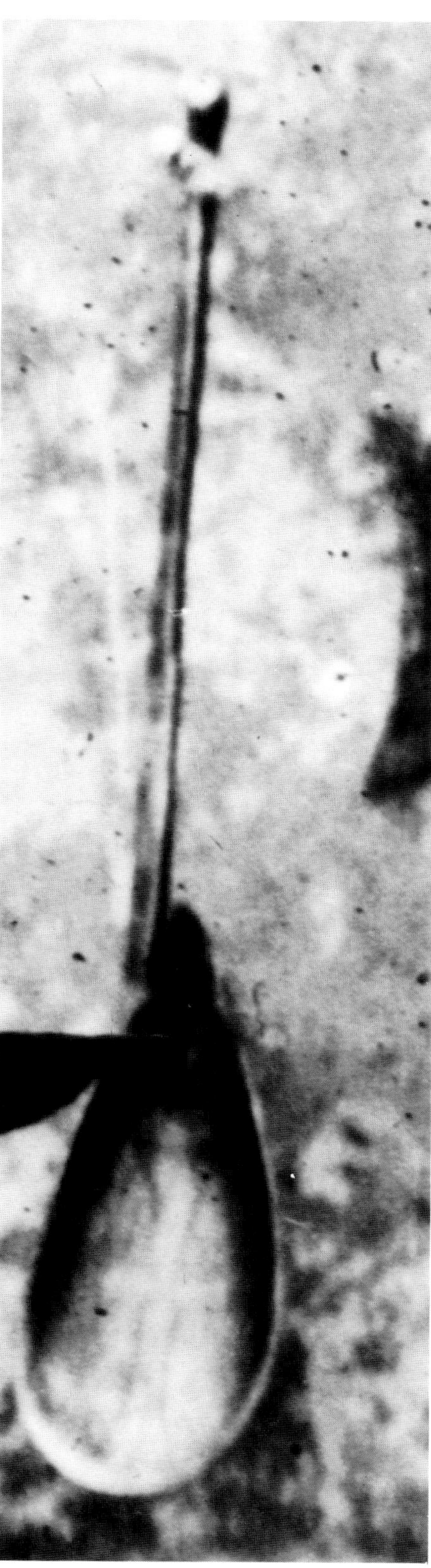

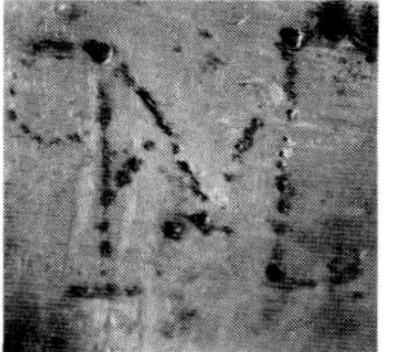

Fig. 22.1

22. SPOON

LIGULA

Figures 22.1–22.4

Baltimore, The Walters Art Gallery, no. 57.648

Hama Treasure, Sixth Century

For technical and compositional analyses, see Chapter III, Appendices III.1 and III.2.

This spoon has an oval bowl joined by a solid disc to a handle which is square in section near the bowl and thereafter round, terminating in a tapering finial (figs. 22.2, 22.3). The bowl has a flat upper rim and, on its reverse, a rat-tail extending from the disc (fig. 22.4), which bears a monogram on the right side (figs. 22.1, 22.3).

This spoon was cast from a single melt of metal, either whole or, more likely, as three separate pieces: the bowl, which was hammered and planished into shape; the disc and its rat-tail extension; and the handle with its finial. The porous joins which are visible under the microscope between bowl and rat-tail, and between disc and handle, suggest soldering. Inside the bowl are drips of what may be silver solder. The black substance in the inscription may be a black corrosion product (see Chapter III, Appendix III.3). The rim of the bowl is worn on the right side near the tip, perhaps from prolonged right-hand use. (On the interpretation of wear on spoons, see Johns and Potter, 1983, 35.)

INSCRIPTION

(Property) of MARIA(?).

Chased, *pointillé,* nielloed(?) (H of monogram = .6 cm). Diehl, 1926, no. 19; *SEG,* vol. 7, no. 105; *IGLS,* no. 2042.

The monogram as published by Diehl (and repeated in *IGLS*) is simplified as *mu-alpha-rho,* yielding *Mara.* While the dotted bar across the diagonals of the *mu* is clearly an embellishment, that at the base of its right vertical is probably part of a *sigma,* which would yield *Maras* (nominative) or *Marias* (genitive).

The fact that this monogram is well centered on the disc and seems to have niello added, strongly suggests that it was contemporary with the object's manufacture. The genitive case ending was probably used to indicate ownership, not dedication (as in "Offering of . . ."). (In *Age,* 1979, no. 539, this monogram was mistakenly attributed to Hama spoon no. 20.) The monogram on this spoon may be repeated, in a confused form, on Antioch spoon no. 52.

COMMENTARY

This spoon differs from Hama spoons nos. 18–21 in three respects: its bowl is oval rather than pear-shaped; it has a rat-tail attachment to its disc; and its handle has a pointed rather than knob finial. The pointed handle of the *cochleare* spoon (see Strong, 1966, 129, 155) came, by the third century, to be used on *ligula* type spoons as well (*ibid.,* 177, 204 ff.; see also Entry no. 18). On this spoon, however, the point is somewhat broad and is worked as a finial. Basically the same handle is found on another Byzantine/Syrian spoon (no. 69), and on two spoons found at Ballana, in Egypt (Emery and Kirwan, 1938, nos. 876, 877). The narrow oval bowl, although less common in this period than the pear-shaped bowl, appears on spoons in the Antioch (no. 56) and Lampsacus treasures (Dalton, 1901, nos. 380–392), and on spoons in the Geneva (Lazović *et al.,* 1977, no. 13) and Istanbul (nos. 2152, 2153) museums. The latter, a pair of spoons from Cotyaeum, also have dotted monograms on their discs. Compared with the other oval bowls, that of this spoon has a less developed rim.

Unlike the monograms on spoon

no. 19 which, taken together, indicate a joint dedication, the monogram on this spoon is probably that of its owner. Presumably after a certain period of use, he gave it to his church for its silver value (see also Entries nos. 18, 49). There is nothing in the decoration of this object to indicate that it had a specifically Christian use. The spoons cited above as formal comparisons all date to the sixth or seventh century; here, the box monogram suggests the sixth century (see Weigand, 1937, 130).

BIBLIOGRAPHY

Diehl, 1926, no. 19; Braun, 1932, 278 f.; *SEG,* vol. 7, no. 105; *Dark Ages,* 1937, no. 108; *Early Christian,* 1947, no. 411; *IGLS,* no. 2042; Milojčić, 1970, 138.

L	24.2 cm
W (bowl)	3.6 cm
Weight	48.5 gr
Roman Weight	1 oz 18 scr
Original Silver Price	14 carats

Fig. 22.2 *Fig. 22.3* *Fig. 22.4*

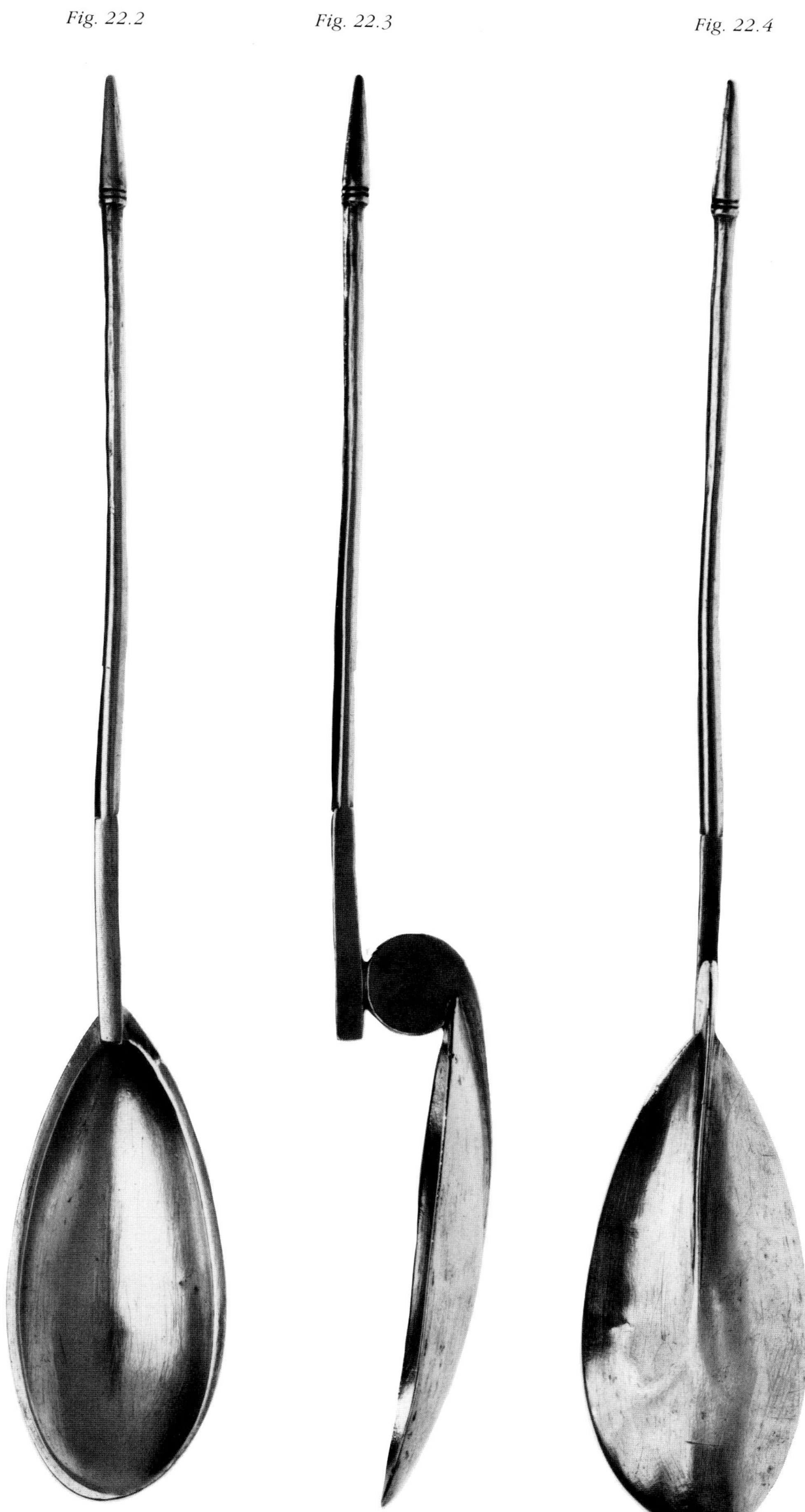

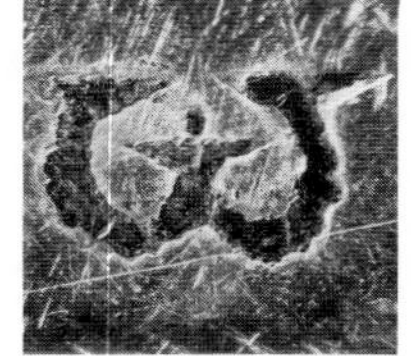

Fig. 23.1

23. LADLE

KYATHOS

Figures 23.1–23.5

Baltimore, The Walters Art Gallery, no. 57.646

Hama Treasure, Sixth to Seventh Century

For technical and compositional analyses, see Chapter III, Appendices III.1 and III.2.

Fig. 23.5

This ladle is composed of a bowl with pouring spout, (nearly) straight sides, and flat base, which is attached to a horizontal handle with perpendicular foot resting on a disc (D 1.8 cm); it is freestanding (figs. 23.2–23.4). An inscription runs the length of the upper surface of the handle (figs. 23.1, 23.2). The beginning of the inscription is framed by an engraved cartouche, which also reappears on the perpendicular end of the handle (fig. 23.5). A narrow line is engraved around the top of the bowl.

This ladle was made in two parts: the bowl, which was hammered, and the handle, which was cast from a separate melt of metal with a higher copper content, for greater strength. The bowl bears stress cracks near the base of its unfinished interior. Similar stress cracks also appear in the bend of the cast handle. The pitted and porous area underneath the juncture of bowl and handle indicates soldering. Niello (see Chapter III, Appendix III.3) is missing from several letters and from the final cross.

INSCRIPTION

+ *For the remission of the sins of STEPHEN.*

Engraved, nielloed (H of letters = .4 cm). Diehl, 1926, no. 20; *SEG,* vol. 7, no. 106; *IGLS,* no. 2043; *Age,* 1979, no. 537.

The letters are well and elaborately formed with heavy serifs. There are no abbreviations or ligatures.

Although this dedicatory formula, *hyper apheseos hamartion,* does not appear on any other object in this catalogue, it does occur in contemporary building and pavement inscriptions in Syria and Palestine, either alone (*IGLS,* nos. 1684, 1993; Brünnow and Domaszewski, 1904–1909, vol. 3, 343; Mittmann, 1967, 42–45), or with *hyper soterias* (Candemir and Wagner, 1978, 227 f.) or *hyper anapauseos* (Milik, 1960, 554). Stephen is not mentioned on any other object among the Stuma, Riha, Hama, and Antioch treasures.

COMMENTARY

This unusual object combines the deep bowl of a type of late Hellenistic ladle with vertical handle (Strong, 1966, 115 f.), with the horizontal handle of a typical fourth-century ladle with wide, shallow bowl (*ibid.,* 193). None of these other ladles has a spout, and the horizontal handles do not have the vertical foot of this example. Although a ladle (*kyathos*) of unspecified material is listed in the Ibion church inventory (no. 91), no other church treasure, attested or surviving, includes one. Three bronze ladles from Egypt, of the late Hellenistic type, are catalogued among the Early Christian objects in Berlin (Wulff, 1909, nos. 1051–1053). The horizontal handle on this example would have impeded its being lowered into ewers like nos. 14, 37, and 38.

BIBLIOGRAPHY

Diehl, 1926, no. 20; *SEG,* vol. 7, no. 106; *Dark Ages,* 1937, no. 106; *Early Christian,* 1947, no. 409; Lassus, 1947, 197 f.; *IGLS,* no. 2043; *Age,* 1979, no. 537.

L	27.5 cm
D (bowl)	7.3 cm
H (bowl)	4.1 cm
Weight	102.2 gr
Roman Weight	3 oz 18 scr
Original Silver Price	1 *solidus* 6 carats
Volume	*ca.* 60 ml

+ΥΠΕΡΑΦΕϹΕΩϹΑΜΑΡΤΙΩΝϹΤΕΦΑΝΟΥ+

+Ὑπὲρ ἀφέσεως ἁμαρτιῶν Στεφάνου.

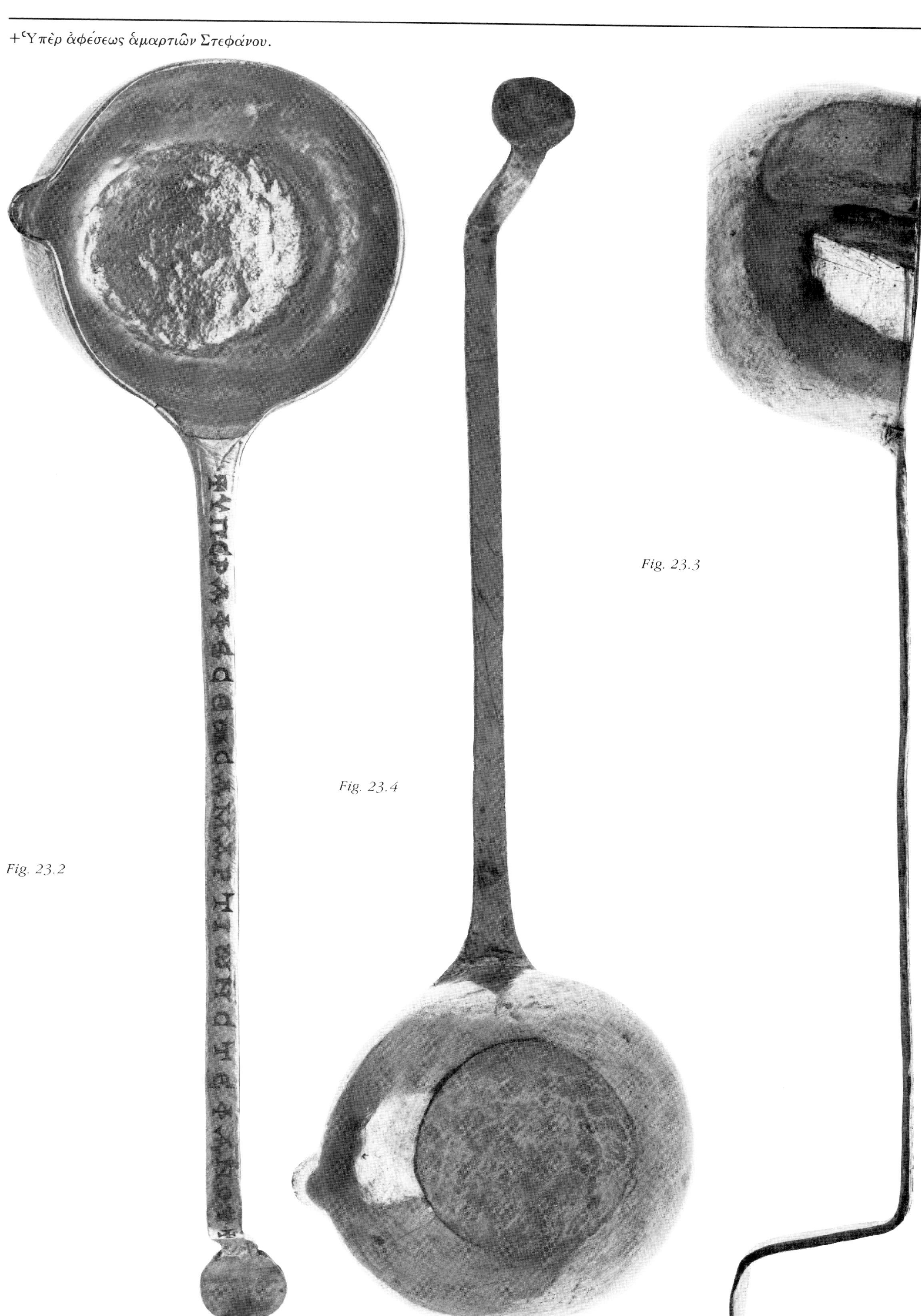

Fig. 23.2

Fig. 23.4

Fig. 23.3

24. STRAINER

Figures 24.1–24.3

Baltimore, The Walters Art Gallery, no. 57.650

Hama Treasure, Sixth to Seventh Century

For technical and compositional analyses, see Chapter III, Appendices III.1 and III.2.

This strainer consists of a pierced hemispherical bowl joined at its upper rim—by a flat, splayed ornament cut as two dolphins—to a handle which is round in section and terminates in a facetted knob threaded with a suspension ring (figs. 24.1–24.3). The holes inside the bowl form a pattern of sixteen radiating lines with small "crosses" incorporated into every other one. The entire handle is decorated with narrow engraved grooves, apparently(?) inlaid with niello (see Chapter III, Appendix III.3).

This strainer was made in three parts, perhaps from three different melts of metal: the bowl, the handle with dolphins, and the ring. The bowl was formed by hammering, and finished inside and out on a lathe. The handle was cast, after which the dolphins were cut out, with their contours left somewhat rough. The handle was soldered to the bowl and the holes punched through from the inside, leaving unfiled edges on the outside. The black fusible substance embedded in the grooves of the handle could be niello, or simply silver corrosion products. The crudely forged ring was inserted through the hole in the terminal knob, and its ends soldered together.

COMMENTARY

This strainer resembles Hama strainer no. 25, which is now lost. The two were too small for filtering wine as it was being poured (contrast strainer no. 26); they were probably used instead to extract spices, insects, dregs or other impurities from the wine already in the cup or chalice. (On this type of small strainer, which is often equipped with a finger[?] ring, see Martin [in Cahn *et al.* 1984] and Johns and Potter [1983, 53 ff.].) Particularly close to these two Hama strainers are two in the Kaiseraugst treasure, which have paired dolphins (Martin in Cahn *et al.,* 1984, nos. 36, 37), and two in the the Thetford treasure (Johns and Potter, 1983, nos. 47, 48). These western fourth-century strainers have twisted rod handles, a type from which the Syrian grooved handle might ultimately derive (see also Antioch spoon no. 56). The arrangement of the holes in this strainer is similar to, but more compressed than, that of the Durobrivae strainer (Painter, 1977 [I], no. 7). For a general discussion of church strainers, see Entry no. 26.

BIBLIOGRAPHY

Diehl, 1926, no. 21; *Dark Ages,* 1937, no. 110; *Early Christian,* 1947, no. 410; *Age,* 1979, no. 538; Cahn *et al.,* 1984, 102, 111 f., 121, no. 295.

L (with ring)	18.9 cm
D (bowl)	3.6 cm
H	1.4 cm
Weight	26.1 gr
Roman Weight	23 scr
Original Silver Price	7 2/3 carats

Fig. 24.1

Fig. 24.2

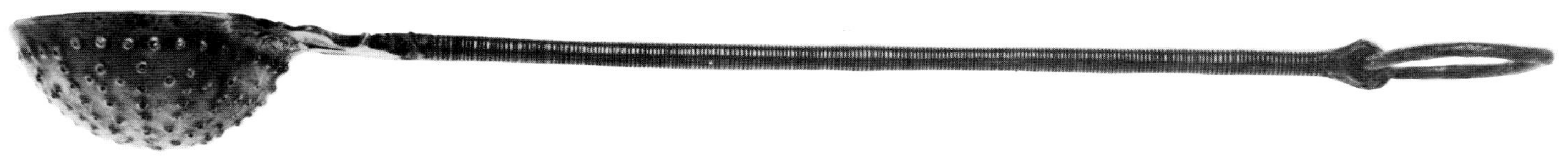

Fig. 24.3

25. STRAINER

Figure 25.1

Present Location Unknown

Hama Treasure, Sixth to Seventh Century

L	*ca.* 17 cm

This strainer is similar in design to strainer no. 24, that is, it consists of a pierced round bowl joined to a handle which is round in section and which has a knob with suspension ring. But in this case, the form of attachment between bowl and handle is plain rather than fashioned as dolphins.

This strainer appears in the 1910 Hama photograph (fig. II.4), and is apparently one of the "2 filtres ou couloirs de vin" mentioned in the 1910 inventory (see Chapter II, above). It and one spoon (no. 21) disappeared from the Hama hoard before it was first published as a unit by Diehl in 1926. This strainer is likewise missing from the photograph taken some time between 1913 and 1929, while the objects were in the Abucasem Collection, in Egypt (fig. II.5).

COMMENTARY

See Entry no. 24.

BIBLIOGRAPHY

Unpublished.

Fig. 25.1

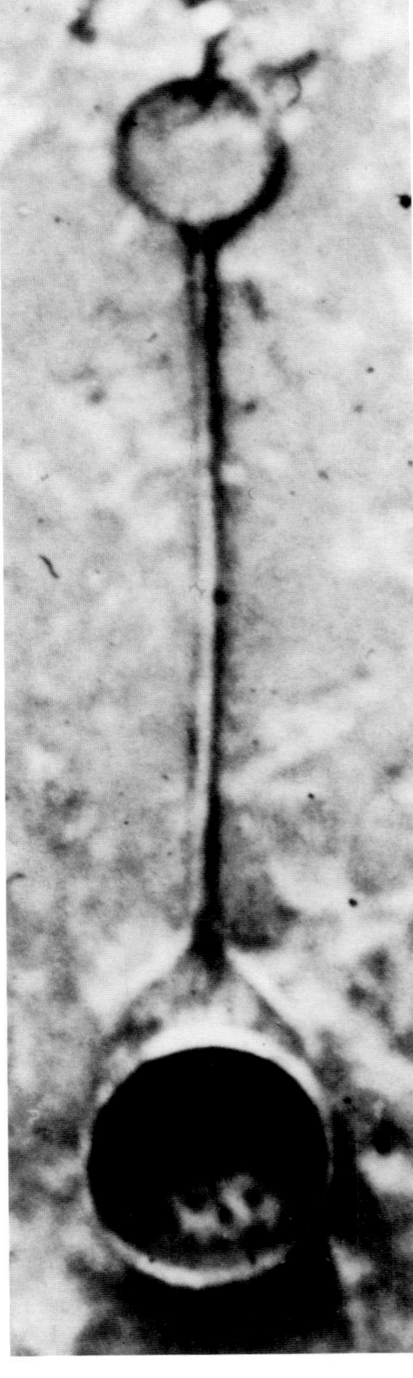

26. STRAINER

ETHMOS

Figures 26.1–26.4

Jerusalem, Museum, Church of St. Anne

Hama Treasure, Sixth to Seventh Century

This strainer consists of a wide, deep bowl with flat rim, and a broad horizontal handle with flared end (figs. 26.2 –26.4). The bottom of the bowl is perforated in a floral pattern of four concentric circles, followed by seventeen vertical ovals and two additional circles (from center to rim). There are two engraved lines on the flat rim. The handle bears an inscription running its length, framed by a simple engraved border (figs. 26.1, 26.2).

This strainer was (apparently) formed by hammering from a single sheet of metal, from which a disc shape with handle was cut. The rim and protruding handle were hammered back flat, away from the bowl, and the straining holes punched from the inside out. There are a few small dents in the rim.

INSCRIPTION

+ *(Treasure) of St. Sergios.*

Engraved, single-stroke (H of letters = .5–.7 cm). Unpublished.

The letters are of consistent size, and serifs are used regularly. There are no abbreviations or ligatures.

The inscription is here understood by analogy with the text of Hama chalice no. 3 and the Sarabaon paten (no. 75). Alternatively, it might be read "(Strainer) of . . . ," as on Hama ewer no. 14, or "(Offering to the church) of. . . ."

COMMENTARY

This strainer differs from the other two in the Hama treasure (nos. 24, 25) in its broad bowl and flat handle; it is of a type that is late Hellenistic in origin (Strong, 1966, 116). In general proportions it corresponds to the Chaourse strainer (which is hinged to a funnel; *ibid.*, pls. 46B, 52), and to several bronze strainers found in Egypt (Emery and Kirwan, 1938, nos. 791–793), one of which, apparently of the sixth century, has an inscription incorporated into its straining holes (*ibid.*, 407). (See also Hayes, 1984, no. 82.) The flat handle of the Jerusalem strainer resembles that of a *trulla* in the Hermitage (Dodd, 1961, no. 30; 582–602). In execution, it recalls the small bowl in the Hama treasure (no. 16), which has a similar rim.

The strainer (Greek = *ethmos;* Latin = *colum*) was traditionally used to filter wine and to cool it with snow (Strong, 1966, 145). Along with other objects of *argentum potorium,* it was adopted for church ritual, wherein it was used to filter impurities from the wine communally collected in the *skyphos,* just as it was poured into the eucharistic chalice (*DACL,* vol. XIII, cols. 2266 ff.). Although both the Latin and the Greek sources which describe the strainer's liturgical function are medieval, earlier evidence of its use in the church is provided by the fourth- and sixth-century strainers of the Durobrivae (Painter 1977 [I], no. 7) and Hama (nos. 24–26) treasures, and by the silver *colum* donated to the church near Tivoli in 471 (see Entry no. 91; Braun, 1932, 450 ff.). While the two smaller Hama strainers clearly had another function (see no. 24), this one could have been made to rest on the rim of a chalice as wine (and water?) was being poured from a ewer. Indeed, Hama ewer no. 14; with its protuding tab, may have provided its resting place when not in use. If these two objects were in fact donated as a set, the inscription on this one might be understood as "(Strainer) of St. Sergios," to complement that on the ewer, which reads "Ewer of St. Sergios."

BIBLIOGRAPHY

Unpublished.

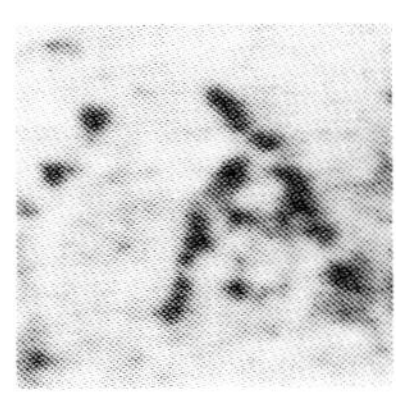

Fig. 26.1

+ Του ἁγίου Σεργίου

L	14.6 cm
D (bowl)	7.8 cm
H	3.7 cm
Weight	32 gr
Roman Weight	1 oz 5 scr
Original Silver Price	9²/₃ carats

Fig. 26.2

Fig. 26.3

Fig. 26.4

27. CHALICE

POTERION

Figures 27.1–27.4

Jerusalem, Museum, Church of St. Anne
Hama Treasure, *ca. 550–565*

This chalice has a broad, slightly bulbous cup which rests on a flaring foot with knob (fig. 27.3). Around the cup's rim runs an inscription (figs. 27.2, 27.3) between two pairs of engraved lines. Other engraved lines ornament the knob—three above and three below—and two others are near the edge of the foot. Four stamps appear inside the foot (figs. 27.1, 27.4).

This chalice has not been examined at first hand, but it appears to belong to our Type A (see Entry no. 1), and was therefore probably made and assembled by the methods described for the London chalice (no. 29). This vessel has apparently never been cleaned, and there are a few shallow dents in its cup.

STAMPS

These stamps were dated by Dodd (1961, no. 18; hexagonal stamp with Justinian's monogram not cited) to the latter part of Justinian's reign (i.e., 550–565) because of their relationship with other, more securely dateable stamps of that period (*ibid.,* no. 17). As classified by Dodd, the stamps may be read, with the addition of the unpublished hexagonal stamp, and one minor emendation (fig. 27.1), as follows:

a. **Round:** nimbed bust; inscribed *LEONTIOU.*
b. **Hexagonal:** monogram of Justinian; unidentified inscription.
c. **Square:** missing.
d. **Long:** nimbed bust; unidentified monogram; unidentified inscription.
e. **Cross:** unidentified monogram; inscribed *EUPHRONIOU.*

INSCRIPTION

+ *In fulfillment of a vow of HELIODOROS and AKAKIOS, children of THOMAS, together with (that) of THOSE WHO BELONG TO THEM.*

Engraved, single-stroke (H of letters = 1.5 cm). Dodd, 1961, no. 18.

The letters are lunate and consistent in size; serifs are regularly used. *Kai* is abbreviated *Ks* and the genitive *omicron-upsilon* is in ligature. Spelling: *omicron* is substituted for the final *omega* in *teknon, ton,* and *diapheronton.*

Except for *omicron, upsilon,* and *omega,* the lettering resembles that on Hama paten no. 5 (also stamped), Hama cross no. 7, and London chalice no. 29, all of which, however, are less cramped in their spacing. On the dedicatory formula and the phrase signifying "household," see Entry no. 1. Heliodoros and Akakios

Fig. 27.2

Fig. 27.1

+ΛΕΟΝ||ΤΙΟV

.И..ΟV

ΕV||ΦΡΟ||Ν[Ι||ΟV]

are also named together, though as deceased, on Hama flask no. 15, given by Megale, to whom they may have been related. Heliodoros dedicated a paten (no. 4) in the memory of his son, Baradatos, and a spoon (no. 18), which was also given *hyper euches,* perhaps together with this chalice (see that Entry). Thomas, father of Heliodoros and Akakios, may be one and the same with Thomas, son of Isaac, who gave one of the two small Hama crosses (no. 9).

Commentary

This chalice is closest in proportions to Hama chalice no. 2 (which is smaller), and is closest in general aspect to London chalice no. 29 (except for the width of the foot). On chalices in general, including the typology of their construction, see Entry no. 1.

Bibliography

Braun, 1932, 78 ff.; Dodd, 1961, no. 18; Ross, 1962, 20; Weitzmann and Ševčenko, 1963, 397; Dodd, 1973, 14, no. 3, 15.

Fig. 27.4

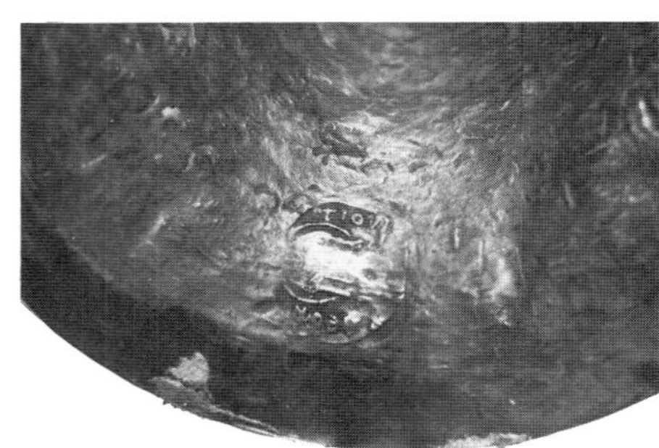

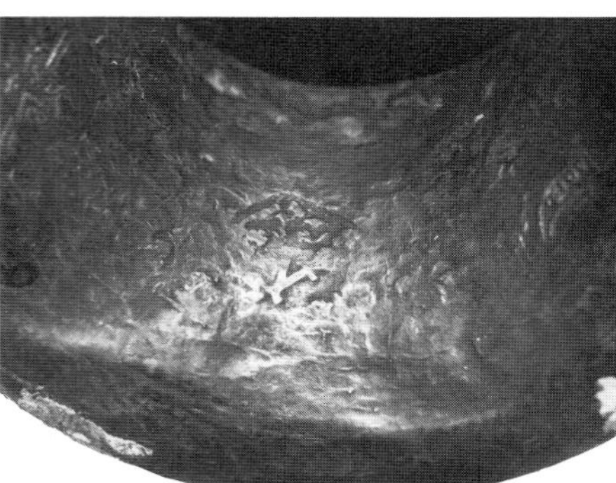

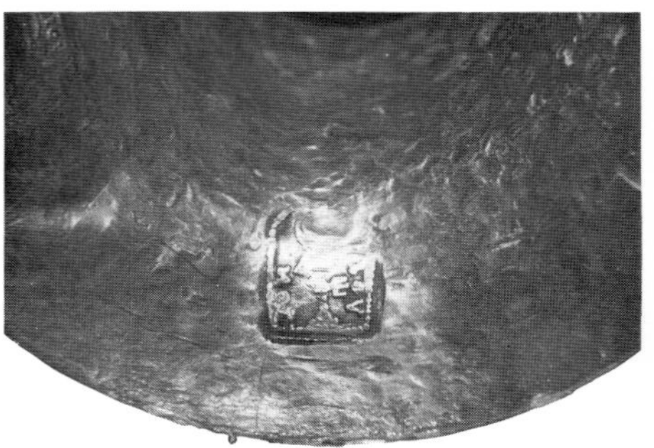

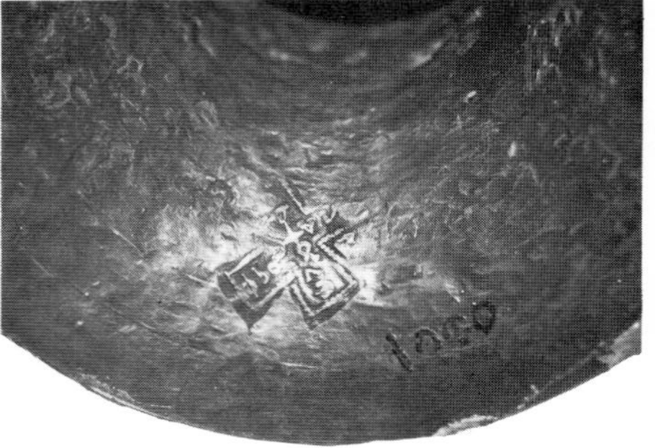

+ΥΠΕΡΕΥΧΗΣΗΛΙΩΔΟΡΥΚΑΚΑΚΙΥΤΕΚΝΟΝ ΘΩΜΑΑΜΑΤΟΝ ΔΙΑΦΕΡΟΝΤΟΝΑΥΤΟΙϹ

+ Ὑπὲρ εὐχῆς Ἡλιοδώρου κ(αὶ) Ἀκακίου τέκνον Θωμᾶ ἅμα τὸν διαφερόντον αὐτοῖς.

H	19.0–19.3 cm
D (cup rim)	*16.5–17.4 cm*
D (foot rim)	*9.2 cm*
Weight	*670 gr*
Roman Weight	*2 lbs 13 scr*
Original Silver Price	*8 solidi* 4 1/3 carats

Fig. 27.3

Fig. 28.1

28. CHALICE

POTERION

Figures 28.1–28.4

Washington, D.C., W. L. Eagleton Collection (on loan to Dumbarton Oaks)

Hama Treasure, Sixth to Seventh Century

This chalice has a relatively deep cup supported on a tall flaring foot with a high knob and a convex flange (fig. 28.2). There is an attachment collar between cup and knob. An inscription encircles the top of the cup (figs. 28.1, 28.2) between pairs of deeply cut turnings, and three double pairs of engraved lines accentuate the foot.

The cup and foot of this chalice were formed by hammering, the marks of which remain on their inner surfaces. Radiography reveals a centering point, either in the bottom of the cup or on the top of the foot. The two parts were joined by means of a silver collar soldered, apparently, to the bottom of the cup and hammered over a flare at the top of the foot to form a mechanical join (see also no. 3, and the discussion to Entry no. 1). Tool marks from the attachment of the collar remain inside the cup, where there is a circular impression (D 3 cm) in the bottom. After assembly, the vessel was lathe-turned to finish the surface, including a (1.5 cm) band inside the top of the cup, and to engrave the decorative lines. The black substance in several engraved letters appeared under microscopic examination to be corrosion products rather than niello. The cup has a shallow dent below the letters *CEP,* and some smaller dents towards the bottom.

INSCRIPTION

+ *(Treasure) of St. Sergios of the village (of) Kapro Koraon.*

Engraved, single-stroke (H of letters = 1.6–2.1 cm). Mouterde, 1926, 365, note 2; *SEG,* vol. 7, no. 108; *IGLS,* no. 2045.

The letters are lunate and vary in height; there are no serifs or ligatures and only one abbreviation (i.e., *ko[mes]*).

This and Hama paten no. 6 are the only objects among the Stuma, Riha, Hama, and Antioch treasures that have single-stroke inscriptions without serifs (see also Phela chalice no. 62). Within this small group, it is further distinguished by its unusual *alpha.* The R-shaped *rho* (i.e., with a small tail) and barred *upsilon* are also found together on several objects in the Hama (no. 14) and Phela (nos. 61, 64, 65) treasures, two objects of which (nos. 14, 65) also have superscript abbreviations

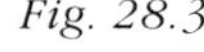

Fig. 28.3

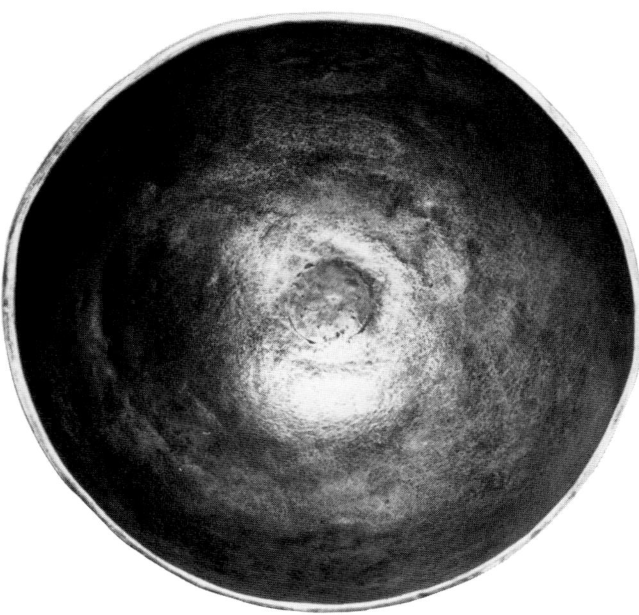

Fig. 28.4

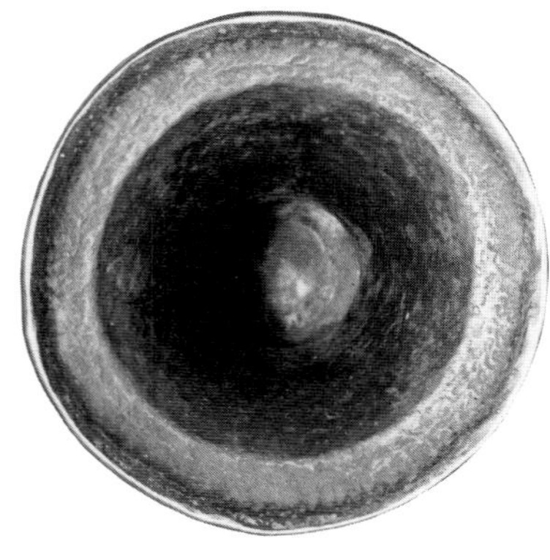

✝ΤΟΥΑΓΙΟΥϹΕΡΓΙΟΥΚΚΑΠΡΟΚΟΡΑΟΝ

\+ Τοῦ ἁγίου Σεργίου κό(μης) Καπρο Κοραον.

H	20.9–21.3 cm
D (cup rim)	17.6 cm
D (foot rim)	9.8 cm
Weight	511 gr
Roman Weight	1 lb 6 oz 17 scr
Original Silver Price	6 *solidi* 5²/₃ carats

Fig. 28.2

similar to that on this chalice. None of these objects is stamped, and while nos. 14 and 61 may be attributed on the basis of their donors to around 550 and 580, respectively, the other objects, including this one, are not easily dateable. The text is rendered by analogy with that of Hama chalice no. 3, and the Sarabaon paten, no. 75. Other possible interpretations include "(Treasure of the church) of . . . ," "(Property) of . . . ," and "(Property of the church) of. . . ."

COMMENTARY

The rather flat, almost "pointed" knob here recalls both the bead on the classical stem cup, from which the chalice foot knob derives (see Entry no. 2), and the later development of its form on the gold Albanian goblets (*Age,* 1979, no. 156). The tall narrow foot of this chalice may be compared with the heavily restored foot of the second Phela chalice (no. 62), and its convex foot flange, with those of Hama chalice no. 3 and Beth Misona chalices nos. 58 and 59. Of all the Type B (i.e., "ring joint") chalices considered here, this one and Phela chalice no. 61 are the only ones without figural decoration (see Entry no. 1).

This, the "Bosworth chalice," was attested early; it was seen on the art market in Paris, measured, and its inscription recorded by A. Héron de Villefosse on March 22, 1911. Although the inscription and Héron de Villefosse's summary description were published in 1926 (by Mouterde, in a discussion of the Hama treasure) and again in 1959 (*IGLS*), it was not realized that the Héron de Villefosse chalice was one and the same with the Bosworth chalice mentioned (but not illustrated) in later art historical discussions (Ross, 1962, 11; Dodd, 1973, 14). Indeed, it was not until a few years ago, when Mr. Bosworth's heir, the Honorable William L. Eagleton, placed the chalice on loan at Dumbarton Oaks, that it was identified from its inscription as an important, presumed lost, part of the Hama treasure. As with another "newly discovered" object from the same treasure, the Jerusalem strainer (no. 26), this object is, in effect, published here for the first time.

BIBLIOGRAPHY

Mouterde, 1926, 365, note 2; *SEG,* vol. 7, no. 108; *IGLS,* no. 2045; Ross, 1962, 11; Dodd, 1973, 14, no. 6.

29. CHALICE

POTERION

Figures 29.1–29.4

London, British Museum, no. 1914.4–15.1

Hama Treasure, First Half of the Seventh Century(?)

For compositional analysis, see Chapter III, Appendix III.2.

This chalice has a broad cup supported on a flared foot with knob and a narrow stem above (fig. 29.2). An inscription, banded by engraved turnings (one above, two below), surrounds the top of the cup (figs. 29.1, 29.2). Additional turned lines encircle the bottom of the cup and the foot, above and below the knob and near the foot rim.

This chalice was made in two parts, cup and foot, probably from the same melt of metal. Each was formed by hammering, the marks of which are still visible on their inner surfaces. The outside of the chalice was finished, and decorative bands engraved, on a lathe. There are hammer marks on the outer surface of the cup and a small vertical tear in the rim under the first *nu* of *Iwannou,* and repairs to the foot, to the left of, and opposite, the registration number. (Examination of this object in the Research Laboratory of the British Museum—by M. J. Hughes, J. Lang, and M. S. Lite [9/17/85]—resulted in the following observations.) Radiography and close visual examination reveal discontinuity of metal in four places: 1) on the outside of the base of the cup between the engraved line and the broad groove around the top of the foot stem; 2) on the inside of the foot close to the base of the cup; 3) on the outside of the stem about one centimeter below the bottom of the cup; and 4) at the corresponding place inside the stem. The inside of the foot contains solder or lead, suggesting that a collar was first affixed to the base of the cup, probably by means of a hard solder, and the join cleaned and decorated by lathe turning. The top of the foot, being slightly cone-shaped, was then fit into the collar, secured with a soft solder, and the surface of the join finished by hand. There is no evidence of niello or gilding.

INSCRIPTION

+ *In fulfillment of a vow of SERGIOS and JOHN.*

Engraved, single-stroke (H of letters = 1.1–1.4 cm). *IGLS,* nos. 210, 2046; Downey, 1951, 353, note 11; Kent and Painter, 1977, no. 155.

The lettering is lunate and of consistent formation; serifs are regularly used. There are no abbreviations or ligatures.

The lettering on this chalice and that on Hama paten no. 5 are so close as to justify the conclusion that they were done by the same hand. On the formula *hyper euches,* see Entry no. 1, and on the donors, see below.

COMMENTARY

This is one of only two Type A chalices in this catalogue (see also no. 73) that is not stamped (see Entry no. 1). The proportions of the vessel (wide cup, thick knob, compact lower foot) are best compared with those of the Riha chalice (no. 30), although the latter has a broader flange to its foot and this one has a taller stem above the knob. The decoration of this chalice, although well executed, is less elaborate than that of the other, which has more engraved lines, a concave moulding, niello inlay, and gilding. Given its links with Type A chalices and other

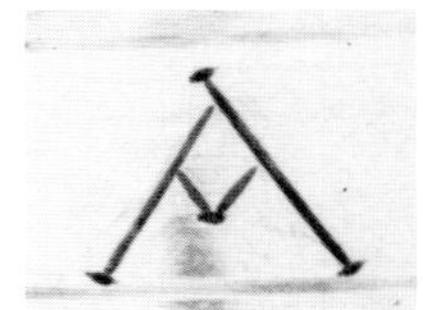

Fig. 29.1

stamped objects (e.g., no. 5), this chalice will be a key piece in future comparative studies of the manufacture of stamped and unstamped silver.

If, as suggested above, the inscription on this object was executed by the same hand as that responsible for the inscription on Hama paten no. 5, certain conclusions follow. As the latter has what are apparently seventh-century stamps, the Sergios and John named here cannot be the same individuals mentioned on Stuma hoard paten no. 36, dated 574–578, where John is already dead. It is suggested in Entry no. 5 that, given the extremely close resemblance between the inscriptions, this chalice and that paten were offered together, as a *diskopoterion* set, by Sergios and John, and Pelagios and Sosanna—the former pair being perhaps the unnamed *tekna* ("children") of the latter. Both objects were presented to the church *hyper euches.* See figure I.1.

Interestingly, this and the Riha chalice (no. 30) were both said to have been offered to or owned by T. E. Lawrence (see Chapter II, above). And during that same period (1908–1913), this chalice was linked with two treasures: in 1910 it was for sale in Aleppo or Beirut with chalice no. 27 of the Hama treasure, and in 1912 Ronzevalle noted that the names of its two donors also appeared on objects of the Stuma treasure. (This latter basis for association is now, of course, in considerable doubt.) This chalice and chalice no. 27 both soon found their way to Jerusalem; the latter by 1910, where it remains today, and the former by 1914, when it was bought there by the British Museum.

BIBLIOGRAPHY

Dalton, 1921, 108; Braun, 1932, 78 ff.; Downey, 1951, 353, note 11; Lawrence, 1954, 246; *IGLS,* nos. 210, 2046; Ross, 1962, 11; *idem,* 1968, 147; *idem,* 1973, 14, no. 4, 15; Kent and Painter, 1977, no. 155.

Fig. 29.4

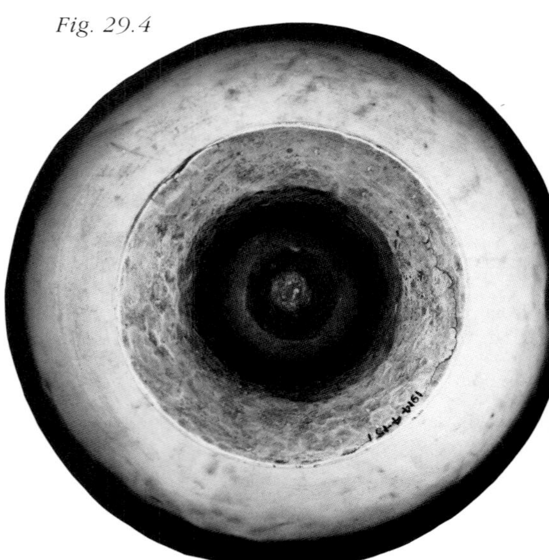

Fig. 29.3

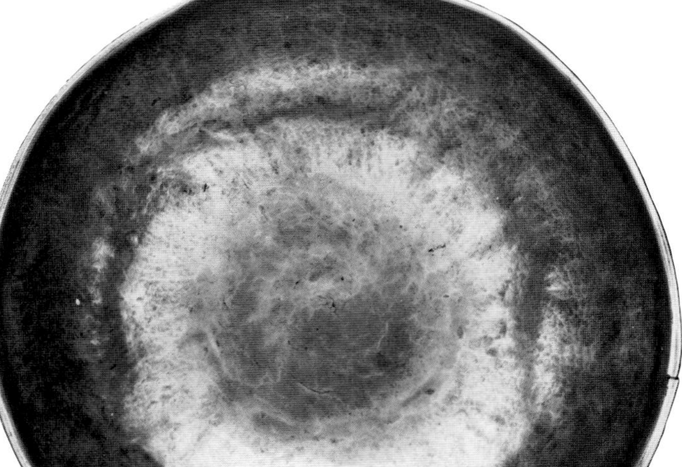

+ ΥΠ ΕΡΕΥΧΗΣΣΕΡΓΙΟΥΚΑΙΙΩΑΝΝΟΥ

+ Ὑπὲρ εὐχῆς Σεργίου καὶ Ἰωάννου.

H	18.6–18.9 cm
D (cup rim)	18.4–18.6 cm
D (foot rim)	9.2 cm
Weight	642.8 gr
Roman Weight	1 lb 11 oz 10 scr
Original Silver Price	7 *solidi* 19 1/3 carats

Fig. 29.2

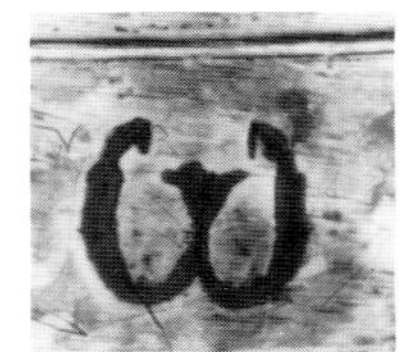

Fig. 30.2

30. CHALICE

POTERION

Figures 30.1–30.5

Washington, D.C., Dumbarton Oaks Collection,
no. 55.18

Riha Treasure, 542(?)

For compositional analysis, see Chapter III, Appendix III.2.

This chalice has a wide, bulbous cup supported by a flaring foot with a knob and short stem above (fig. 30.3). An inscription surrounds the top of the cup (figs. 30.2, 30.3), banded by one turned line above, and a shallow concave moulding between two lines below. Three sets of lines encircle the foot. Gilding still highlights the upper turned borders and spills over onto the inscribed band. Five stamps appear inside the foot (figs. 30.1, 30.5).

(The following is based in part on personal examination of the object in the company of S. Boyd, curator, and in part on observations made at the Center for Conservation and Technical Studies, Fogg Art Museum, Harvard University [E. Holmberg, C. Forsythe, A. Beale: 9/76, 10/76; C. Craine: 1/77].) This chalice was made in two parts, cup and foot, probably from the same melt of metal (a single sheet having an average thickness of .1 cm). Both were formed by hammering, the marks of which are still visible on their interior surfaces. Since no join is visible on the outside, the cup and foot were perhaps affixed to one another by the method described for chalice no. 29, that is, by a silver collar soldered to the base of the cup, used as a seating for the foot stem, and subsequently worked smooth. In the bottom of the cup is a flattened mass of silver (D *ca.* 1 cm) with six hexagonally arranged tool marks. The chalice was lathe-turned to finish the surface and engrave the decorative lines. The letters of the inscription were chased and keyed for the niello inlay, which has a shiny gray surface, and can be seen to be in two layers inside the second *epsilon* of *prospheromen.* The presence of mercury and the smeared edges of gilded areas may indicate the mercury gilding method (Lechtman, 1971, 10). Until restored in 1976, this chalice was thoroughly blackened, and its foot was bent. There are dents, scratches, and abrasions all over the surface and a vertical crack (1.5 cm) in the rim above the *sigma* of *soi.* The niello is missing from most letters, and it has bubbled in the letters *prospher,* perhaps in antiquity.

STAMPS

These stamps were dated by Dodd (1961, no. 8) to 542 because of the presence of the monograms of Justinian (527–565) and Peter, whom she took to be Peter Barsymes, *comes sacrarum largitionum* in 539–542(?) (and 547–550+). (See Entry no. 1.) The secondary box monograms (as opposed to cross monograms) suggest a dating relatively early in Justinian's reign (Weigand, 1937, 130). These are the earliest stamps among the four treasures of Stuma, Riha, Hama, and Antioch. There is no square stamp, and the hexagonal stamp was applied twice.

Fig. 30.4

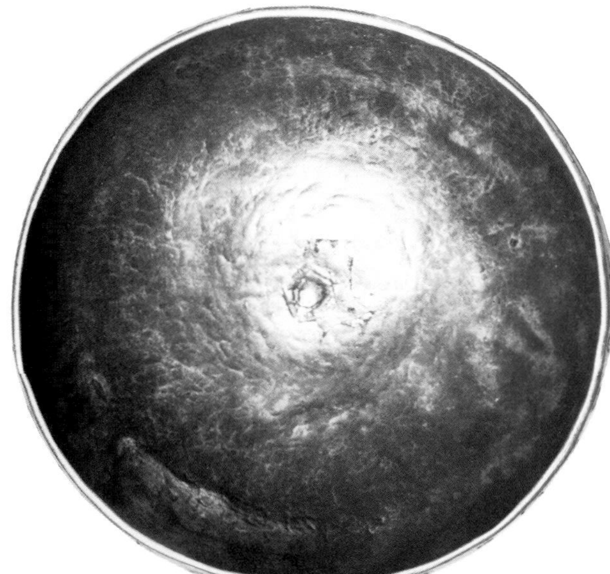

ϮΤΑϹΑЄΚΤωΝϹωΝϹΟΙ
ΠΡΟϹΦЄΡΟΜЄΝΚ̅Є

\+ Τὰ σὰ ἐκ τῶν σῶν σοὶ προσφέρομεν Κ(ύρι)ε.

As classified by Dodd, they may be read as follows:

a. Round: nimbed bust; inscribed *BACCHOU.*

b. Hexagonal: monogram of Justinian (or Anastasius); inscribed *PIENTIOU.*

b. Hexagonal: monogram of Justinian (or Anastasius); inscribed *PIENTIOU.*

c. Square: missing.

d. Long: nimbed bust; monogram of Peter; inscribed *SERGIOU.*

e. Cross: monogram of Peter; inscribed *THOMAS.*

H	17.5 cm
D (cup rim)	15.9 cm
D (foot rim)	10.0 cm
Weight	527.7 gr
Roman Weight	1 lb 7 oz 8 scr
Original Silver Price	6 *solidi* 10 2/3 carats

Fig. 30.3

Fig. 30.1

BAX||XOV

ΠΙЄΝ||[ΤΙ]ΟV

[ΠΙЄΝ]||ΤΙΟV

ϹϹΡ||[ΓΙΟV]

Θ||[ω||ΜΑ]||Ϲ⁎

Inscription

+ *Thine own, from Thine own, we offer Thee, Lord.*

Chased, engraved, nielloed (H of letters = 1.0 cm). *IGLS,* no. 694; Downey, 1951, 351; Dodd, 1961, no. 8; Ross, 1962, no. 9.

The letters are lunate and consistent in size; serifs are used regularly. One *omega* (of *ton*) has a distinctive cross barring the center vertical and *Kyrie* is abbreviated with a bar.

The barred *omega* is found in other sixth-century contexts, including some inscriptions on Sion treasure objects, and the superscript bar abbreviation appears also on the Phela paten and seal (nos. 60, 66). The inscription was first published in *IGLS,* where *Kyrie* was mistakenly written out in full. The text was there identified as coming from the liturgy of John Chrysostom (Brightman and Hammond, 1896, 386), and as being used as well in sixth-century dedicatory inscriptions in Constantinople (on the altar of Hagia Sophia; Cedrenus, I, 677), Ephesos, and Syria (*IGLS;* Downey). It appears also at Mount Nebo (*ca.* 597), Nicaea, and, most relevant here, in precisely the same form on the large bronze cross at Mount Sinai (on all these examples, see Weitzmann and Ševčenko, 1963, 393 f.).

Commentary

In its very broad cup and relatively thick foot, this, the Riha or "Tyler chalice," most closely resembles another of our Type A chalices (on which, see Entry no. 1): that in London (no. 29). The concave moulding on the cup of the vessel reappears on the Riha ewers (nos. 37, 38), and on one Hama chalice (no. 2). The Riha chalice is, therefore, formally linked to other objects in the reconstructed Kaper Koraon Treasure, although at the same time it differs from them by the impersonal nature of its inscribed text, and by the early date of its stamps. That this chalice was shown after cleaning to have a "pitted" surface supports its association with the Riha treasure, whose two ewers (nos. 37, 38) are in a similar condition. Its early purchase date (1913) in Paris, where the Riha paten then apparently was, provides further corroboration (see Chapter II, above).

Selected Bibliography

For earlier bibliography, see Ross, 1962, no. 9. See also, Bréhier, 1919, 420; *IGLS*, no. 694; Downey, 1951, 351; Dodd, 1961, no. 8; Weitzmann and Ševčenko, 1963, 394, note 53; Elbern, 1963; Dodd, 1973, no. 1, 14 f.

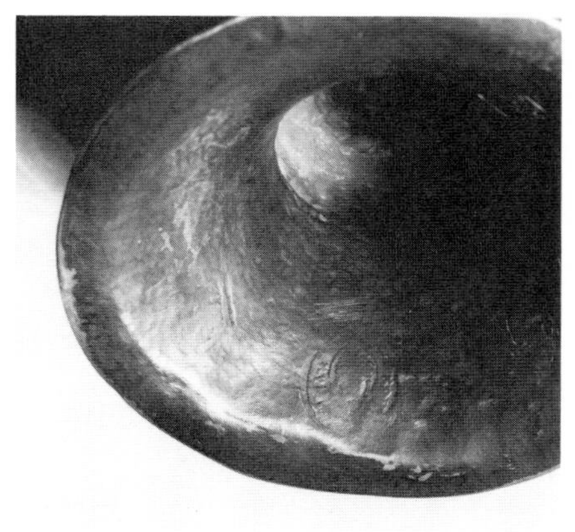

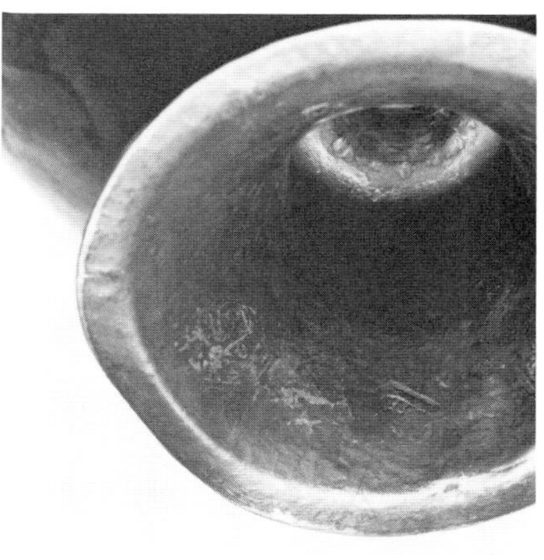

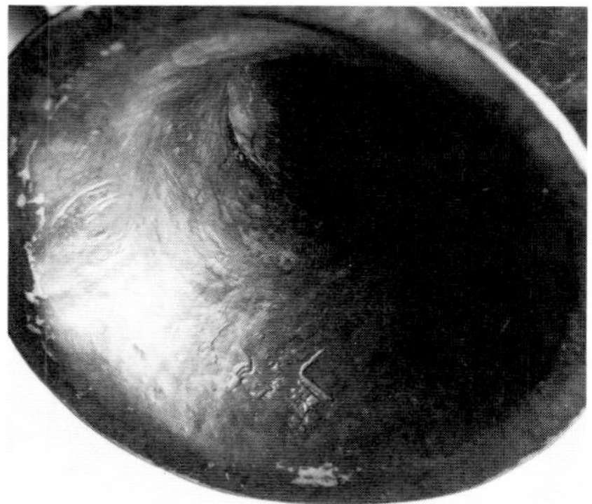

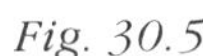

Fig. 30.5

31. FAN

RHIPIDION

Figures 31.1–31.6

Istanbul, Archaeological Museum, no. 3758

Stuma Treasure, 577(?)

This fan, which consists of a disc with scalloped edges and tang, forms a pair with no. 32 (the Riha fan). Each of its faces is decorated with a seraph flanked by fiery wheels, and its sixteen scallops are worked as peacock feathers (figs. 31.2, 31.3). The incised line decoration is given greater definition on the front, where the face of the seraph is in relief (contrast figs. 31.4, 31.5). Gilding was applied on both sides to seraphs (except hands and feet), wheels, and border. Four stamps were applied to the front of the tang, which has a hole for attachment to a staff (figs. 31.1, 31.6).

This fan was apparently cast as one piece, but not in the same mold as the Riha fan, as their contours differ slightly. The thick edges of both fans turn up slightly towards the front, and on this one there is a depression (D .4 cm) in the front just below the seraph's head, which was probably made when the object was turned on a lathe to cut the lines of the circular field. The metal is thick at the center of the fan where it was worked from the front to form the seraph's head. Both surfaces were burnished horizontally (see also nos. 34–36) before the execution of the decoration, which is incised to two different depths on both sides. The feathers on the front are defined by short, firm strokes, and those on the back in loose, shallow strokes. At least some of the gilding was applied as foil, torn pieces of which are visible in the tool marks of the feathers of both seraphim, and of the borders. The stamps were apparently struck before the decoration, as the feathers are arranged around the top stamp (see Dodd, 1973, 36 ff.). The hole for attachment to a staff was punched from the back, after stamping. The fan's lobed border has been broken off on the right side in three places, and from the largest of these, a crack runs to the top of the right wheel. Its tang, like that of no. 32, has a groove impressed into it from having been affixed to a staff.

Fig. 31.1

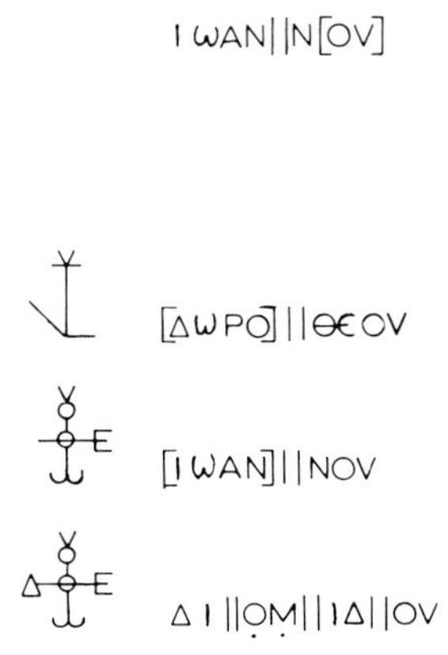

IWAN||N[OV]

[ΔWPO]||ΘЄOV

[IWAN]||NOV

ΔI||OM||IΔ||OV

Fig. 31.6

STAMPS

These stamps were dated by Dodd (1961, no. 22) to 577 because of the monograms of Justin II (565–578) and Theodore, whom she took to be Theodore Petri, *comes sacrarum largitionum* of 577. (See Entries nos. 32, 35.) As classified by Dodd, the stamps may be read, with one minor emendation (fig. 31.1), as follows:

a. **Round**: nimbed bust; inscribed *IWANNOU.*
b. **Hexagonal**: ? (border only).
c. **Square**: monogram of Justin II; inscribed *DOROTHEOU.*
d. **Long**: nimbed bust; monogram of Theodore; inscribed *IWANNOU.*
e. **Cross**: monogram of Theodore; inscribed *DIOMIDOU.*

COMMENTARY

See Entry no. 32.

BIBLIOGRAPHY

Ebersolt, 1911, 407 ff.; Bréhier, 1920, 175, 186; Rosenberg, 1928, vol. 4, 634 f.; *Exposition,* 1931, no. 757; Braun, 1932, no. 646; *DACL,* vol. 5, cols. 1623 f.; Dodd, 1961, no. 22; *Byzantine Art,* 1964, no. 684; Dodd, 1968, 147; Wessel, 1971, cols. 550 f.; *Age,* 1979, no. 553.

Fig. 31.2

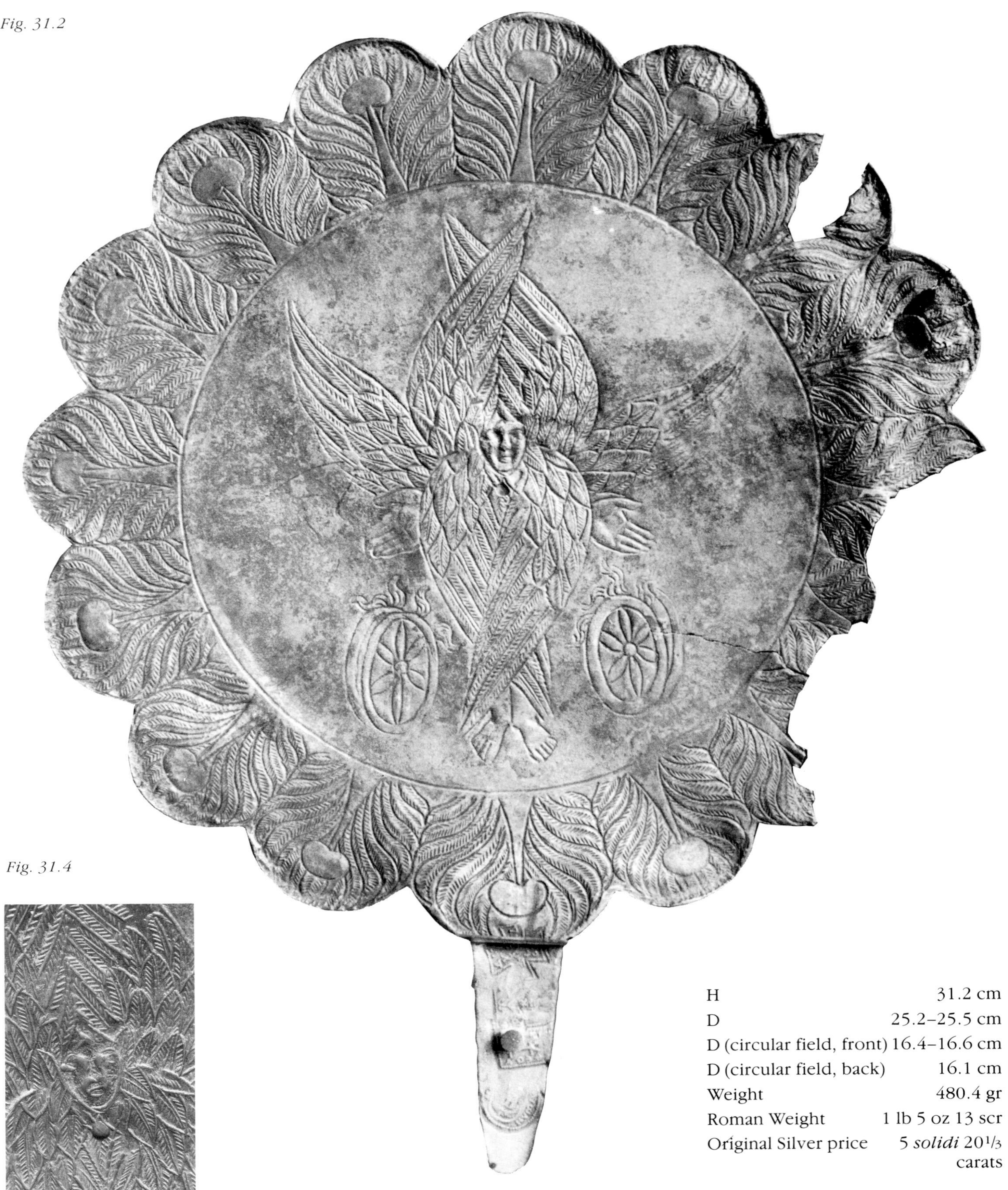

Fig. 31.4

H	31.2 cm
D	25.2–25.5 cm
D (circular field, front)	16.4–16.6 cm
D (circular field, back)	16.1 cm
Weight	480.4 gr
Roman Weight	1 lb 5 oz 13 scr
Original Silver price	5 *solidi* 20 1/3 carats

Fig. 31.3

Fig. 31.5

32. FAN

RHIPIDION

Figures 32.1–32.7

Washington, D.C., Dumbarton Oaks Collection,
no. 36.23

Riha Treasure, 577(?)

For compositional analysis, see Chapter III, Appendix III.2.

This fan, which consists of a disc with scalloped edges and a tang, forms a pair with no. 31 (the Stuma fan). Each of its faces is decorated with a cherub, or *tetramorph,* flanked by fiery wheels, and its sixteen scallops are worked as peacock feathers (figs. 32.2, 32.3). The incised line decoration is given greater definition on the front, where three of the cherub's four heads are in relief (contrast figs. 32.4, 32.5). Gilding was applied on both sides to cherubim (except hands and feet), wheels, and border. A black substance (niello?) fills the mouths and feather eyes of the beast. Four (or five) stamps appear on the back of the tang, which has a hole for attachment to a staff (figs. 32.1, 32.6).

The stages of manufacture described for Stuma fan no. 31 apply to this one as well, except that the obverse central turning point (D .4 cm) here coincides with the human mouth of the *tetramorph.* Oval and crescent punches (the former struck inside chased circles) were used for feather eyes front and back, respectively. The stamps on the reverse of the tang were said by Dodd (1973, 36 ff.) to have been applied after the decoration, as the top stamp seems to overlap the border feathers. However, it should be pointed out that part of the feather cuts into the left side of the cross stamp which, furthermore, was struck higher up on the tang than was that on the Stuma fan. This suggests that here, as there, the stamps were struck before the decoration was applied.

The one and a half scallops which have been torn from the right border of this fan correspond to the (greater) damaged area on Riha fan no. 31 (see Chapter I, above). There are also small holes in the adjoining scallops, and in others as well. Two patches (L 3.2 and 2.3 cm) of (modern?) silver have been soldered onto the back of the broken scallops, and another repair (L 1.6 cm) has been made to the top feather. The area below the missing scallops (at 4 o'clock on the front) was further damaged in 1978 and subsequently restored (report of C. Craine, Center for Conservation and Technical Studies, Fogg Art Museum, Harvard University, 6/78). The tang, like that on fan no. 31, has a groove impressed into it from having been affixed to a staff.

STAMPS

These stamps were dated by Dodd (1961, no. 21) to 577, because of the monograms of Justin II (565–578) and Theodore, whom she took to be Theodore Petri, *comes sacrarum largitionum,* in 577 (see Entries nos. 31, 35). As classified by Dodd, the stamps may be read as follows:

a. Round: nimbed bust; inscribed *IWANNOU.*
b. Hexagonal: ? (obscured by square stamp?).
c. Square: monogram of Justin II; inscribed *DOROTHEOU.*
d. Long: nimbed bust; monogram of Theodore; inscribed *IWANNOU.*
e. Cross: monogram of Theodore; inscribed *DIOMIDOU.*

Fig. 32.1

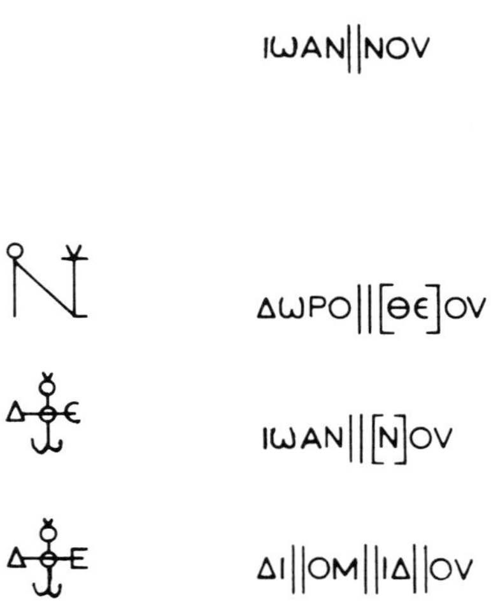

ΙωΑΝ||ΝΟV

ΔωΡΟ||[ΘЄ]ΟV

ΙωΑΝ||[Ν]ΟV

ΔΙ||ΟΜ||ΙΔ||ΟV

Fig. 32.6

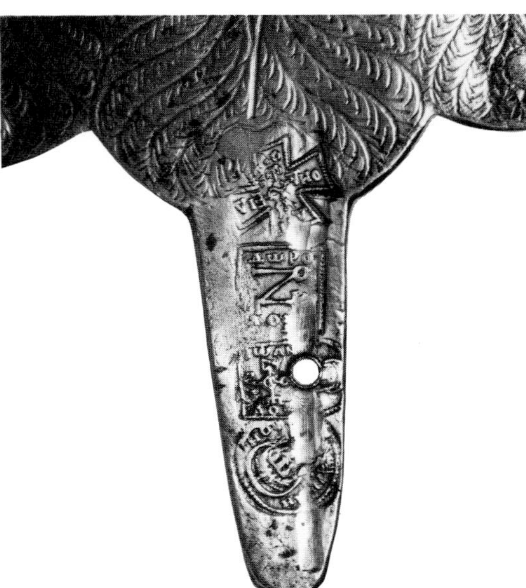

Commentary

The fan (Greek = *rhipidion;* Latin = *flabellum*) is attested in the liturgy by the end of the fourth century. In the Clementine rite, as preserved in the *Apostolic Constitutions* (VIII.12.3–4; *ca.* 375), two deacons stand by the altar and wave fans "of fine skin, peacock feathers or cloth" to prevent flies from settling on the sacrament. The number of fans used in one service reached twelve (Connolly and Codrington, 1913, 22). Although not listed among donations in the *Liber Pontificalis* between 312 and 642, the liturgical fan is mentioned by John Moschos (*PS,* ch. 150) as being employed in an Italian church in 535/6. The pair from the Stuma and Riha treasures, stamped in the year 577(?), are the earliest extant fans, and predate the "precious *rhipidia*" in use in 624 in Hagia Sophia, Constantinople (*Chron. Pasc.,* I, 714).

In the center of the Stuma fan (no. 31) is portrayed a *hexapterygon,* or six-winged creature, with face and feet, one of the seraphim which cried the *Tersanctus* before the Throne of God in the Vision of Isaiah (Isaiah 6.3). In the center of the Riha fan is a cherub, the four-winged creature that guarded the Gates of Eden (Genesis 3.24) and the Throne of God in the Vision of Ezekiel (Ezekiel 1.5 ff.; 10), where their wings were covered with eyes and they each had hands, feet, and four faces (of a lion, an eagle, a man, and an ox)—whence they are also called *tetramorphs.* Between them were fiery wheels. In the Book of Revelation (4.7 f.), the two creatures are fused; there, the beasts that sing the *Tersanctus* combine the seraph's six wings covered in cherub's eyes with the latter's four heads as revealed to Ezekiel. It is not surprising, therefore, that the two were often confused in the Byzantine mind (Mango, 1962, 85 f.), and that the cherubim's wheels accompany the seraphim on the Stuma fan. The seraphim and cherubim were two of the nine orders of angels guarding the Throne of God, and so, like the gold-encrusted cherubim placed over the Ark of the Covenant in the Temple of Solomon, their presence on the fans protecting the sacrament is particularly appropriate. Cherubim stood before the sanctuary of Hagia Sophia in Edessa (McVey, 1983, 95; after 525)—that is, on a ten-columned chancel screen and not, as often stated (*ibid.,* 105), on the ciborium (which had only four columns [*Chron. 1234,* I, 180])—and seraphim hover in the ninth-

Fig. 32.2

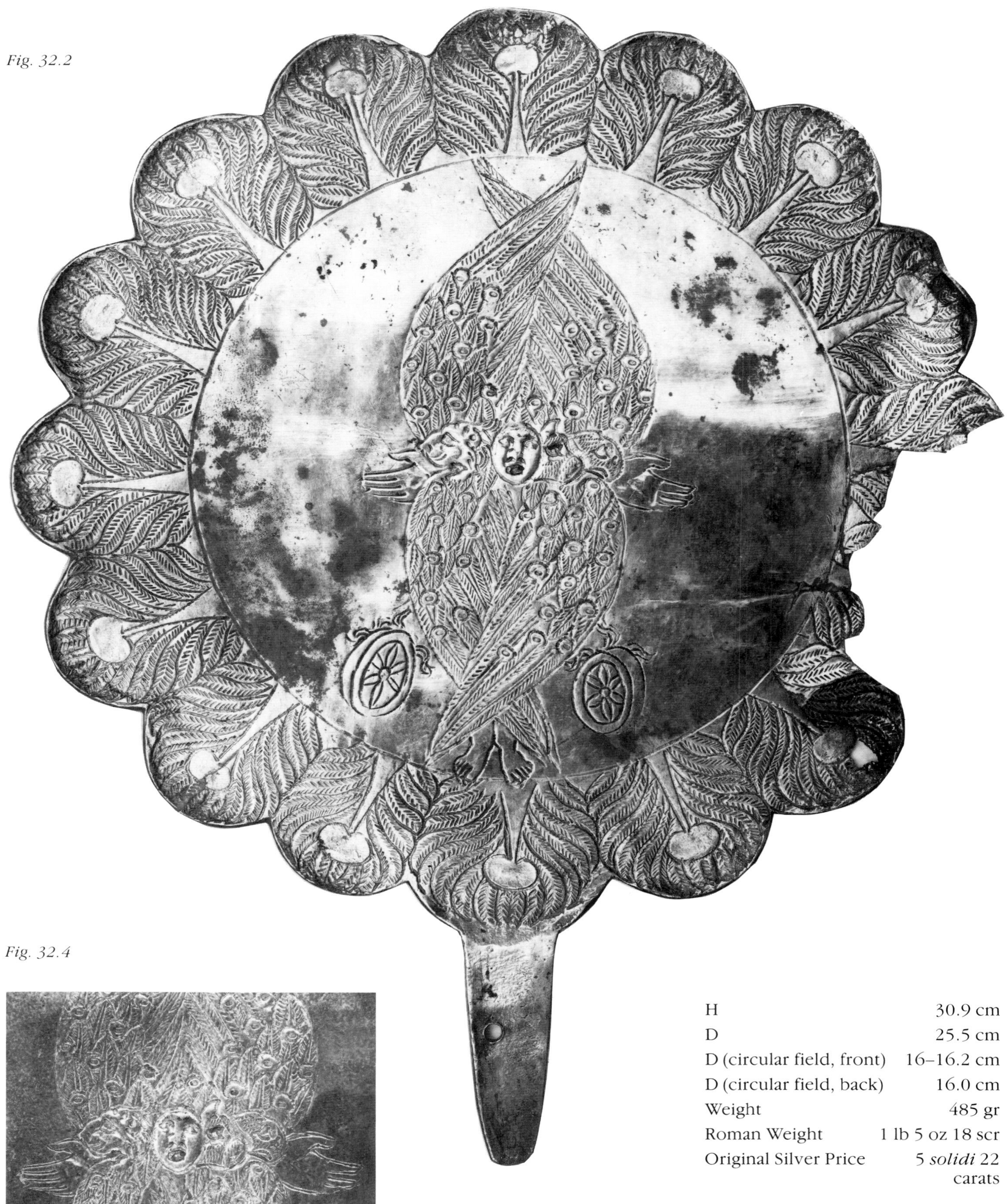

Fig. 32.4

H	30.9 cm
D	25.5 cm
D (circular field, front)	16–16.2 cm
D (circular field, back)	16.0 cm
Weight	485 gr
Roman Weight	1 lb 5 oz 18 scr
Original Silver Price	5 *solidi* 22 carats

Fig. 32.3

Fig. 32.5

century mosaics on the central dome pendentives of Hagia Sophia in Constantinople (Mango, 1962, 83 ff.). The peacock feathers bordering these fans recall both the use of such feathers for *rhipidia* from Hellenistic times (Daremberg and Saglio, 1151 f.; a tradition still observed in the seventeenth-century Vatican [*Euchologion,* 137]), and the eyes of the *tetramorph's* wings.

The name of the seraph, *hexapterygon,* was eventually extended to the fan itself. The description by Job the Monk (sixth century; Photios, *Bibliotheca,* cod. 222 [*PG* 103, col. 769B]) of fans of feathers bearing symbols of *hexapteryga,* is taken further in a contemporary prayer. The offertory *anaphora* preceding the *Tersanctus* of the reconstructed Syrian liturgy (fifth to eighth century) identifies the fans themselves as *hexapteryga,* and intertwines that name with those of their supernatural prototypes: "angels serving with *hexapteryga* covering the mystical table in the presence of the cherubim and seraphim . . ." (Brightman and Hammond, 1896, vol. 1, 482).

While not in use, silver-gilt *rhipidia* like these, mounted on staffs, may have been exhibited in the sanctuary by the altar together with other liturgical treasures (see the *Chron. Pasc.,* I, 714, where they were removed to the *skeuophylakion*). The eleventh-century commentary on the liturgy by Yahya Ibn Jarir speaks of *flabella* placed to the right and left of the altar, which he compares both to the two thieves on the crosses and to the two cherubim that guarded the Temple sanctuary (McVey, 1983, 104). A Syriac manuscript of around 1220 seems to illustrate precisely such a display (fig. 32.7; Leroy, 1964, 303, pl. 74.1), and a partially destroyed mosaic of 512 at Qartamin Monastery in Mesopotamia may likewise have shown a cherub-decorated *flabellum* standing over an altar (Hawkins and Mundell, 1973, 293).

The sequence of decoration of both fans as proposed by Dodd (1973, 35 ff.) does not take adequate account of the four surfaces involved, only three of which figure in her scheme. The obverse of the Stuma fan is identified by Dodd as the reverse, because the stamps were applied to that side of the tang; the true reverse, which is virtually identical in technique to the reverse of the Riha fan, is thus omitted from the discussion. In fact, the obverse of the Stuma fan shows no trace of Dodd's suggested "reworking" from a "preliminary sketch" (of the type on the reverse). A conclusion that the two fans were finished in separate workshops is thus difficult to accept, considering the close similarity of craftsmanship observed in every detail.

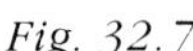
Fig. 32.7

Selected Bibliography

For earlier bibliography, see Ross, 1962, no. 11. See also, Dodd, 1961, no. 21; *DO Handbook,* 1967, no. 62; Dodd, 1968, 147; Wessel, 1971, cols. 550 f.; Dodd, 1973, 25 ff.; Kent and Painter, 1977, no. 145; *Age,* 1979, no. 553.

33. LAMP

FARUM CANTHARUM?

Figures 33.1–33.5

Bern, Abegg Stiftung, no. 8.114.64

Stuma Treasure, 574–576/578

This standing lamp with footring has a convex base and flaring sides that terminate in a short, upright rim with a rounded edge (fig. 33.3). The convex base is worked in a series of interlocking lobes, with sixteen pointing down and sixteen up. Encircling the sides above is a band of four palmettes alternating with four spear-shaped leaves, joined at their bases by a simple swag. The upright rim bears a niello inscription (figs. 33.2, 33.3). Thick gilding highlights the rim, the plant motifs, and the outlines of the ovoid lobes on the base, creating a bold contrast of silver and gold patterns. Five stamps appear on the bottom of the lamp (figs. 33.1, 33.5).

This lamp was formed by hammering from a single sheet of metal. The top of the upright rim was hammered into a rounded edge, like that on several patens in this catalogue (e.g., nos. 4–6, 34–36). There is no sign of attachment for the footring, which may have been formed, like that of Hama lamp no. 13, by folding the metal back on itself. Hammer marks are visible inside the lamp and within the footring. The final shaping and exterior finishing were done on a lathe, whose clamping mark is found within the footring. Decorative lines were also cut on the lathe, including those at the top and bottom of the upright rim, and the faint ones on the footring. The set of pronounced lines running through the base of the plant and the top of the lobed motifs corresponds to similar turned bands on Hama lamp no. 13, and here probably represents an early, abandoned stage of decoration. The repoussé ornament on the vertical surfaces of this lamp was probably pushed out from behind and finished from the front. A combination here of drop-shaped gouging and dotted, chased outlines recalls the tool marks on the Stuma and Riha patens (nos. 34, 35), and on Antioch plaques nos. 44 and 45. No trace of gold foil was discernible under microscopic examination, and the fact that thick gilding has run over some of the outlines suggests mercury gilding (Lechtman, 1971, 10). The stamps were applied after the lamp was hammered and turned on a lathe.

One large area of the lamp—including one whole leaf and more than half a palmette—was replaced at an unknown period with a palmette differing in detail from the others (fig. 33.4). While the silver of the restored area has, on the outside, a different surface and patina than the original, and lacks all trace of gilding, there is little evidence of the repair on the inside. There are several unrepaired holes in the lamp, including three to the left of the restored area, one in a palmette, and others in the lobed base. Niello is missing from only one letter.

STAMPS

These stamps were dated by Dodd (1968, no. 27.1) to 578–582, because of the presence of the monogram of Tiberius Constantine. It is probable, however, that the appearance of the monogram of Justin II (565–578) in another stamp (see also Entry no. 36) indicates the period 574–578, during Justin's insanity

Fig. 33.2

and Tiberius' caesarship, when the latter took the name Constantine (John of Ephesos, *HE,* III.5). (Alternatively, though less likely, the stamps could date specifically to their joint reign of September 26 to October 5, 578 [Grumel, 1958, 356]. On their joint coinage at Antioch in that short period, see Bellinger, 1966, 263.) Peter, a *comes sacrarum largitionum* whose monogram appears in two stamps, could therefore be placed either 574–576 or 578; that is, before or after Theodore Petri, who is known to have held that office in 577? The stamps on this lamp are virtually identical to those on Stuma paten no. 34. As classified by Dodd, they may be read, with one very minor emendation (fig. 33.1), as follows:

a. Round: nimbed bust; inscribed *STEPHANOU.*
b. Hexagonal: bust; monogram of Justin II; inscribed *MEGALOU.*
c. Square: monogram of Tiberius Constantine; unidentified inscription.
d. Long: nimbed bust; monogram of Peter; inscribed *IWANNIS.*
e. Cross: monogram of Peter; inscribed *SEBASTOU.*

Fig. 33.1

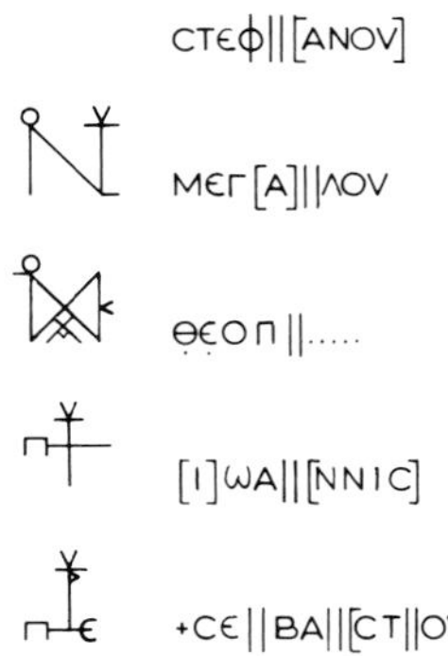

Inscription

+ *In fulfillment of a vow and (for) the salvation of SERGIOS, tribune and argyroprates, and (for) the repose (of the soul) of MARIA, his wife, and (of those) of THEIR PARENTS.*

Engraved, chased, nielloed (H of letters = .7 cm). Dodd, 1968, no. 27.1; Dodd, 1973, 8.

The lettering is lunate and uniform in size; serifs are used regularly. Except for *goneon* (the unique mistake, found also on Stuma paten no. 34), the spelling is correct. *Kai* is abbreviated *Ks* (see no. 34), and S is also used as an abbreviation sign after *TRIB* (as on no. 34). The genitive *omicron-upsilon* is here consistently put in ligature, as are *eta-sigma* and *alpha-upsilon.*

The lettering of this inscription most closely resembles that of the Stuma paten (no. 34), which also bears the identical text. The additional ligatures and closer lettering (.1–.2 cm *versus* .8–.9 cm apart), are the result of fitting this text into a shorter space. For remarks on the combination of dedicatory formulae used here (i.e., *hyper euches kai soterias* and *[hyper] anapauseos*), see Entry no. 15. *Tribounos* was a title given to, among others, a state factory official (*PW, tribunus fabricae*) and an *argyroprates* was, literally, a "silver-seller" (and not a silversmith, which would be an *argyrokopos* or *argyropoios*). Taken together, the two titles suggest that Sergios held a position in a state silver factory. This Sergios may well be one and the same as the Sergios who offered a Stuma paten (no. 36) with Anna (then, necessarily, his second wife) in 574–578. It may also be that this Sergios is the son of the John who is named as father of Sergia (that is, his sister) on the Riha paten (no. 35) of 577?. (The Sergios who dedicated the London chalice [no. 29] with a certain John, was probably another individual [see Entries nos. 5, 29].) Because the texts inscribed on this lamp and the Stuma paten (no. 34) are identical, and their stamps virtually so, it may be assumed that the pair formed a joint offering, by Sergios. See figure I.1.

Commentary

This lamp may be described as a type of *kantharos* on a broad foot (Strong, 1966, 163, fig. 34a), and may be a standing version of the suspended *farum cantharum* mentioned in Latin sources (see Entry no. 13). Such lamps are portrayed on the Riha paten (no. 35). The form of the Abegg lamp has been compared by Dodd (1973, 11 f.) to that of contemporary hanging lamps in the Hama (no. 13) and Mytilene treasures (Vavritas, 1957, 319, fig. 3, no. 8), as well as to that in the Hermitage (*idem,* 1973, fig. 3), with which it also shows decorative parallels. Its similarity to the hanging lamp on the Stuma paten may well carry special significance (see Entry no. 34).

†ΥΠΕΡΕΥΧΗϹϗϹΩΤΗΡΙΑϹϹΕΡΓΙȢΤΡΙΒϗΑΡΓΥΡΟΠΡΑΤȢ
ϗΑΝΑΠΑȢϹΕΩϹΜΑΡΙΑϹΤΗϹΑΥΤȢϹΥΜΒΙȢϗΤΩΝΑΥΤΩΝΓΩΝΕΩΝ

+ Ὑπὲρ εὐχῆς κ(αὶ) σωτηρίας Σεργίου τριβ(ούνου) κ(αὶ) ἀργυροπράτου
κ(αὶ) ἀναπαύσεως Μαρίας της αὐτοῦ συμβίου κ(αὶ) τῶν αὐτῶν γωνέων.

H	14.4–14.7 cm
D (rim)	15.8–16.4 cm
D (foot)	8.0 cm
Weight	493 gr
Roman Weight	1 lb 6 oz 1 scr
Original Silver Price	6 *solidi* 1/3 carat

Fig. 33.4

Fig. 33.3

The shape and decoration of this lamp may be traced back to a deep bowl lamp type of Achaemenid origin, which was popular in the Hellenistic period (Strong, 1966, 99 ff.). A late second-century "*vaso*" in the Bosco Marengo treasure could be cited as another prototype in size, shape, and decoration (Bendinelli, 1937, 32 f., pl. XII.2), and attention should also be drawn to the form of the top cup on the fourth-century Kaiseraugst lampstand (Cahn *et al.*, 1984, pl. 51). The palmettes on the Abegg lamp have been compared by Dodd (1973, 12) with those on the Stuma paten (no. 34), the Hermitage lamp, and the cross of Justin II. Such palmettes are related both to the classical acanthus and cornucopia motifs, and to the Sasanian split palmette, which was introduced into Byzantine ornament in the sixth century at Constantinople (St. Polyeuctos, Sts. Sergios and Bacchos, Hagia Sophia), Ravenna (S. Vitale), and Thessaloniki (St. George). (See Spieser, 1984, 135 ff.) These spreading palmettes with interposed spear-shaped leaves correspond, respectively, to the alternating acanthus and *nymphaea caerulea* of Hellenistic ornament (e.g., Strong, 1966, 109, pl. 31A), and recall the classical bands of honeysuckle and acanthus still used throughout the fifth century in Syrian architecture (Beyer, 1925, 46 f.; Strube, 1979).

The lobed ornament on the lower part of this lamp is in the tradition of ancient *phiale* decoration (Strong, 1966, 56 f., 76 f.), but may derive from the later, fourth-century interest in boldly fluted and faceted surfaces (Shelton, 1981, 42 ff.). Similar surface treatment, contemporary with this object, is to be found on the Sion and Stuma patens (see no. 34), in the over-lapping leaf ornament on Hama flask no. 15, and on objects in the Luxor treasure (Strzygowski, 1904, nos. 7201–7210). It also appears on the many amphorae with lobed bodies shown in tessellated pavements, and considered characteristic of the latest mosaics at Antioch (see Hawkins and Mundell, 1973, 285). The heavy outlining of the eggs on this lamp is comparable to the treatment of the border on a Traprain Law flagon (Curle, 1923, no. 8). Here, the striking coloristic contrast achieved through gilding emphasizes and transforms the ornament. The gilt outlines of the interlocking lobes suggest a reticulate pattern on the base, faintly reminiscent both of two-zone plaited capitals and of *à jour* lamps (e.g., in the Sion treasure).

Bibliography

Dodd, 1968, no. 27.1; *idem,* 1973, no. 3; Kent and Painter, 1977, 83; Feissel, 1985, 470; Boyd, 1986; Mundell-Mango, 1986.

Fig. 33.5

34. PATEN

DISKOS

Figures 34.1–34.8

Istanbul, Archaeological Museum, no. 3759

Stuma Treasure, 574–576/578

This paten has high, sloping sides, a flat narrow rim, but no foot (figs. 34.3, 34.5). The inner surface is decorated with the Communion of the Apostles in relief (fig. 34.6): Christ, represented twice standing behind an altar under a ciborium, distributes wine from a chalice to six Apostles on the left, and bread to six others on the right. The scene is framed by a border of egg and palmette motifs, which fills the sloping sides. The flat outer rim bears an inscription (figs. 34.2, 34.3). The rim, the border between the eggs, and the figural decoration were gilded. Five stamps appear on the back (figs. 34.1, 34.4, 34.7).

This paten was formed by hammering, the marks of which remain visible on the reverse. The outer edge of its rim was rolled forward to form a raised border which is round in profile. The front of the object was burnished smooth, apparently in two stages, for concentric turnings appear on the rim and horizontal ones on the inner surface. Two turning points are visible, one in the center of the back and one in the front. The inscription was chased (note impression on back of plate). The relief decoration was apparently first hammered out from behind; the heads of the two Christs and the legs of four Apostles in the foreground are in very high relief, while the heads of the other Apostles are slightly less prominent. A variety of techniques and tools was used to finish the decoration on the front; blunt and round tools were employed, respectively, for straight lines (of noses, mouths, hair, palmettes, pleated drapery, and sandal straps) and for tear-drop gouges (for drapery folds, canopy foliage, and the groundline). Two punches (the larger = .1 cm) were used for eye pupils, and for borders and ornamental patterns on the canopy, hanging lamp, haloes, garment borders, and table cloth; tonsures were stippled. Gilding was applied in foil, large rectangular patches of which are clearly visible on the lower right side of the central composition.

Most of the damage to this paten is confined to its right side. As on the other two Stuma patens (nos. 36, 39), there is here a long diagonal dent, in this case extending from the center of the altar top to about 2 o'clock on the outer side, where a section of the rim has been lost. Metal is also missing from the inscription to either side of this hole, and from letters at about 10 o'clock. There are tears in the egg border near 3 o'clock, and a second, curved dent (made by another plate?) is in the lower egg border (visible on the back). The upper right border has apparently been straightened out since 1908 (contrast figs. 34.3, 34.8; Ebersolt, 1911), but there is still corrosion on both sides of the plate, so that much of the inscription is obscured. There is a coppery glow to the surface, and its gilded areas have a greenish cast. Niello is missing from the inscription, particularly at the top of the plate and on the right along the tear; niello has flowed out of the words *autou symbiou* (near 10 o'clock), perhaps in antiquity.

STAMPS

These stamps were dated by Dodd (1961, no. 27) to 578, because of the monograms of Justin II (565–578) and Peter, a *comes sacrarum largitionum* who apparently served after Theodore Petri (577), and later, under Tiberius Constantine (578–582). It is probable, however, that the second square-stamp monogram, which Dodd read as that of Justin II, is in fact that of Tiberius Constantine, making these stamps

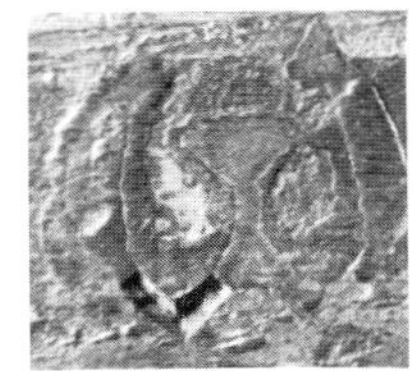

Fig. 34.2

virtually identical to those on lamp no. 33 in the Abegg Stiftung, which also has a dedicatory inscription identical to this one (see that Entry for details). As classified by Dodd, the stamps may be read, with some emendation, as follows:

a. Round: nimbed bust; inscribed *STEPHANOU.*
b. Hexagonal: bust; monogram of Justin II; inscribed *MEGALOU.*
c. Square: monogram of Tiberius Constantine; unidentified inscription.
d. Long: monogram of Peter; inscribed *IWANNIS.*
e. Cross: monogram of Peter; inscribed *SEBASTOU.*

Inscription

+ *In fulfillment of a vow and (for) the salvation of SERGIOS, tribune and argyroprates, and (for) the repose (of the soul) of MARIA, his wife, and (of those) of THEIR PARENTS.*

Engraved, chased, nielloed (H of letters = .8 cm). Ebersolt, 1911, 417; *IGLS,* no. 698.

All the observations made regarding the inscription on lamp no. 33, which has the identical text, apply here, except that in this case *kai* is abbreviated once as *K,* and the genitive *omicron-upsilon* is written out, as well as put in ligature.

The inscription as published by Ebersolt has one serious omission, which follows *Sergiou* in the second line. Ebersolt completed this as *t(ou),* whereas the text clearly reads *trib(ounou) k(ai),* just as on lamp no. 33. The omission is repeated in *IGLS,* and the supplied *tou* led Dodd (1973, 8 ff., 46) to conclude that Sergios had acquired a second title, that of tribune, by the time he donated the lamp. In fact, the two inscriptions are identical and contemporary. For remarks on the text of this inscription, see Entry no. 33. See also figure I.1.

Commentary

This plate and the related one, no. 35, were both dedicated donations, intended, as indicated by their size and form, to be church patens (see Entry no. 4). They differ from all other contemporary patens in being decorated with a narrative scene: the Communion of the Apostles, a symbolic/liturgical portrayal of the Last Supper. These two patens, of 574–578, bear the earliest dated examples of this composition, which is also found in the sixth-century Rossano Gospels in a more symmetrical and elongated form, which itself was apparently derived from a monumental painting (Ainalov, 1900) once found on the apse wall of the Church of the Last Supper on Mount Sion (Loerke, 1975; see also Schrader, 1979, 147 ff.).

Because of their obvious resemblance and related provenance, these two patens have often been discussed together, although it is their differences in style and details of composition that have usually been emphasized. Their similarities, nevertheless, are striking. It is known—or has been established here—that: 1) the two were found together (see Chapter II, above); 2) their stamps are dated to virtually the same years; 3) the name of the donor of the Riha paten, Megas (an unusual name; see Feissel, 1985), appears as an official in a stamp applied to the Stuma paten (Dodd, 1973, 46); and 4) Sergios, the donor of the latter, was both tribune and silver-seller, a fact suggesting employment in a state silver factory (see no. 33). The broader implications of the relationship of Megas and Sergios, and of their careers in the state silver industry (see Chapter I, above) predispose one to reconsider their patens as objects manufactured, decorated, and stamped in the same workshop.

Fig. 34.1

+CTEΦ||ANȢ
MEΓA||ΛOV
OCIN||...
IW[A]||NN[IC]
+CE||[BA]||CT||[OV]

Fig. 34.7

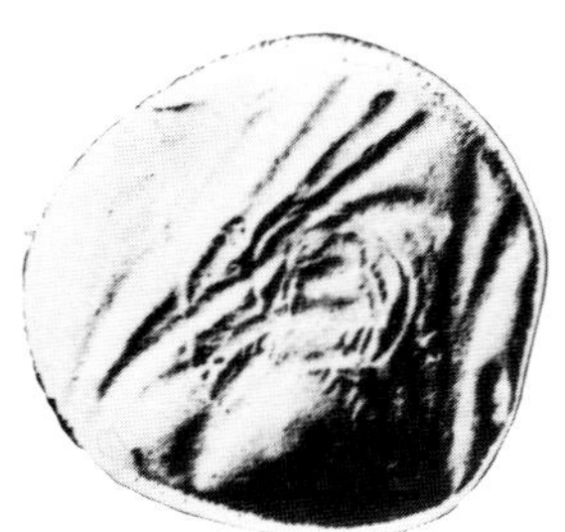

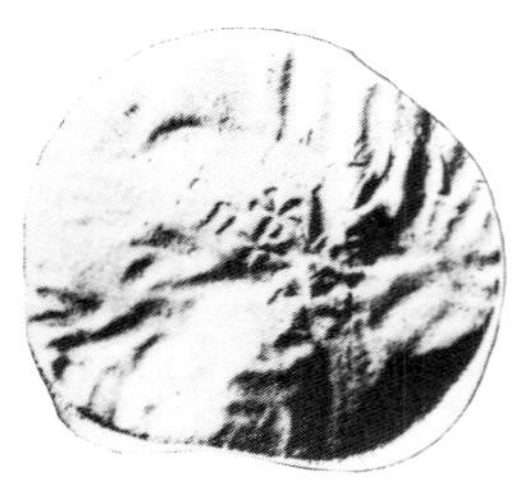

+ ΥΠΕΡΕΥΧΗϹ ϏϹ[…] ΙΑϹϹΕΡΓΙΟΥΤΡΙΒˢ ϏΑΡΓΥΡΟΠΡΑΤΟΥϏ
ΑΝΑΠΑΥϹΕΩϹΜΑΡΙΑϹΤΗϹΑΥΤΟΥϹΥΜΒΙ ϏΤΩΝΑΥΤΩΝΓΩΝΕΩΝ

+Ὑπὲρ εὐχῆς κ(αὶ) σ[ωτηρ]ίας Σεργίου τριβ(ούνου) κ(αὶ) ἀργυροπράτου κ(αὶ) ἀναπαύσεως Μαρίας τῆς αὐτοῦ συμβίου κ(αὶ) τῶν αὐτῶν γωνέων.

D	36.5–36.8 cm
H	2.8–3.1 cm
Weight	836.6 gr
Roman Weight	2 lbs 6 oz 7 scr
Original Silver Price	10 *solidi* 2 1/3 carats

Fig. 34.3

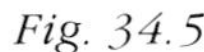
Fig. 34.5

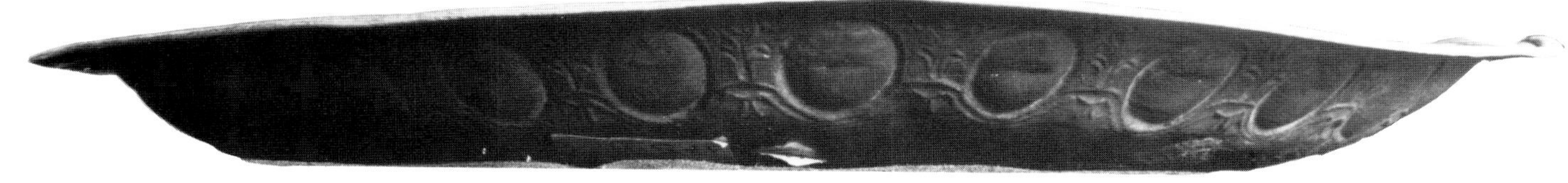

The dimensions of the two patens are particularly close and, most importantly, their inner surfaces bearing the figural composition are of precisely the same diameter (27 cm). The burnishing technique used on both patens (and on Sergios' second paten, no. 36) differs from that used on other contemporary silver plates. Also highly distinctive among eastern patens is the positioning of the inscription on the rim of these two and of Sergios' paten no. 36. Moreover, the letter forms on both objects (and on Sergios' contemporary lamp, no. 33) virtually coincide.

Although very similar techniques and tools were used to execute the figural compositions on both patens, the two craftsmen responsible worked in different styles and composed their scenes somewhat differently. The view (Dodd, 1973, 40 ff.) that the individual who decorated the Riha paten was a more gifted artist than the individual responsible for the Stuma paten may provide the key to the production of the two objects. In seeming contradiction to this appraisal, it can be argued that not only is the Stuma paten as well executed in its own way as is the Riha, but that the Stu-

Fig. 34.4

Fig. 34.6

ma's figures are, in fact, superior in anatomy, volume, and drapery to the cramped Apostles on the other plate. This is observed most clearly in the lower half of the four profile figures in the foreground of the Stuma paten, where the legs emerge solidly from their softly pleated garments, which are no more "turned into conventional pattern" (Kitzinger, 1958, 19) than are those on the David plates (*Age,* 1979, nos. 425–33). In fact, the two inner figures can be compared for quality with those on the Sinai "Moses cross" (Weitzmann and Ševčenko, 1963, figs. 3, 4). Equally competent are the two end figures rendered in foreshortened perspective. But where the Stuma paten figures are indisputably weak is in the construction of their heads (aptly described as "watermelons" by Peirce and Tyler, 1934, vol. 2, 114). With the exception of that of the Apostle gazing upwards on the left, they are uniformly bland, and their "schematized and lifeless" (Kitzinger, 1958, 19) faces totally lack the individuality of those on the Riha paten. (The almond-shaped eyes of the Stuma faces are found nowhere else on contemporary silver.) More in keeping with the traditional drapery style on the Stuma paten is its classicizing egg and palmette border (see Schrader, 1979, 150 ff.), which can be compared to the borders on the Homs Vase (no. 84), and those on the Sion patens (e.g., *DO Handbook,* 1967, no. 63), which have a similarly placed cusped band of alternating palmettes and upright leaves. Moreover, the Stuma paten palmette is repeated in a more elaborate and larger form on the companion Stuma lamp (no. 33), where the ovoid lobes are reminiscent of the paten's eggs.

The differences in composition between the two versions of the Communion of the Apostles on these patens are difficult to reconcile with what we know to have been standard copying practices in this period. Indeed, the arrangement of the figures is in itself too different to support the notion (Dodd, 1973, 47 f.) that one paten (the Stuma) was simply copied from the other (the Riha). A more likely hypothesis would have each artist making his own adaptation from a single large paten—on the scale, perhaps, of one of the Sion plates (*DO Handbook,* 1967, nos. 63–65)—decorated with an elongated and symmetrical composition like that of the Rossano Gospels (Loerke, 1975). Into his reduced working area (which is only about 60 percent that afforded by the Sion plates) each artist copied the figures of Christ and four "profile" figures of Apostles, chosen from the available twelve, and then filled in the others "free hand" in the remaining background space. Such a hypothesis could explain the classical overtones of the Stuma paten; the artist, while revealing his native inability in treating the human head, might have used mechanical means to copy the figures (but only one head?) from the larger, no doubt superior, prototype, which may also have had a cusped border executed on the high technical level of the Sion patens.

The actual distribution of the figures on the two patens, and the choice of background "props," may have been influenced by the circumstances of their donations. One very prominent but seemingly anomalous figure on the Stuma paten is that just in front of the altar. Ebersolt (1911, 411 f.) suggested that this Apostle, Peter, had received the bread, uncovered his hands, and was now crossing to receive the wine. Another interpretation, however, might focus on the compositional link between this figure and the lamp which hangs prominently in the center over the altar, for the hands of the crouching Apostle seem to respond simultaneously to it and to Christ. As the lamp bears in its general form and lobed decoration a marked similarity to the lamp offered by Sergios (no. 33; Dodd, 1973, 52) together with this very paten, a connection between the two objects (and their donor) may intentionally have been incorporated into the scene. Indeed, what may be a faintly indicated paten on the altar beneath the lamp and at the center point between the two Christs, could be taken to refer to the Stuma plate itself. Other possible donations, within the range of the Apostle's gesture, include the chalice in use on the left, and the voluminous altar cloth. And of course, a similar interpretation may be placed on the vessels portrayed on the Riha paten (no. 35).

In effect, the scenes on the two patens enact the presentation to Christ of objects used during the eucharistic liturgy, by portraying their use in this scene. That *ex-voto* objects would be introduced into the solemn iconography of the Communion of the Apostles is not without parallel in contemporary art. Such "donation portraits," where Christ and the donated objects are shown without the donors (whose names, nevertheless, are adjacent to the image), are variations on contemporary compositions wherein Christ is presented by the donor with the church building (Grabar, 1960), eucharistic vessels (as at S. Vitale), books (Weitzmann, 1977, pl. 34), *et cetera.*

Bibliography

Ebersolt, 1911, 407; Bréhier, 1920, 174; Volbach, 1921, no. 6; *IGLS,* no. 698; Wilpert, 1926, 118 ff.; *idem,* 1927, 305 ff.; Rosenberg, 1928, vol. 4, 686 f.; *Exposition,* 1931, no. 760; Braun, 1932, 202, 210; Peirce and Tyler, 1934, vol. 2, 114; de Francovich, 1951, 14; Downey, 1951, 350; Alföldi and Cruikshank, 1957, 244, note 30; *Edinburgh,* 1958, no. 9; Rice, 1958, no. 8; Dodd, 1961, no. 27; Volbach, 1961, no. 247; Weitzmann and Ševčenko, 1963, 395; *Byzantine Art,* 1964, no. 485; Dodd, 1968, 147 ff.; *idem,* 1973, 9 ff., 40 ff.; Kent and Painter, 1977, 83; Schrader, 1979; Feissel, 1985, 470; Mundell-Mango, 1986.

Fig. 34.8

35. PATEN

DISKOS

Figures 35.1–35.9

Washington, D.C., Dumbarton Oaks Collection,
no. 24.5

Riha Treasure, 577(?)

For compositional analysis, see Chapter III, Appendix III.2.

This paten has high sloping sides, a flat narrow rim but no foot (figs. 35.3, 35.5). As on the Stuma paten (no. 34), the inner surface here is decorated in relief with a representation of the Communion of the Apostles (fig. 35.6). The iconography is essentially the same: Christ is shown twice behind an altar distributing wine and bread to two groups of Apostles. The architectural setting is more elaborate than on the other paten, but the sloping sides of this paten are left plain. An inscription fills the flat rim (figs. 35.2, 35.3). The figures (except feet), altar front, columns, shell, and vessels are gilded. Five stamps appear on the back (figs. 35.1, 35.4, 35.7), and two modern French duty stamps are on the rim (fig. 35.8).

The manufacture of this paten closely paralleled that of paten no. 34—that is, the hammering, formation of the round rim border, and burnishing of the object may all be described in the same terms. Here there is a turning point (D .4 cm) visible front and back between the wine skins on the table. As on Stuma patens nos. 34 and 36, there is evidence of two stages of burnishing: concentric on the rim and side, and horizontal on the flat inner surface. The inscription and figural decoration were also executed in techniques closely related to those used on the Stuma plate. The inscription was chased, scored, and filled with niello—the upper layer of which is lustrous black and the lower (revealed in areas of loss) is leaden in color and uneven. (In some letters the niello has bubbled.) The relief decoration was raised from behind and finished from the front with a variety of tools, as was the case with the Stuma paten (no. 34), and other repoussé objects in this catalogue. Straight incisions by a sharp tool define some areas (e.g., arch, altar top, ground line, *clavi,* and some pleats), while a series of round punch marks outline others (e.g., the figures, vessels, and columns). Round punches (D .15 and .075 cm) were also used for eye pupils and surface patterns on the altar cloth, and a round-ended tool was employed to cut tear-shaped gouges in diagonal drapery folds. Shorter though basically similar strokes mark the hair, while tonsures are stippled, and *clavi* hatched.

A photograph of 1909 (fig. 35.9; see Chapter II, above) shows the paten heavily encrusted with corrosion at the top, and with its rim misshapen and torn on the upper right and bottom left. The object was cleaned before 1921 (Diehl, 1921, pl. XIV), and again in 1946 and in 1977, when soil deposits were removed from the back (DO files). In addition to the damage to the rim, the silver is torn along the edge of the lower surface of the plate, from about 10 to about 12 o'clock, and down over the arch, and at 2 and 6 o'clock.

Fig. 35.2

There are small tears along the outlines of the chalice, the communion bread, and both Christs' beards. Niello has fallen from parts of the inscription, and the gilding has rubbed off the faces and arms of the Apostles.

STAMPS

These stamps were dated by Dodd (1961, no. 20) to 577 because of the monograms of Justin II (565–578) and Theodore, whom she took to be Theodore Petri, *comes sacrarum largitionum* in 577. (See Entries nos. 31, 32.) As classified by Dodd, the stamps may be read as follows:

a. **Round**: nimbed bust; inscribed *IWANNOU*.
b. **Hexagonal**: ? (only corner of stamp).
c. **Square**: monogram of Justin II; inscribed *DOROTHEOU*.
d. **Long**: nimbed bust; monogram of Theodore; inscribed *IWANNOU*.
e. **Cross**: monogram of Theodore; inscribed *DIOMIDOU*.

On the front of the outer rim are two tiny rectangular stamps, above the *pi* and to the right of the *rho* in *hyper*. These are countermark duty stamps of a type introduced in France in 1893; the particular devices shown here were applied at Marseilles, probably in 1912 when G. Marcopoli, who then owned the paten, was expelled from Aleppo (see Chapter II, above).

Weevil = countermark for imported silver; M = Marseilles.

INSCRIPTION

+ *For the repose (of the soul) of SERGIA, (daughter) of JOHN, and of THEODOSIOS, and (for) the salvation of MEGAS and of NONNOUS and of THEIR CHILDREN.*

Engraved, chased, scored, nielloed (H of letters = 1.0 cm). *IGLS*, no. 695; Ross, 1962, 12; Dodd, 1961, no. 20; *Age*, 1979, no. 547.

The lettering is lunate and uniform in size; and serifs are used regularly. *Kai* is abbreviated *Ks*.

This lettering most closely resembles that of Hama chalice no. 2, the Stuma lamp (no. 33), the Stuma

Fig. 35.8

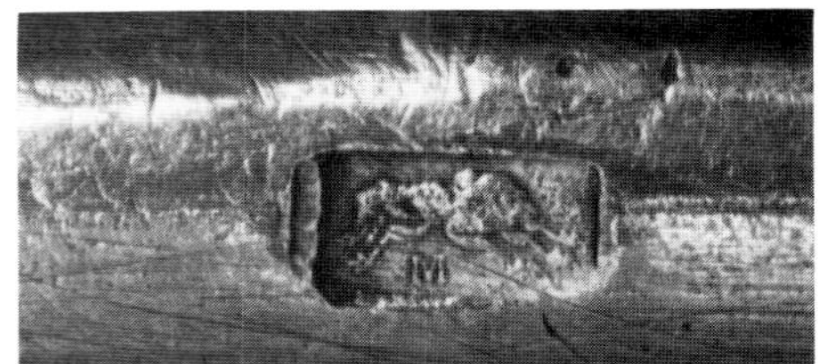

Fig. 35.7

Fig. 35.1

IWAN||NOV

ΔWPO||[ΘEOV]

[IWAN||N]OV

ΔI||OM||I[Δ]||OV

+ΥΠΕΡ·ΑΝ ΑΠΑΥϹΕѠϹ ϹΕΡΓΙΑϹ ΙѠΑΝΝΟΥϗ ΘΕΟΔΟϹΙΟΥϗ
ϹѠΤΗΡΙΑϹ ΜΕΓΑΛΟΥϗ ΝΟΝΝΟΥϗ ΤѠΝ ΑΥΤѠΝ ΤΕΚΝѠΝ

+ Ὑπὲρ ἀναπαύσεως Σεργίας Ιωάννου κ(αὶ) Θεοδοσίου κ(αὶ) σωτηρίας Μεγάλου κ(αὶ) Νοννοῦ κ(αὶ) τῶν ἀυτῶν τέκνων

D	35.0 cm
H	2.5 cm
Weight	904 gr
Roman Weight	2 lbs 9 oz 3 scr
Original Silver Price	11 *solidi* 1 carat

Fig. 35.3

Fig. 35.5

Fig. 35.4

Fig. 35.6

paten (no. 34), and another Stuma treasure paten, no. 36. The combination of the formulae *hyper anapauseos* and *soterias* (corresponding to "dead and living"), which is also found on the second Antioch treasure chalice (no. 41), was attributed by Downey (1951) to Syrian liturgical usage. The reverse of the same (i.e., "living and dead") is on the ewers given by the same donor, Megas (nos. 37, 38), and on objects nos. 15, 33, 34, and 36 (the latter three of which match this paten in their lettering). The reading of the name as *Megas* as opposed to *Megalos,* as it was previously rendered (from the quoted genitive form *Megalou*), was recently put forward by Feissel (1985). On Megas, whose high official titles are listed on his ewers, and whose name (apparently) appears in silver stamps on three objects dedicated by Sergios (again, nos. 33, 34, and 36), see Chapter I, above, and Entry no. 37. It is possible that Megas is the brother of Megale, who dedicated the Hama flask (no. 15), and that Sergia, daughter of John is the sister of Sergios, who dedicated the Stuma lamp and patens (nos. 33, 34). (On attested "paired naming" of siblings, see Mundell-Mango, 1986.) See Figure I.1.

COMMENTARY

It is proposed in the discussion on the Stuma paten (no. 34) that this plate and that one were made, decorated, and stamped in the same workshop. It is further argued that this paten is not, as often asserted, superior in style to the other. Indeed, their "shortcomings" offset each other, for while the Stuma paten displays weak character portrayal but a fair command of the classical figural and ornamental vocabulary, the Riha paten displays relatively awkward figures but strong facial characterization. The two artists, working perhaps from a larger prototype (see the discussion to Entry no. 34), seem to have adjusted the composition of the Communion of the Apostles to their own purposes. The one working on the Stuma paten allowed his figures to obscure the altar table, so that the one object in sharp focus is the lamp hanging over it. On the other hand, the artist working on the Riha paten "held his figures back," so that the central focal area is the table top and the four objects neatly framed upon it: a chalice, a paten, and two wine skins (for the latter, see *Antioch* II, pl. 55). Equally prominent are the *cherniboxeston* set (*trulla* and ewer) in the exergue, and the lamps (similar to nos. 13, 33) set on the epistyle behind the altar. As on the Stuma paten, a chalice is being used at the left.

Although most of these objects have an immediate role to play in the eucharistic rite, those in the exergue attract undue attention. It could be argued (as was argued for the Stuma paten) that all these objects, so pointedly displayed, were other gifts given to the church by Megas, the donor of this paten—namely, chalices, a paten, two or more lamps, and a *cherniboxeston.* The wine skins may represent a supply of wine; similarly, the tall flames issuing from the two lamps could signify a provisioning of oil. The prominent arched epistyle on columns, pictured on the Riha paten, may even allude to a silver furniture revetment for a ciborium or chancel screen, and the patterned altar cloth may also have been a gift. Certainly, Megas was (or became) a powerful man. He may in 577 already have possessed the string of titles he had by 582 (see no. 37; the titles may have been omitted here for lack of space). The presentation of a number of silver objects, plus textiles, oil, wine, and even revetments to his local church would have been lavish proof of both his piety and his worldly success. Megas later gave a pair of ewers (nos. 37, 38) which together are the heaviest and therefore the costliest surviving donations to this church.

Selected Bibliography

For earlier bibliography, see Ross, 1962, no. 10. See also, Wulff, 1918, vol. 1, 199; Bréhier, 1919, 256; *idem,* 1920, 176 ff.; Wilpert, 1927, 303 f.; *IGLS,* no. 695; Downey, 1951, 350; Dodd, 1961, no. 20; Weitzmann and Ševčenko, 1963, 395; *Byzantine Art,* 1964, no. 484; Elbern, 1964, 134; Wessel, 1964, 9 ff.; *DO Handbook,* 1967, no. 61; Dodd, 1968, 147; Wessel, 1969, 367 ff.; Cecchelli *et al.,* 1959, 65; Dodd, 1973, 10 ff., 40 ff.; Kent and Painter, 1977, no. 144; *Age,* 1979, no. 547; Schrader, 1979; Feissel, 1985, 469 ff.; Mundell-Mango, 1986.

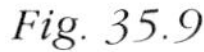

Fig. 35.9

36. PATEN

DISKOS

Figures 36.1–36.7

Istanbul, Archaeological Museum, no. 3761

Stuma Treasure, 574–578

This paten has high sloping sides, a flat narrow rim, but no footring (figs. 36.3, 36.5). In the middle is a large cross with flaring arms; engraved with sharp and gouged outlines and with diagonal strokes at its center, it is set upon a hill, within a medallion formed by a pair of engraved lines. Engraved lines also accentuate the top and bottom of the sloping sides, and an inscription fills the flat rim (figs. 36.2, 36.3). Traces of gilding (possibly foil) are visible in the cavities of the cross outline. Five stamps appear on the reverse (figs. 36.1, 36.4, 36.6).

This paten was formed by hammering, the marks of which are visible on its reverse. The outer edge of its rim was rolled and folded forward to form a rounded border. In the center of both sides are turning points (D .4 cm) formed when the plate was mounted on a lathe for burnishing and for engraving the ornamental lines. As on the Stuma and Riha patens (nos. 34, 35), two stages of burnishing lines are here visible: the first, on the sloping sides and rim, are concentric, while the second, within the central field, are on axis with the horizontal arms of the cross. The condition of the cruciform stamp on the back, which overlaps the centering hole, is so sharp that the stamps must have been applied after the paten was turned on the lathe and, therefore, after at least the preliminary decoration. The side of the paten is torn away from the bottom, from about 2 to 7 o'clock. Further tears appear in the bottom at 11 and 1 o'clock, and on the flat rim, through the inscription, from 3 to 4 o'clock, where the rim is nearly "pleated." This part of the paten has been straightened out since 1908 (fig. 36.7; Ebersolt, 1911). A diagonal dent runs across the lower left quadrant of the plate. Niello is missing from several letters, particularly along the tear. There is corrosion on both the front and back.

STAMPS

These stamps were dated by Dodd (1961, no. 29) to 578–582 because of the monogram of Tiberius Constantine. The monogram of Justin II in another stamp, however, indicates instead the period 574–578 (see Entry no. 33). As classified by Dodd, these stamps may be read, with emendations (fig. 36.1), as follows:

a. **Round**: unnimbed bust; unidentified inscription.
b. **Hexagonal**: bust; monogram of Justin (struck twice?); inscribed *MEGALOU.*
c. **Square**: monogram of Tiberius Constantine; unidentified inscription.
d. **Long**: bust; unidentified monogram; unidentified inscription.
e. **Cross**: unidentified monogram; inscribed *THOMA.*

INSCRIPTION

+ *In fulfillment of a vow and (for) the salvation of SERGIOS and ANNA and (for) the repose (of the souls) of DOMETIOS and of JOHN.*

Engraved, chased, nielloed (H of letters = .9–1.0 cm). Ebersolt, 1911, 417; *IGLS,* no. 697.

The inscription as published by Ebersolt (1911, 417) is correct with the exception of the final *S* (i.e., *kai*), which he did not see, and supplied. (This is repeated in *IGLS.*) The lettering is lunate, and serifs are used consistently. Letter size is uniform, and letter forms are regular and, in some cases, elegantly attenuated (e.g., *epsilon* has a long tongue and *alpha* and *mu* have a central pendant stroke). *Kai* is abbreviated both as *Ks* and, between names, as *S.*

Fig. 36.2

The lettering can be compared with that on the Stuma lamp (no. 33), and the Stuma and Riha patens (nos. 34, 35). The combination of dedicatory formulae used here (*hyper euches kai soterias* and *[hyper] anapauseos*) is the same as that on the Hama flask (no. 15), as well as on the Stuma lamp and paten (nos. 33, 34), which were most likely gifts of the same Sergios mentioned here. (On Sergios, tribune and *argyroprates,* see Entry no. 33.) Sergios gave the two other objects (nos. 33, 34) in the names of his deceased wife, Maria, and of their parents. Perhaps Anna is his second wife, and the two named deceased, Dometios and John, are her father and his father, respectively. See figure I.1. The concentration of memorial dedications at Kaper Koraon in the 570s may be associated with the devastation of the Persian seige of nearby Apamea, in 573 (see Chapter I, above).

Commentary

This paten is closely associated with two groups of objects: 1) those having niello inscriptions on their flat rims (i.e., nos. 34, 35; the Stuma and Riha patens), rather than incised inscriptions on their inner surface; and 2) those with monumental crosses in their centers. As previously observed by Dodd (1973, 24 f.), this Stuma paten has the incised band around its cross usually allocated for the dedicatory inscription. But that the text was instead applied to the rim is, along with the object's distinctive burnishing, a point of association with the patens of Sergios, tribune and *argyroprates* (no. 34; Stuma) and Megas (no. 35; Riha), both of which, however, are decorated with the Communion of the Apostles. Dodd (*ibid.,* 24 f.) listed four other patens (nos. 4, 5, 63, 74) with monumental crosses, to which may be added the paten from Sarabaon (no. 75). The cross on this paten most closely resembles that on the Phela paten (no. 63), which is dated 577. A notable difference between these two crosses, however, is the hill under this one, which Dodd (*ibid.,* 28) compared to that on the Phela paten with a smaller cross (no. 64). As there are no Rivers of Paradise flowing from the hill on the Stuma paten, the reference may be to Golgotha rather than to the Garden of Paradise (Ebersolt, 1911, 410). The double outline of the crosses on the Stuma and Phela patens may be compared to the incised border on the crosses included in this catalogue (e.g., nos. 7–10, 42, 65, 67, 68). At 767 grams, this paten is among the least heavy of those of the period; only the Beth Misona (no. 60: 542 grams) and Gallunianu (no. 81: 200 grams) patens are lighter in weight.

Bibliography

Ebersolt, 1911, 407, 410 f., 417; Bréhier, 1920, 174, 182; *IGLS,* no. 697; *Exposition,* 1931, no. 758; Braun, 1932, 210; Downey, 1951, 350; Dodd, 1961, no. 29; Weitzmann and Ševčenko, 1963, 395; Dodd, 1973, 24 f., 28; Feissel, 1985, 470; Mundell-Mango, 1986.

Fig. 36.6

Fig. 36.1

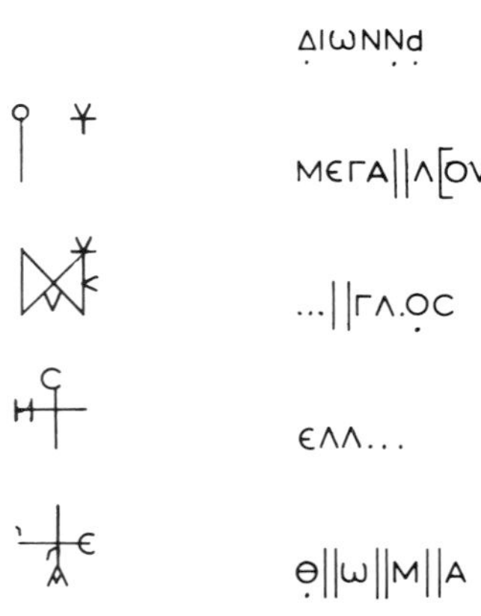

+ ΥΠΕΡΕΥΧΗϹ Κ ϹΩΤΗΡΙΑϹ ϹΕΡΓΙΟΥ S ΑΝΝΑϹ
Κ ΑΝΑΠΑΥϹΕΩϹ ΔΟΜΕΤΙΟΥ S ΙΩΑΝΝΟΥ

+ Ὑπὲρ εὐχῆς κ(αὶ) σωτηρίας Σεργίου (καὶ) Ἄννας
κ(αὶ) ἀναπαύσεως Δομετίου (καὶ) Ἰωάννου.

D	35–36.0 cm
H	3.0 cm
Weight	767 gr
Roman Weight	2 lbs 4 oz 3 scr
Original Silver Price	9 *solidi* 9 carats

Fig. 36.3

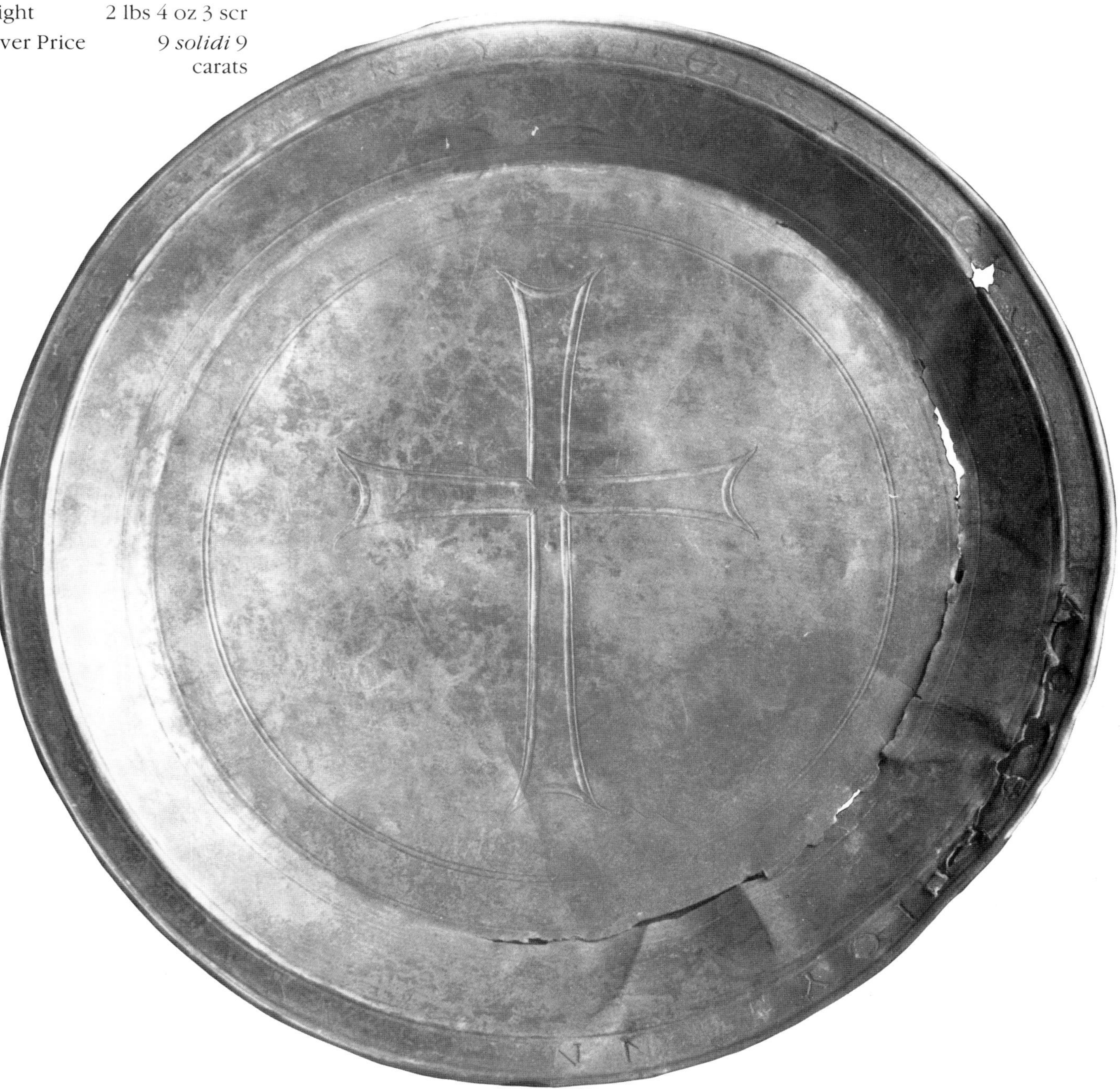

Fig. 36.5

Fig. 36.4

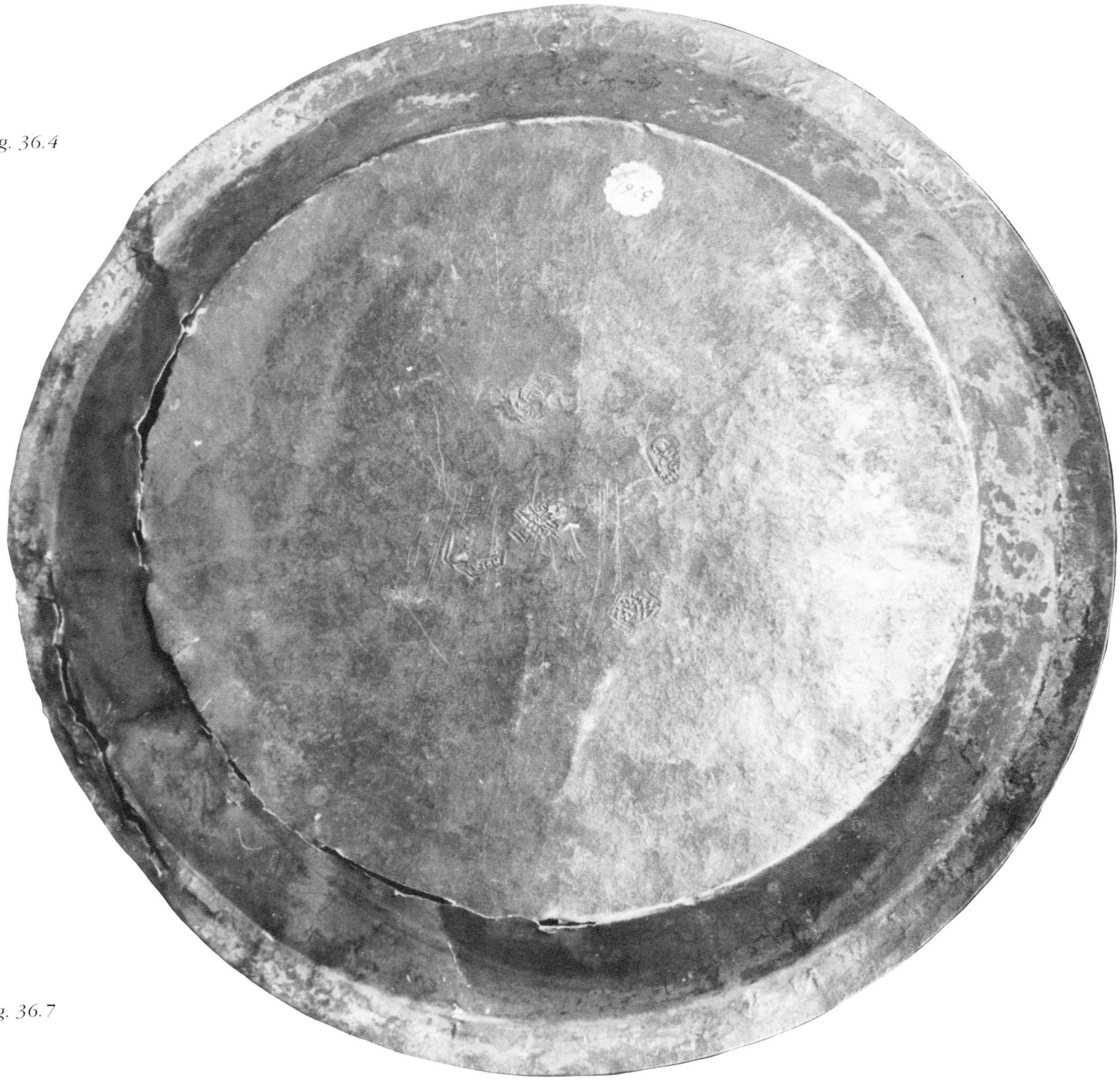

Fig. 36.7

37. EWER

XESTION

Figures 37.1–37.4

Bern, Abegg Stiftung, no. 8.112.64

Riha Treasure, 582–602

This ewer forms a pair with Riha ewer no. 38. It has a raised base and a wide body tapering to a tall neck with an upright rim having a shallow *cyma recta* profile (fig. 37.3). A long (60 cm) inscription in niello with shiny gray surface runs around the middle of the body (figs. 37.2, 37.3) banded by a pair of concave mouldings with turned lines. There are pairs of turnings under the rim, under the body, and on the base, which consists of a flat, closed foot. Four stamps appear on the bottom (figs. 37.1, 37.4).

This vessel was formed by hammering from a single sheet of metal. Its outer surface was burnished and the linear and concave ornament engraved on a lathe, the turning point of which is visible in the center of the bottom. The object was once highly polished, as can still be seen in some areas. Its stamps were struck after it was hammered and turned. The vessel's surface is pitted. There is one dent in the inscribed band, which has lost some of its niello inlay. There is a small hole in the upper rim, and on the inner, opposite side of the rim, a repair to another hole.

STAMPS

These stamps were dated by Dodd (1968, no. 31.1) to (early in) the reign of Maurice (582–602), whose monogram appears once. (See no. 38.) The hexagonal stamp is missing. As classified by Dodd, the stamps may be read, with very minor emendations (fig. 37.1), as follows:

a. Round: nimbed bust; inscribed *MAXIMOS.*
b. Hexagonal: missing.
c. Square: monogram of Maurice; unidentified inscription.
d. Long: nimbed bust; monogram of Marianos (*comes sacrarum largitionum?*); inscribed *PATRIKIS.*
e. Cross: monogram of Marianos (*comes sacrarum largitionum?*); inscribed *THOMAS.*

INSCRIPTION

+ *For the salvation of MEGAS, glorious ex-consul, patrician, and curator of our most pious sovereign, and (for) the repose (of the soul) of PETER, (son) of PELAGIA, and (of that) of NONNOUS.*

Engraved, nielloed (H of letters = 1.2–1.3 cm). Dodd, 1968, no. 31.1; *idem,* 1973, 7.

The lettering is lunate, and serifs are used regularly. Letter forms are unusually tall and narrow, and have a mannered, "spidery" appearance, due, no doubt, to the demands of fitting a long text onto a limited space. Signs that the spacing of the letters was not carefully planned in advance include the use of the full genitive *omicron-upsilon,* despite economizing with *S* for *kai,* until the final *Nonnou,* which shows two hasty ligatures (*nu-nu* and *omicron-upsilon*). *Endoxotatos* is abbreviated with a crescent sign.

For the combination of the formulae *hyper soterias* and *hyper anapauseos,* and the form of the name *Megas,* see Entry no. 35. Nonnous, the wife of Megas, mentioned on the Riha paten (no. 35; stamped in 577?), is, according to this inscription, dead. The deceased Peter, son of Pelagia, must have been a close relative (a nephew?) to merit mention before Megas' wife. Pelagia may have been his second wife, and Peter, his stepson. Another solution would be to supply a *kai* after Peter and to make him and Pelagia the

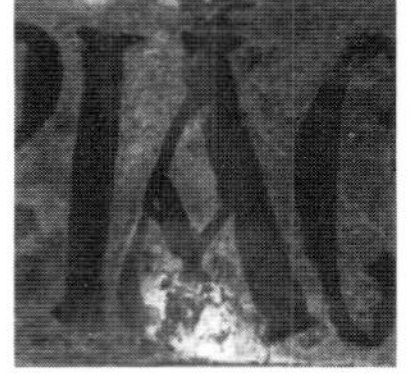

Fig. 37.2

"children" of Megas and Nonnous (cited on paten no. 35). Megas, whose name appears not only in dedications of objects dateable to 577 (Riha paten no. 35) and 582-602 (Riha twin ewers nos. 37, 38), but also (presumably) in stamps applied to other pieces between 574 and 578 (Stuma lamp no. 33, and Stuma patens nos. 34 and 36) is attested in Constantinople in 587/8. (On his career as curator of an imperial domaine and holder of high honorific titles, see Feissel, 1985; and Chapter I, above).

COMMENTARY

The two Abegg ewers have been compared in their shape with several contemporary silver vessels, including the Homs Vase (no. 84), the Hama (no. 14) and Albanian ewers (*Early Christian,* 1947, no. 415), and the amphora in the Hermitage (Dodd, 1973, 7), with the latter providing the closest parallel. Whereas the first vessels have straight, "defined" necks (see no. 14), the Abegg ewers have the form of the ancient *pelike* (without its handles)—that is, they show a tapering neck on a wide body, whose greatest fullness is at one third of its height. The fourth-century silver amphorae from the Durobrivae (Painter, 1977 [I], no. 5) and Esquiline (Shelton, 1981, nos. 19, 20) treasures have their fullness placed higher on the body. Closer in contour to ewers nos. 37 and 38 are several earlier silver pitchers found in the East; namely, in Asia Minor (first century AD; Oliver, 1980, fig. 13); at Dura Europos (third century; Oliver, 1977, no. 106); and in Syria (fourth century; Milliken, 1958, 37, ill. after p. 41). Squatter in proportions are several first-century amphorae in silver, including one from Homs (Seyrig, 1952, no. 12) and another from Asia Minor (Oliver, 1980, fig. 19), as well as bronze examples from Oum Hauran and in Ontario (Hayes, 1984, no. 152). Another, more contemporary group of vessels with related form are the five bronze pitchers found with the second Cyprus treasure (late sixth to seventh century), all of which, however, have an even broader, flat base (Dalton, 1906, fig. 17).

Although lacking the characteristic handles, the two Abegg ewers may have served as amphorae for storing eucharistic wine in quantity—the equivalent of the *amae* of the Latin inventories (*Liber Pontificalis*). It is possible that the wine skins displayed on the altar on the Riha paten refer to a donation of wine made by Megas, the paten's donor (see no. 35). If so, these two wine-storing ewers would have made an appropriate supplementary gift, presented by him a few years later. On the function of the Hama ewer (no. 14), inscribed *xestin,* see its Entry.

BIBLIOGRAPHY

Dodd, 1968, no. 31.1; *idem,* 1973, no. 1; Kent and Painter, 1977, 83; *Age,* 1979, no. 552; Feissel, 1985, 470; Mundell-Mango, 1986.

Fig. 37.4

Fig. 37.1

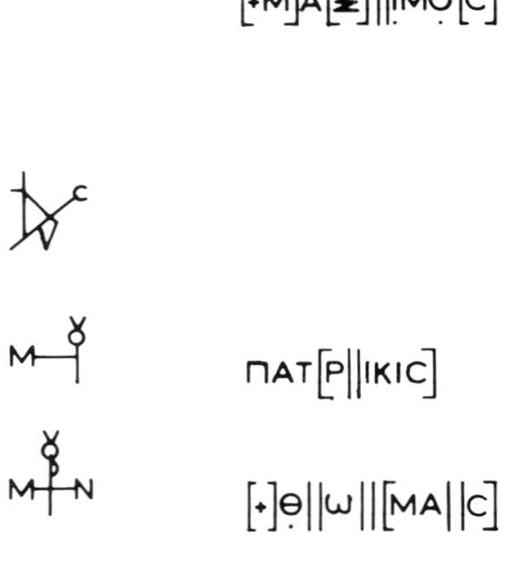

+ΥΠΕΡϹΩΤΗΡΙΑϹΜΕΓΑΛΟΥΕΝΔΟΞ ΑΠΟΥΠΑΤΩΝΠΑΤΡΙΚΙΟΥϚΚΟΥΡΑΤΟΡΟϹΤΟΥ

ЄΥϹЄΒЄϹΤΑΤΟΥΗΜΩΝΔЄϹΠΟΤΟΥϚΑΝΑΠΑΥϹЄΩϹΠЄΤΡΟΥΠЄΛΑΓΙΑϹϚΝΟΝΝΟΥ

+ Ὑπὲρ σωτηρίας Μεγάλου ἐνδοξ(οτάτου) ἀπὸ ὑπάτων πατρικίου (καὶ) κουράτορος τοῦ εὐσεβεστάτου ἡμῶν δεσπότου (καὶ) ἀναπαύσεως Πέτρου (καὶ) Πελαγίας (καὶ) Νοννοῦ.

H	33.0 cm
D (rim)	10.0 cm
D (base)	12.5 cm
Weight	2162 gr
Roman Weight	6 lbs 7 oz 2 scr
Original Silver Price	26 *solidi* 8⅔ carats

Fig. 37.3

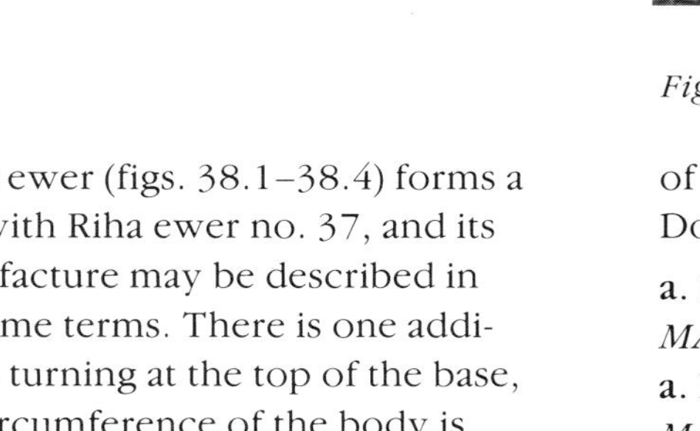

Fig. 38.2

38. EWER

XESTION

Figures 38.1–38.4

Bern, Abegg Stiftung, no. 8.113.64

Riha Treasure, 582–602

This ewer (figs. 38.1–38.4) forms a pair with Riha ewer no. 37, and its manufacture may be described in the same terms. There is one additional turning at the top of the base, the circumference of the body is two centimeters greater, but the object is seventy-seven grams lighter than its mate. Four stamps appear on the bottom (figs. 38.1, 38.4). The present condition of this ewer is similar to that of no. 37; that is, its surface is pitted and there are shallow dents in the body. There is an oblong hole in the rim and some niello is missing from the inscription.

STAMPS

These stamps are very similar to, though better preserved than, those of its mate (no. 37), and were dated by Dodd (1968, no. 31.2) with it to (early in) the reign of Maurice (582–602). Both vessels lack the hexagonal stamp, and this one lacks the square one as well, whose place is in effect taken by a second impression of the round stamp. As classified by Dodd, they may be read as follows:

a. **Round:** nimbed bust; inscribed *MAXIMOS.*

a. **Round:** nimbed bust; inscribed *MAXIMOS.*

b. **Hexagonal:** missing.

c. **Square:** missing.

d. **Long:** nimbed bust; monogram of Marianos (*comes sacrarum largitionum?*); inscribed *PATRIKIS.*

e. **Cross:** monogram of Marianos (*comes sacrarum largitionum?*); inscribed *THOMAS.*

INSCRIPTION

+ *For the salvation of MEGAS, most glorious ex-consul, patrician and curator of our most pious sovereign and (for) the repose (of the soul) of PETER, (son) of PELAGIA, and (that) of NONNOUS.*

Engraved, nielloed (H of letters = 1.2 cm). Dodd, 1968, no. 31.2; Dodd, 1973, 7.

The remarks made concerning the inscription on ewer no. 37 apply here, except that the abbreviation sign over *endox* is a full circle and the double *nu* in *Nonnou* is not in ligature.

COMMENTARY

See Entry no. 37.

BIBLIOGRAPHY

Dodd, 1968, no. 31.2; *idem,* 1973, no. 2; and see Entry no. 37.

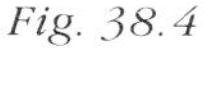

Fig. 38.4

Fig. 38.1

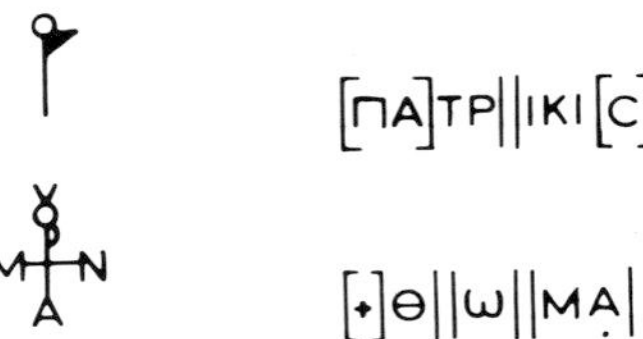

+ΥΠΕΡϹΩΤΗΡΙΑϹΜΕΓΑΛΟΥΕΝΔΟΞ̇ΑΠΟΥΠΑΤΩΝΠΑΤΡΙΚΙΟΥϚΚΟΥΡΑΤΟΡΟϹΤΟΥ
ЄΥϹЄΒЄϹΤΑΤΟΥΗΜΩΝΔЄϹΠΟΤΟΥϚΑΝΑΠΑΥϹЄΩϹΠЄΤΡΟΥΠЄΛΑΓΙΑϹϚΝΟΝΝΥ

+ Ὑπὲρ σωτηρίας Μεγάλου ἐνδοξ(οτάτου) ἀπὸ ὑπάτων πατρικίου (καὶ) κουράτορος τοῦ εὐσεβεστάτου ἡμῶν δεσπότου (καὶ) ἀναπαύσεως Πέτρου (καὶ) Πελαγίας (καὶ) Νοννοῦ.

H	32.5 cm
D (rim)	9.5–9.9 cm
D (base)	12.0 cm
Weight	2085 gr
Roman Weight	6 lbs 4 oz 10 scr
Original Silver Price	25 *solidi* 11 1/3 carats

Fig. 38.3

39. PATEN

DISKOS

Figures 39.1–39.3

Istanbul, Archaeological Museum, no. 3760

Stuma Treasure, Sixth to Seventh Century

This paten has high sloping sides, and a flat narrow rim, but no foot-ring (figs. 39.1–39.3). A small cross with slightly flaring arms is engraved in the center. There are no decorative lines, inscription, gilding or niello.

This paten was formed by hammering, the marks of which remain visible on its reverse. Its outer edges were made to form an upright, rather than rounded border to its flat rim. Lathe-made burnishing lines are clearly visible on the front, in the center of which are two turning points (D .4 cm). The outer sides and a narrow band extending (*ca.* 1.5 cm) onto the bottom were also burnished. Part of a compass-drawn line, equal to the height of the cross, arcs to the left of the cross and continues faintly to the right. The cross itself is rather crudely drawn; the foot has been heavily engraved twice, and the line of the vertical cross bar intersects the horizontal arm. This object is very damaged. Its bottom is torn from the sloping side in a line extending from 1 to 8 o'clock. Metal is missing along this tear at 4 o'clock, from the upper rim at 9 o'clock, and from the top left part of the cross. The top rim is cracked at 5 o'clock, and crumpled along the left side. A pronounced dent runs diagonally across the paten from the upper right corner of the cross to the sloping side. Both surfaces are very scratched, and corrosion covers parts of the rim and much of the back. A small deposit of silver directly to the left of the cross may be the result of a repair.

Commentary

This paten differs in several respects from others included in this catalogue. It is the only one with neither a dedicatory inscription nor ornamental lines; moreover, its decoration is limited to a somewhat clumsy cross, which itself is unusual in being constructed of nearly straight lines and in having the vertical arm intersect the horizontal (see also Strzygowski, 1904, no. 2701). Dodd (1973, 27 f.) has associated this paten with others having a small cross at the center, including Hama no. 6, a paten in the Phela treasure (no. 64), and the Beth Misona paten (no. 60). It is noteworthy, moreover, that the burnished band extending onto the bottom of this plate recurs on the Hama plate (no. 6); yet at the same time, it must be added that the Hama plate has a decorative band and an inscription, as do the other two. Despite its relatively rough decoration, and the losses of silver it has suffered, this, the third Stuma paten, is the heaviest among all Syrian examples assembled here; it could, therefore, well have been the costliest.

Bibliography

Ebersolt, 1911, 407, 410; Bréhier, 1920, 174; *Exposition,* 1931, no. 758; Braun, 1932, 202, note 14; Dodd, 1973, 28.

D	35.5–36.5 cm
H	2.9–3.5 cm
Weight	1090 gr
Roman Weight	3 lbs 3 oz 22 scr
Original Silver Price	13 *solidi* 7 1/3 carats

Fig. 39.1

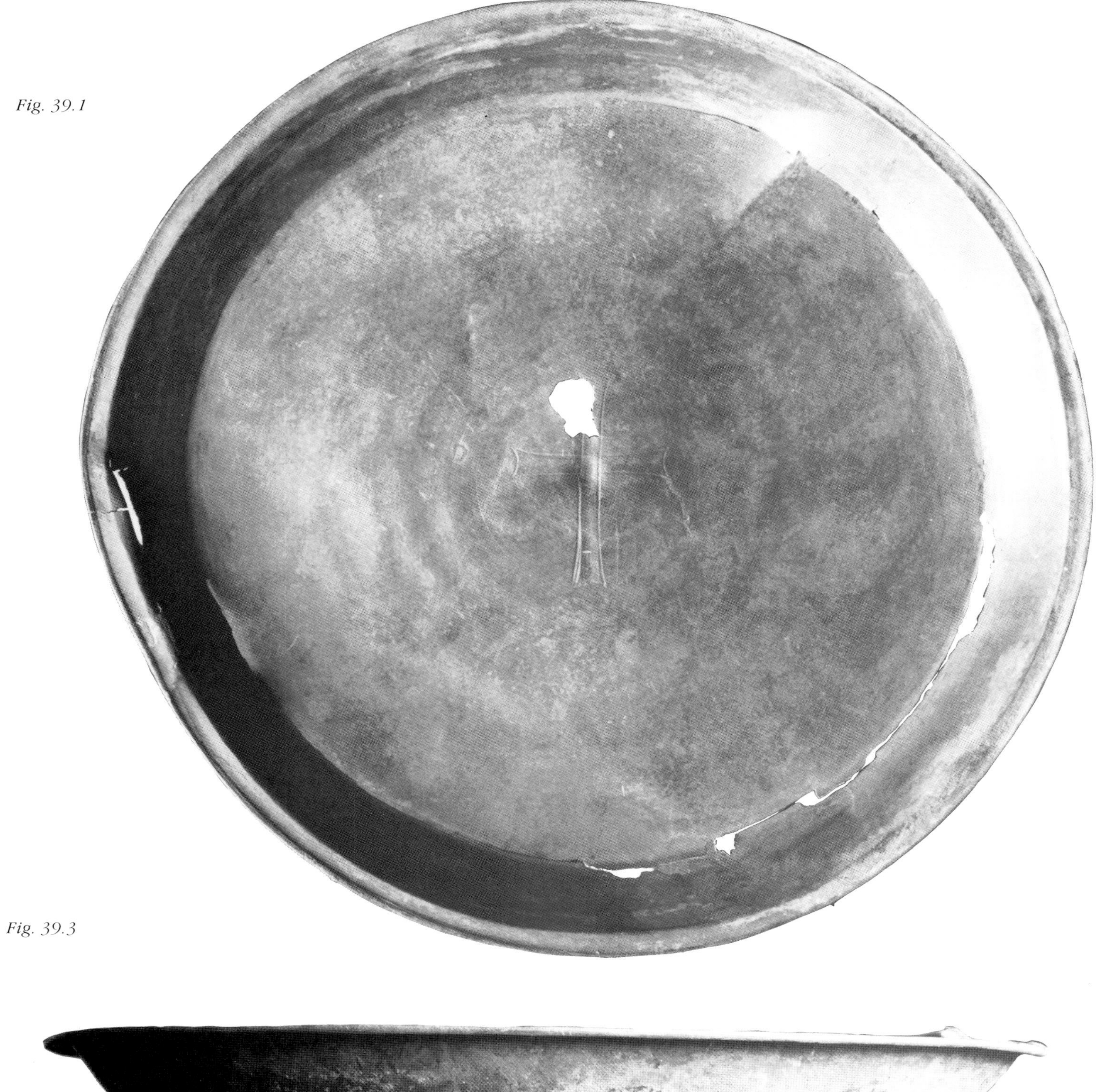

Fig. 39.3

Fig. 39.2

40. LAMP

FARUM CANTHARUM?

Figures 40.1–40.6

New York, The Metropolitan Museum of Art, no. 50.4 (The Cloisters Collection, 1950)

Antioch Treasure, Sixth Century

For compositional analysis, see Chapter III, Appendix III.2.

This object is composed of a plain inner cup set within an openwork cup which rests on a splayed foot with knob (figs. 40.1–40.4). The outer cup is divided into two decorative zones, and much of it is gilded. The much larger upper part is worked as a reticulate pattern of vine scrolls in which twelve seated figures are symmetrically distributed and interspersed with various creatures (lamb, rabbit, grasshopper, butterfly, birds, snails) and two baskets; the vines are heavily hung with grapes and leaves. Above this openwork zone runs a row of rosettes along the lower edge of a plain band which forms the top of the outer cup. Below the openwork zone is a flat band which has small square beads above, and is attached below to the bottom part of the cup—that composed of a calyx of overlapping pointed leaves. The outer cup appears to have been soldered to the hollow foot, whose knob is covered with a pattern of horizontal overlapping leaves "pointing" toward the right. From a short stem under the knob, the foot spreads out to a raised rim (H .7 cm) which has a pair of turned lines on its vertical edge. The upper, horizontal surface of the foot is covered with a frieze of overlapping pointed leaves. The top of the inner cup is folded over the upper rim of the outer cup.

(The following observations concerning the manufacture and condition of the object owe much to conversations with Mr. Richard Stone and Mr. Edmund Dandridge, conservators, and to Dr. Margaret Frazer, curator, all of The Metropolitan Museum, as well as to a report on the object by Ms. Terry Weisser and Ms. Carol Snow, conservators at The Walters Art Gallery.) The inner cup was apparently hammered and then lathe-turned, the marks of which are visible on its exterior surface. The outer cup was made in two main parts: the foot, which was hammered and decorated by chasing, and the openwork cup. The latter was probably first formed (by hammering) as a cup with thick walls, which were then cut through to create the scrolled decoration and the calyx and border at the base (Stone). The human figures, which project up to .4 centimeters from the surface of the outer cup were carved from solid metal; they and the other decorative elements were chased from the front to finish details. The grapes were struck with a circular punch. The upper rosette border of the outer cup may have been made separately and soldered to the cup.

Photographs taken of the object before it was restored in 1913 by the firm of Léon André of Paris, show that it had been "somewhat flattened," front to back (figs. 40.5, 40.6; Rorimer, 1954, 162; and Chapter II, above), and that it was covered inside and out with a thick layer of corrosion. A hole (D *ca.* 3 cm) to the right of one central figure was cut through both the inner and outer cups. A declaration of restoration signed by André in 1916 cites cleaning, and states that part of the inner cup was remade "afin de nous permettre de réappliquer les sujets dessus" (MMA files). The latter operation may have included the addition of three missing rosettes, part of the vine (Rorimer, 1954, 165), and, possibly, the arm of a central figure. Plaster restorations and modern paint were removed in 1951, after the object entered The Metropolitan Museum (MMA files). The vessel still incorporates extraneous material, and its surfaces have been roughened by cleaning and restoration. The inner cup has a jagged edge and a thick coat of gesso on its inner walls, which almost totally obscures their metal surface (Stone and Dandridge). There are several cracks in the piece, and parts are missing from its fabric.

Commentary

Almost from the time of its first appearance, in 1910(?), this, the so-called Antioch Chalice, has been the subject of intense controversy (see also Chapter II, above). This stems from the fact that it was early identified (by Gustavus Eisen; see especially his 1923 publication) as the Holy Grail—its battered inner cup supposedly that used by Christ at the Last Supper, and now set into a "commemoratively decorated" outer cup of first century manufacture. (The Holy Grail was said to be an onyx cup in the sixth century and a silver cup with handles in the seventh [see Wilkinson, 1977, 83, 97].) Not surprisingly, this identification and dating were strongly disputed (Jerphanion, 1926; see Arnason, 1941; *idem,* 1942, for the history of the dispute). Some (Wilpert, 1926; *idem,* 1927; and Glenny *et al.,* 1985) have labelled the object a modern forgery, while as early as 1924, others were already proposing datings for it in the sixth century (Conway, 1924, 110; Jerphanion, 1926, 159)—a view still widely held today (e.g., *Age,* 1979, no. 542).

Although no longer believed to be a holy relic, this object is still almost universally described as a chalice (an early *calyx imaginatus,* according to Elbern [1963]), even though it bears no dedicatory inscription and is totally unlike any other Early Byzantine chalice in its form and decoration. Yet, as early as the 1920s, it was compared with a small group of *à jour* vessels having glass (rather than metal) liners (Volbach, 1921[1], 13; Conway, 1924, 109; Zahn, 1928, col. 568). (On metal liners, see Entry no. 16.) The double-shell, openwork silver vessels found in Denmark (third century) and Georgia have liners of blue or violet glass (Kisa, 1908, 602 ff.), and the latter resembles the Antioch Chalice in its high relief work and its rosette border. The loose metal liner of a related gold cup in a private collection (Kondoleon, 1979) may not be original—and the same may be true of the ill-fitting and rough inner cup of the Antioch Chalice, which could well have had a glass liner when made, with the present cup being either an ancient or a modern replacement (if modern, it might have been an element of deception related to the object's identification as the Holy Grail). These double-shell, openwork cups have in turn been compared in technique and appearance to fourth-century *diatreta* cage-cups (Zahn, 1928, col. 568) and related glass work (e.g., the Lycurgus Cup; Coche de la Ferté, 1956, 150 ff.).

The Antioch "Chalice" (and the similar Georgian vessel?) may, in fact, belong to quite a different group of

Fig. 40.4

Fig. 40.3

objects—namely, that of openwork (standing or hanging) lamps, such as those in silver found in Rome (Shelton, 1981, 37, fig. 15) and Lycia (Boyd, 1986), as well as one in bronze found in Bithynia (Firatlı, 1969, 198, fig. 18). Indeed, it seems quite possible that the original function of the Antioch Chalice was really that of a lamp (with glass liner), rather than that of a chalice or drinking goblet.

The figures on this object have always been identified as Christ and the Apostles—a youthful Christ appearing twice, surrounded and acclaimed by ten Apostles. While *ten* Apostles might be acceptable at an earlier date, by the sixth century their number was quite strictly set at twelve, unless restricted by space (Jerphanion, 1930, 194 f.), which cannot be convincingly argued in this case (compare *idem,* 1926, 104). Furthermore, Jerphanion found it odd that in the mixed iconography

Fig. 40.1

H	19.5 cm
D (cup rim)	13.5–18.0 cm
D (foot rim)	7.3 cm

of the Antioch Chalice—which portrays Christ as "teaching doctor" and "acclaimed King"—He is apparently delivering His Mission to Apostles who are "nailed to their chairs," rather than standing. The iconography of Christ flanked by seated Apostles has been associated with similar portrayals of philosophers grouped around a central figure of Socrates, Diogenes or Kalliope (Hanfmann, 1951; Richter, 1965, 81 ff.). Indeed, group portraits of the Seven Sages who gathered at a *symposion* held by Periander survive in several forms (*ibid.*). The traditional Sayings of the Seven Sages accompany two such pavement compositions and were inscribed on spoons, a set of which, in fact, was found together with some "Apostle spoons" (see Entry no. 49). The precise membership of the group varied, and although their number was set at seven by 44 BC, representations of eleven or twelve wise men are also known (*ibid.*, 82).

It is possible that the composition on the Antioch Chalice is a deliberate mix of both traditions, the Christian and the pagan, designed to illustrate an important contemporary theme. In addition to the apho-

Fig. 40.2

ristic Sayings of the Seven Sages, another collection of pagan statements, known as the Theosophy, had been compiled by the late fifth century in order to demonstrate that pagan philosophers had prophesized the advent of Christ, just as the Old Testament prophets had done. Variations of the text are known, from Alexandria(?), from Malalas writing at Antioch, and from Harran in Mesopotamia *ca.* 600 (Brock, 1983; *idem,* 1984), the latter group apparently intended for converting the pagan Sabians. Many of these sayings—those of Orpheus, Hermes Tresmegistos, Pythagoras, Porphyry, *et cetera*—proclaim Christ, who Himself said "I am the Light," in Neo-Platonic terms of radiance and light. It is possible that the ten figures holding scrolls and proclaiming Christ on the Antioch Chalice represent some of these prophesying philosophers, thus echoing, for example, the proclaiming Old Testament prophets of the Rossano Gospels (Muñoz, 1907). The acclamation of Christ as "the Light" would, of course, be particulary apt for a lamp decoration. It is further relevant to recall that at Apamea (near Kurin) there was documented until at least 361, the Neo-Platonic school of Iamblichus of Chalcis, disciple of Prophyry (Balty, 1972, 209 ff.), and that two pavements of Sages have been found there, one under the cathedral built in 533 (itself a symbol of suppression; *ibid.*) and another, in the "governor's palace," perhaps dating as late as the sixth century. In conclusion, the "Antioch Chalice" is here provisionally identified instead as the "Apamea lamp"—a theory which will be pursued at length elsewhere.

Selected Bibliography

Eisen, 1916; *idem,* 1923; Woolley, 1924; Diehl, 1926, 105; Jerphanion, 1926; Mouterde, 1926; Wilpert, 1926; Dodge, 1927; Eisen, 1933; for other publications up to 1940 see Arnason, 1941; *idem,* 1942; after which, see Weitzmann, 1947, 404; Dodge, 1950; de Francovich, 1951, 3 ff.; Rorimer, 1951, 102 ff.; *Art Treasures,* 1952, 51, 221; Rorimer, 1954; Coche de la Ferté, 1956, 160; Elbern, 1963, 120; *Middle Ages,* 1969, no. 6; Kondoleon, 1979, 48 f.; *Age,* 1979, no. 542.

Fig. 40.5

Fig. 40.6

Fig. 41.1

41. CHALICE

POTERION

Figures 41.1–41.5

New York, The Metropolitan Museum of Art,
no. 47.100.34 (Fletcher Fund, 1947)

Antioch Treasure, Sixth to Seventh Century

For compositional analysis, see Chapter III, Appendix III.2.

This chalice, now badly damaged, has a broad cup supported on a flared foot with a knob (fig. 41.2). An inscription runs around the top of the cup between a border of turnings, one above and two below, with the latter banding a concave moulding (figs. 41.1, 41.2). It continues on the foot, where it is framed by a pair of engraved lines. Other lines mark the bottom of the cup and the top (two) and bottom (three) of the knob. According to notes taken around 1910–1913 (MMA files), the chalice was gilded "inside" and on the inscribed bands; there are three stamps inside the foot.

This chalice was made in two parts, cup and foot, probably from the same melt of metal. Both were formed by hammering. They were soldered together, probably by the method described for chalice no. 29, which involves the use of a silver collar and leaves no distinguishable join (see Entry no. 1). The outside of the chalice and the inside of its cup were finished and their decorative lines engraved on a lathe. Gilding was probably applied by mercury.

This chalice was dropped and both its cup and foot were shattered, apparently before 1913 (see Chapter II, above). An early photograph (fig. 41.5), taken while the chalice was at Kouchakji Frères in Paris, shows its intact state before the damage. It was restored by the firm of Léon André in Paris, around 1913 (see also Entry no. 40). There, the fragments of the cup were mounted on a modern silver cup and the foot was reassembled (minus much of its inscription) and reinforced with a cone of modern silver. The same procedure was later used by the same firm to restore the Phela chalices (nos. 61, 62). This vessel was said (MMA files) to have been cleaned by André, but it was apparently still corroded on entering The Metropolitan Museum in 1947, where C. J. Langlais then subjected it to a four-step cleaning process which "removed incrustation." There is still, however, much silver chloride corrosion present on the object.

Fig. 41.4

Fig. 41.3

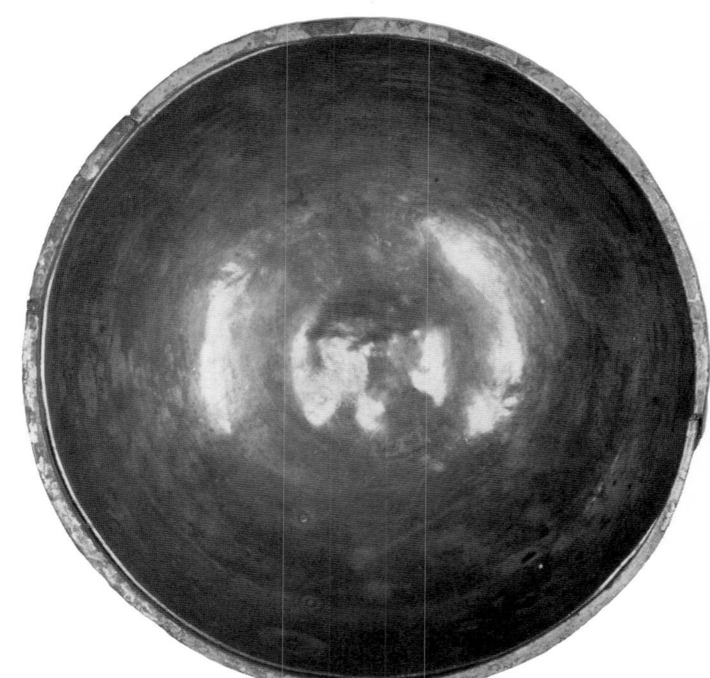

+ΥΠΕΡΑΝΑΠΑΥCCΕΩCΧΑΡΟΥΦΑΚCΩΤΗΡΙΑCΘΕΚΛΗC

ΚΑΙΤΩΝΤΕΚΝΩΝΑΥΤΩΝ

+ Ὑπὲρ ἀναπαύσεως Χαρουφα κ(αὶ) σωτηρίας Θέκλης [*καὶ τῶν τέκ*]νων αὐ[*τῶν*].

H	18.5 cm
D (cup rim)	17.9 cm
D (foot rim)	10.2–10.4 cm

Fig. 41.2

STAMPS

According to a letter written by Fahim Kouchakji to W. H. Forsyth, on November 8, 1948 (MMA files), two or three stamps were noticed inside the foot by Constaki Kouchakji of Aleppo, before the chalice was damaged. According to that letter, all three read *APRAM, APRM,* and *EPRAM* or *ABPAM,* while according to Downey (1951, 350), they read *ABPAM.* The latter could be read *ABRA(HA)M* in Greek, while *EPRAM* could be read *EP(H)RA(I)M* in Latin; Ephraim was the name of the *comes Orientis* at Antioch in 524–526, who was (honorary?) *comes sacrarum largitionum* (*IGLS,* no. 1142). These stamps were classified as "undated" and "imperial(?)" by Dodd (1961, no. 80), who did not cite the Kouchakji readings. Unfortunately, the stamps, which are now obscured by the modern cone inserted in the foot, did not show up in radiographs taken in 1985 by Richard Stone and Edmund Dandridge of the Conservation Department of The Metropolitan Museum.

INSCRIPTION

+ *For the repose (of the soul) of CHAROUFAS and (for) the salvation of THEKLA and of THEIR CHILDREN.*

Engraved(?), double-stroke (H of letters = 1.5–1.6 cm [cup]; .9 cm [foot]). Downey, 1951, 349; Dodd, 1961, no. 80.

The letters are lunate. The form of the *alpha* on the cup differs from that on the foot. There are no serifs or variations in the thickness of the letters except for *phi. Kai* is written in full and abbreviated *Ks.*

The double-stroke lettering on this object differs from that on the Hama flask (no. 15), the large Antioch cross (no. 42), and on objects in the Luxor treasure (Strzygowski, 1904, nos. 7201 ff.), where there is some flaring of the extremities. The combination of the dedicatory formulae *hyper anapauseos* and *(hyper) soterias* is discussed at length by Downey (1951; see also Entry no. 35). The persons named on this chalice do not reappear on other objects herein catalogued. As noted by Downey (*ibid.,* 350, and note 4), Charoufas is a Semitic name, well attested near Apamea in the sixth century. See figure I.1.

COMMENTARY

This chalice, which by its construction apparently belongs to our Type A (see Entry no. 1), has concave mouldings at the top of the cup like those on chalices nos. 2 (Hama) and 30 (Riha), and ewers nos. 37 and 38 (both Riha). The positioning of part of the inscription on the foot is unparalleled among Early Byzantine chalices, but occurs on western chalices of the eighth century and later (Elbern, 1963, 13 ff.). Also unusual is the gilding on the inside of the cup, which is normally not even burnished (see Entry no. 1).

BIBLIOGRAPHY

Eisen, 1916, 426; Volbach, 1918, 23 ff.; Bréhier, 1920, 175; Volbach, 1921 [I], 13, no. 2; *idem,* 1921 [II], 110 f.; Watts, 1922, 11 f.; Eisen, 1923, vol. 1, 3; Diehl, 1926, 105, note 2; Jerphanion, 1926, 17 ff.; Mouterde, 1926, 364; Wilpert, 1926, 136; *Exposition,* 1931, no. 396; Volbach, 1931/1932, 107; Braun, 1932, 78 ff.; Eisen, 1933, 20 f.; *Dark Ages,* 1937, no. 81; *Early Christian,* 1947, no. 392; Downey, 1951, 349 ff.; Rorimer, 1954, 161; *IGLS,* no. 2044; Dodd, 1961, no. 80; Ross, 1962, 11; Weitzmann and Ševčenko, 1963, 395, 398, note 53; Dodd, 1973, 14, no. 5, 15, 20 ff.

Fig. 41.5

42a–c.
Cross Revetment

STAUROS

Figures 42.1–42.8

42a. New York, The Metropolitan Museum of Art,
no. 50.5.3 (Fletcher Fund, 1950) (arm revetments)
42b, c. Paris, Musée du Louvre, Département des Antiquités Grecques et Romaines, nos. MNE 632, 633 (medallions I, II)

Antioch Treasure, Sixth to Early Seventh Century

For compositional analysis, see Chapter III, Appendix III.2.

This cross revetment can be reconstructed from parts preserved in The Metropolitan Museum of Art and the Musée du Louvre (figs. 42.2–42.8). (Thanks are due to Dr. Margaret Frazer, Curator of the former museum, and to Dr. Catherine Metzger, Conservateur of the latter, for their help in the present reconstruction.) Both sides of the cross had the same decoration: in the center, a bust portrait of Christ in relief set within a circle of large beads (figs. 42.5, 42.6). The flaring arms of the cross are covered with a slightly raised inscription framed by a flat border (figs. 42.1–42.3).

This revetment, composed of eight hammered sheets of metal wrapped around the four arms of a wooden core, is joined and secured to the wood along its thickness by a series of silver nails (now numbering 108) placed one centimeter apart (fig. 42.4). Silver nails, used to attach the central medallions to the core, remain within the beaded border and on the lower arm stub. The medallions had projecting stubs that fit over the ends of the silver sheathings on the arms. Although the decoration of the two medallions is nearly identical (including a wedge in the same position within the series of beads), differences in Christ's beard and some measurements preclude manufacture from a common matrix. Examination of the medallions in the Laboratoire de Recherche des Musées de France in May 1985 revealed surface abrasion and the absence of mercury. This suggests that the gilding, traces of which remain on the halo, garments, books, and beads, was in gold leaf.

It is now unclear whether the cross revetment and fifteen nails were removed from the original wooden core before burial. This cross has been restored twice, once around 1913 by Léon André, in Paris, and again in 1953 at The Metropolitan Museum. The first restoration was described thus by Downey (1954, 276): "(The metal was) skillfully mounted . . . on a new wood core covered with plaster which simulates the texture and appearance of the original metal." It is now very difficult to differentiate the original from the restored parts, to determine whether the cross had hoops to hold *pendelia* (on which, see Entry no. 7) or if the revetment on the foot surrounded a wooden tang for positioning in a stand. During the second restoration, the inscriptions on the lower arm were reversed and thereby corrected, apparently by sawing off the lower arm and reattaching it to the cross. The present proposed reconstruction (figs. 42.7, 42.8) would reduce the length of the lower arm and slightly increase that of the upper, in keeping with demands made by the length of the inscribed text, which is fullest on the reverse side. All the

Fig. 42.4

H	149.0 cm	*Fig. 42.2*
W	95.0 cm	
TH	4.5 cm	
D of medallion I (with beads)	13.2 cm	
D of medallion II (with beads)	12.7 cm	

arms would be set further away from the crossing to allow the insertion of the two Louvre medallions, whose surviving stubs with borders would overlap the ends of the arms (the nail under medallion II would fit into the nail hole at the top of the lower arm, side II), thus concealing the arm joints. The two medallions are at present backed with wax and a white substance covered by a piece of cloth. The backing was apparently applied before, or while, they were in the possession of their first known owner, A. Kann (1910–1931?), as a ticket bearing his name adheres to the covering.

ΑΓΙΟϹΟΘΕΟϹΑΓΙΟϹΙϹΧΥΡΟϹΑΓΙΟϹΑΘΑΝΑΤΟϹΕΛΕΗϹΟΝΗΜΑϹ

ΥΠΕΡΕΥΧΗϹΗΡΟΔΟΤΟΥΚΑΙΚΟΜΙΤΑΠΑΝΤΑΛΕΟΝΤΟϹ

Ἅγι[ος ὁ Θεός,] ἅγιος ἰσχυρ[ός, ἅγι]ος [ἀθά]νατος ἐλ[έησ]ον ἡμᾶς.
Ὑπὲ[ρ εὐχῆς] Ἡροδότου καὶ Κομιτᾶ Παντ[α]λέοντος

Fig. 42.1

Inscription

Side I: *God is Holy, the All-Powerful is Holy, the Immortal is Holy, Have mercy on us.*
Side II: *In fulfillment of a vow of HERODOTOS and KOMITAS, (sons) of PANTALEON.*

Double stroke, raised (H of letters = 3.0–6.0 cm). Downey, 1951, 352, note 1; *idem,* 1954, 280.

Originally mounted with Pantaleon's name incorrectly set on side I, the text was emended by Downey (1951, 352, note 1) and the inscription was properly rearranged on the cross in 1953 (*idem,* 1954). The two final letters (*OC*) on the right arm of side I, however, were left in their upside down, reversed position. The letters are lunate, and in some cases show flared extremities rather than serifs. Individual letter size varies more or less according to its position on the flaring arms of the cross. There are no abbreviations or ligatures.

Double-stroke lettering occurs on the Antioch treasure chalice (no. 41) and on the Hama flask (no. 15). This type of lettering approximates stone inscriptions executed in relief, many of which are found in Syria, particularly in the basalt stone regions (*IGLS, passim*). The combination of the *Trisagion* on one face of the cross with a dedication on the other occurs also on the silver-plated cross in the Louvre (Metzger, 1972). The *Trisagion,* which is first attested in the fifth century (and should not be confused with the *Tersanctus* of Isaiah 6.3 [see Entry no. 32]), was subject to both Trinitarian and Christological interpretations (see Brock, 1985, 29 f.). In the latter case, the phrase "Who was crucified for us" was added for emphasis. While this longer form is often called Monophysite, and the shorter, Trinitarian form (used on this cross) is considered Chalcedonian (Downey, 1954, 278 ff.), usage was, in fact, along geographic rather than sectarian lines (Brock, 1985, 29 and note 18). The former version was prevalent in the West, Constantinople, and Jerusalem, while the latter was favored in Asia Minor, Syria, and Egypt. While the three names inscribed on the Antioch cross do not otherwise recur on Syrian silver objects, two of them are attested in other inscriptions from Northern Syria. A Komitas was honored on a bronze cross (*IGLS,* no. 211) belonging to G. Marcopoli of Aleppo, an early owner of the Riha paten (see Chapter II, above), and the name Pantaleon (or Pantoleon) is recorded at Antioch (a *klerikos*), at Kaper Pera (a *commerciarius,* who built a church there in 595/6), and at Igaz (*IGLS,* nos. 1473, 1600; Dagron, 1985, 456 f.).

Commentary

This is one of the largest crosses extant from the Early Byzantine period. At a meter and a half high, it is surpassed by the bronze cross of S. Vitale at Ravenna (present height 168 cm; Cavallo *et al.,* 1982, no. 35), while the bronze "Moses cross" at Mount Sinai is just over one meter (Weitzmann and Ševčenko, 1963, *passim*). Tall silver revetted crosses survive from medieval Georgia; that from Katskhi (eleventh century), for example, is two and one-third meters high (Mepisashvili and Tsintsadze, 1979, 266). Textual evidence indicates that monumental crosses featured prominently in some important Early Byzantine churches, the earliest being the 150-pound gold cross donated after 324 by Emperor Constantine to St. Peter's in Rome (*Liber Pontificalis,* 176). When the metal cross set up around 378 by Poimnia on the Church of the Ascension in Jerusalem (Wilkinson, 1981, 51) was struck by lightning in 448, the Empress Eudocia was said to have replaced it with a 6000(!) pound bronze cross (Rufus, ch. 12). A second large cross—a gemmed gold cross on steps—was erected on Golgotha by Emperor Theodosius II and Pulcheria in 421/2 (Holum, 1982, 103). Later imperial donations, such as the pearl-studded cross given to the Holy Sepulchre by Empress Theodora (Malalas, p. 423) and the gemmed cross sent to Sergiopolis by her and Justinian (Evagrius, *HE,* VI.21) may also have been on a large scale. The gold gemmed cross presented by the Persian King Chosroes II in 591, also to St. Sergios, must have been of considerable size as its dedicatory inscription fills sixteen lines of printed text (*ibid.*).

Although the Antioch cross has been described as a "processional cross supported by two men," as portrayed on two of the Antioch plaques (nos. 46, 47; Downey, 1954, 278), it was probably on permanent display inside its church. As observed above, it is unclear whether the original wooden core of the cross may have had an extended foot, like the tang on solid metal crosses (e.g., nos. 7, 8), to insert in a stand. There is an eastern tradition of large crosses being prominently displayed before the altar—a tradition probably based on the cross erected on Golgotha by Theodosius. According to the sixth-century description of the Cathedral of Edessa (McVey, 1983, 107), a large "luminous" cross stood on a "column that . . . portrays Golgotha," situated between the ambo and the chancel (*ibid.,* 95). A similar arrangement reappears in 1050 at Antioch, where in the cathedral three large silver-gilt gemmed crosses stood on wooden "stools" to the west of the altar (LeStrange, 1890, 372 f.). The tall medieval Georgian crosses referred to above likewise stood on bases before the altar (Mepisashvili and Tsintsadze, 1979, 155 f.). In the Church of the Holy Cross built at Rusafa in 559 (Ulbert, 1977) there is, in the second phase of construction of the U-shaped Syrian bema which stood in the nave, a stone socle before the throne (Baccache and Tchalenko, 1979/1980, vol. 1, 316) which may have served as a base for a monumental cross of the type donated to that city by Justinian and Theodora and, later, by Chosroes II (Evagrius, *HE,* VI.21). There are similar bases or sinkings on bemas in Syrian villages in the area of Kaper Koraon (Baccache and Tchalenko, 1979/1980, vol. 1, 75, 97, 137) and several bema thrones are decorated with, or support, a sculptured cross (*ibid.,* 101, 122, 219, 227). Moreover, a Syrian pavement from that area apparently portrays such an arrangement (Sotheby's 1973, no. 98) which is evocative of the *Hetoimasia.* It is possible, therefore, that the Antioch cross was set up within a Syrian bema where both of its decorated sides would have been visible to the congregation.

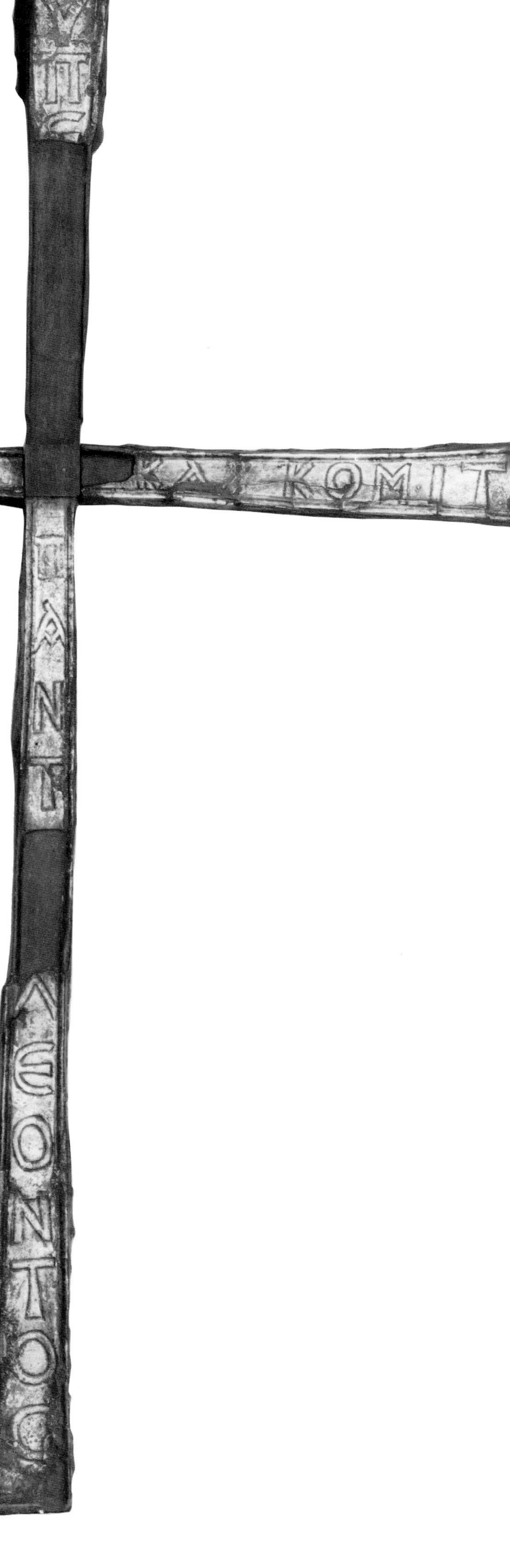

Fig. 42.3

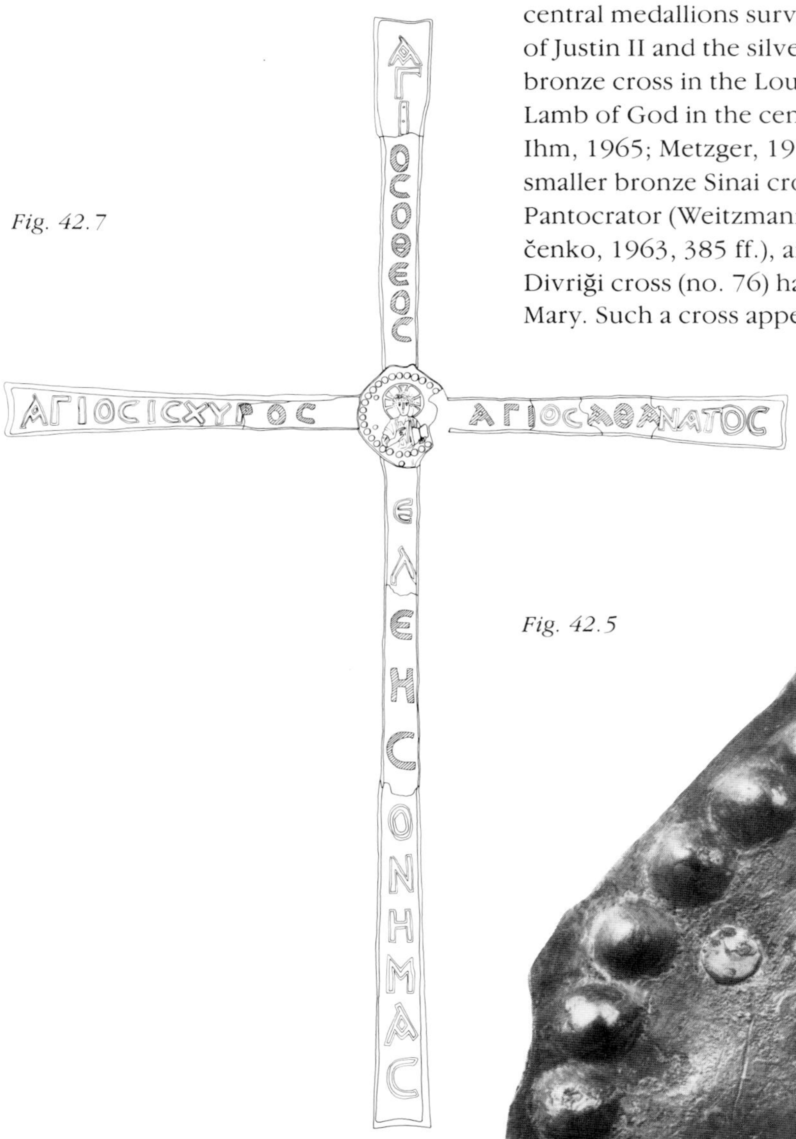

Other Early Byzantine crosses with central medallions survive: the cross of Justin II and the silver-plated bronze cross in the Louvre have the Lamb of God in the center (Belting-Ihm, 1965; Metzger, 1972); the smaller bronze Sinai cross has the Pantocrator (Weitzmann and Ševčenko, 1963, 385 ff.), and the Divriği cross (no. 76) has the Virgin Mary. Such a cross appears in the apse mosaic of S. Apollinare in Classe, and in a Syriac manuscript of 633/4 from Beth Hala (Leroy, 1964, pl. 2). The type of Christ portrayed in the Antioch cross medallions is the "Syrian" type, with triangular face and frizzy hair, but only one (I) has the characteristic short beard found in the Rabbula, Diyarbakir, and Beth Hala Gospels, and on the coinage of Justinian II (*ibid.,* pls. 2, 24, 26, 27, 29–31; Breckenridge, 1959, 59 ff.).

Despite its size, the Antioch cross is closely related in form and decora-

Fig. 42.7

Fig. 42.5

tion to the smaller solid metal crosses in this catalogue. It bears comparison with the four Hama crosses (nos. 7–10), and those from Phela (no. 65), Divriği (no. 76), Ma'aret en-Noman (nos. 67, 68), and Luxor (Strzygowski, 1904, no. 7201). The cross which is perhaps closest is that in the Louvre, which has a central medallion and the same distribution of similar inscribed texts (Metzger, 1972).

Bibliography

Eisen, 1916, 426; Volbach, 1921 [II] 110 ff.; Eisen, 1923, vol. 1, 3; Diehl, 1926, 105, note 2; Jerphanion, 1926, 12; Mouterde, 1926, 364; *Exposition,* 1931, no. 397, 398; Eisen, 1933, 20 f.; *Dark Ages,* 1937, no. 82; *Early Christian,* 1947, no. 389; Downey, 1951, 352, note 1; *idem,* 1954; Rorimer, 1954, 161; Coche de la Ferté, 1958, no. 41; Weitzmann and Ševčenko, 1963, 398, note 53.

Fig. 42.8

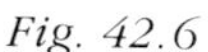

Fig. 42.6

43. CROSS

STAUROS

Present Location Unknown

(formerly, W. Froehner Collection, Paris)
Antioch Treasure, Sixth to Seventh Century(?)

H = "smaller" than 150 cm (i.e., than Antioch cross no. 42)

In the first report published on the Antioch treasure, Eisen (1916, 426) listed the six pieces belonging to Kouchakji Frères of Paris and added that "A smaller cross, also of silver, supposed to be from the same find, was procured by M. Froehner, the well known archaeologist. It is now in Paris and has remained in his possession." The larger cross is no. 42. This cross has not been located. With the exception of two tiny, possibly medieval, pendant crosses (inv. nos. 1299, 1300), which are of silver, the dozen or so crosses now preserved in the Froehner Collection in the Bibliothèque Nationale, are all of bronze.

BIBLIOGRAPHY

Eisen, 1916, 426; Eisen, 1923, 3.

44. Plaque

Figures 44.1–44.3

New York, The Metropolitan Museum of Art, no. 50.5.1 (Fletcher Fund, 1950)

Antioch Treasure, Sixth to Seventh Century

For compositional analysis, see Chapter III, Appendix III.2.

This plaque, which forms a pair with no. 45, bears a repoussé portrait of St. Paul holding a book, standing on a small platform under an arch flanked by peacocks (fig. 44.1). The spirally fluted columns, with twisted rope-carved mouldings at the top and bottom, stand on vertically fluted bases and support single-zone acanthus capitals. The arch is ornamented with an overlapping leaf pattern culminating in a small wreath. Surrounding the central panel, framed by two twisted rope mouldings, is an animated scroll border issuing from a vase below and a cross above, with trefoil leaves at its four corners. The edges of the plaque were bent back for attachment to a (wooden?) panel by means of nails fitted through holes, some of which survive. There are six holes in the upper surface of the plaque (one each in the upper left corner, on the left side, and the top, and three on the right), and two or three additional holes where the plaque bends back, presumably for attachment in the thickness of its supporting panel (fig. 44.2).

Fig. 44.3

The decoration of this plaque was executed in repoussé technique from behind, and details (such as the linear definition of hair, beard, sandals, leaf patterns, and peacock feathers) were engraved and chased from the front. Several circular punches were used to produce stippling and other flat patterns; the largest (D .18 cm) was used on the peacocks, border grapes, and platform; a smaller one (D .10 cm) on the arch wreath and book; and the two smallest ones on the platform (D .05 cm) and the halo, undergarment, and border of the mantle (D .03 cm).

A photograph taken before 1913 (fig. 44.3) shows the plaque heavily corroded, with its plain outer edge and rope border broken off from the lower left corner halfway up the left side and along the bottom. The missing metal was replaced and the front of the plaque cleaned by Léon André of Paris, in 1913 (MMA files), and the object was thus published by Volbach in 1918 (25, fig. 3). But, when W. Young examined the plaque in 1937 (MMA files), the rear surface retained what he described as "the heaviest silver deposit that I have ever seen on any antique silver object . . . (being) . . . from 1/16–3/16 of an inch thick." When the plaque entered The Metropolitan Museum in 1950, it was said to have had modern light brown paint on its reverse, the latter being subsequently filled with wax. Stains were then removed from the obverse and the surface polished.

Commentary

See Entry no. 45.

Bibliography

See Entry no. 45.

H 26.8–27.5 cm
W 21.1–21.2 cm

Fig. 44.1

Fig. 44.2

45. PLAQUE

Figures 45.1–45.3

New York, The Metropolitan Museum of Art, no. 50.5.2 (Fletcher Fund, 1950)

Antioch Treasure, Sixth to Seventh Century

For compositional analysis, see Chapter III, Appendix III.2.

This plaque, which forms a pair with no. 44, bears a repoussé portrait of St. Peter, holding a cross staff and keys, standing on a small platform under an arch flanked by peacocks (fig 45.1). The spirally fluted columns, with twisted rope-carved mouldings at the top and bottom, stand on vertically fluted bases and support single-zone acanthus capitals. As on plaque no. 44, the arch here is ornamented with an overlapping leaf pattern culminating in a small wreath. Surrounding the central panel, framed by two twisted rope mouldings, is an animated scroll border issuing from a vase below and a cross above, with trefoil leaves at its four corners. Plaques nos. 44 and 45 differ slightly in their dimensions, and in the motifs of their scroll borders.

Some of the attachment holes in this plaque contain silver/copper nails with green corrosion on the reverse. Eight nail holes appear in the obverse surface (one each in the upper and lower left corners, and on the bottom; two on the left side; and three on the right), and two additional holes pierce the plaque where it was turned back around the thickness of its supporting (wooden?) panel (fig. 45.2).

This plaque was decorated in the same way as no. 44; indeed, the same punches were employed for identically placed ornaments (e.g., on grapes, feathers, garments, *etc.*). Although the platform upon which Peter stands has been recently damaged, it retains, on its far right side, the same patterns found on the platform in plaque no. 44. Chisel marks are visible all over the background of this panel.

This plaque shares the history of repair (contrast figs. 45. 1 and 45.3 [pre-1913 photograph]) outlined for plaque no. 44. Present defects include a horizontal crack across its center and a patch of silver (.6 × 1.3 cm) between Peter's feet, which was lost and recently replaced. Much of the surface is worn smooth, such as the stippling on halo and *clavi,* and Peter's keys.

COMMENTARY

The format and architectural framework of plaques nos. 44 and 45 resemble those of the five Sion treasure plaques, which include a set of three, each with three figures under a gable (Firatlı, 1965, figs. 7, 8; *DO Handbook,* 1967, no. 69), and a pair with a cross under an arch (Kitzinger, 1974). The peacocks in the spandrels of the Antioch plaques recur in almost identical form on the gabled Sion plaques. Furthermore, the large trefoil leaves that point outward in the border corners of

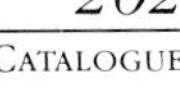

Fig. 45.3

these plaques appear there as well, though pointing inward. All seven (Antioch/Sion) plaques have similar columns which may, in turn, be compared with those on Hama chalice no. 3 and the Riha paten (no. 35). Moreover, they show basically the same distribution of ornamental patterns, albeit of differing motifs, on the arches or gables, and borders.

The figure styles of Paul (no. 44) and Peter (no. 45) differ in several respects. Top-heavy, with a tiny ear (like Peter's) and a large hand, Paul is rendered in a flat and angular manner. His sharp features and furrowed brow endow him with an aura of intensity and intelligence. Linear definition flattens his drapery which, except for one leg, hangs loose from the body in the manner of Venus' robe on the Anchises plate in the Hermitage (Dodd, 1961, no. 16; AD 550). By contrast, Peter is a softer figure (made more so by surface wear). His appearance is dominated by his heavy mantle, which resembles that of St. Symeon on the Louvre plaque (no. 71) and those worn by the figures on Hama chalice no. 3. The peacocks on both plaques are executed in high relief profile views, and are covered with textured patterns, as are the animals and fish on many other Byzantine and Sasanian silver objects (e.g., Kent and Painter, 1977, nos. 158, 161, 178, 183, 184, *etc.*).

The arch had, for the Early Byzantines, a "vaguely honorific" function of "singling out persons and objects deserving of reverence" (Kitzinger, 1974, 12), and as such enjoyed wide popularity in secular and sacred contexts—including Gospel canon tables, which offer striking formal similarities with these silver plaques. Although martyred and honored at Rome, Peter and Paul were long associated with Antioch, where they preached the Gospel. As chiefs of the Apostles, they were often portrayed together (e.g., *Age,* 1979, nos. 506, 507), sometimes flanking a *Chrismon* or cross (as on plaques nos. 46, 47). They appear on other Syrian silver objects, such as Hama chalice no. 3, where they flank a cross, and the Beth Misona chalices (nos. 57–59), where they flank Christ. If, contrary to their widely accepted designation as "bookcovers" (*ibid.,* nos. 554, 555), these plaques instead formed part of an iconic revetment, they may have flanked a central panel with a cross or the figure of Christ. (See the discussion to Entry no. 46.)

BIBLIOGRAPHY

Eisen, 1916, 426; Volbach, 1918, 25 ff.; Bréhier, 1920, 175; Volbach, 1921 [II], 110 ff.; Eisen, 1923, vol. 1, 3; Diehl, 1926, 102, note 5, 121; Jerphanion, 1926, 17 ff.; Mouterde, 1926, 364; Wilpert, 1926, 138 f.; *idem,* 1927, 338 ff.; *Exposition,* 1931, nos. 393, 394; Eisen, 1933, 20 f.; *Dark Ages,* 1937, nos. 83, 84; *Early Christian,* 1947, no. 390; Downey, 1954, 276; Rorimer, 1954, 161; *Bookbinding,* 1957/1958, nos. 3, 4; Dodd, 1973, 20 ff., 54; Kent and Painter, 1977, nos. 148, 149; *Age,* 1979, no. 554.

H	27.1–27.2 cm
W	21.1–21.4 cm

Fig. 45.1

Fig. 45.2

46. Plaque

Figures 46.1–46.4

New York, The Metropolitan Museum of Art, no. 47.100.36

Antioch Treasure, Sixth to Seventh Century

For compositional analysis, see Chapter III, Appendix III.2.

Fig. 46.3

This plaque, which is a near twin to and likely forms a pair with the fragmentary plaque in the Louvre (no. 47), bears a repoussé composition consisting of two nimbed and bearded saints who each hold a book in one hand and a large silver cross between them, in the other (fig. 46.1). The composition is surrounded by a scrolled border issuing from four corner amphorae and framed by two twisted rope mouldings. This and plaque no. 47 were, like plaques nos. 44 and 45, presumably made to fit onto a wooden backing. Most of the outer edges are now lost except on the lower left side, where there survives one of the holes for attachment by nails of silver/copper alloy, which have left green corrosion on the reverse (fig. 46.2).

Like Antioch plaques nos. 44, 45, and 47, this one was decorated in repoussé technique from behind, and details, such as the linear definition of haloes, hair, pleats, and sandals, were finished by chasing and engraving on the front. Two circular punches (D .15 and .05 cm) were used to ornament the book covers, the hatched *clavi,* and, possibly, the border grapes. Another (D .23 cm) formed the pupils.

A photograph taken before 1913 (fig. 46.3) shows the plaque heavily corroded, and missing the entire upper right border area, the lower right and upper left corners, and the plain outer edge beyond the left scrolled border. The restoration undertaken by Léon André in Paris, in 1913, is described in The Metropolitan Museum files in the following terms: the plaque "was mounted in metal frame, chased to complete border, backed by silk gauze and wax." One might also observe that sections of the surviving scrolled border were moved from the upper border down to the lower right side. (The plaque thus restored was published by Diehl in 1926, 121.) The backing must have been removed if, as stated (MMA files), the reverse was studied by W. Young in 1937. When the plaque entered The Metropolitan Museum (in 1947), it was said, like plaque no. 44, to have had modern brown paint on its reverse. The reverse was subsequently reinforced with beeswax (fig. 46.2), and incrustations and stains were removed from the front, which was then polished. Yet, corrosion remains, and it is difficult to distinguish the original parts of the border. The plaque is cracked around the top and bottom of the cross, and on the lower left side.

Commentary

Stylistically, the figures on plaques nos. 46 and 47 may best be compared with those of the Sion silver plaques (Firatlı, 1965, figs. 7, 8; *DO Handbook,* 1967, no. 69), which are likewise conceived in geometrical terms. They have the same symmetrical faces under rigid fringes of hair, and the same stiff parallel drapery folds, although anatomical distortions differ between the swollen shoulders on the Sion plaques and the tiny hands and feet on the Antioch panels. This schematization may also be observed in the Rabbula Gospels Evangelists (fig. 46.4 [St. Mark]; Cecchelli *et al.,* 1959, fol. 10a) who, while of broader girth and with bigger hands and feet, are enveloped in drapery similar to that on these plaques. It is significant that the Rabbula Gospels, dated 586, may have been produced at a site only seven kilometers from Kaper Koraon/Kurin (see Mundell-Mango, 1983; and Chapter II, above). The Rabbula Evangelists, these two Antioch plaques, and some local pavements may therefore represent a regional "style" which, however, was but one of several, as demonstrated by the multiplicity of hands and styles evident elsewhere in the same Gospels, and on the other pair of Antioch plaques (nos. 44, 45).

The similarities, not only in drapery style but in physiognomy, between the four Rabbula Evangelists and the four (now three) figures on these plaques permit an identification of the latter as Evangelists, holding their books. The figure on the left on this plaque resembles the youthful, unbearded John, also on the left in the Gospels, and that on the right, the bearded full-faced Matthew on the same page (Cecchelli *et al.,* 1959, fol. 9b). The surviving bearded figure on the Louvre plaque can be compared to either Mark or Luke in the Rabbula Gospels.

The composition on these two plaques is found in a similar style on the alabaster reliquary-*sedia* in Venice, attributed to sixth-century Alexandria (*Treasury,* 1984, no. 7), where the Evangelists are accompanied by their symbols. Both there and on the Stroganoff silver plate (Volbach, 1958, pl. 245), there are streams or Rivers of Paradise flowing from the cross, as also on Phela paten no. 63. Here, as on the Sarigüzel sarcophagus in Istanbul (*ibid.,* pl. 75), the cross without rivers is receiving the homage of a pair of flanking figures. (On the relic of the True Cross then kept at nearby Apamea, see Entry no. 3).

The function most often proposed for the Antioch and Sion silver plaques (*Age,* 1979, nos. 554, 555; Kitzinger, 1974) is that of book covers; presumably the four Evangelists who hold books and a large cross (nos. 46, 47) were intended for the Gospels, while Peter and Paul (nos. 44, 45) were intended for the Epistles. If, as Kitzinger (1974, 3) has suggested, book covers could reflect a frontispiece inside, it would do well to recall that the arched and gabled frames of the Rabbula Gospels canon tables (often with flanking birds) were transferred to frame other illuminations that prefaced the written text, and that among them are Evangelist portraits (e.g., fig. 46.4) which, as noted above, bear comparison with the Antioch and Sion figural plaques. Manuscripts of the Gospels and Epistles were essential even for village churches (see Entry no. 89), and the dimensions of contemporary books (from 30 × 26 cm to 38 × 30 cm; Weitzmann, 1977, 27 ff.) generally correspond to those of our silver plaques.

Fig. 46.4

In the case of the Sion plaques, a difficulty arises from the fact that one matching set consists of three (*DO Handbook,* 1967, no. 69; Firatlı, 1965, fig. 8), not two plaques. This raises the possibility that they served as wall, door or furniture revetments. Indeed, figural panels in precious metal are known to have adorned *confessiones* in Rome (*Liber Pontificalis,* 181, 233, 262).

H	28.1–28.5 cm
W	22.1–23.2 cm

Fig. 46.1

Fig. 46.2

Silver also covered the main portals of Hagia Sophia in Constantinople (*Book of Ceremonies,* I, 192), and St. Peter's in Rome (*Liber Pontificalis,* 323); *confessiones* were also endowed with silver doors at Rome (*ibid.,* 242), and even in a country church near Tivoli (see Entry no. 91). That such silver doors could be enhanced with figural panels is documented in the case of the ciborium of St. Demetrios at Thessalonike (Cormack, 1985, figs. 23, 27). Silver plaques like those in the Antioch (attested ninth century) treasure may have been attached to a chair; the patriarchal throne of Antioch, for example, was composed of silver plates on a palm wood frame (Michael, III, 99). Indeed, silver revetments on all types of church furnishings—such as ciboria, chancel screens, ambos, and altars—were commonplace in the Early Byzantine period, and some, such as the chancel screen in Hagia Sophia, are known to have incorporated figures (including Apostles; see Mango, 1972, 87).

Although the possible functions for plaques nos. 44–47 are seemingly numerous, they were, in fact, probably limited by the type of church in which they were dedicated, which in this case was very likely rural and small. Revetments in such churches were most likely restricted to the immediate altar area. It was suggested in Entry no. 35 that specific donations were displayed on the Riha paten, and that they may have included a silver revetment represented by that plate's prominent, arched epistyle on columns. Alternatively, the four Antioch plaques could have covered a cubic base anchoring a wooden tang under a monumental cross, like Antioch cross no. 42. If so, the two plaques with the four Evangelists and crosses may have covered the east and west faces of the base, while the Peter and Paul plaques would have covered the north and south faces. Georgian sixth-century stone stelae supporting crosses had framed figural panels (Mepisashvili and Tsintsadze, 1979, 235), which in metallic form later covered the crosses themselves (*ibid.,* 266, 268 f.), or became incorporated into the staff-holders (Seibt and Sanikidze, 1981, no. 23). It is relevant to note that the Syrian bema, a possible "base" for a monumental cross, often had stone thrones with fan-shaped tops, like that on the reliquary-*sedia* in Venice (*Treasury,* 1984, no. 7), which is carved on both sides with figures very similar to those on our plaques. It is tempting, therefore, to suggest that silver plaques nos. 44–47 were revetments attached to the wooden superstructure of a Syrian bema, to which was affixed a monumental cross, itself composed of revetted wood (see Entry no. 42). On silver votive plaques, see Entries nos. 71 and 72.

Bibliography

Eisen, 1916, 426; Volbach, 1918, 25 ff.; Bréhier, 1920, 175; Volbach, 1921 [II], 110 ff.; Eisen, 1923, vol. 1, 3; Diehl, 1926, 121; Jerphanion, 1926, 17 ff.; Mouterde, 1926, 364; Wilpert, 1926, 138 f.; *idem*, 1927, 338 ff.; *Exposition,* 1931, no. 395; Eisen, 1933, 20 f.; *Dark Ages,* 1937, no. 85; *Early Christian,* 1947, no. 391; Downey, 1954, 276, 279; Rorimer, 1954, 161; Grabar, 1954, 22; *Bookbinding,* 1957/1958, 3; Coche de la Ferté, 1958, no. 42; Buschhausen, 1967, 282; Ostoia, 1970, no. 9; Dodd, 1973, 20 ff., 54; *Age,* 1979, no. 555; *Treasury,* 1984, no. 7.

47. Plaque Fragment

Figure 47.1

Paris, Musée du Louvre, Département des Antiquités Grecques et Romaines, no. MNE 659

Antioch Treasure, Sixth to Seventh Century

This is a fragment from the left side of a plaque which probably formed a pair with Antioch plaque no. 46. What remains is part of a nimbed and bearded figure holding a book in one hand and, in the other, a large cross, of which only the flaring tip of the left arm remains (fig. 47.1). On the lower left edge of the piece is a surviving segment of a twisted rope border frame like that on its companion plaque.

Fig. 47.1

This plaque was manufactured by the techniques described for Antioch plaque no. 46. The figure has lost over half his halo and his feet. There are cracks in the area of the neck, to the right of the head, and across the cascading mantle. There is no wax backing as on the other three plaques.

Commentary

See Entry no. 46.

Bibliography

Exposition, 1931, no. 398; *Bookbinding,* 1957/1958, 3; Coche de la Ferté, 1958, 45, 104 f., no. 42; *Age,* 1979, no. 555; *Treasury,* 1984, no. 7.

H	17.5 cm
W	6.0 cm

48. MIRROR

Figures 48.1–48.4

New York, The Metropolitan Museum of Art, nos. 47.100.35 (Fletcher Fund, 1947); 52.37 (Gift of Fahim Kouchakji, 1952; handle)

Antioch Treasure(?), Sixth to Seventh Century(?)

For compositional analysis, see Chapter III, Appendix III.2.

This mirror consists of a disc with raised rim and a handle on the reverse (figs. 48.1, 48.2); the slightly convex obverse was polished to reflect. The spatulate handle grip has a narrow collar across the middle and is decorated to resemble two fingers though, incongruously, it is engraved with a leaf design. The soldering plates are spade-shaped, and a tight overlapping leaf pattern covers the mirror's rim. A lathe-turned circle (D 3.7 cm) marks the center of the reverse, and two concentric lines run just inside the rim.

This mirror was cast, and the turning marks on the reverse indicate that it was finished on a lathe; its cast handle was soldered in place. The dealer Brummer had the disc cleaned, and it was cleaned again in 1948, after its acquisition by The Metropolitan Museum. A hole near the disc's edge and several split areas were repaired with soft solder in 1949 (fig. 48.3; pre-restoration photograph, without handle). Upon its acquisition in 1952, the handle was repaired, straightened, cleaned, and reattached. The soldering plates are fragmentary, and a diagonal dent, like those on the Hama and Stuma patens (nos. 4–6, 34, 36, 39), creases the surface of the object. The back side is very damaged, with a pitted surface.

Fig. 48.4

COMMENTARY

Called a paten in publication, before the presentation of its handle to The Metropolitan in 1952, this mirror belongs to a lesser known type of such objects having handles on the reverse side—a type introduced by the second century AD (Strong, 1966, 179; Lloyd-Morgan, 1981, 90 ff.). A fourth-century(?) example from Syria, now in The Cleveland Museum of Art (Milliken, 1958, ill. after p. 41) has a "reef-knot" handle, while two others, both in a London private collection, have finger-shaped handles like this example. (Finger-shaped hooks project from many objects of Early Christian/Early Byzantine date; see *Age,* 1979, no. 557.) A third such handle may be on a mirror at Nijmegen (Lloyd-Morgan, 1981, 92, no. 7). One of the London mirrors, with elaborate and well-executed guilloche patterns on its handle and rim, has been attributed to the fourth century; it was recently offered for sale together with a platter and a bowl similar to one in the Mildenhall treasure (*Apollo Magazine* [April 1984], 46). The second London mirror, said to be "from the environs of Constantinople" (and, like this, formerly belonging to Brummer; see Brummer, 1979, no. 42), bears close resemblance to this one. Because this Antioch mirror has unusually shaped soldering plates, and

D	23.2–23.3 cm
H	2.8 cm
Weight	510 gr
Roman Weight	1 lb 6 oz 16 scr
Original Silver Price	6 *solidi* 5 1/3 carats

Fig. 48.1

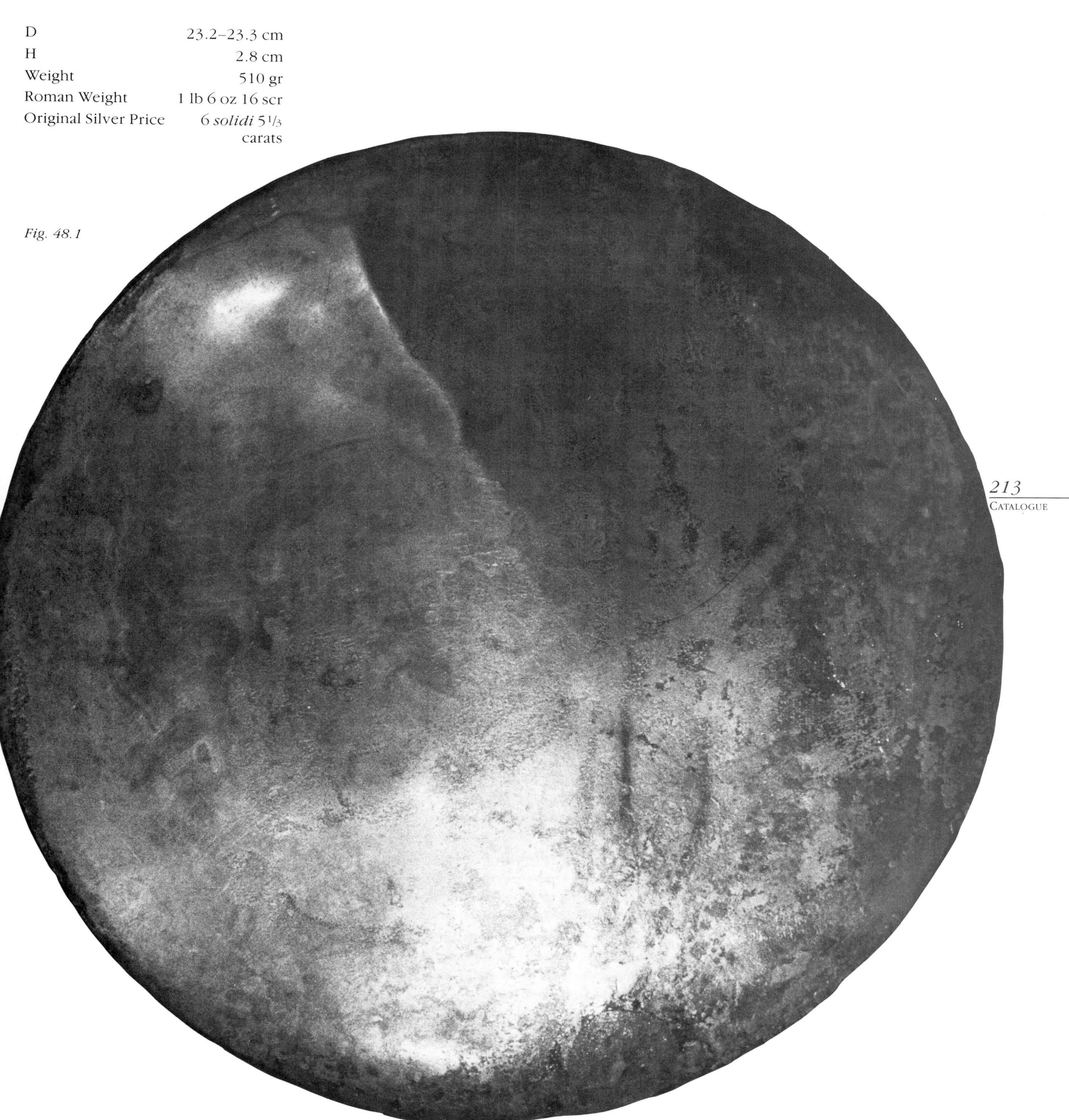

because its border ornament recalls patterns used on various sixth-century silver objects (e.g., nos. 3, 31, 32, 40), it (and the second London mirror) may well be considerably later than the two attributed to the fourth century—that is, basically contemporary with the Antioch treasure proper. While portrayed in use on seventh-century objects (fig. 48.4; Dodd, 1961, no. 75 [AD 641–651]), no extant published mirror of this type has hitherto been dated after the fourth century (see Cahn *et al.,* 1984, 319, notes 10 ff.). The most patently "domestic" article among the reconstructed Kaper Koraon treasure, this mirror was probably donated to a church for its monetary value.

BIBLIOGRAPHY

Early Christian, 1947, no. 393.

Fig. 48.2

Fig. 48.3

49. SPOON

LIGULA

Figures 49.1, 49.2

Washington, D.C., Dumbarton Oaks Collection, no. 37.35

Antioch Treasure(?), Sixth to Early Seventh Century

One of a set of seven (nos. 49–55), this spoon has a plain oval bowl with broad tip, joined by a solid disc to a handle that begins by being hexagonal and then becomes round in section (fig. 49.2). The front of the handle, above the disc, is fashioned into a boar's head. The round section has four wide bands, and the terminating finial is composed of a triple set of mouldings below a vase-like element banded at the top by a double moulding and ending in an oblong knob. There is an inscription on the upper three sides of the hexagonal part of the handle, and a monogram on the right side of the disc (fig. 49.1; compare fig. 55.3 [Diehl, 1930, fig. 1]). The disc extends in a rat-tail on the undecorated back of the bowl (compare fig. 55.3).

This spoon was cast, probably in three parts, as was Hama spoon no. 22: bowl, disc with rat-tail, and handle with boar's head and finial. The bands were engraved on the round part of the handle, and linear and stippled details were added to the boar's head. There are slight differences among the boars' heads on the seven spoons in the set, as well as among the mouldings of the finials; the lengths of the hexagonal parts of the handles vary from 3.0 to 3.3 centimeters. Some niello has been lost from the inscription.

INSCRIPTION

Handle: + *Blessing of St. Thomas.*
Disc: + *(Property) of DOMNOS* +

Engraved, nielloed (H of letters = .24 cm). Diehl, 1930, 210; Ross, 1962, 18.

The letters are of uniform size and serifs are used regularly. The *mu* form used in the inscription has no parallel among the objects of the reconstructed Kaper Koraon treasure.

On the word *eulogia,* see below. (On the Byzantine choice of Apostles, see Jerphanion, 1930, 194.) Monograms appear frequently on silver spoons, and most often they take the box form, which dominated Byzantine monograms generally into the sixth century (see Entry no. 22). Cross monograms, introduced during the reign of Justinian (Weigand, 1937, 130), appear less frequently (see Entry no. 19), and the bar monogram found on one spoon would date to the sev-

Fig. 49.2

L	26.5 cm
W	4.3 cm
Weight	79.5 gr
Roman Weight	2 oz 22 scr
Original Silver Price	23 1/3 carats

+ϵ ΥΛΟΓΙΑ ΤΟΥ ΑΓΙΟΥ Θ Ω Μ Α

+ Εὐλογία του ἁγίου Θωμᾶ + Δόμνου +

Fig. 49.1

enth century (Lazovic *et al.*, 1977, nos. 12, 13; Grierson, 1968, 108). The monogram of Domnos on this set of spoons is distinct from all three types. It may instead be compared with Latin box monograms, which have "floating" letters (see Milojčić, 1970, fig. 7.3, 5–7), in contrast to Greek box monograms, where every letter is usually incorporated into the main letter (often a *nu* or *mu*). The inclusion of a cross within the monogram occurs on the Lampsacus "Sages spoons" (Dalton, 1901, no. 390), on the spoons from Cotyaeum (Istanbul, Archaeological Museum nos. 2152, 2153), and is implicit in the very form of the cross monogram. The name Domnos appears on two objects in the Beth Misona treasure (nos. 57, 60), and is common in other Syrian inscriptions (e.g., *IGLS,* nos. 168, 474, 597, 616, 921, 922, 1378, 1547, 1578, 1579, 1584, 2112, 2113).

Commentary

This type of spoon, having a handle with finial and a bowl which is a cross between oval and pear-shaped, can be described as a *ligula* (see Entry no. 18). The baluster finial is very common on spoons of this period (see Dalton, 1901, nos. 380–391, 400–413). Animal heads appear at the juncture of bowl and handle on spoons dating from the late third century on (Strong, 1966, 178), first as part of the scroll offset, then as an extension of the handle (Johns and Potter, 1983, 38 f.), as they are here, on a larger scale. The solid form and overall pattern of stippling on the boars' heads of these Antioch spoons recall the treatment of the animals embossed in the bowls of the Cyprus spoons (Dalton, 1901, nos. 414–424).

The significance of the inscriptions on this set of spoons must be considered in light of these animal ornaments. The boar and lion were favorite quarries of the royal and aristocratic hunt, and as such were frequently portrayed in both late Roman and Sasanian art. While animals of the sort involved in such hunts were the most popular subjects of mosaic pavements in all types of Syrian buildings of this period, the boar virtually never appears in church decoration, nor does it have any Christian symbolism; indeed, it appears in the Bible as a destructive animal (Psalm 79.13). By contrast, the boar assumed divine and royal significance in enemy Persia (Garsoian, 1982, 160 ff.).

The names on this set of spoons are clearly those of seven Apostles (Thomas, Luke, Mark, Peter, Matthew, Philip, and Paul). Diehl (1930) rightly suggested that their number was originally twelve, and found in two meanings of the word *eulogia* used in the inscriptions preceding them, two possible explanations of the spoons' function. According to one explanation, they were "holy souvenirs" like the ampullae inscribed *eulogia* (i.e., "blessing"; Grabar, 1958, *passim*) obtained at pilgrimage shrines; these, assumedly, would have come from the Apostoleion in either Jerusalem or Constantinople, and Domnos would simply have added his personal monogram. According to Diehl's second interpretation, Domnos gave to his church a set of twelve "used" spoons bearing his monogram. Then, to suit their use in the liturgy, the word *eulogia* (referring to fragments of the eucharist) was inscribed on them, together with the names of the twelve Apostles who were, Diehl conjectured, symbolically represented in the Holy Thursday service in the Apostoleion at Jerusalem by a dozen deacons employing such spoons.

In both cases Diehl presumed that the inscription and monogram were added to the spoons at different times. Yet, two points argue against Diehl's theories. One, countering his first theory, is the boars' heads, which are distinctly inappropriate to Christian pilgrimage manufacture. The other, countering his second theory, is that part of another set of spoons with Apostles' names and a personal monogram ("of Matthew") belongs to the clearly domestic silver treasure from Lampsacus to which amusing afterthoughts in Greek have been added. (Dalton, 1901, nos. 380–384; de Ridder, 1924, no. 2049). Moreover, it is noteworthy that the Lampsacus treasure also contains eight or nine spoons from a set (of twelve ?; see Cahn *et al.,* 1984, 83) engraved with Greek *Sayings of the Seven Sages* and quotations from Vergil and other Latin sources to which amusing afterthoughts in Greek have been added. (Dalton, 1901, nos. 387–392; de Ridder, 1924, no. 2050). The *Sayings of the Seven Sages* are portrayed on two *triclinium* pavements in Syria (at Apamea and Baalbek; see Entry no. 40), an appropriate location given that the *Sayings* were delivered at the "Banquet of the Sages." It is tempting to see these "Sages spoons" as a part of Late Antique, pagan "dining iconography," and the "Apostles spoons" as their Christianized version, serving to remind the diners of the Communion of the Apostles (a "type," in a sense, of all Christian meals).

It seems likely, then, that Domnos had made his set of twelve spoons complete with boars' heads, monograms, and Apostles' names, as domestic dining spoons. *Eulogia* could here be taken in its third sense, that of "blessing" of food (Festugière, 1970, 193, note 35), akin to Latin blessings, such as *De donis Dei,* inscribed on contemporary silver plate shown by Engemann (1972) to be domestic and not liturgical or ecclesiastical in use. The fact that the eighth spoon surviving from the set (no. 56) is, apparently, a poor replacement, and that, while lacking an Apostle's name and owner's monogram, it has an animal's head, suggests that these spoons were still in private hands some time after their manufacture. They were eventually presented to a church for their silver value, perhaps by the individual whose monogram was added to spoon no. 52. Patently part of the domestic *ministerium* was the similar lion-headed spoon in Geneva which has an aphorism ("love your friend") on the handle, like on the Lampsacus "Sages spoons," and is matched to a bowl having the same monogram (Lazovic, *et. al.,* 1977, nos. 12, 13).

BIBLIOGRAPHY

Diehl, 1930; *Exposition,* 1931, no. 375; Ross, 1962, no. 13; *DO Handbook,* 1967, no. 72; Milojčić, 1970; Bruce-Mitford, 1983, 137.

+ Εὐλογία τοῦ ἁγίου Λουκᾶ + Δόμνου +

Fig. 50.1

50. SPOON

LIGULA

Figures 50.1, 50.2

Washington, D.C., Dumbarton Oaks Collection,
no. 37.36

Antioch Treasure(?), Sixth to Seventh Century

For a description of this spoon (fig. 50.2) and its manufacture, see Entry no. 49. The bowl of the spoon is slightly bent and niello is missing from the inscription (fig. 50.1).

INSCRIPTION

Handle: + *Blessing of St. Luke.*
Disc: + *(Property) of DOMNOS* +

For dimensions and commentary on the inscription, see Entry no. 49.

COMMENTARY

See Entry no. 49.

BIBLIOGRAPHY

See Entry no. 49.

Dimensions as for spoon no. 49.

Weight	81.5 gr
Roman Weight	3 oz
Original Silver Price	1 *solidus*

Fig. 50.2

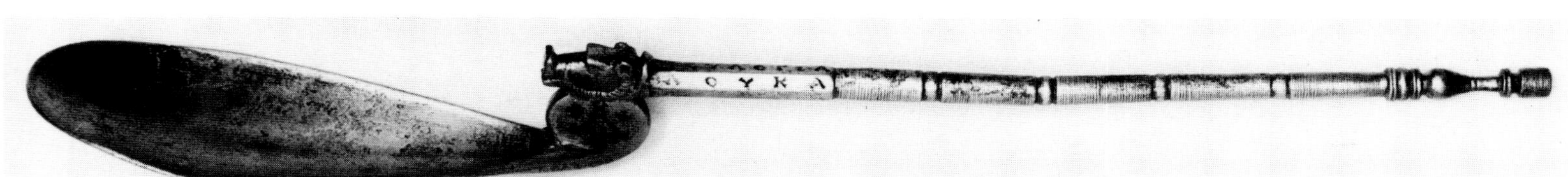

+ΕΥΛΟΓΙΑ ΤΟΥΑΓΙΟΥ ΜΑΡΚΟΥ

+ Εὐλογία τοῦ ἁγίου Μάρκου + Δόμνου +

Fig. 51.1

51. SPOON

LIGULA

Figures 51.1, 51.2

Washington, D.C., Dumbarton Oaks Collection,
no. 37.37

Antioch Treasure(?), Sixth to Seventh Century

For a description of this spoon (fig. 51.2) and its manufacture, see Entry no. 49. The tip of the bowl is broken off and the niello is missing from the inscription (51.1).

INSCRIPTION

Handle: + *Blessing of St. Mark.*
Disc: + *(Property) of DOMNOS* +

For dimensions and commentary on the inscription, see Entry no. 49.

COMMENTARY

See Entry no. 49.

BIBLIOGRAPHY

See Entry no. 49.

Dimensions as for spoon no. 49.

Weight	74.3 gr
Roman Weight	2 oz 17 scr
Original Silver Price	21 2/3 carats

Fig. 51.2

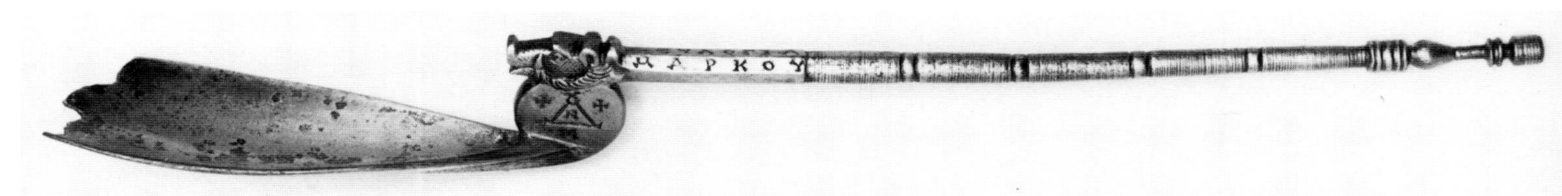

52. SPOON

LIGULA

Figures 52.1–52.4

Washington, D.C., Dumbarton Oaks Collection, no. 37.38

Antioch Treasure(?), Sixth to Early Seventh Century

For a description of this spoon (fig. 52.2)—which has a secondary, *pointillé* monogram on the left side of its disc (fig. 52.3)—and of its manufacture, see Entry no. 49. Niello is lost from the inscription (fig. 52.1).

INSCRIPTION

Handle: + *Blessing of St. Peter.*
Disc (I): + *(Property) of DOMNOS*+
Disc (II): *(Property) of MARAS(?)*

(The secondary monogram is unpublished but see Ross, 1962, pl. XVII.B).

For dimensions and commentary on inscription, see Entry no. 49 (and Entry no. 22). The monogram seems to include the letters M or N, R, and A.

COMMENTARY

See Entry no. 49.

BIBLIOGRAPHY

See Entry no. 49.

Dimensions as for spoon no. 49.	
Weight	83.3 gr
Roman Weight	3 oz 1 scr
Original Silver Price	1 *solidus* 1/3 carat

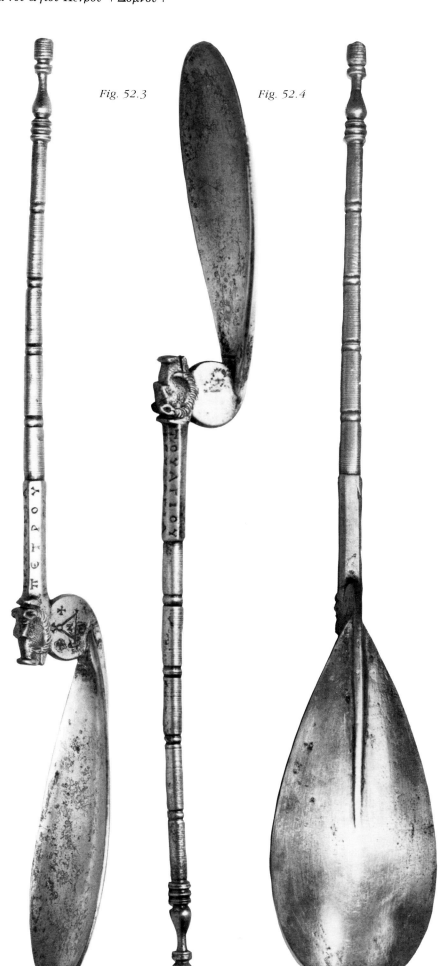

+ΕΥΛΟΓΙΑ ΤΟΥ ΑΓΙΟΥ ΠΕΤΡΟΥ 

+ Εὐλογία τοῦ ἁγίου Πέτρου +Δόμνου+

Fig. 52.1

Fig. 52.2

Fig. 52.3

Fig. 52.4

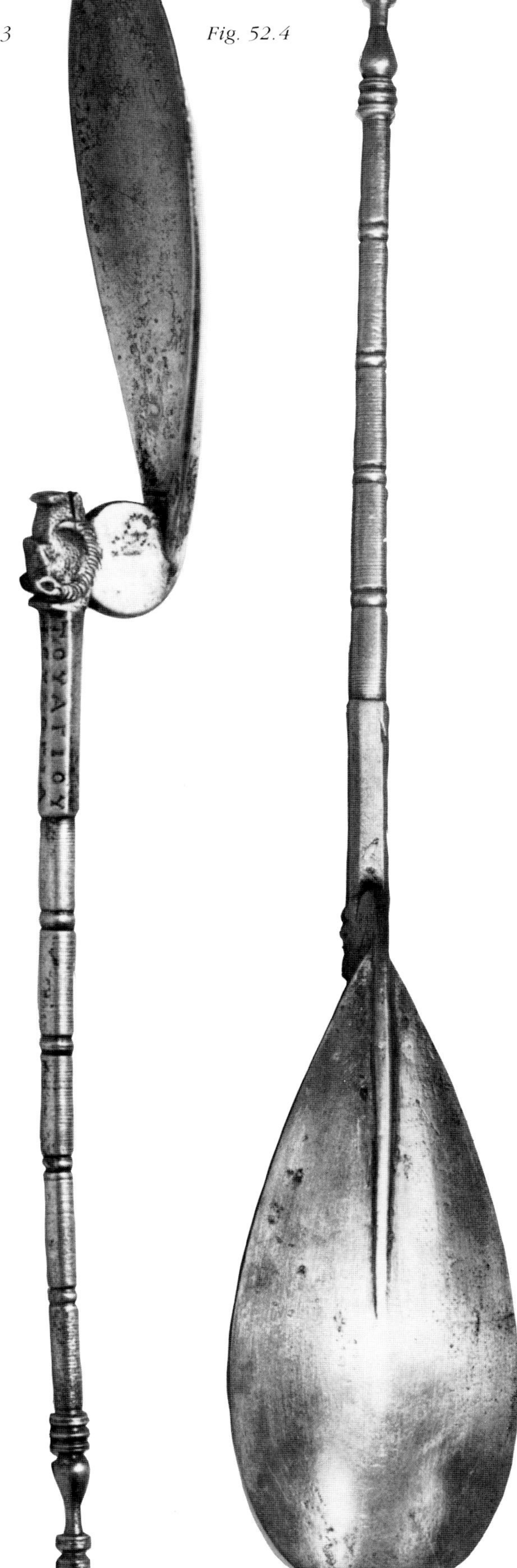

+ЄΥΛΟΓΙΑ ΤΟΥ ΑΓΙΟΥ ΜΑΘΘЄΟΥ

+ Εὐλογία τοῦ ἁγίου Μαθθέου + Δόμνου +

Fig. 53.1

53. SPOON

LIGULA

Figures 53.1, 53.2

Washington, D.C., Dumbarton Oaks Collection,
no. 37.39

Antioch Treasure(?), Sixth to Seventh Century

For a description of this spoon (fig. 53.2) which differs slightly from the others in the details of its finial and of its manufacture, see Entry no. 49. Niello is lost from its inscription (fig. 53.1).

INSCRIPTION

Handle: + *Blessing of St. Matthew.*
Disc: + *(Property) of DOMNOS*+

For dimensions and commentary on the inscription, see Entry no. 49.

COMMENTARY

See Entry no. 49.

BIBLIOGRAPHY

See Entry no. 49.

Dimensions as for spoon no. 49.

Weight	85.5 gr
Roman Weight	3 oz 3 scr
Original Silver Price	1 *solidus* 1 carat

Fig. 53.2

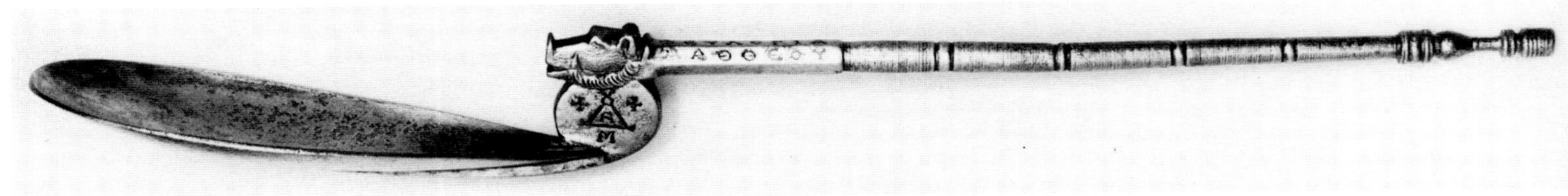

+ΕΥΛΟΓΙΑ ΤΟΥΑΓΙΟΥ ΦΙΛΙΠΠΟΥ

+ Εὐλογία τοῦ ἁγίου Φιλίππου + Δόμνου +

Fig. 54.1

54. SPOON

LIGULA

Figures 54.1, 54.2

Washington, D.C., Dumbarton Oaks Collection,
no. 37.40

Antioch Treasure(?), Sixth to Seventh Century

For a description of this spoon (fig. 54.2) and its manufacture, see Entry no. 49. Niello is lost from its inscription (fig. 54.1).

INSCRIPTION

Handle: + *Blessing of St. Philip.*
Disc: + *(Property) of DOMNOS* +

For dimensions and commentary on the inscription, see Entry no. 49.

COMMENTARY

See Entry no. 49.

BIBLIOGRAPHY

See Entry no. 49.

Dimensions as for spoon no. 49.	
Weight	79.5 gr
Roman Weight	2 oz 22 scr
Original Silver Price	23 1/3 carats

Fig. 54.2

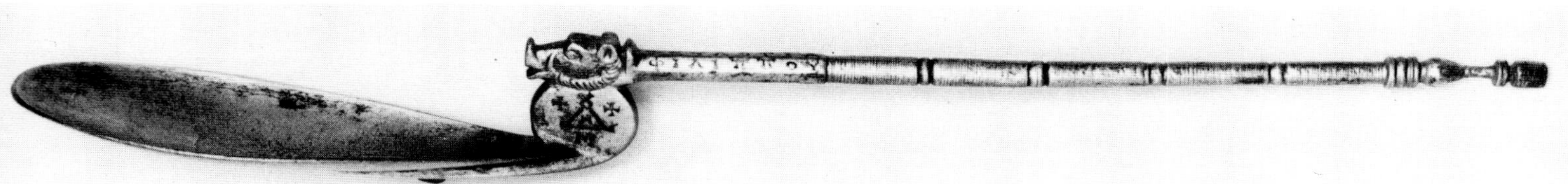

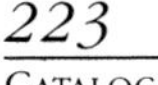

+ Εὐλογία τοῦ ἁγίου Παύλου + Δόμνου +

Fig. 55.1

55. SPOON

LIGULA

Figures 55.1–55.3

Washington, D.C., Dumbarton Oaks Collection,
no. 37.41

Antioch Treasure(?), Sixth to Seventh Century

For a description of this spoon (figs. 55.2, 55.3) and its manufacture, see Entry no. 49. A part of the bowl is missing near its tip. There is a small gash in the hexagonal part of the handle and the inscription (fig. 55.1) has lost its niello.

INSCRIPTION

Handle: + *Blessing of St. Paul.*
Disc: + *(Property) of DOMNOS* +

For dimensions and commentary on the inscription, see Entry no. 49.

COMMENTARY

See Entry no. 49.

BIBLIOGRAPHY

See Entry no. 49.

Dimensions as for spoon no. 49.

Weight	77.7 gr
Roman Weight	2 oz 20 scr
Original Silver Price	22 2/3 carats

Fig. 55.2

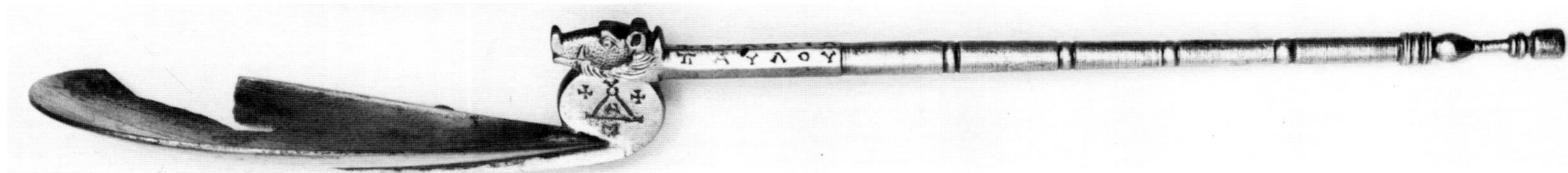

Fig. 55.3

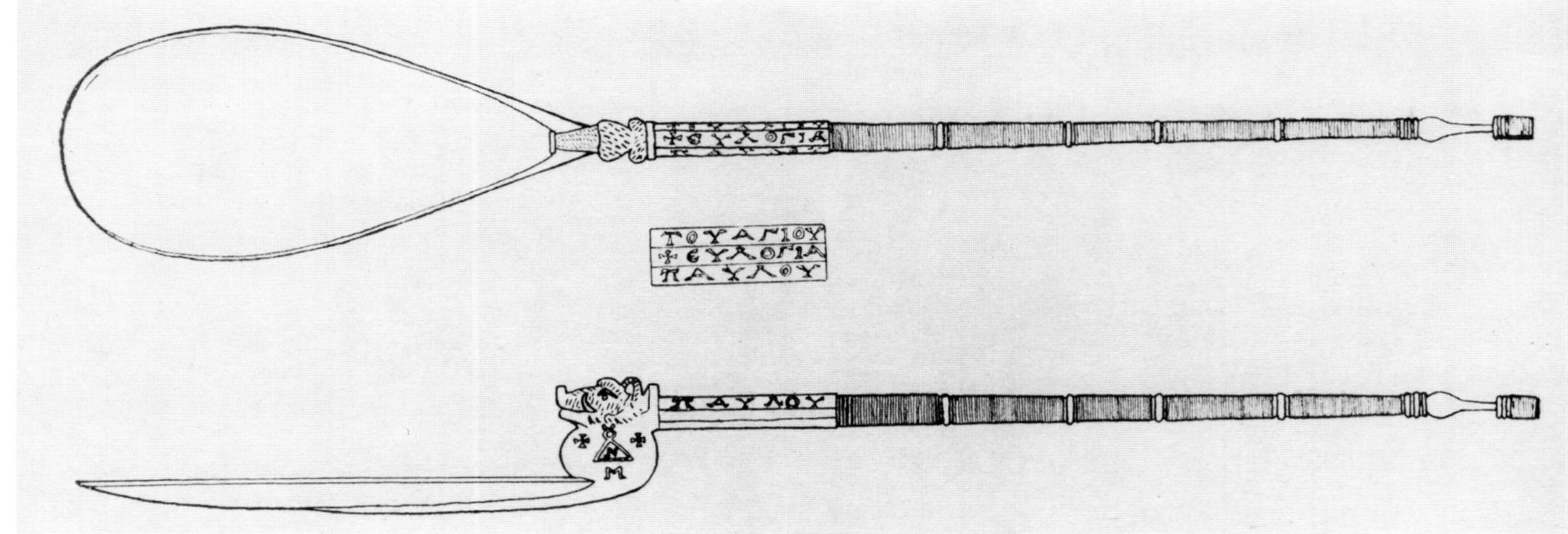

56. SPOON

LIGULA

Figures 56.1, 56.2

Washington, D.C., Dumbarton Oaks Collection, no. 37.42

Antioch Treasure(?), Sixth to Seventh Century

This spoon has an oval bowl attached by a solid disc to a handle which is round in section, except at the bowl end where it is fashioned as a schematic animal head, and at the opposite end, where it terminates in a baluster finial (figs. 56.1, 56.2). A series of deep grooves with five smooth intervals covers the handle, and the finial is composed of a vase element with double mouldings at both ends and a knob. The disc extends in a rat-tail on the back of the bowl which is decorated with a leaf having scalloped edges, gouged parallel veins, and a thin spine. The animal's head has summarily engraved features and stippled fur.

This spoon was cast (Ross, 1962, 19), perhaps in three parts (as was no. 22): bowl, disc with rat-tail, and handle. The grooves were then engraved on the handle, the details of the animal's head added, and the leaf pattern engraved on the bowl. There is a hole in the bowl of the spoon beside the rat-tail.

COMMENTARY

While presumably manufactured later, to fill out the (partially decimated) set of boar's head spoons catalogued in Entries nos. 49–55, this spoon is shorter (by 2.5 cm), lighter, and different in the shape and decorative details of bowl, handle, and finial. Moreover, there is neither inscription nor monogram, and this animal's head lacks the elongated snout and curving tusks of the boars on the other spoons. While its ruff and square nose approximate in summary fashion the lion's head on a spoon in Geneva (compare Lazovic *et al.*, 1977, no. 12), a third type of animal may have been intended here. Foliage patterns that ornament the obverse of some spoon bowls in the fourth century (Painter, 1977 [II], nos. 32–34) are often found on their reverse in the sixth to seventh centuries (see Entry no. 69; e.g., Dalton, 1901, nos. 400–413; *Byzantine Art,* 1964, nos. 508–510). In contrast to the linear sprigs found on most of those spoons, the rigid leaf on this one resembles more the spear-shaped leaves on Stuma lamp no. 33, while in technique it recalls the gouged acanthus frieze and other motifs on those fourth- and sixth-century objects cited in connection with Hama box no. 17. An unpublished spoon in the Staatliche Museen, Berlin is nearly identical to this one in its leaf decoration, grooved handle, and finial.

BIBLIOGRAPHY

See Entry no. 49.

L	24.0 cm
W (bowl)	3.9 cm
Weight	43.5 gr
Roman Weight	1 oz 14 scr
Original Silver Price	12 2/3 carats

Fig. 56.1

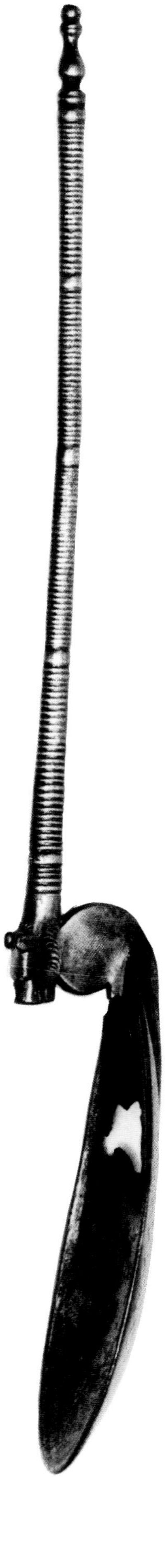

Fig. 56.2

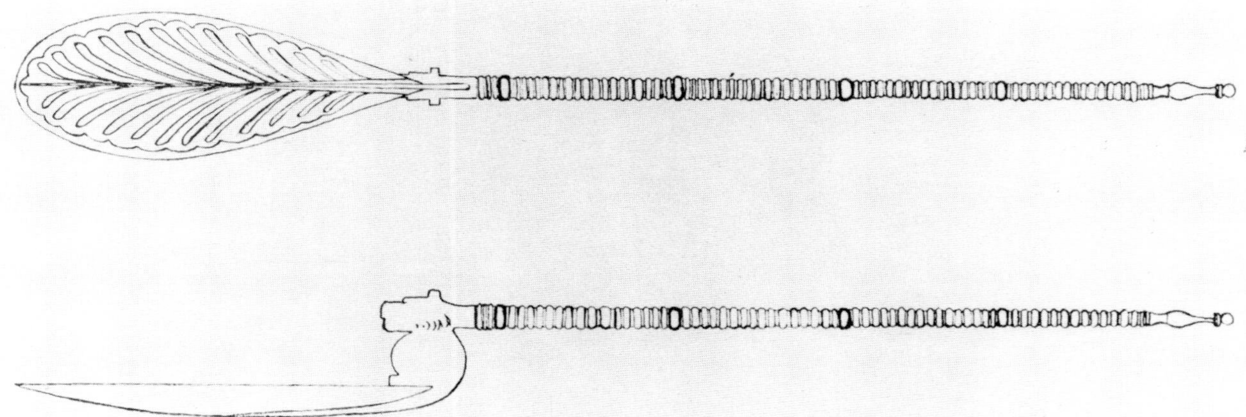

Catalogue: Entries Nos. 57–106

Other Silver Treasures and Related Objects

THE BETH MISONA TREASURE (nos. 57–60)

This treasure, composed of four objects, has no recorded find-spot, and is unattested before the Mallon family sold it to The Cleveland Museum of Art in 1950 (Milliken, 1951). Bréhier's association (1951, 261) of the dedication to St. Sergios (nos. 57, 60) with the city of Rusafa/ Sergiopolis was taken a step further by Milliken (1951), who implied that the objects were actually found there. Both Downey (1953, 144 f.) and Seyrig disputed this, and recognized in the village name inscribed on the paten (no. 60) the true destination of the objects, which the latter successfully deciphered as *chorion Beth Misona* (in Tchalenko, 1953–1958, vol. 3, 39, note 3). A *chorion* is a smaller settlement than a *kome,* and *beth* is the Semitic equivalent word meaning, literally, "house." Here, it refers to an estate or domain, hence "the village of the domain of Misona." Elsewhere (Mundell-Mango, 1986) the suggestion has been made that Beth Misona may be identified with modern Msibina (metathesis of Bamisina, a postulated modern version of Beth Misona), 3.5 kilometers southeast of Stuma (fig. II.2).

57. CHALICE

Cleveland, The Cleveland Museum of Art, no. 50.378 (purchase from the J. H. Wade Fund)

Beth Misona Treasure, Sixth to Seventh Century

H	16.8 cm
D (cup rim)	13.5–13.8 cm

This chalice has a broad cup supported on a flaring foot with narrow flange and knob, above which is a short stem and an attachment collar. Around the cup are four repoussé medallions, each containing a nimbed bust portrait in relief; Christ and the Virgin are on opposite sides, with Sts. Peter and Paul in between. The medallions have plain frames in relief, and details of the busts are defined by chasing and engraving. Concave mouldings surround the cup below and above the zone of medallions. At the top, under an engraved line, runs an inscription. The knob is covered with overlapping leaves, and beneath that is a twisted rope moulding. There is a "blob" of silver in Peter's left eye.

Fig. 57.1

INSCRIPTION

+ *The priest, KYRIAKOS, son of DOMNOS, (has presented this chalice) to St. Sergios, under Zeno the priest.*

+ Πρ(εσβύτερος) Κυριακὸς υἱὸς Δόμνου τῶ ἁγίω Σεργίω επὶ Ζήνωνος πρεσβυτέρου.

Like the chased inscription of Hama paten no. 4, individual strokes of this lunate lettering are unconnected. Its letter forms bear a general resemblance to those of Hama objects nos. 7, 9, 10, and 14. A certain (presumably different) Kyriakos was the donor of Hama cross no. 7. Domnos (presumably the same individual as this) donated the Beth Misona paten (no. 60). (The name Domnos also appears on the Antioch spoons nos. 49–55, though here again, it is very likely another individual.)

COMMENTARY

See Entry no. 59.

SELECTED BIBLIOGRAPHY

Bréhier, 1951, 259 f.; Milliken, 1951; Downey, 1953; *SEG,* 1958, no. 852; Ross, 1962, 11; Dodd, 1973, 17 f.; *Age,* 1979, no. 544.

Fig. 58.1

58. Chalice

Cleveland, The Cleveland Museum of Art, no. 50.379 (purchase from the J. H. Wade Fund)

Beth Misona Treasure, Sixth to Seventh Century

H	16.6–16.9 cm
D (cup rim)	13.6–14.5 cm

This chalice forms a pair with no. 59, and is also closely related to no. 57; it may be described in the same terms as the latter with regard to its shape and decoration. Its slight differences include a more highly placed knob and a broader flare in the foot above a raised, rather than flat, flange. Instead of an inscription, this chalice has near the top of its cup a frieze of debased egg and palmettes between unevenly executed beaded bands. A braided band around the bottom of the cup replaces chalice no. 57's concave moulding. The four medallions differ only in minor details from those on the other chalice, but there are (modern?) "blobs" of silver in the eyes of Christ and Paul. The edge of the foot has been repaired.

Commentary

See Entry no. 59.

Bibliography

See Entry no. 57.

59. Chalice

Cleveland, The Cleveland Museum of Art, no. 50.380 (purchase from the J.H. Wade Fund)

Beth Misona Treasure, Sixth to Seventh Century

H	16.7–17.1 cm
D (cup rim)	14.2–13.9 cm

This chalice forms a pair with no. 58, and is also closely related to no. 57; it may be described in the same terms as the former with regard to its shape and decoration. One slight difference is that the braided band on the bottom of the cup here runs in the opposite direction. This chalice is further distinguished from the other two by the less precise workmanship of its medallion busts: the crosses on Christ's book and nimbus are misstruck, the outlines of Peter's cross extend beyond the raised area, and hatching is omitted in some places. The face of Christ and that of the Virgin are worn very smooth. There is heavy incrustation inside the foot. The edge of the foot, under the Virgin's medallion, has been repaired and there are some hammer marks on the surface between those of Christ and Peter.

Commentary

Chalices nos. 57–59 consist of separately hammered cups and feet joined by hammered collars. Hama chalice no. 3 has a knob decorated in a manner very similar to these. Moreover, it has a concave moulding (on its arcade) very much like that of chalice no. 57 (which reappears on objects nos. 30, 37, and 38). The egg and palmette frieze on chalices nos. 58 and 59 is similar to the border on the Stuma paten (no. 34) and the braided band is found as well on the Hama flask (no. 15).

These three chalices are very close to one another in nearly all details of their design and decoration; their medallions are especially alike, even in their dimensions. Indeed, the coincidence of their measurements

Fig. 59.1

in raised areas suggests that preliminary repoussé blocking of the busts was done with a single set of matrices.

These medallions bear comparison with their (much more skillfully executed) counterparts on the Homs Vase (no. 84). In addition to the rendering of drapery by a series of finger-shaped gouges, and punching the shape of the mouth from the front, the chalices and the Homs Vase share similar facial types. Christ, although unbearded on the chalices, has the same high, broad crown of hair that falls straight over His shoulders—a type which Dodd (1973, 48 f.) identified in a series of contemporary silver objects, with the Hermitage reliquary (*Age,* 1979, no. 572) providing the closest parallel. The Paul, Peter, and Virgin on these chalices also match the types on the Homs Vase, with only minor variations. Much cruder in execution, the chalice medallions should perhaps be seen as less expensive, mass-produced (i.e., matrix) copies of contemporary types exemplified by those on the Homs Vase. The chalices were relatively inexpensive in another respect—namely, they are among the lightest weight for their size at 305, 332, and 330 grams respectively (H *ca.* 17 cm), together with the three Hama chalices (nos. 1–3) which weigh even less.

These three chalices were undoubtedly all made in the same workshop and at the same time, and may all have been presented to the Beth Misona church by the priest Kyriakos. Alternatively, the two uninscribed (i.e., "anonymous") chalices may have been bought by the church with its institutional funds.

Bibliography

See Entry no. 57.

60. PATEN

Cleveland, The Cleveland Museum of Art, no. 50.381 (purchase from the J. H. Wade Fund)

Beth Misona Treasure, Sixth to Seventh Century

D	32.4 cm

This hammered, lathe-turned paten has slightly convex sides, a narrow rim, and no foot. At its center is an engraved cross with flaring arms, oval serifs, and a gouged spine. Just below the center of the cross is the lathe turning point in the center of a plain disc (D 2cm). The cross is surrounded by an engraved, single-stroke inscription which is enclosed by two pairs of engraved turnings. Two further pairs band the base of the sloping sides and the rim. There is a repair to the end of the left arm of the cross and to the rim directly below the cross foot.

Fig. 60.1

Inscription

+ *Having vowed, DOMNOS, son of ZACHEOS, has offered (this paten) to St. Sergios of the village of Beth Misona.*

+ Εὐξόμενος Δόμνος υἱὸς Ζαχέου προσήνενκεν τῶ ἁγίω Σεργίω χω(ρίου) Βεθ Μισωνα.

The lettering belongs to a group distinguished by an R-shaped *rho* and a barred *upsilon* (the latter lacking here); included are nos. 14, 28, 61, 64, and 65. Downey (1953, 143 f.) successfully rebutted Bréhier's contention (1951, 259) that the mixture of square and lunate letter forms indicated an early (i.e., fourth-century) date. The dedicatory formula *euxamenos . . . prosenegken* is also found on Hama cross no. 7 and on chalice no. 73. On Domnos, see Entry no. 57. On the name of the village, read as *Benmisona* by Downey (1953, 145), see Seyrig (in Tchalenko, 1953–1958, vol. 3, 39, note 3).

Commentary

This paten is closest in shape to Hama paten no. 4, which also has convex sides. This one's smaller cross, set in a medallion, belongs to a type of decoration discussed in Entry no. 6. The cross serifs are paralleled on Phela paten no. 64, as well as on many extant contemporary crosses (see Entry no. 8). The gouging technique used in the center of the cross is a survival from fourth-century craftsmanship (see no. 17), and is found on many objects of the sixth century (see no. 56).

This paten was given by the father of the priest Kyriakos, who gave chalice no. 57 "to St. Sergios." The latter, and the nearly identical chalices nos. 58 and 59, bear a close resemblance in their ornament to Hama chalice no. 3, given to the St. Sergios church at Kaper Koraon by Pelagios Basianos. As this Pelagios may be one and the same as the Pelagios who presented a paten to the same church in the seventh century (no. 5), all these other stylistically related objects could thus be so dated. However, this identification is far from certain (e.g., they could belong to different generations of the same family), and as the egg and palmette borders on chalices nos. 58 and 59 resemble the ornament on the Stuma paten (no. 34), dated 578, the dating of objects nos. 3, 57, and 60 should probably remain open for the present.

Bibliography

Bréhier, 1951, 257 ff.; Milliken, 1951; Downey, 1953, 143 ff.; *SEG*, 1958, no. 852; Tchalenko, 1953–1958, vol. 3, 39, note 3; Weitzmann and Ševčenko, 1963, 398; Dodd, 1973, 27.

The Phela Treasure (nos. 61–66)

This treasure, composed of at least seven objects (two chalices, two patens, one cross, one seal—and fragments of a cross staff fitting [Ross, 1962, 20; Dodd, 1973, 5, note 2]), is first attested in 1955 when John S. Newberry presented to Dumbarton Oaks a cross (no. 65) which he had bought from the dealer George Zacos. In a letter addressed to Marvin Ross (DO files), Zacos explained that the cross was first acquired in Beirut and that it must, "consequently," have been found nearby. On September 29, 1956, Ross received a letter from Henri Seyrig concerning the remainder of the Phela treasure, which was then in the possession of the dealer E. Bustros, in Beirut (WAG files). Seyrig provided descriptions of two chalices and two patens, the latter "in fine condition," including stamps and inscriptions, and said that they had been found "somewhere near Latakiya." In another letter, of December 29, 1956 (WAG files), Seyrig said that Phela was "entre les anciennes villes de Balanée et de Gabala" on the seacoast (fig. II.1). By 1959, the Paul Mallon family had acquired these objects, which were then photographed in their unrestored condition; in those photographs the fragments (no. 65a) may also be seen (DO files; Ross, 1962, 20). The two chalices, two patens, and the seal were restored by the firm of Léon André in Paris, apparently before 1961 (Dodd, 1961, no. 25, where paten no. 63 is shown restored), and acquired by the Abegg Stiftung, Bern in 1963.

(In a letter of December 14, 1956 to W.M. Milliken, Seyrig reported that two objects [a bowl and spoon] acquired that year by The Cleveland Museum of Art [nos. 56.29, 56.36] may have belonged to the same treasure [CMA files]. These two objects are part of a domestic treasure composed of thirteen pieces said to be "from Syria," and mostly attributed to the fourth century [Milliken, 1958; *Age,* 1979, no. 131]. In view of the tentative nature of Seyrig's suggestion, the apparent differences in dates between the domestic and the church objects, and the marked differences in condition of the pieces in the two treasures, the possibility of common find-spot and origin must be considered remote.) Elsewhere (Mundell-Mango, 1986) it is proposed that ancient Phela is Feilun, a village less than two kilometers east of Stuma (fig. II.2). Attempts to locate a village of comparable name on the seacoast and in Cyprus (in view of the inscription on stamp no. 66) have proved unsuccessful (DO files).

61. CHALICE

Bern, Abegg Stiftung, no. 8.39.63

Phela Treasure, Sixth to Seventh Century

H	20.0–20.2 cm
D (cup rim)	16.3–16.8 cm

Fig. 61.1

This chalice has a broad, somewhat shallow cup supported on a flaring foot with a small flange and a knob, above which is an attachment collar (on its construction, see Entry no. 1). Around the upper rim of the cup is an engraved single-stroke inscription above a pair of engraved turnings. Four pairs of turnings decorate the flared foot. This chalice was reconstructed by the firm of Léon André of Paris from a series of fragments, which were mounted on a modern silver cup and reinforcing foot cone (compare chalices nos. 41, 62).

INSCRIPTION

+ *In fulfillment of a vow and (for) the salvation of MARIA and of HER CHILD and of THEODORE.*

+ Ὑπὲρ εὐχῆς (καὶ) σωτηρίας Μαρίαε (καὶ) τοῦ τέκνου αὐτῆς (καὶ) Θεοδώρου.

This inscription belongs both to the group with square letter forms (nos. 6, 60, 65; see Entry no. 6), and to the group with the R-shaped *rho* and barred *upsilon* (nos. 14, 28, 60, 64, 65; see Entry no. 14). Small lettering at the end of the inscription is found also on Hama chalice no. 1. For the dedicatory formulae, see Entry no. 1. Maria may be the individual mentioned on Phela paten no. 64, where she is apparently referred to as deceased. Theodore may be the husband of Maria (although one would then expect to read "their" child), or else a close relative; he may also have been the *excubitor* who was a co-donor of paten no. 63, dated 577(?).

COMMENTARY

The distribution of paired turned lines on the foot of this vessel links it to Hama chalice no. 28 (with double paired lines), which also has square letter forms and the same type of join between cup and foot.

BIBLIOGRAPHY

Ross, 1962, no. 14; Dodd, 1973, no.4.

62. CHALICE

Bern, Abegg Stiftung, no. 8.38.63

Phela Treasure, Sixth to Seventh Century

H	17.7–18.0 cm
D (cup rim)	14.3 cm

This heavily restored chalice has a broad cup supported on a flared foot with a knob, above which is an attachment collar (on its construction, see Entry no. 1). Around the top of the cup is an engraved, single-stroke inscription between turned lines. The cup shows six chased figures nimbed and standing on a twisted rope band between two turnings. Directly under the cross which marks the beginning of the inscription stands Christ (only the top of His halo and lower torso are preserved), who is flanked by two archangels holding staffs. On the opposite side of the cup stands an orant Virgin (only the top of her cap and veil remain) flanked on the left by an unbearded deacon (St. Stephen?) holding a censer, and on the right by a military saint (St. Sergios?) dressed in a *chiton* and *chlamys,* with a lance in one hand and a shield in the other. The facial features were formed by straight lines and the eyes by the same punches used on the deacon's censer. The drapery is composed of a mixture of straight incisions and tear-shaped gouges. Two pairs of turnings decorate the foot of the chalice below the knob, the lower being composed of several lines. There are traces of gilding on Christ and one archangel. Like Phela chalice no. 61,

Fig. 62.1

this one was reconstructed by the firm of Léon André, from fragments, many of which are mounted on a modern cup. A modern foot was inserted inside the base as far as the second turning from the bottom.

Inscription

+ *ELPIDIOS, in thanksgiving to the Theotokos, presented (this chalice) for his salvation and (that) of HIS HOUSE(HOLD).*

+'Ελπίδ[ιο]ς εὐχαριετῶν τῆ Θεοτόκω ὑπὲρ σωτηρίας αὐτοῦ καὶ τοῦ ὄίκου προ[σένεγκε]ν.

This is one of just three single-stroke inscriptions without serifs in this catalogue (nos. 6, 28). The *alpha* form with diagonal bar is also found, mixed with the inverted V-shaped bar, on Hama objects nos. 10 and 14. The formula *eucharistōn . . . prosenegken* recurs on the second Sinai cross (given "to the Holy Trinity"; Weitzmann and Ševčenko, 1963, 397, note 48; see also nos. 7, 60, 76). The Theotokos is mentioned on two other objects in this treasure (nos. 64, 65), but the name Elpidios does not recur among Syrian silver objects, although the feminine form is found combined with Pelagios and Stephen—two names appearing in the Hama treasure—on a sixth-century pavement from Ain el-Bad, near Hama (*IGLS,* no. 2016; Balty, 1977, no. 64).

Commentary

The decorative format of this chalice (i.e., standing frontal figures) recurs on Hama chalice no. 3 (where there is an arcade), and on Hama flask no. 15. The twisted rope on the base of the cup corresponds to the braided band on the Beth Misona chalices (nos. 57–59). In terms of craftsmanship this chalice could be described as the least sophisticated among the objects catalogued here (compare the Beth Misona medallions; nos. 57–59). The circular faces and splayed feet are singularly crude and the multiple lines of the drapery are not suggested to the same geometric control exercised on plaques nos. 46 and 47.

Six similar figures, in bust form, are found on the Homs Vase (no. 84), where the Virgin is flanked by archangels, and Christ by Peter and Paul, an arrangement found also on the Hermitage reliquary (*Age,* 1979, no. 572). More commonly portrayed in ceremonial costume, wearing the *maniakion* and holding a cross staff (see Entry no. 15), Sergios(?) is here shown in military pose and armed for battle, and in that form he can be compared with the figures of Sts. Theodore and Longinus on capitals at Aila in *Palestina Tertia* (Glueck, 1965, pl. 216 B, C). St. Stephen holding a censer, similar to the figure on this chalice, but inscribed, stands at the center of a contemporary votive cross in The Metropolitan Museum (*Age,* 1979, no. 557).

Bibliography

Ross, 1962, no. 14; Dodd, 1973, no.5.

63. PATEN

Bern, Abegg Stiftung, no. 8.37.63

Phela Treasure, 577(?)

D	37.0–37.2 cm

This paten has high sloping sides, a flat rim turned forward to form an edge that is round in profile, and no footring. At its center is a large engraved cross defined by narrow and gouged lines; it has flared arms with curved terminals and diagonal strokes at the center crossing (below which are two or three centering points within a plain disc). This paten must have slipped on the lathe, resulting in "wavy" turnings to the left of the cross. Around the cross is an engraved single-stroke inscription between turned lines. Two more lines decorate the sloping

Fig. 63.1

sides and the flat rim, respectively. Five stamps appear on the reverse. This paten (like Phela chalices nos. 61, 62) was restored by the firm of Léon André, Paris; metal was replaced to losses from the sloping sides, the inscribed band above and below the cross, and to the rim on the upper right side.

STAMPS

These stamps were dated by Dodd (1961, no. 25) to 577, because of the monograms of Justin II (565–578) and of Theodore, whom she took to be Theodore Petri, *comes sacrarum largitionum* in 577.

INSCRIPTION

+ *In fulfillment of a vow and (for) the salvation of AGATHANGELOS and of THEODORE, excubitor.*

+Ὑπὲρ εὐχῆς καὶ σωτηρίας Ἀγα[θ]αγγέλου καὶ Θεοδώρου ἐξκουβίτορος.

The letter forms may be compared with those on several Hama objects (e.g., nos. 7, 9, 14) and on the inscribed Beth Misona chalice (no. 57). For the dedicatory formulae, see Entry no. 1. Agathangelos is not mentioned elsewhere on contemporary silver objects, while Theodore may be identified with a donor of Phela chalice no. 61. An *excubitor* was a palace guard and a member of an elite corps established by Emperor Leo to assume the duties no longer exercised by the *scholae,* which had become a ceremonial guard. The *comes excubitorum* was a position of great authority, held by the future emperors Justin I, Tiberius, and Maurice (Jones, 1972, vol. 2, 658). Although intended to serve the emperor at Constantinople, the *excubitores* were sometimes sent abroad in war; they were sent to the eastern front under the command of Maurice in the 570s (John of Ephesos, *HE,* VI.14), at precisely the time Theodore donated this paten at Phela.

COMMENTARY

See Entry no. 6.

BIBLIOGRAPHY

Dodd, 1961, no. 25; Ross, 1962, no. 14; Weitzmann and Ševčenko, 1963, 397; Dodd, 1973, no. 6.

64. PATEN

Bern, Abegg Stiftung, no. 8.36.63

Phela Treasure, Sixth to Seventh Century

D	34–34.2 cm

This paten has high slopping sides, a flat rim turned forward to form an outer edge which is round in section, and no footring. In the center is a small engraved cross with equal flaring arms bearing oval serifs and with a tang, which is emplanted in a stippled hill with scalloped edges. On the hill are the Four Rivers of Paradise, indicated by wormlike forms, and above the cross is a stippled dove. The cross is inscribed with the legend *Phos, Zoe* ("Light, Life"), and around it runs a dedicatory inscription banded by two pairs of engraved turnings. Another engraved line decorates the rim. This paten was apparently first burnished in a diagonal direction, the marks of which are still visible in the disc (D 2.5 cm) surrounding the turning point in the lower arm of the cross, which was made when the paten was subsequently finished in circular motion on a lathe. This paten, in contrast with other pieces in its treasure (nos. 61–63, 66), was found in good condition, with only a crack on its rim at about 9 o'clock.

INSCRIPTION

Cross: + *Light, Life.*
Field: + *For the salvation and (for) the repose (of the soul) of SABINIANE and MARTHA and MARIA. (Paten) of the Theotokos of the village of Phela.*

Φῶς Ζωή +Ὑπὲρ σωτηρίας καὶ ἀναπαύσεως Σαβινιανῆς (καὶ) Μάρθας (καὶ) Μαρίας τῆς Θεοτόκου κώμ(ης) Φελα.

Fig. 64.1

This inscription belongs to a group having an R-shaped *rho* and a barred *upsilon* (nos. 14, 28, 60, 61, and 65). This inscription is also close in its letter forms, in its *tes* in ligature, and particularly in its use of serifs, to that on Phela chalice no. 61, which likewise mentions a Maria—who, however, may have been deceased when this paten was dedicated. Although often used successively in the same dedication (i.e., applied to different people), *hyper soterias* and *hyper anapauseos* are otherwise never, as here, used in combination for the same individuals. *Soteria* is used for the living, as explicitily stated (*soterias zonton*) in one inscription of 601 at Zorava, in Arabia (Robert, 1953, 188, no. 218), and *anapausis* for the dead (e.g., the *anapauson tas psychas*), as attested at Mount Sinai (Ševčenko, 1966, no. 3). The coupling on the paten of the two phrases with reference to the three women is therefore ambiguous, and at least one of them was presumably still alive. The reading "(Paten) of . . . " is based on analogy with the inscription on the Hama ewer (no. 14). Alternatives include: "(Treasure) of . . ." (see nos. 3, 75), "(Offering to the church) of . . ." (see no. 83) or "(Property of the church) of. . . ."

COMMENTARY

On this type of paten decoration—a small cross within a medallion—see Entry no. 6. The style of the decoration, executed like that on the reverse sides of the Stuma and Riha fans (nos. 31, 32; i.e., exclusively in incised lines), is diagrammatic. Unlike the "simple" craftsmanship displayed on Phela chalice no. 63, there is here a sense of economical yet bold composition. On the iconography of the cross standing on Golgotha (as on no. 36), from which flow the Four Rivers of Paradise, see Dodd (1973, 26 ff.), where its significance is linked to the paten's dedicatory inscription invoking the repose of the soul in paradise. The legend "Light, Life," commonly found on crosses (e.g., Ross, 1965, nos. 100, 179 H), is taken from John 8.12, and refers specifically to Christ: "I am the Light of the World . . . ." Its combination here with the dove of the Holy Spirit could be said to have Trinitarian overtones, and like the cross alone and the Communion of the Apostles, found on other patens (nos. 4–6, 34, 35, *etc.*), it is an appropriate decoration for the eucharistic plate.

BIBLIOGRAPHY

Ross, 1962, no. 14; Dodd, 1973, no. 7.

65. CROSS

Washington, D.C., Dumbarton Oaks Collection, no. 55.17

Phela Treasure, Sixth to Seventh Century

H	47.6 cm
W	28.4 cm

This medium-sized, cast cross has flaring arms with tear-shaped, spherical serifs and a tang at the base. Its obverse bears an inscription between a double border of narrow and broadly gouged engraved lines; a similar border, though formed by one engraved line, is on the reverse, where there is a centering point at the crossing of the arms. The arms on both sides were burnished on their axes. The top right corner of the cross is now broken off and there is a crack in the right arm.

Fig. 65.1

INSCRIPTION

+ *Under JOHN, the priest (of the Church) of the Theotokos of the village of Phela (this cross was bought/presented).*

+ Ἐπὶ Ἰωάννου πρεσβυτέρου τῆς Θεοτόκου κώμ(ης) Φελα.

On the significance of *epi* with regard to the type of donation made to the Church, See Chapter I, above. John the priest may be the same as John the Bishop, whose name is on the Phela Seal (no. 66). The Church of the Theotokos of Phela is specified on other objects here (see no. 64).

COMMENTARY

See Entries nos. 7, 8.

BIBLIOGRAPHY

Ross, 1962, no. 14; Dodd, 1973, 5; Kent and Painter, 1977, no. 146.

65a. FRAGMENTARY FITTING FOR A CROSS STAFF(?)

Present Location Unknown, (formerly P. Mallon Collection)

Phela Treasure, Sixth to Seventh Century

A. D of slotted end	*ca.* 4.2 cm
B. D of rimmed base	*ca.* 4.2 cm

One fragment (above) is spherical in shape with a broad slot in its flat end. It has two sets (of two and three) engraved lines around its middle. The other fragment (below) is tubular in shape with a squared rim at its preserved end above which runs a pair of engraved turnings.

COMMENTARY

One fragment resembles in its general appearance the spherical box in the Ma'aret en-Noman treasure (no. 70). While its slot apparently led Ross (1962, 20) to describe it as "a collection box?," it is more likely that the opening was designed as a means of attachment to another object. While this fragment resembles a chalice knob in its shape, none of the Syrian chalices is constructed, as are those from Gallunianu (nos. 77–80), by means of rivets or other fastening devices, which could be used with such an opening (see Entry no. 1). More plausible is the suggestion made by Susan Boyd that the two fragments together formed the knobbed fitting of a cross (or fan) with staff (see e.g., Ross, 1962, no. 19). The tang of Phela cross no. 65 (H 7 cm; greatest W 3 cm) could have fit at least part way into the upper slot, and a wooden staff would have gone into the lower, "sleeve" opening.

Fig. 65.1

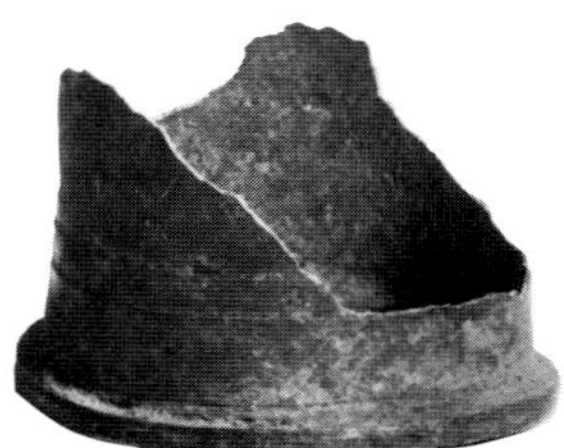

BIBLIOGRAPHY

Ross, 1962, 20; Dodd, 1973, 5, note 2.

66. SEAL

Bern, Abegg Stiftung, no. 8.41.63

Phela Treasure, Sixth to Seventh Century

L	3.4 cm
D (max.)	1.8 cm

This hollow seal is formed of a rolled sheet of hammered silver, to which discs are attached at both ends; their edges were hammered down and decorated with grooves. Two rings, one now broken off, were soldered upright to the smaller disc end, and an inscription surrounded by punched dots chased into the larger. A tear in the seal's side has been repaired and the extant ring reattached, presumably by the firm of Léon André of Paris.

INSCRIPTION

+ *Seal (of) JOHN, bishop of Kerania.* +

+ Ἰω[άννου] ἐπισκό[που] Κηρανίας +

The lettering is lunate and abbreviations indicated by superscript bars. There are two types of *alpha* used.

This tiny script bears a general resemblance to the equally small lettering on Hama spoon no. 18, which is likewise "erratic" in its letter forms. Dodd (1973, 30) suggested that John the bishop may, in his younger days, have been the priest John named on the Phela cross (no. 65). His see is probably to be identified with Cypriote Kyrenia (*ibid.*), although its ancient name was spelled *Kerynia* and not, as here, *Kerania*.

Commentary

This seal may be described as an early example of a cone seal in metal (Vikan and Nesbitt, 1980, 20 ff.). The typical Early Byzantine cone seal is made of rock crystal, and shows a pictorial and not an inscriptional device. This specimen is closer in concept and design to the typical Middle Byzantine cone seal, which is made of metal (bronze), has a suspension ring, and shows an inscriptional device. Silver is unusual for such seals at any period (see Vikan, 1984, note 1) as are indications of occupation, dignity, rank, *et cetera*. Bishop John may have used this seal for correspondence, or for documents issued from his cathedral. But in any case, it was probably a personal and not an ecclesiastical implement, and as such, it probably entered the Phela church treasure as a personal gift, for its metal value. Perhaps, as Dodd has suggested (1973, 30), this is the same John who was earlier presbyter of the Church of the Theotokos at Phela, which may have been his native village.

Bibliography

Dodd, 1973, no. 8.

Fig. 66.1

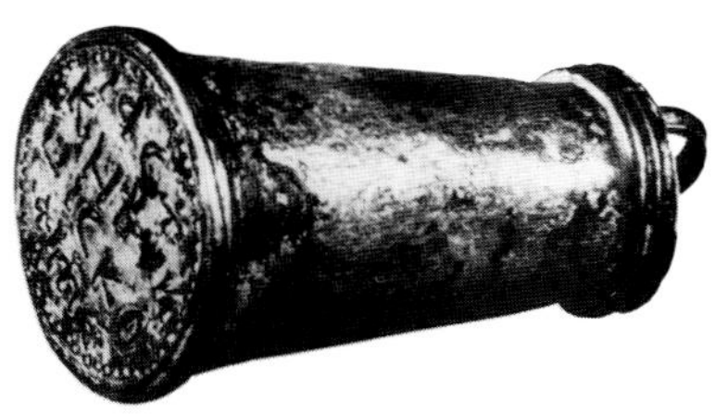

The Ma'aret en-Noman Treasure (Nos. 67–72)

This treasure, composed of two crosses, a spoon, a box, a plaque, and a number of plaquettes, has, with no compelling reason, been known as the "Second Hama Treasure," from the time of its first publication (*Early Christian,* 1947, nos. 381, 382; Ross, 1950). The larger cross (no. 67) and one plaquette (no. 72a) had been seen by René Mouterde in Beirut in 1945 (*IGLS,* nos. 2047, 2048). There may, however, be a much earlier attestation, for grouped with these objects, at least by Mouterde, is a square bronze seal with the name *Eustathios,* transcribed in 1913 by Tawfic Abucasem (*ibid.,* no. 2049), then (or soon to be) owner of the Hama treasure (see Chapter II, above). The provenance of this "Second Hama Treasure" was corrected by Henri Seyrig in a letter to Marvin Ross of September 29, 1956, to be "the immediate outskirts of Ma'aret en-Noman, to the south of that little town" (fig. II.1; WAG files [a correction made also in *IGLS,* 1959, 318; nos. 2047–2049]). As the precise find-spot is unknown, the treasure is placed under the above name for convenience.

In his 1956 letter to Ross, Seyrig noted that there had been two main lots to the treasure: one of four major pieces (two crosses, a spoon, and a box; nos. 67–70) and a single plaquette (no. 72a), acquired by the dealer Joseph Brummer before 1947 (*Early Christian,* 1947, nos. 381, 382), and another of one large plaque (with St. Symeon Stylites; no. 71), the lid to the box (no. 70), and many more, mostly fragmented, plaquettes (nos. 72b–72n)—this lot had gone to Paris, with the lid and plaquettes having been acquired by Seyrig himself. He presented the latter to The Walters Art Gallery in 1957 (WAG files), after already having presented the lid in 1952 (Ross, 1953; Seyrig, 1956 letter). Moreover, Henry Walters had bought three of the first lot of Brummer objects (nos. 68, 70, 72a) in the 1949 Brummer sale, from which the other two pieces (nos. 67, 69) went to Fahim Kouchakji, owner of the Antioch treasure (*IGLS,* nos. 2047–2049; and Chapter II, above); Kouchakji, in turn, sold them to The Toledo Museum of Art in 1953. The remaining object in Paris—the St. Symeon plaque—was acquired in 1952 by the Louvre (Louvre files). The present location of the bronze seal once belonging to Abucasem is unknown.

67. CROSS

Toledo, The Toledo Museum of Art, no 53.48a (Gift of Edward Drummond Libbey)

Ma'aret en-Noman Treasure, Sixth to Seventh Century

H	18.0 cm
W	13.2 cm

This rather small cross has slightly flaring arms and a tang; on its obverse is a niello-inlaid inscription within an engraved border.

Fig. 67.1

INSCRIPTION
+ *Save us, Son of God, who was crucified for us.*

Σῶσον ἡμᾶς υἱέ τοῦ Θεοῦ, Ὁ σταυρωθὶς ὑπὲρ ἡμῶν.

The lettering is lunate and well formed. Spelling: the *omicron* is dropped from *hyios* and the *epsilon* from *staurotheis.* The formula used here is a variation on the *Trisagion* of Peter the Fuller, which is considered by some to be Monophysite (*IGLS,* no. 2047; Downey, 1954, 279), but which was, in fact, distinguished by geographical rather than sectarian usage (see Brock, 1985). For the "Orthodox" *Trisagion,* see Entry no. 42.

COMMENTARY
This is the only known Early Byzantine cross with a niello-inlaid inscription (compare no. 7). As with the two medium-sized Hama treasure crosses (nos. 7, 8), this and Ma'aret en-Noman cross no. 68 might have formed a *de facto* pair, being very close in dimensions. As with the Hama "pair," one is inscribed and one plain. On crosses of this type, see Entry no. 7.

BIBLIOGRAPHY
Early Christian, 1947, no. 381; Ross, 1950, 162 f.; *IGLS,* no. 2047.

Fig. 68.1

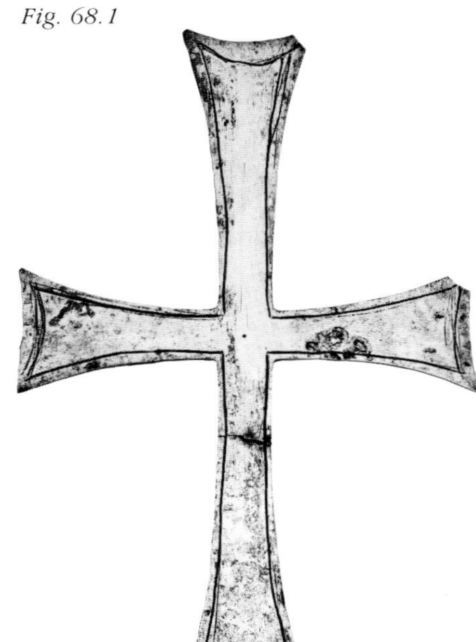

68. CROSS

Baltimore, The Walters Art Gallery, no. 57.1827

Ma'aret en-Noman Treasure, Sixth to Seventh Century

H	17.0 cm
W	11.5 cm

This rather small cross has flaring arms, a tang now broken off, and an engraved border on the obverse, the reverse being plain. It was cut from a cast sheet of metal with the centering point at the crossing used to determine the lengths of the arms. In addition to the tang, the (brittle) metal has broken off at the right corner of the upper arm and the upper corner of the right arm; a strip of lead solder has been used (on the back) to repair the break in the lower arm.

COMMENTARY

This is the only cross herein catalogued not to have its engraved border repeated on the reverse. In terms of design, it could be described as a compact version of Hama cross no. 7, which is twice as large. The tang on this specimen is proportionally much broader and the quality of the linear border much cruder than on the Hama crosses. On its function, see Entry no. 7.

BIBLIOGRAPHY

Ross, 1950, 162 f.

69. SPOON

Toledo, The Toledo Museum of Art, no. 53.48b (Gift of Edward Drummond Libbey)

Ma'aret en-Noman Treasure, Sixth to Seventh Century

L	25.4 cm
W	4.2 cm

Fig. 69.1

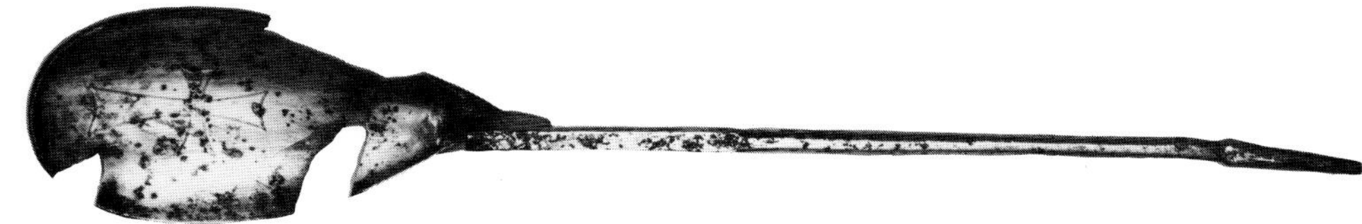

This spoon has an oval bowl with engraved cross attached by a disc to a raised handle, which is square in section near the bowl, and then becomes round, terminating in a pointed finial. The bowl has a flat upper rim, and on its reverse there is a rat tail and a fine, engraved leaf pattern. Metal is broken off the bowl in three places.

COMMENTARY

This spoon is very similar to Hama spoon no. 22 in its general form and, particularly, in the shape of its finial. The reverse of that spoon is, however, plain, but the type of leaf pattern used here is common on sixth- and seventh-century spoons generally. A less naturalistic version decorates the reverse of Antioch spoon no. 56, while the "feathery" leaf on this example may be compared with those on spoons in the Lampsacus and Cyprus treasures (Dalton, 1901, nos. 380–384, 400–413; de Ridder, 1924, no. 2049; Ross, 1967/1968, no. 9; Wulff, 1909, no. 2267). The cross on this spoon is very similar to that on Hama spoon no. 18 (of *ca.* 550–565) and, in its placement, to the crosses on that spoon, Hama spoons nos. 19–21, and the Ghiné spoon. On their decoration and function, see Entry no. 18.

BIBLIOGRAPHY

Ross, 1950, 162 f.

70. BOX

Baltimore, The Walters Art Gallery, no 57.1835

Ma'aret en-Noman Treasure, Sixth to Seventh Century

H (with lid)	8.0 cm
D (max.)	5.9 cm

Fig. 70.1

This spheroid box has a flat base and a sloping lid with a large hollow knob on top. Both lid and box have highly polished surfaces decorated with sets of deeply cut turnings. Lid and body were formed by hammering, the marks of which are visible on the inner surfaces. The object was lathe-turned for burnishing and engraving; centering points appear in the top of the knob and the bottom of the box. There is a tear extending from the lid down the side of the box, and two more tears in the opposite rim.

COMMENTARY

This small apple-shaped box bears a general resemblance to a larger and rounder silver box at Dumbarton Oaks (*Age,* 1979, no. 550), and to a small silver bowl with footring in Kiev, dated 577(?) (Dodd, 1961, no. 23). The Dumbarton Oaks and Hama (no. 17) boxes are marked with *Chrismons,* probably signifying a sacred function (see Entry no. 17). Although it has been suggested that this box had a similar application (Ross, 1953; "for wafers"), it may well have been put to a secular use (see Duffy and Vikan, 1983, 96 ff.), and only later given to the church for its metal value.

BIBLIOGRAPHY

Early Christian, 1947, no. 382; Ross, 1950, 162 f.; *idem,* 1953.

71. PLAQUE

Paris, Musée du Louvre, Département des Antiquités Grecques et Romaines, no. Bj 2180

Ma'aret en-Noman Treasure, Sixth to Seventh Century

H	29.6 cm
W	25.5 cm

On this hammered plaque with relief decoration, which is bordered on all but the bottom by a triple garland, stands a stylite on his column. Above is a cockle shell and below, a bearded serpent wraps itself around the column, against which a ladder is set. The bearded saint wears a cowl and voluminous robes, which cover the hands in which he holds a scroll. He stands within a trellised enclosure set upon a single-zoned Corinthian capital with volutes. The column has a three-stepped base and a small door(?) halfway up the shaft. The serpent is covered with a scale pattern which echoes that of the border. There is gilding on all the decorated areas except the column shaft and ladder. An inscription runs in two lines along the lower edge. Metal has broken off the plaque at the upper left, the top, and especially the upper right. A photograph was taken of the object in Beirut before it was cleaned (Institut français d'archéologie; neg. no. F3475).

INSCRIPTION

In thanksgiving to God and to St. Symeon, I have offered (this plaque).

Εὐχαριστῶν τῶ Θεῶ καὶ τῶ ἁγίω Συμεονίω προσήνεγκα.

The same dedicatory formula, *eucharistōn . . . prosenegken,* is found on two crosses—in Greek on the smaller Sinai cross (Weitzmann and Ševčenko, 1963, 397, note 48) and in Armenian on the Divriği cross (no. 76)—and on one chalice (no. 62). The Luxor cross (Strzygowski, 1904, no. 7201) was given as a *eucharisterion* ("a thanksgiving").

COMMENTARY

Symeon's full, forked beard and general facial type (with strong nose and somewhat "tragic" eyes) are related to those on the Homs Vase (no. 84) and Hama chalice no. 3. The Cherchel *trulla,* dated 547(?) (Dodd, 1961, no. 14), recalls in certain of its qualities (e.g., its shell, Poseidon's head and softly modelled figure, the eagles' heads) comparable features on this plaque.

Fig. 71.1

It is a matter of dispute whether the Symeon portrayed here is the Elder (389–459) or the Younger (521–592) stylite, although the absence of the latter's identifying epithet (i.e., "of the Wondrous Mountain") could favor the former; if the latter, this might be a contemporary portrait. The Symeons were, together with Sergios, among the most prominent saints of nothern Syria. The *vitae* of the Elder and the Younger contain episodes upon which this particular scene could theoretically have been based (Lassus, 1960, 139 ff.). It has also been suggested that this iconography is symbolic rather than literary, with the serpent personifying evil. But another interpretation is also possible. In the ancient world the snake was associated, as a symbol of regeneration, with the healing god Asklepios, and *ex-votos* representing snakes were offered at *Asklepieia* to commemorate cures (Rouse, 1902, 209). On one such plaque (third century AD?) a snake stands erect under an aedicula (Vincent and Abel, 1926, 695, pl. LXIX).

As both Symeons performed cures (Lassus, 1960, 139 ff.; Vikan, 1984, 67 ff.), the inscribed dedication could refer to a healing (see Entry no. 72), and the figure of the Stylite with a snake could allude to portrayals of Asklepios (e.g., *Age,* 1979, no. 133). This plaque, offered anonymously to Symeon, *eucharistōn* (in "thanksgiving"), may thus be identified as a *charisterion,* like those offered in thanksgiving to St. Thekla at Seleucia Isauriae by the *magister militum* Saturninus (Dagron, 1978, mir. 13).

Although this plaque was classed as a casket revetment by H. Buschhausen (1971, no. B25), I. Ševčenko (*Age,* 1979, no. 529) has cited a passage in the *vita* of Daniel Stylites, imitator of Symeon the Elder, in which Daniel was honored by the dedication of a (ten-pound) silver votive plaque portraying him and inscribed, "Request of God that we may be pardoned for our sins against you Father." Dedicated as an act of atonement, it was affixed to the wall of his sanctuary on the Bosphoros. This Symeon plaque may likewise have been set up as a votive plaque on the wall or *templon* (Lassus, 1960, 130, note 2) of a village church near Ma'aret en-Noman. In this respect it is noteworthy that the format of the Symeon plaque recalls that of pagan silver and bronze votive plaques in which the god is shown inside an aedicula (Walters, 1921, nos. 230–236).

Selected Bibliography

Lassus, 1960; Elbern, 1965, 296; Buschhausen, 1971, no. B25; Kent and Painter, 1977, no. 156; *Age,* 1979, no. 529.

72a-n. FOURTEEN PLAQUETTES

Baltimore, The Walters Art Gallery, nos. 57.1826; 57.1865.560–572

Ma'aret en-Noman Treasure, Sixth to Seventh Century

72a. FEMALE ORANT
(57.1826)

H	3.0 cm
W	2.4 cm

This rectangular plaquette, whose analysis has revealed a surprisingly low silver content (*ca.* 32 percent *versus ca.* 60 percent copper and *ca.* 8 percent tin), bears a female orant figure wearing a tunic, *himation,* and a crown with two pair of *pendelia.* Above each hand is an eight-pointed star, and an inscription runs vertically on both sides of the figure, from the lower left corner to the lower right. A beaded frame surrounds the composition. There is a large attachment hole stuck through the first word.

INSCRIPTION

Lord, help.

Κύριε βοήθι.

(Because some of the remaining thirteen plaquettes [nos. 72b–n] have since disintegrated, the following descriptions are based on a list made by H. Seyrig, dated September 9, 1956 [WAG files].)

72b. FEMALE ORANT
(57.1865.565)

H	3.5 cm
W	2.8 cm

This plaquette is similar to no. 72a, but the head is flanked by birds rather than stars.

INSCRIPTION

(May they be) acceptable.

[Εὐπρόσ]δεκτα.

72c. FEMALE ORANT
(57.1865.566)

H	4.8 cm
W	3.5 cm

This plaquette is similar to nos. 72a and 72b, but has nothing in the upper corners; a star and a crescent mark the end of the inscription.

INSCRIPTION

(May they be) acceptable.

Εὐ[π]ρό[σδ]εκτα.

72d. FEMALE ORANT
(57.1865.570)

Only a small piece of this plaquette survives.

INSCRIPTION

(May they be) acceptable.

[Ε]ὐπρ[όσδεκτα].

72e. FEMALE ORANT
(57.1865.568)

Only the inscription and one hand survive of this plaquette.

INSCRIPTION

Lord, help. (May they be) acceptable.

[Κ]ύριε β[οήθι]. Εὐπρόσδεκτ[α].

72f. Female Orant
(57.1865.567)

Only the inscription and one foot remain of this plaquette.

Inscription

Lord, help. (May they be) acceptable.

Κύριε βοήθι. Εὐπρόσδεκ[τα].

72g. Female Orant
(57.1865.569)

This plaquette is like no. 72f.

Inscription

Lord, help. (May they be) acceptable.

Κύριε βοήθ[ι]. Εὐπρ[ό]σδεκ[τα].

72h. Female Orant
(57.1865.571)

This tiny fragment preserves only two letters.

Inscription

Lord, help. (May they be) acceptable.

[Κύριε βοήθι]. Εὐ[πρόσδεκτα].

72i. Female Orant
(57.1865.572)

This fragmentary plaque is similar to no. 72a, but apparently is uninscribed.

72j. Eyes (57.1865.563)

H	2.6 cm
W	3.6 cm

This rectangular plaquette, whose analysis has revealed nearly 97 percent silver, bears a large pair of almond-shaped eyes with oval iris and pupil. Large bushy eyebrows composed of parallel strokes follow the contours of the eyes. Below runs an inscription, and the entire composition is enclosed in a beaded frame. A twisted length of silver remains knotted through one of three attachment holes.

Inscription

In fulfillment of a vow.

Ὑπὲρ [ε]ὐχῆς.

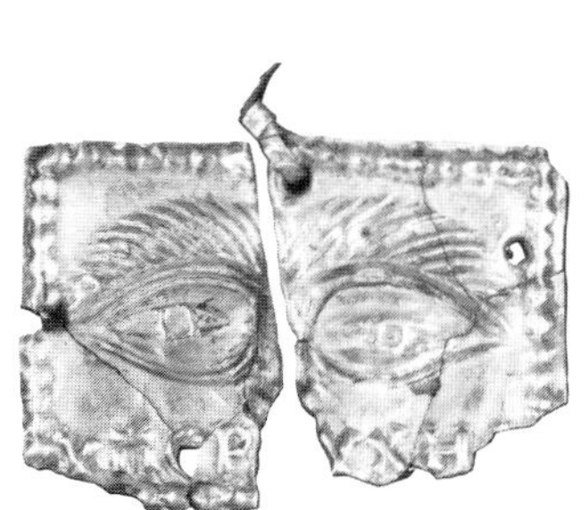

72k. Eyes (57.1865.564)

This plaquette, of which only part of the right side remains, is of the same type and dimensions as no. 72j, except that the eyes are rounder and the top was triangular in shape.

Inscription

In fulfillment of a vow.

[Ὑπὲρ ε]ὐ[χ]ῆς.

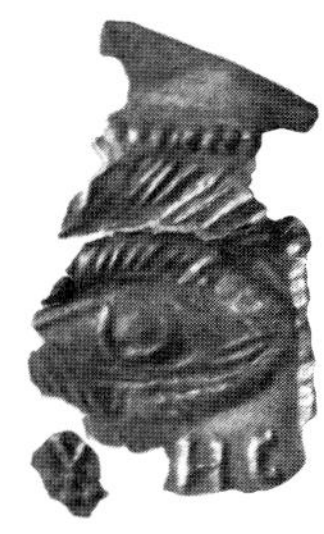

72l. Eyes (57.1865.561)

H	4.0 cm
W	4.5 cm

This plaquette is broader, but like nos. 72j and 72k, it had a triangular top. The eyebrows are somewhat shorter, and the inscription, arranged around a cross, is placed in two lines above, rather than below, the eyes. The bottom is broken off.

Inscription

Lord, help.

Κύριε βοήθι.

72m. EYES (57.1865.560)

H	4.0 cm
W	4.5 cm

This rectangular plaquette bears a pair of eyes, the lower line of which is straight, and parallel to the bottom of the surrounding beaded frame. The eyes themselves, which have upturned iris and pupil, are defined by smaller beaded lines. As on no. 72l, the inscription is at the top and, as on no. 72j, an attachment hole remains above it.

INSCRIPTION

Lord, help + *Amen* +
Κύριε βοήθι. Ἀμήν.

72n. EYES (57.1865.562)

H	3.5 cm
W	4.6 cm

This plaquette has lost all its outer edges. The eyes are oval, as on nos. 72k and 72l, and, as on nos. 72l and 72m, the inscription is above them.

INSCRIPTION

(May they be) acceptable.
Εὐπρόσδ εκτα.

COMMENTARY

These fourteen plaquettes comprise one of only two groups of as yet published small votive plaques known to have survived from the Early Christian period. The other group, that in the Durobrivae (Water Newton) treasure, includes leaf-shaped silver plaques and one gold disc (Painter, 1977[I], 36 ff.). The former continue a pagan type (e.g., Baratte, 1981, 76), to which *Chrismons* have been added in some cases. The Walters plaquettes may likewise continue pagan types, but their significance, considered below in the light of their texts and images, remains unclear.

There are three texts inscribed on all but one (no. 72i [uninscribed]) of these plaquettes: 1. "In fulfillment of a vow" (*hyper euches*), which appears on many dedicated objects in this catalogue (see Entry no. 1), accompanies eyes on two plaquettes (nos. 72j, 72k); 2. "Lord, help" (*Kyrie boethei*), a very common Byzantine invocation, appears alone with one female orant (no. 72a) and with two pair of eyes (nos. 72l, 72m); 3. "(May they be) acceptable" (*euprosdekta*) is used alone with three female orants (nos. 72b, 72c, 72d) and with one pair of eyes (72n). The second and third phrases are combined on four female orant plaquettes (nos. 72e, 72f, 72g, 72h), and thus may constitute the full legend. With regard to *euprosdekta,* H. Seyrig (1956 list) noted that the word recalls a passage in the Epistles (Romans 15.16), ". . . that the offering up of the Gentiles might be acceptable, being sanctified by the Holy Ghost," and that, as the adjective on the plaquettes is in the neuter plural, it ought to signify "une intention d'offrande agréable"; he further suggested the word might occur in the liturgy. It would seem, then, that taken with the phrase *Kyrie boethei* (as on nos. 72e, 72f, 72g, 72h), the sense could be, "If the offerings are acceptable, the Lord will help (me)."

Although the female orants (nos. 72a–72i) bear some resemblance to the taller orant figures of St. Thekla on the Cirga casket (Grabar, 1962), the latter are flanked by lions. While the Walters figures have been identified as the Virgin (Ross, 1950, 163; Seyrig, 1956 list), at least one of them (no. 72a) clearly wears a crown. This iconography presents a problem, for although diademed personifications are known at Antioch (*IGLS,* nos. 998, 1014, 1015), the crowned Virgin or crowned female saints (as portrayed in the West) are, with the possible exception of St. Helena, unknown in the East in this period.

The intrepretation of the eyes is equally problematic. They were probably not intended to be apotropaic symbols, as the usual "attacking" element of a spear, scorpion, *et cetera* is missing (Perdrizet, 1922, 27 ff.). A second possibility, suggested by G. Vikan (1984, 66 f.), is that these were *ex-votos* offered in recognition of a healing, as attested by Theodoret (*Graec. affec. cur.,* 8, 64) who mentions "images of eyes . . . feet, . . . hands . . . made of gold, . . . wood." This practice, which was widespread in the ancient world (Rouse, 1902, 210 ff.), still survives today (Anguili, 1977). The curative powers believed to be exercised by pagan deities were transferred to Christian saints (see Entry no. 71), such as Thekla at Seleucia who, in fact, specialized in diseases of the eyes (Dagron, 1978, mir. 23–25, 37), as did Symeon Stylites the Younger (Van den Ven, 1962/1970, chs. 41, 59, 80, 117). It is noteworthy, perhaps, that the orant female on these plaquettes resembles representations of St. Thekla, and that the Louvre plaque of St. Symeon (no. 71) forms part of this same treasure.

Whatever interpretation is placed on these images, the words which accompany them are related to those on dedicated liturgical objects—that is, they were clearly offered in return for something, whether before or after the favor was granted (see Chapter I, above).

These plaquettes were probably mass-produced by matrices, perhaps at the shrine where the favor was requested. As they apparently were found outside Ma'aret en-Noman, they were probably not offered at a pilgrimage shrine but rather in a village, at, one might suppose, a "branch office" of the healing saint, to whom the local church, or a shrine within it, was dedicated (see Chapter I, above). The holes in these plaquettes indicate that, once taken to a church, they were either attached by a nail or, as was clearly the case with no. 72j, suspended, as their modern equivalents are in some Greek churches today.

Final mention should be made of several fragments of at least two plaquettes which have a circular beaded frame enclosing two facing *erotes*(?); there are undecipherable letters on some. It is difficult to see any Christian significance to these fragments, which look like pieces from a woman's casket (see Buschhausen, 1971). If plaquettes nos. 72a–72n were manufactured at the village church where they were offered, then perhaps such scraps as these, from domestic use, were recycled for this purpose.

Bibliography

Ross, 1950, 163 (no. 72a); *IGLS,* no. 2048 (no. 72a); Vikan, 1982, 45 f. (no. 72m); Vikan, 1984, 66 f. (no. 72m).

The Marato tes Myrtes(?) Treasure (Nos. 73, 74)

This treasure is made up of two silver objects, a chalice now in Boston and a paten (stamped 498–518) now in Beirut (Dodd, 1973, 15, note 32; 25). According to Dodd, these two objects were dug up in a Syrian village (and not at Rusafa, as stated in *Age,* 1979, no. 543) *ca.* 1969; about that time a series of pavements were similarly unearthed and appeared on the international art market. The identity of the find-spot of the pavements has been given as a village near Gergenaz, called Tell Minnis (fig. II.1; Canivet, 1979, 352, note 4), the antique name of which was perhaps the *kome* of *Marato tes Myrteś* ("the cave of the myrtle tree") mentioned in one of their many inscriptions (of 516/7; see Rey-Coquais, 1977, 157, note 2). This identification for the chalice and paten, however, is highly speculative, and requires further investigation.

73. CHALICE

Boston, Museum of Fine Arts, no. 1971.633 (Edward J. and Mary S. Holmes Fund)

Marato tes Myrtes(?) Treasure, Fifth to Seventh Century

H	18.0 cm
D (cup rim)	16.0 cm

This hammered chalice has a broad cup, to whose upper rim are soldered cast lunate, tabbed handles resting on vertical rings with short soldering plates below. The flared foot has a small flange and a knob with a short stem above. The cup and foot were apparently joined by the "concealed joint" construction of Type A chalices (see Entry no. 1). On each side of the cup is a large engraved *Chrismon* with pendant *alpha* and *omega.* Around the top runs a niello-inlaid inscription, interrupted by the handles and banded above by an engraved line and below by a concave moulding between turned lines; further turned lines ornament the foot. The gilding which highlights the *Chrismon,* the two bands framing the inscription, the knob, and the foot flange is smeared in places and may have been applied by the amalgam technique (see Chapter III, above). The damaged foot and bowl (Dodd, 1973, fig. 7) have been repaired.

Fig. 73.1

Inscription

+ *Having vowed, SARA offered (this chalice) to the First Martyr.*

Σάρρα εὐξαμένη τῶ πρωτομάρτυρι προσήνεγκα.

The dedicatory formula, *euxamene . . . prosenegka,* occurs on objects nos. 7 and 60. The "First Martyr" is St. Stephen, whose portrait may be among those on Phela chalice no. 62; it was, furthermore, to this saint that box no. 83 was dedicated.

Commentary

The cup of this chalice, with its ring handles under a horizontal thumb plate, follows a late Hellenistic type, which became very popular by the first century AD (Strong, 1966, 112 f., 134). The form of its flared foot with knob is a later development (see Entry no. 2). Similar thumb plates, without vertical rings, appear on the Ardaburius chalice at Dumbarton Oaks (Ross, 1962, no. 5). The concave moulding on this chalice resembles those on three Riha objects (nos. 30, 37, 38). A *Chrismon* is not known to be used on such a large scale on any other chalice of the period, although a cross is similarly placed on the cup of at least one Sion chalice (Firatlı, 1965, fig. 14) and, together with standing figures, it appears on Hama chalice no. 3.

Bibliography

Dodd, 1973, 15, 25, no. 9; *Barbarians,* 1976, no. 225; *Age,* 1979, no. 543.

74. PATEN

Beirut, F. Alouf Collection

Marato tes Myrtes(?) Treasure, 498–518

D	36.8–37.0 cm

This paten has high, sloping sides, a flat upper rim, but no footring. At its center is a large engraved cross, which has flaring arms with curved ends and diagonal strokes at the crossing. Surrounding it is an engraved, single-stroke inscription between turned lines; other turned lines decorate the upper rim. There are two stages of burnishing (concentric and horizontal) evident, comparable to that on Stuma/Riha patens nos. 34–36. On the reverse are stamps dated by Dodd (1973, 25) to the reign of Anastasius (498–518). The object is heavily restored.

INSCRIPTION

+ *In fulfillment of a vow and (for) the salvation of HIM WHOSE NAME GOD KNOWS.*

Ὑπὲρ [εὐχῆς καὶ σ]ωτηρίας [οὗ τὸ] ὄνομα ὁ Θεὸς οἶδε.

The lettering is very regular and, except for *alpha, upsilon,* and *omega,* resembles that of Hama objects nos. 5 and 29. For the formula *hyper euches kai soterias,* see Entry no. 1. The anonymous reference to the donor is found also on the Louvre cross (Metzger, 1972), as well as in building inscriptions (e.g., Brünnow and Domaszewski, 1904–1909, vol. 3, 346; Murray, 1896, 126 f.; MAMA, vol. 2, 107 f.).

COMMENTARY

This paten shares much in common with Hama paten no. 5, which, however, was apparently stamped in the seventh century.

BIBLIOGRAPHY

Dodd, 1973, 15, note 32; 25; Dodd, forthcoming.

Fig. 74.1

The Sarabaon Treasure (No. 75)

This "treasure" is composed of only one known object, a paten which belonged to the church of the village of that name. It is said to have been found in Syria or Lebanon, and was purchased in Geneva around 1970, together with a chalice inscribed *Hyper euches Patrikiou presbyterou + kai mnemes Timotheou,* which is thought to have been discovered elsewhere. E. Dodd (forthcoming) has identified Sarabaon with Sarba, in Lebanon (see Jalabert, 1922, 101, no. 19).

75. Paten

Switzerland, Private Collection

Sarabaon Treasure, Seventh Century(?)

D 30.5–30.8 cm

This relatively small paten has very high, sloping sides, a flat rim with round edge, and a footring, which appears to have been raised from the plate rather than having been a separate piece soldered in place. In the center of the obverse is a large engraved cross having flaring arms with lunate ends. Around it runs a *pointillé* inscription between pairs of turned lines, another one of which appears on the upper rim. There is one centering point on the cross and another on the reverse, around which is a disc shape, evidence of lathe turning. Also on the reverse are four stamps (two stars and two figures) which are dated by Dodd (forthcoming) to the seventh century(?), on the basis of their similarity to the stamps on Hama paten no. 5.

Inscription

+ *Treasure of the most holy church of the village of Sarabaon.*

+ Κιμήλιον τῆς ἁγειωτάτης ἐκλησίας χωρίου Σαραβαον.

The text, *keimelion tes . . . ,* is equivalent to that on Hama chalice no. 3. The use of the word *ekklesia* is unparalleled among eastern objects in this catalogue, and the phrasing, "church of . . . Sarabaon," without naming a patron saint, is comparable only to "church of Gallunianu" on chalice no. 79.

Commentary

This paten is unusual in having a footring, although the Paternus paten also has one (Matzulevich, 1929, no. 6), as do the Sion patens (*DO Handbook,* 1967, nos. 63–65). (On the raising of a footring from the plate itself, see Bruce-Mitford, 1983, vol. 3, 169 ff.) This also has the highest and steepest sides of the patens included here, and the smallest diameter. On the decoration of patens with a large cross, see Entry no. 4, and Chapter I, above. Like the anonymous Hama chalice (no. 28) and the Phela cross given "in the time of" a priest (no. 65), this object may have been bought with general church funds.

Bibliography

Dodd, forthcoming.

Fig. 75.1

The Čaginkom(?) Treasure (No. 76)

This treasure comprises two crosses with Armenian inscriptions found near Divriği in eastern Turkey around 1969, when they entered the Archaeological Museum in Istanbul (Firatlı, 1969, 197, no. 2). The one cross included here is inscribed with what may be the name of a village called Čag, Čagin, or Čaginkom. The other cross, composed of five joined crosses, has a lengthy Armenian inscription (unpublished) on one side and a Greek monogram on the other.

76. Cross

Istanbul, Archaeological Museum, no. 8051

The Čaginkom(?) (Divriği) Treasure, 527–547(?)

H	58.0 cm
W	32.2 cm

This rather large cross has a tang, flaring arms with flat, circular serifs, and two holes with chains for *pendelia,* one of which, an *omega,* survives. The obverse (on which the *omega* is at the right) bears an engraved, single-stroke inscription between an engraved border composed of narrow and broadly gouged lines. An identical border decorates the reverse, which has five medallions at the extremities and intersection of the arms. Each medallion contains a nimbed bust: Christ is at the top, the Virgin at the center, an unidentified female saint at the foot, and two angels on the horizontal arms. On the obverse of the tang (with hole) are four stamps dated to 527–547 (see Dodd, 1961, nos. 11, 14; and *idem*, forthcoming). The medallions and border on the reverse are gilded.

Inscription

+ *In gratitude . . . (X) . . . offers to his/her intercessor, St. George (of) Čaginkom.*

(Translation by Robert Thomson.)

The epigraphic technique used here is very similar to that of contemporary Greek inscriptions. This anonymous dedication corresponds in its combination of "gratitude" and "offers" to several Greek dedications in this catalogue, including Hama cross no. 7, and Phela chalice no. 62; those, however, do not describe the recipient as an "intercessor." *Čaginkom* (called *Opsikom* in Firatlı, 1969) could be taken to be *Čagin kome*—that is, the "village of Čagin," or if, as Professor Thomson points out, Čagin is genitive singular, "the village of Čag"—perhaps an Armenian settlement within the Byzantine Empire.

Commentary

Despite its Armenian inscription (believed by Firatlı [1969] to be a

Fig. 76.1

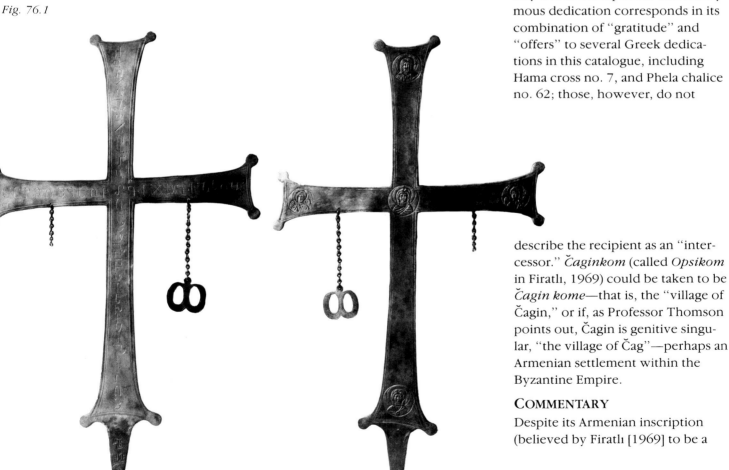

later addition), this cross is thoroughly Byzantine in its design, decoration, and, most importantly, in its stamps. On its function and design—with tang, serifs, and *pendelia*—see Entry nos. 7 and 8. The flat, circular serifs on this cross are like those on the Louvre cross (Metzger, 1972), another from Madaba (Piccirillo, 1982, pls. 24, 25), and one in Berlin (Wulff, 1909, no. 945). This is the only cross in this catalogue to preserve at least one of its *pendelia*. The medallion busts could be described as abbreviated versions of those on the Homs Vase (no. 84), by virtue of their prominent noses, "tragic" eyes, and gouged drapery. The angels' hatched *clavi* are repeated on objects nos. 35, 45–47, and 57–59, and the crescent strokes of their hair are paralleled on heads of objects nos. 15 and 35. Why a cross dedicated to St. George should bear the portraits of five other figures is a matter for speculation.

Bibliography

Firatlı, 1969, 197, no. 2; *Anatolian*, 1983, no. C48; Dodd, forthcoming.

The Gallunianu Treasure (nos. 77–82)

This treasure, which is composed of six objects—four chalices, a paten, and a spoon—was dug up in 1963 in a field in the Val d'Elsa (at Pian de' Campi, close to Poggibonsi, and about two and one-half kilometers from Galognano [Von Hessen *et al.*, 1977, 9 f.]). The village mentioned on chalice no. 79, Gallunianu, has been identified with Galognano. This is only the second western treasure, after the fourth-century Durobrivae treasure (Painter, 1977[I]), to contain explicit Christian dedications to a church, and here also, a village church. (On the non-ecclesiastical Canoscio treasure, see Engemann, 1972.) This modest treasure, with an aggregate weight of 1805 grams (Von Hessen *et al.*, 1977, 29), has been described as being of Italian manufacture, as dating to the mid-sixth century, as having been donated by "middle-class" Goths, and as having been buried at the time of the Lombard invasion of Italy in the second half of the sixth century (*ibid.*, *passim*). The Gallunianu Treasure, as restored, appears below.

77. Chalice

Siena, Pinacoteca, no. I.S.B. 22 (Soprintendenza per i Beni Artistici e Storici di Siena)

Gallunianu Treasure, Sixth Century

H	24.3 cm
D (cup rim)	16.5 cm

This chalice has a tall narrow cup supported on a tall flaring foot without knob. There are three turned lines at the top of the cup and one on the foot. The cup and foot were formed by hammering, the marks of which remain on their inner surfaces. The two parts were joined by means of a silver rivet attached to the bottom of the cup which was introduced into the foot, hammered flat from the inside, and secured with silver solder (see also no. 80; Von Hessen *et al.,* 1977, 11). The chalice was then turned on a lathe to finish its outer surface and a one-centimeter strip inside the cup. The several tears in the side of the cup were repaired with silk and resin (Bonfioli, in *Mostra,* 1981, 15).

Commentary

This chalice is both the largest and the simplest in decoration of the four in this treasure. It differs in design from the typical Byzantine Syrian chalice, which has a broad cup and, with one exception (Hama chalice no. 1, with which these chalices have been compared), a foot knob. The tapering cup of this vessel most resembles that of the smallest Gallunianu chalice (no. 80). This method of joining cup and foot is similar to that used for the Durobrivae chalice (Painter, 1977[I], no. 6), but differs notably from the external collar on eastern chalices (see Entry no. 1). It has been suggested above

Fig. 77.1

(in Entries nos. 1, 28) that the finished band inside the cup may indicate the use of a glass liner inserted to cover the otherwise rough interior.

Like chalices nos. 78 and 80 in this treasure, this one is unusual in not having a dedicatory inscription. Although Beth Misona chalices nos. 58 and 59 lack inscriptions, they presumbably formed a set with inscribed chalice no. 57. On the date, place of manufacture, and the church to which this treasure was dedicated, see Entry no. 79.

Bibliography

Von Hessen *et al.,* 1977; Bonfioli, in *Mostra,* 1981, 12 ff.; Cavallo *et al.,* 1982, no. 205.

78. Chalice

Siena, Pinacoteca, no. I.S.B. 23 (Soprintendenza per i Beni Artistici e Storici di Siena)

Gallunianu Treasure, Sixth Century

H	16.3 cm
D (cup rim)	11.0 cm

This chalice has a tall cylindrical cup with a somewhat flat bottom, supported on a wide flaring foot. There are thick turned lines at the top of the cup and at the top and bottom of the foot. This vessel was manufactured by the techniques described for chalice no. 77. The upper rim of the cup, which bears a finished band (H .8 cm) on the inside, was thickened and bent outwards. This object was very damaged when found and, like two other Gallunianu chalices, was repaired with silk patches (see Entry no. 77). It remains dented and bent.

Commentary

The general aspect of this chalice corresponds to that of the medieval(?) Lamon chalice which, however, has a knob (Elbern, 1963, no. 18). For commentary on the shape and manufacture of these Italian chalices, see Entry no. 77, and for their date and origin, see Entry no. 79.

Bibliography

See Entry no. 77.

Fig. 78.1

79. Chalice

Siena, Pinacoteca, no. I.S.B. 24 (Soprintendenza per i Beni Artistici e Storici di Siena)

Gallunianu Treasure, Sixth Century

H	13.0 cm
D (cup rim)	11.7 cm

Fig. 79.1

This chalice has a tall, slightly tapering cup with a full bottom, resting on a flaring foot with broad rim. Around the top of the cup runs a *pointillé* inscription between pairs of turned lines. Other engraved lines encircle the top and bottom of the foot, and the inside of the cup, just under the rim, where there is a finished band (H 1 cm). The chalice was manufactured by the methods described for chalice no. 77 (and no. 78), except that the rivet was introduced from the foot up into the cup and hammered down inside it. This vessel, unlike the others, was in very good condition when found.

Inscription

+ *HIMNIGILDA gave this chalice to the church of Gallunianu.*

The lettering resembles that of Greek *pointillé* inscriptions on objects nos. 3, 11, 12, and 75 in its use of dotted serifs and many letter forms. Like paten no. 75, this chalice was offered to a "church" rather than a saint. Gallunianu has been identified with modern Galognano, a village in the vicinity of the findspot (Von Hessen *et al.,* 1977). The otherwise unattested name of Himnigilda is thought to be of Germanic origin.

Commentary

The four Gallunianu chalices (nos. 77–80) are similar in contour and are related in their manufacturing techniques, although they differ from each other in dimensions and decoration, indicating that they were probably made and donated separately. This particular design, without a foot knob, contrasts with nearly all early eastern and many western medieval chalices (see Entry no. 2). Their sequential manufacture suggests that they represent an established "Italian" (or residual Roman) type hitherto unknown. Italian manufacture is suggested for all these objects, and a date in the mid-sixth century (*ibid.,* 35) would mean they were made under Byzantine occupation. The inscribed names on chalice no. 79 and paten no. 81 suggest that the donors were Goths, who presented these objects to their village church at Gallunianu sometime before the Lombard invasion (*ibid.*).

Bibliography

See Entry no. 77.

80. Chalice

Siena, Pinacoteca, no. I.S.B. 25 (Soprintendenza per i Beni Artistici e Storici di Siena)

Gallunianu Treasure, Sixth Century

H	10.4 cm
D (cup rim)	8.0 cm

This chalice has a tall tapering cup supported on a conical foot with flange. There are three turned lines at the top of the cup and two at the top and three at the bottom of the foot. It was made like the others, with the rivet joining the cup and foot hammered flat inside the foot. This chalice was very damaged when found (Von Hessen *et al.,* 1977, pl. 4), but has since been repaired with silk and resin (Bonfioli, in *Mostra,* 1981, 13).

Commentary

For commentary on the shape and manufacture of the Gallunianu chalices, see Entry no. 77, and for their date of manufacture, see Entry no. 79.

Bibliography

See Entry no. 77.

Fig. 80.1

is represented by the diagonal marks visible in a large circular area around the central turning point; this area was subsequently covered by the clamping device of a lathe when the final, concentric burnishing took place. Niello inlay remains in only one letter.

INSCRIPTION

+ *SIVEGERNA made (this paten) for her soul.*

These letters are very well formed, and may be compared with other niello-inlaid inscriptions, both from the east (e.g., nos. 1, 2, 34–36, *etc.*) and the west (e.g., the medieval[?] Lamon chalice; Elbern, 1963, no. 18). Like the name of Himnigilda on chalice no. 79, that of Sivegerna is thought to be of Germanic origin—probably Gothic rather than Lombard (Von Hessen *et al.,* 1977). Unlike the similar Greek formula, *hyper anapauseos* (see e.g., Entry no. 15), where the word "soul" is implied, "*anima*" is here stated, and "salvation" implied.

COMMENTARY

Although basically similar to Byzantine/Syrian patens in manufacture and form, this paten differs from them in its proportions (with shorter and steeper sides), and in having no decoration at its center. The placement of the niello-inlaid inscription recalls the format of the stamped Stuma/Riha patens nos. 34–36. It has been suggested (*ibid.,* 56 ff.) that this plate and spoon no. 82 formed an offering for a paraliturgical (*agape* feast) rather than a liturgical use. On its dating, place of manufacture, *et cetera,* see Entry no. 79.

BIBLIOGRAPHY

See Entry no. 77.

81. PATEN

Siena, Pinacoteca, no. I.S.B. 26 (Soprintendenza per i Beni Artistici e Storici di Siena)

Gallunianu Treasure, Sixth Century

D 20.3 cm

This paten has steeply sloping sides, a flat broad upper rim, but no footring. On the upper rim is a large, niello-inlaid inscription between two turned lines. The edge of the rim turns slightly upward. This paten was hammered, the marks of which remain on the reverse. There is evidence of two stages of burnishing on the obverse: the preliminary

Fig. 81.1

82. SPOON

Fig. 82.1

Siena, Pinacoteca, I.S.B. 27 (Soprintendenza per i Beni Artistici e Storici di Siena)

Gallunianu Treasure, Sixth Century

L	15.6 cm
W (of bowl)	3.0 cm

This cast spoon has a bowl which is between oval and pear-shaped. It is attached by a disc to a raised handle which is polygonal in section, terminating in a point. There is an engraved *Chrismon* on the right side of the disc, and scratched crosses on the other side and on the handle, the end of which is bent.

COMMENTARY

The spoon with pointed handle was known from Antiquity as a *cochlearia* (see Entry no. 22). It was suggested above (in Entry no. 18) that the Hama (nos. 18–21), Ma'aret en-Noman (no. 69), and Ghiné spoons may have been donated with chalices and had a specifically liturgical function. On the other hand, it has been suggested (Von Hessen *et al.,* 1977, 56 ff.) that this spoon and similar ones may have been donated and used with plates, such as no. 81, for paraliturgical use at an *agape* dinner, whose cessation in the seventh century coincided with the disappearance of this type of spoon.

BIBLIOGRAPHY

See Entry no. 77.

83. BOX

St. Louis, The St. Louis Art Museum, no. 44.1924

Syria, Sixth to Seventh Century

H	8.7 cm
D	10.8 cm

This cylindrical hammered box with lid is decorated with a series of wide vertical flutes banded top and bottom by engraved scallops. Pairs of turned lines encircle the box above and below the fluting. The slightly concave top of the lid has at its center a pattern of radiating flutes, each terminating in a scallop. Surrounding this is a concave moulding between turned lines, followed by a plain band with *pointillé* inscription, and then a pair of engraved lines. On the bottom of the box are two lines of a graffito inscrition.

INSCRIPTION

Lid: *Offering of TIBERINE, the deaconess, to St. Stephen.*

Προσφορὰ Τιβερίνης διακο(νίσσης) τῷ ἁγίω Στεφάνω.

Bottom (graffito): *Offering: two pounds, two ounces, four grams.*

Προσφορὰ λί(τραι) β', οὐ(γγίαι)β', γρ(άμματα) δ'.

One would expect the word order *prosphora diako(nias) Tiberines* if it were a question of a diaconate (Buschhausen, 1971, no. 13)—which, in fact, are rarely mentioned in the east (Marrou, 1940, 95 ff.). Tiberine is an attested name in greater Syria (e.g., *IGLS,* no. 2720), and deaconesses were frequent donors to churches (see also Entry no. 88). Although the word *prosphora* does not appear on other silver objects in this catalogue, it is found in pavement dedications (e.g., at Kome Nebo [Saller and Bagatti, 1949, 139, 166 ff., 172 ff.]; at Birosaba [Alt, 1923, 57 f.]; and at Khisfin [Tsaferis and Bar-Lev, 1976, 114 f.]).

COMMENTARY

For gouged fluting with a scalloped edge, see the sixth- to seventh-century Antioch spoon no. 56. The radial flutes on the box lid resemble those on a small bowl with a fifth-century(?) stamp and several plates of the seventh century (Dodd, 1961, nos. 55, 67, 73, 83).

Fig. 83.1

To facilitate the compilation of inventories, craftsmen, by the fourth century BC, often wrote the weight of an object on its underside (Strong, 1966, 20). Weights are less commonly given on Byzantine silver; exceptions include the Paternus paten, (at least) two Sion patens, and a stamped plate in Berlin, all of the sixth century (Matzulevich, 1929, no. 6; *DO Handbook,* 1967, nos. 64, 65; Wulff, 1909, no. 1107). Sometimes the aggregate weight of a set of objects was indicated on one piece (e.g., the four *scutellae* in the Esquiline treasure; Strong, 1966, 20). Thus, Zahn suggested (1921, vol. 2, 43, no. 99) that because the weight written on this box is about twice that of the object itself, it may have referred to a pair or set of boxes. According to a more recent theory, the box contained an offering of precious metal (Duffy and Vikan, 1983, 98). On the uses of such small boxes, see Entry no. 17.

Formerly in the Gans Collection, Berlin.

Bibliography

Zahn, 1921, vol. 2, 43, no. 99; *Early Christian,* 1947, no. 376; Buschhausen, 1971, no. C3; *Age,* 1979, no. 573; Duffy and Vikan, 1983, 98.

84. Ewer

Paris, Musée du Louvre, Département des Antiquités Grecques et Romaines, no. Bj 1895 (Gift of J. A. Durighello of Sidon.)

Syria, Sixth to Seventh Century

H	45.0 cm
D (upper rim)	11.5 cm
D (base)	29.0 cm

This hammered ewer has a flat base, bulbous body, and tall straight neck. There are convex mouldings at the top and bottom of the neck, the latter being decorated with a braided rope pattern, which is repeated on the raised base, and above and below a repoussé frieze which encircles the body at its fullest part. The frieze contains eight medallion bust portraits separated by cornucopiae rising from acanthus leaves. There are engraved lines on the neck of the vessel. A large hole in its side, under the frieze, has been repaired with a thin sheet of silver.

Fig. 84.1

Commentary

The shape of this, the "Homs Vase," is best compared with that of the Hama ewer (no. 14) which, however, has a handle. While the shape, mouldings, and braided rope ornament of this vessel resemble those of other objects found in Byzantine Syria (e.g., nos. 14, 15, 71), the high quality of its repoussé frieze sets it apart. Most often noted are its illusionistically rendered cornucopiae and the classical character of the portrait busts. Heads and drapery are solidly executed in a combination of gouging and engraving techniques that are echoed in the figural work on other objects in this catalogue (e.g., nos. 3, 15, 34, 35, 42, 44–47, 57–59, 62, 71). Likewise, the juxtaposition of the frieze with a wide expanse of plain, polished silver is paralleled on, for example, the Stuma and Riha fans (nos. 31, 32).

Despite these technical links to objects found in Syria, the absence of "imperial" (presumably Constantinopolitan) control stamps, and its find-spot in the ruins of a Syrian village church (Héron de Villefosse, 1892, 239), the Homs Vase is often attributed to Constantinople because of its superior quality (e.g., *Age,* 1979, no. 552). Moreover, the suggestion has recently been made (Dodd, 1983, 148) that it was decorated by the same hand that made at least one David plate. These two objects may differ technically, however, for while the David plates were worked entirely from the front (Foltz, 1975), the Homs Vase was apparently first worked from behind, in repoussé technique, and finished on the front (a technical examination of the object is currently being undertaken, and will be published in a study by Dr. C. Metzger).

The medallion figures, none of whom is nimbed, have been identified as Christ between Peter and Paul on one side, and the Virgin between two archangels on the other. Between Paul and one archangel is a beardless saint holding a book, who is perhaps John the Evangelist, and between Peter and the other archangel is a bearded bust thought to be that of John the Baptist (*Age,* 1979, no. 552). Christ is the full-bearded Zeus/Pantocrator type, seen also on the Divriği cross (no. 76) and the Stuma and Riha patens (nos. 34, 35; contrast nos. 15, 42, 57–59). Similar arrangements of single figures—both full length and in medallions—are found on several other sixth- and seventh-century silver objects (see Entry no. 15, and Dodd, 1973, 48 ff.); indeed, the busts on the Divriği cross (no. 76) may be described as "compressed versions" of those on this object. Although it lacks a dedicatory inscription, its find-spot inside a church and the sacred character of its decoration suggest that the Homs Vase was put to the same liturgical use as the Riha ewers (nos. 37, 38; see Entry no. 38).

Found near Homs.

Selected Bibliography

Héron de Villefosse, 1892; Coche de la Ferté, 1958, 50 f. 107 f.; *Masterpieces,* 1958, no. 44; Volbach, 1958, no. 246; Dodd, 1973, 7; *Age,* 1979, no. 552.

85. CENSER

New York, The Metropolitan Museum of Art, 1985.123 (Rogers Fund, 1985)

Constantinople, 582–602

H	8.9 cm
W	13.2 cm

This censer is decorated with standing figures of Christ, Peter, Paul, and an orant Virgin flanked by archangels. They are placed under segmented arches which are raised on spirally fluted columns with acanthus capitals. The object is made from at least four pieces: footring, base, sides, and chains. The sides were probably formed from a single sheet that was bent into hexagonal shape after the figural decoration was raised, chased, and engraved. The sides and footring were joined to the base with hard solder, and then the figures and arches were gilded. The silver of the chains contains a high percentage of copper, making it stronger. They appear to be an integral part of the censer, although one link, which joins the chains to the censer's tab, is broken, and another is lost. An inscription appears just below the censer's rim, but above the arches under which the figures stand. Breaks in the silver and the distortion of the sides and base are consistent with damage caused by continuous use over centuries. The application of solder to the interior walls, especially in the heads of the figures, testifies to their periodic need for repair. The object exhibits no certain evidence of burial.

Inscription

The God of St. George pray for thy servant LEONTIOS.

Ὁ Θ(εὸ)ς τοῦ ἁγίου Γεωργίου βοήθι τοῦ δούλου σου Λεοντίου.

Fig. 85.1

Leontios has not been identified. Since the letters intrude upon the area of the arches, it is likely that they were added after the censer was completed.

Stamps

(We owe the following to Erica Dodd.) Six stamps are visible on the bottom of the censer, within the footring: two round, one long, and three cross-shaped. The round stamps show the nimbed bust of the Emperor Maurice (582–602); they are inscribed *Lamprotatos.* The long stamp shows the monogram of Maurice, and a nimbed bust above the monogram; it is inscribed *Patrikiou.* The cross stamps contain the monogram of Peter, and are inscribed *Patrikis.* The stamps belong to the normal imperial series and were most likely applied in Constantinople. The monogram of Peter (Barsymes?) suggests that the stamps were applied early in the reign of Maurice. (These stamps show features that are not "regular" for the imperial series, in that there are six, rather than the usual five stamps, and the monogram of the emperor occurs in a long stamp rather than in a hexagonal or a square stamp. These irregularities are found in other stamps from the reign of Maurice, however, and therefore they are "regular" for the imperial series during his reign. [See Dodd, 1961, nos. 14, 15; *idem,* 1968, 148; *idem,* forthcoming].)

Another hexagonal censer, made in the reign of Phocas (602–610), comes from the first Cyprus treasure and is now in the British Museum (*Age,* 1979, no. 562). Its structure is very similar to that of this one, but being considerably smaller, it bears busts, not full-length images, of the same figures. These censers are also linked by a communality of style. The caplike hair styles of the figures and the softly modelled folds of the draperies, for example, resemble such contemporary work as the figures on a chalice in the Hama treasure (no. 3).

Said to have come from Mesembria, Bulgaria.

BIBLIOGRAPHY

Unpublished.

86. FLASK

New York, The Metropolitan Museum of Art, 1984.196 (Purchase, Rogers Fund and Schimmel Foundation Inc. Gift, 1984)

Constantinople (?), Sixth Century

H	31.5 cm
D	10.0 cm

This slender flask stands on a tall foot with flaring base that supports a richly decorated pear-shaped body. The tall, narrow neck and wide mouth of the vase repeat in smaller scale the profile of the base. Six registers of decoration animate the surface. Beginning at the top, there are: three incised turnings above a raised band with a formalized ivy vine; a row of pendant acanthus leaves and flowers; a portrayal of the Adoration of the Magi (which is the flask's principal decoration); a grape vine scroll; a row of tall, elaborately formed acanthus leaves and flowers behind which emerge displayed eagles; and another raised band of ivy. Each register is divided from the next by thin raised strips of zigzag pattern, of beading, or of slightly concave border. Turned lines also frame the bottom edge of the lower acanthus band and the border of ivy directly below it. The figures in the Adoration of the Magi, decorative bands and vine scrolls, and parts of the neck and base are gilded.

There is a break through the neck of the flask below the ivy band, and a shallow V-shaped section of the rim on a line above Joseph in the Adoration has been repaired in Antiquity with a section of a lip from another vessel. The flask has also suffered a large dent in its lower register in line with the angel.

COMMENTARY

This flask represents a type of silver vessel decorated with pagan or Christian imagery that was popular from the fourth to the sixth centuries (see Strong, 1966, 191 f.). It may have been used during the celebration of the eucharist, perhaps to hold the water that was mixed with the wine, judging from its eucharistic ivy and vine borders and the image of the Magi bringing gifts to the Christ Child. The closest comparison for the shape of the flask is the earlier, fourth-century bottle from the Esquiline treasure (Shelton, 1981, 82 f.), but the organization of the decoration here resembles more that of the sixth-century silver flask in The Cleveland Museum of Art,

Fig. 86.1

which depicts an animated Dionysiac *thiasos* (*Age,* 1979, no. 131). A similar liveliness of posture and gesture characterizes the scene of the angel and the three Magi bearing gifts on The Metropolitan Museum's flask, where the central Magus stops and turns back to the third king, pointing out the star of Bethlehem to his companions. The angel who guides the kings also looks over his shoulder as he strides toward the outstretched arms of Christ, seated in His mother's lap. Joseph witnesses the event from behind the Virgin's wicker chair. The star of Bethlehem above the Christ Child's head is shaped like a six-pointed rosette of a type that frequently occurs in pilgrimage art of the sixth and early seventh centuries.

The vigor with which the Adoration scene is depicted characterizes its portrayal on other sixth and seventh century works, like a lead flask only recently published (Engemann, 1984, 115 ff.), and an ivory pyxis in the Archaeological Museum in Istanbul (Volbach, 1976, nos. 173a and 171). The acanthus and eagle design in the flask's lower register recalls the decorative language of the presbytery mosaics of San Vitale in Ravenna, where lush variations of acanthus plants fill the vaults, and eagles rise from cornucopiae on the main apse's archivolt. The decoration on the flask is more static and regimented, but the manner of display and especially the slightly "wind blown" bending of the central plant are reminiscent of Justinianic decoration. Similar playful use of this age-old motif is found on the Homs Vase (no. 84), where a cornucopia rises between the leaves of an abstract acanthus plant.

BIBLIOGRAPHY

Unpublished

87. VELLUM LEAF FROM A CODEX

New York, Pierpont Morgan Library, cod. M874

Syria(?), Sixth Century

1 folio; 30.5 × 25.5 cm (8th folio of quire 7)
2 columns; 16 lines
New Testament; Matthew 15.38–16.17
Greek

This folio was removed before 1896 from the codex *Purpureus Petropolitanus* ("Codex N"), a New Testament which had been divided by the seventeenth century, rebound in 1820, and is now dispersed in libraries or collections in Patmos, the Vatican, London, Athens, Thessalonike, Vienna, Leningrad, and Lerma, Italy. The volume is written in silver Greek uncials on purple tinted vellum with *nomina sacra* and *titloi* in gold; it bears no illustrations. The Arabic pagination was added in Ephesos in 1820 (see below).

COMMENTARY

The codex *Petropolitanus* and the three other extant purple vellum New Testaments in Greek—the *Sinopensis,* the *Rossanensis,* and the *Beratinus*—are all thought to descend from the same "none too orthodox ancestor" (Rypins, 1956, 31), although there are variations in format among them, and two have illustrations. These manuscripts are said to have been produced in the same scriptorium, in Constantinople or Asia Minor (*ibid.,* 29), or in Syria or Palestine (*Age,* 1979, no. 444), where major centers of book production were located at Antioch, Berytus, Caesarea, Edessa, and Nisibis (Mundell-Mango, 1981, 3 ff.).

Fig. 87.1

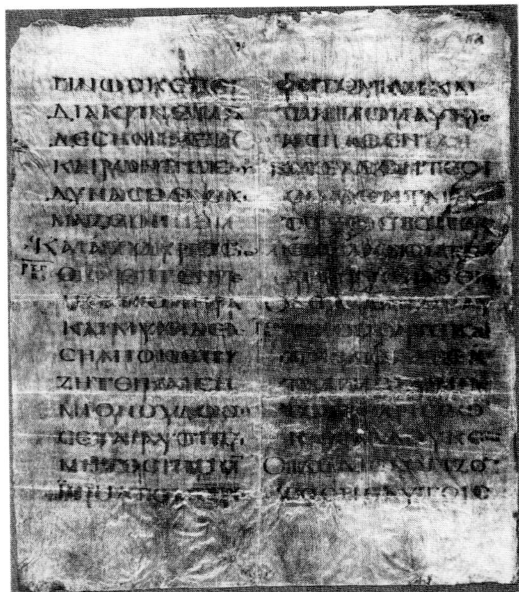

Wherever this volume was written, it was undoubtedly expensive. A Bible mentioned in the *Life of Epiphanios* (p. 10) as costing forty *solidi*—eighty times the price of codex no. 89 in this catalogue—may have been as luxurious as this one, but there are few other price comparisons to make from this period. This purple New Testament, bound probably in precious metal, may have been destined for a cathedral or other large church well endowed with rich and showy offerings in silver and silk. Its humble counterpart, bought for a few carats and destined for a village church, was a codex like no. 89, which took its place in a treasury alongside donations like the silver objects from Kaper Koraon.

Acquired in 1955; in Sarumsahi, Cappadocia in 1847–1896; in Ephesos in 1820.

SELECTED BIBLIOGRAPHY

Rypins, 1956; Cavallo, 1967, 98 ff.; *Age,* 1979, no. 444.

88. VELLUM CODEX

London, British Library, cod. Add. 12156

Northern Syria(?), ca. 562

137 folios; 30.8 × 23.8 cm (18 quires signed with letters)
3 columns; 43–51 lines
Various anti-Chalcedonian works
Syriac

This manuscript contains anti-Chalcedonian works compiled by Timothy Aelurus, twice Monophysite patriarch of Alexandria (457–460, 475–477). There is a bilingual (Syriac and Greek) index of heresies on folios 130r and 137r. The scribe Tayla, who copied the manuscript in a "fine Edessene hand" (Wright, 1870–1872, vol. 2, 648), terminated on folio 136v with the usual doxology ("Glory to God . . ."), and then wrote (Mundell-Mango, 1984, MS-30):

> Through the prayer of the whole glorious church may Tayla, scribe of Edessa, who wrote this book, be shown mercy in the hour of which there are judgments on Judgment Day, so be it, amen.

At the top of the middle column, a different hand recorded the following long note, the first five lines of which have been erased:

> And in the days of the priest Mar Bacchos who is from Gamal, (who was) steward, and the priest Mar 'Aziz, who was the librarian, and the priest Mar Shemun, who was from Karmil, who is the doorkeeper. In the year 873 in the month Nisan, the deaconess Megala, who is from Beth Mana, gave it, then, for her memorial and for the salvation of her soul; because in the name of God she offered this gift. He (God) shall give to her (. . . 5 lines erased . . .) a good reward, and shall write her name in the Book of Life, and Our Lord shall make a good memorial to the departed and (grant) mercy and compassion to the living, through the prayers of the upright and the righteous who do His will, for ever and ever, amen and amen. And towards the monks (*ahē*), Sergios, from Shagura, and Shemun from Tell She, who take care of the scriptorium (*beth katoba*), God shall exercise mercy, amen and amen.

COMMENTARY

This manuscript was presented by its donor, Megala the deaconess, in 562 (873 of the Seleucid era) to an institution whose name was undoubtedly given in the introductory lines, which are now unfortunately erased. That it was a village church could be inferred from the fact that the positions of steward, librarian, and doorkeeper were held by priests, but the fact that custodians of the scriptorium were monks makes it more likely that it was a monastery. Whether or not Tayla himself worked in this scriptorium is unclear. He does not identify himself as a monk, and his pseudo-title, "scribe of Edessa," was used by at least four other scribes working 552–593 in the area immediately to the south of Kaper Koraon, and one in the village of Sarmin (figs. II.1, II.2; Mundell-Mango, 1983). To this group may be attributed seven manuscripts (including the Rabbula Gospels) copied for various monasteries whose current abbots signed docu-

Fig. 88.1

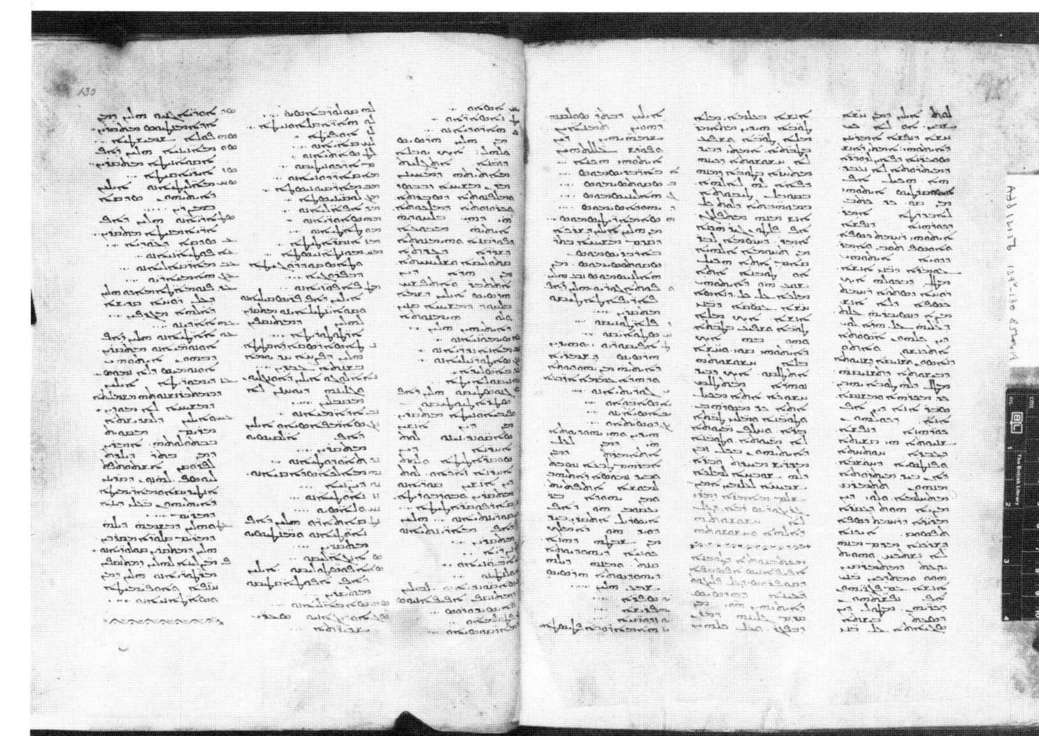

ments (567/8) related to the Tritheist quarrel then dividing the Monophysite world. It is possible that this collection of theological texts may have been copied in the same area and circumstances (*ibid.*, 421 f.). Megala, who apparently paid for the book, was probably deaconess of a nearby village church, perhaps in her native village of Beth Mana. She gives it as her memorial (*dokrana*), and for the salvation of her soul; the latter is comparable to the *hyper soterias* of Greek dedications (see Entry no. 1), and the former, to *hyper mnemes* (see Entry no. 4), but which in Semitic contexts is used also for the living. The "good reward," the inscription in "the Book of Life," and the reference to "the departed" and "the living" are all formulae recurring as often in contemporary Syriac manuscripts as their Greek counterparts do on the silver objects here catalogued. Unlike codex no. 89, the price here is not given. A manuscript of comparable length, but having only about half the number of written lines, was bought for three *solidi* and twenty-one carats by a recluse in a village near Bostra in 604 (Wright, 1870–1872, vol. 2, 458).

This manuscript was found in Egypt, at Deir es-Suriane.

Selected Bibliography

Wright, 1870–1872, vol. 2, 639–648; Brock, 1977; Mundell-Mango, 1984, MS-30.

89. Vellum Codex

London, British Library, cod. Add. 14472

Northern Syria(?), 624(?)

73 folios; 23 × 16 cm (cut down) (8 quires signed with letters)
2 columns; 21–28 lines
Acts and Epistles
Syriac

This manuscript contains the Acts of the Apostles and three Catholic Epistles (James, Peter, and John), according to the Peshitta or "Simple" version, the earliest Syriac translation of the New Testament. The text, "written in a fine, clear Estrangela" (Wright, 1870–1872, vol. 1, 82), ends at the top of the right hand column of folio 72v with the Epistle of John (I), where the scribe has written a subscription, colophon, and doxology, under which is a later note stating that the manuscript then belonged to a deacon of Tagrit. The following, earlier (non-scribal) note starts at the top of the left hand column and continues onto folio 73r (Mundell-Mango, 1984, MS-80):

> Before God and His Christ may this be a good memorial to the community who has a partnership in this book, whose (= the community) life may He preserve through His grace and mercy; and to the departed it shall be a good memorial with the upright and with the righteous through the prayers of all who shall please and have been pleasing to His will; and to the sinner who possessed the diligence to deposit this book in the church of Gadaltha, Christ shall consider her (= the sinner) worthy of hearing the beloved voice which says, 'Come ye blessed of My Father, inherit the kingdom which is prepared for you from before the foundation of the world' (Matthew 25.34), through the prayers of the upright and righteous, yea and amen. For anyone who borrows this book in order to read in it or to collate from it is under (= bound by) the word of God until it is returned to its owners. This book was bought then, in the year 935 in the month of Ab on the fifteenth with twelve carats. For all who read in it shall pray for (her) who bought it and for the sinner who wrote the record, that they be pitied as the thief on the cross, yea and amen.

Commentary

This manuscript was given to a church in the village of Gadaltha by an unnamed woman, "a sinner," who hoped thereby to "inherit the kingdom" of God. The donation was to be a "good memorial" to all who participated in its production, as well as to "the departed." The volume, bought in 624 (935 of the Seleucid era), cost twelve carats—that is, exactly half a *solidus*. Where and by whom the codex was written is not stated, and Wright (1870–1872, vol. 1, 82) was cautious about describing the text as contemporary with the note of 624, although mention of those who "participated" may imply that they were personally known to the donor. There remains, however, the possibility that the book was bought second hand in 624, and that the price was consequently reduced. Two years previously another scriptural book (the Pauline Epistles) which was twice as long as this, was bought by John bar Sergios, resident of a village in the province of Edessa, for fourteen carats (*ibid.*, 90 f.). Again, however, it is not absolutely clear whether the book was new. John Moschos (*PS*, ch. 134) gives the price of an entire(?) New Testament as three *solidi*.

The location of Gadaltha is unknown, although Wright (1870–1872, vol. 1, 82) suggests that it may be the village of that name near Mosul—hence outside of the Byzantine Empire. That its price is quoted in carats suggests it may have been bought in a Byzantine city, although in 624 all of *Oriens* was still under Persian control. The manuscript note has nine spelling mistakes, which suggest relative illiteracy in Syriac (in favor of Greek or Pehlevi). The verb used to describe the offering of this book (*etsim* = "deposited") has the same root as the word for "treasure" (*simtha*)—a word often used in Syriac manuscripts to describe the book itself. Indeed, the Scriptures were considred part of the treasures of rural as well as urban churches. The *keimelia* inventoried in the village church at Ibion included twenty-one vellum and three papyrus books (see Entry no. 91), and Pancratius, the legendary bishop of Taormina, is credited with including one or two copies of the New Testament as essential equipment, along with two silver *diskopoteria* (see Entry no. 1) for every church (Mango, 1972, 137).

Fig. 89.1

That village churches had other books—the works of Eusebius and Aphraates, and the Acts of Symeon Stylites—is known from preserved manuscript notes (Mundell-Mango, 1981, 6). Some villagers obtained their books in cities like Edessa and Amida, much as the donors to the Kaper Koraon church traveled to a city to buy at least their stamped silver objects (see Chapter I, above).

This manuscript was found in Egypt, at Deir es-Suriane.

SELECTED BIBLIOGRAPHY

Wright, 1870–1872, vol. 1, 81 f.; Mundell-Mango, 1984, MS-80.

90a, b. Two Silk Textile Fragments

Washington, D.C., Textile Museum, nos. 11.21 (a), 11.26 (b)

No. 90a	
H	33.5 cm
W	25.5 cm
No. 90b	
H	16.0 cm
W	15.0 cm

Fragment no. 90a is decorated with a scrolled grid into which are set alternating medallions and eight-lobed rosettes enclosing birds, confronted or addorsed, on palmettes. The warp is cream-colored silk and the weft, red silk and cream-colored silk. The weave is complementary-weft, with five span floats in diagonal alignment.

Textile fragment no. 90b is decorated with a symmetrical composition of two armed men attacking two tigers. They are set within a circular frame ornamented with an ivy scroll. At the top and bottom of the medallion are plant motifs—a winged palmette and a trefoil. The hunters wear short tunics and spotted leggings. The warp is cream-colored silk and the weft red silk and cream-colored silk. The weave is complementary-weft with five-span floats in diagonal alignment.

Commentary

Fragment no. 90a belonged to a silk cloth, other fragments of which are known (Trilling, 1982, no. 114). A grid pattern enclosing ornamental motifs or objects was a popular Early Byzantine decorative device in wall and pavement mosics (Spieser, 1984, 143 f., pl XIX–1; Levi, 1947, 470 ff., pls. CXXIV, CXXVI, CXXVIII, CXXXI, CXXXVII, CXCI) and manuscripts (Weitzmann, 1977, pl. 20), as well as on textiles (Trilling, 1982, 97 f.). The medallion on fragment no. 90b was part of a repeating pattern on a large cloth (*ibid.,* no. 115). Although of neutral or secular iconography (on the hunt, see Entry no. 101), these silks are of a type that was donated—sometimes secondhand—to churches. Next to precious metal, the most valued donations to Early Byzantine churches were textiles (see Guillou, 1979), especially purple silks, and those woven or embroidered with gold or silver threads.

Imperial donations of textiles to churches include the purple silk altar cloths with gold-woven images given by Justinian to Hagia Sophia in 563 (Mango, 1972, 89), some years after he and Justin I had sent comparable *pallea aurotexta* to Rome (*Liber Pontificalis,* 276, 285). Chosroes II sent to St. Sergios at Rusafa a "Hunnic" curtain fashioned from gold (Evagrius, *HE,* VI, 21). At the episcopal level, Victor, bishop of Ravenna, had made for his cathedral (*ca.* 543) an altar cloth "of pure gold and silken thread," with his and other portraits on it, and a purple inscription. About two years later his successor, Maximian, gave the same church a purple cloth with his portrait and New Testament scenes, and a gold-woven cloth. Among titled laymen, Flavius Vlalila gave his country church near Tivoli

Fig. 90.1

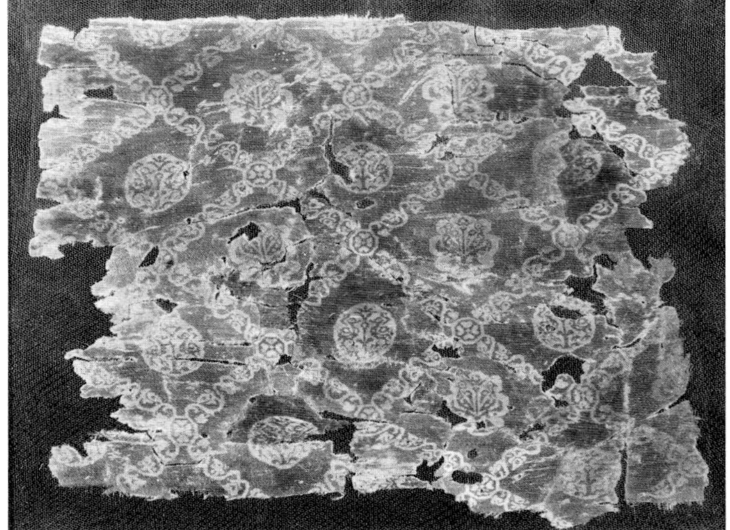

about eighty cloths (*pallea* and *vela*) of silk, gold thread, and linen in 471 (see Entry no. 91), and the Ibion church had a number of textiles—cloths (*mamparia* and *ouela*) in linen and wool, some described as "hanging" (*kremaston;* see, e.g., *Age,* 1979, no. 476), and one "triply-woven web" (*histos triyphantos;* see Entry no. 91). Some textiles were given secondhand, as the Constantine inventory (e.g., 82 women's tunics and 16 men's tunics, *etc.;* Entry no. 91), and the story of Sosiana (Entry no. 18) testify. The latter gave several loads of silk (*holoserikos* and *metaxa*) garments, of the type worn by the imperial couple and their courtiers, each worth over one pound of gold (72 *solidi*), to churches of Constantinople to be refashioned into altar cloths, veils, and *mandele* (John of Ephesos, *Lives,* ch. 55).

Although garments, especially silk, dyed the purest purple by the *murex* shellfish were restricted to imperial use, the public was allowed to use other grades of purple—some achieved by mixing indigo and madder (Trilling, 1982, 29, note 5). The red silk fragments here may be other such approximations. Justinian eventually liberalized the laws even further so that women could wear purple silk (Reinhold, 1970, 65 ff.), perhaps to increase revenue from what was a state monopoly. Both purple-dyeing and silk weaving were protected state industries based in *Oriens*—and, like some trade in silver, were regulated by state officials (Stein, 1949–1959, vol. 2, 769 f. 843 ff.).

Fragment no. 90a was acquired from P. Mallon, Paris, in 1949; fragment no. 90b was acquired in 1950 from P. Tano, Cairo.

BIBLIOGRAPHY

Trilling, 1982, nos. 114, 115.

91. PAPYRUS INVENTORY

Oxford, Bodleian Library, cod. gr. th. d.2[P]

Ibion, Egypt, Fifth to Sixth Century

H	29.2 cm
W	14.2 cm

The text of this inventory is as follows (Hunt and Edgar, 1932–1934, 432 ff.): "Inventory of the holy treasures (*ton hagion keimelion*) and other utensils of the holy church of Apa Psaius of the village (*kome*) of Ibion [in Egypt], entrusted to the most discreet John, presbyter and steward (*oikonomos*), Choiak 15, thirteenth indiction, being as follows:

3 silver chalices (*poteria*)
1 silver ewer (*xestes*)
2 hangings (*katapetasmata*)
1 iron rod (*rhabdos*)
1 other, small
1 marble (*trapeza*)
1 bronze tripod (*tripous*) for the slab
23 linen cloths (*mamparia*) for the slab
5 woollen cloths
6 door-curtains (*ouelothyra*)
1 other, old
1 hanging woollen curtain (*ouelarion ereinoun kremaston*)
1 hanging cover (*stroma kremaston*)
4 bronze lampstands (*lychniai*)
2 iron lampstands
1 bronze altar (*bomos*)
1 bronze basin (*lebes*)
1 bronze flagon (*kokkoumion*)
2 bronze fonts (*louteria*)
6 handlamps (*cheirolychniai*) with 6 nozzles (*myxai*)

Fig. 91.1

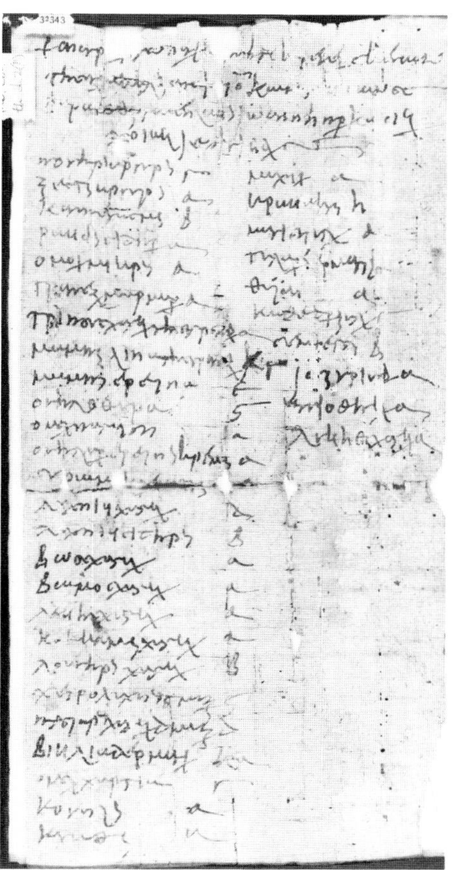

4 boat-shaped lamps (*ploiaria*) with 4 nozzles
21 parchment books (*biblia dermatina*)
3 others of papyrus (*chartia*)
1 cup (*kotyle*)
1 ladle (*kyathos*)
1 knife (*machaira*)
1 bier (*krabaktion*)
1 wooden tray (*magis*)
2 leather cushions (*tylaria*)
1 mortar (*thyian*)
3 wooden chairs (*kathedrai*)
2 stools (*sempsellia*)
1 triply woven web (*histos triyphantos*)
1 cupboard (*apaiotheke*)
1 bronze flask (*lykethos*)

(verso): Made by me, Elias, archdeacon, on behalf of the holy Apa George."

This translation is taken from Hunt and Edgar, with the exception of the word *xestes* (see below). This fifth- or sixth-century inventory may be compared with two others in Latin: (a) one from an early fourth-century African church, and the other (b) from a fifth-century Italian church.

(a) Inventory of the church at Constantine in Numidia (May 19, 303; see Ziwsa, 1893, 186; Painter, 1977[I], 46, note 28):

"1 book (*codex*)
2 gold chalices (*calices*)
6 silver chalices
6 silver ewers (*urceola*)
1 silver paten(?) (*cuccumellum,* i.e., "pan")
7 silver lights (*lucernae*)
2 (silver?) wax lights (*cereofala*)
7 bronze short lamps (*candelae breves*) with their lights
11 bronze lights with their chains
82 women's tunics (*tunicae*)
38 veils (*mafortea*)
16 men's tunics
13 pair, men's shoes (*calligae*)
47 pair, women's shoes
19 thongs (*coplae rusticanae*)
1 small silver bust (*capitulata argentea*)
1 silver light
4 jars (*dolia*)
6 chests (*arcae*)"

(b) The silver objects from the extensive inventory (the *Charta cornutiane*) of the church built by Flavius Vlalila near Tivoli in 471 (*Liber Pontificalis,* CXLVI f.): ". . . I expend also of silver for the embellishment of the same church or for the celebration of the above mentioned most holy rites, namely, there is:

1 silver paten (*patena*)
1 large silver chalice (*calyx*)
2 small silver chalices
1 silver ewer (*urceum*)
1 small ama for offering
1 strainer (*colum*)
1 censer (*thimiaterium*)
1 silver cantharus lamp (*farum cantharum*) with 18 chains and dolphins
4 silver polycandela (*coronae*) with their little chains
1 silver lampstand (*stantarea*)
and in the confessio its 2 silver doors (*ostia*) with fastenings (*clavi*)

which all kinds, weighed by the city scales have by weight of silver fifty-four (pounds), seven ounces."

Commentary

The exact location of Ibion, a common village name in Egypt, is unknown (Drew-Bear, 1979, 122 ff.). "Apa Psaius" is the Abyssinian St. Besoi (Grenfell and Hunt, 1897, 162, note 2). This inventory is cumulative, including, apparently, all the objects then belonging to the church, as is the inventory of the Constantine church. By contrast, the Tivoli list is limited to the founders' donations, of which only the silver objects are cited here. The Ibion inventory covers furniture, liturgical vessels, lighting equipment, cloths, and books. It lists both the valuable (silver chalices) and the banal (iron rods). The inventory is of great interest for the study of Early Christian church treasure because it contains the Greek equivalents of the Latin terms utilized in the *Liber Pontificalis* and other western sources, such as the two supplementary lists given in this Entry.

The translation of *xestes,* noted above, was a matter of speculation in the original edition of the inventory, where F. E. Brightman's suggestion of "paten" was first proposed (*ibid.,* 162, note 6), and later repeated by Hunt and Edgar (1932–1934). On *xestes,* which on most accounts should be translated "ewer" (Latin = *urceum* and *urceola*), see Entry no. 14; on other terms in the inventory, see Grenfell and Hunt (1897, 162 f.). Although rendered as "flagon" by Hunt and Edgar (1932–1934), the Ibion bronze *kokkoumion* may be comparable to the Numidian silver *cuccumellum,* a term normally designating a flat cooking pan. Those two objects may, therefore, have served as patens, although one would expect both to have been of silver.

The Constantine and Tivoli churches owned more silver (including silver door revetments at Tivoli and secular silver[?] [i.e., bust and lamp] at Constantine) than did the Ibion church, but otherwise the possessions of all three churches were comparable. They included precious and non-precious metals, textiles, and books (for the eighty-three-odd textiles and books at Tivoli, see *Liber Pontificalis,* CXLVII). While having, apparently, only linen (23) and woollen (5) cloths, as compared with the large numbers of silks and other precious textiles at Tivoli, the Ibion inventory far surpasses the two Latin lists in its number of books: twenty-four as opposed to one codex at Constantine and the *evangelia IIII apostolorum, psalterium et comitem* at Tivoli (*ibid.*). (On textiles and books included in this catalogue, see Entries nos. 87–90, and for silver objects, see the index and Chapter I, above.) (For a Merovingian inventory, giving object prices in *solidi,* see Knögel, 1936; and on two Coptic inventories [seventh to eighth century], see Crum, 1909, nos. 238, 244.)

Bibliography

Grenfell and Hunt, 1897, no. CXI; Hunt and Edgar, 1932–1934, no. 192; Drew-Bear, 1979, 122 ff.

92. RING

Houston, Menil Foundation Collection, no. R24

East Mediterranean, Sixth to Seventh Century

D (hoop)	2.0 cm
D (bezel)	2.0 cm

At the center of the large, thin bezel is a hairless oval head from which sprout six serpentlike "rays." Along the upper edge are three magical "ring signs" (on which, see Bonner, 1950, 58 f.; 194 f.): an N-shaped form, a *pentalpha,* and an asterisk. Below the head is a hatched bar, a seventh, unattached serpent, and a second asterisk. The flat, octagonal hoop, which is soldered to the bezel, bears an engraved inscription.

INSCRIPTION

+ *He that dwells in the help (of the Highest)*+

ʽΟ κατοικων ἐν βοηθία

The letters bear serifs and the *beta* takes the form of a Latin R, with a bar across the bottom. This inscription, from the beginning of Psalm 90, had a specific association with apotropaic jewelry in early Byzantium (*ibid.,* 5, nos. 294 ff.; and Vikan, 1984, 75 ff.).

COMMENTARY

Like the inscription from Psalm 90, the octagonal shape of the hoop had a specifically apotropaic association for the early Byzantines (*ibid.,* 76); moreover, the Gorgon-like head on the bezel seems to have had a specifically medico-magical function. A closely related silver ring with octagonal hoop in the British Museum (Dalton, 1901, no. 142) is inscribed "Lord, help the wearer," with "wearer" bearing a feminine case ending, while another, excavated at Corinth, reads "Womb amulet" (Davidson, 1952, no. 1947).

Fig. 92.1

A group of contemporary and later pendant amulets shows basically the same device, and some bear incantations against the womb (see Entry no. 93). This is consistent with an identification of the bezel device as neither Gorgon nor Medusa, but rather as Chnoubis, the popular "gem amulet" of Greco-Egyptian origin which was invoked against abdominal pains and problems of the uterus (Vikan, 1984, 75 ff.). The process whereby the Chnoubis—with its serpent body, lion head, and seven (or twelve) solar rays—came, as here, to resemble Gorgon can be traced on yet another group of Early Byzantine jewelry amulets related to this ring—namely, on medico-magical armbands like that in Entry no. 94. Significantly, there is a strong correlation between these three closely interrelated categories of *women's* amuletic jewelry—Chnoubis rings (as here), pendants (no. 93), and armbands (no. 94)—and silver, which was clearly the preferred medium for all three. This is especially striking, since in this period silver is only rarely used (in place of bronze or gold) for other types of jewelry. Interestingly, in the Byzantine marriage ceremony (as attested from the Middle Byzantine period; see Trempelas, 1940), the groom received a gold ring, and the bride one of silver.

Said to have come from Anatolia (G. Zacos).

BIBLIOGRAPHY

Vikan and Nesbitt, 1980, 20; Vikan, 1984, 76 ff.

93. PENDANT

Houston, Menil Foundation Collection, no. 824

East Mediterranean, Sixth to Seventh Century

D	4.5 cm

This pendant bears dense but iconographically confused apotropaic imagery and words on both its surfaces. Its obverse is filled by a Gorgon-like oval head sprouting seven serpent "rays," while its reverse shows a series of magical characters and symbols: above are the *pentalpha,* two crescent moons, a star, an erect snake(?), and a figure—perhaps a misunderstood archangel—holding a long cross staff, while below are a pair of "Z"s and a six-pointed asterisk, both "ring signs" (on which, see Bonner,

Fig. 93.1

1950, 58 f., 194 f.). Figures and symbols are only summarily rendered, although the serpents are surprisingly vigorous. Inscriptions, between incised lines, encircle both compositions, and are found within the two fields as well. The pendant's suspension hoop, which was apparently soldered in place, has broken off.

Inscription

Obverse: *Holy, Holy, Holy, Lord Sabaoth, Heaven is full. Amen. IAW. Grace of God.* (within field)

Ἅγιος ἅγιος, ἅγιος Κύριος σαβαώθ, πλήρης οὐρανός ΙΑΩ (χ)άρις Θεοῦ.

Reverse: *Womb, dark (and) black, eat blood, drink blood.*
As the serpent you coil, as a lion you roar, as a sheep, lie down; as a woman. (within field)

+ Ὑστέρα μελάνη μελανομένη ἕμαν τρόη ἕμαν πη.
+ Ὃς ὄφης ἤλησσε, ὃς λέον ὄρυλσε, ὃς πρόρατον κυμοῦ, ὃς γυνή. . .

Although many individual letters are elegantly formed (especially on the reverse), missing letters and mistakes in spelling—as well as unfinished phrases—strongly suggest that the craftsman responsible for this inscription understood little of the meaning (or even the language) of what he was transcribing. For example, the initial *chi* of *charis* ("grace") was dropped, while in the *Trisagion, alphas* appear for *lamdas* and a *kappa* for a *beta* (in Sabaoth). This latter confusion suggests that the form of the *beta* in the model was that characteristic of the sixth to eighth centuries (see, e.g., nos. 75, 92, 94), which looks like a Latin "R" with an (overlooked) bar across the bottom.

While "Grace of God" appears, in one form or another, on a variety of inscribed objects of the Early Byzantine period, the *Trisagion* and especially *IAW* are often associated specifically with amulets—with the latter commonly used as a magical expression for divine power (see Bonner, 1950, 134 f.). The incantation on the reverse, however, is even more explicitly apotropaic and amulet-related (see Drexler, 1899, 594 ff.; and Laurent, 1936, 303 ff.). Like others of its type, it addresses the womb (*hystera*) directly, as though a living creature; the organ is labeled with a damning double epithet ("dark and black"), is accused of behaving like a snake and a lion, and is admonished to be still like a sheep, and to eat and drink blood.

Commentary

This is one of the earliest and finest in a long and closely interrelated series of pendant amulets distinguished by a Gorgon-like head and an incantation addressed to the uterus; moreover, it, and the others, are close relatives of the Early Byzantine ring and armband amulet types represented by objects nos. 92 and 94 in this catalogue (see Vikan, 1984, 78 ff.). Among all three categories of amulet, words, symbols, and images converge toward magical medicine. Moreover, that this magic was invoked specifically on behalf of women is (especially) clear from the uterine incantations found on the pendants. Typically, the womb is admonished to "lie down" and here, moreover, to consume blood—presumably the blood that it would otherwise discharge. This suggests that these objects functioned specifically to enhance fertility—that is, a bloodless uterus will presumably avoid miscarriage (*ibid.*).

There is little doubt that the apotropaic creature on these pendants (rings and armbands) is neither Gorgon nor Medusa, but rather Chnoubis, the popular "gem amulet" of Greco-Egyptian origin which was invoked against abdominal pains and problems of the uterus (Bonner, 1950, 54 ff.; and Vikan, 1984, 75 ff.). Especially distinctive of this magical polymorph—which originally was a lion-headed serpent—are its seven "rays" (for the seven planets), and the Z-shaped "ring signs." These amulets, like their related rings (no. 92) and armbands (no. 94), were apparently made specifically for women; it is clear, moreover, that the preferred, "magical" medium for all three was silver (see also Entry no. 92).

Said to have come from Anatolia (G. Zacos).

Bibliography

Vikan, 1984, 78 f.

94. ARMBAND

New York, Private Collection

East Mediterranean, Sixth Century

D	*ca.* 7.7 cm
H (medallions)	*ca.* 3.2 cm

This armband consists of a flat, ribbonlike band with four oval medallions. The band and one of the medallions bear inscriptions only (respectively, Psalm 90 and the *Trisagion*), while the other three medallions show figurative compositions, in two cases with accompanying words. One bears a highly schematic, uninscribed scene of the Women at the Tomb (with just one of the Holy Women and a crude aedicula for the Tomb), another shows a nimbed Holy Rider with cross staff (inscribed "Health"), and the third has a thoroughly abstract portrait of the enthroned Virgin with Christ Child, accompanied by an invocation on behalf of a certain Anna. Although the technique is very simple, the horse bearing the Holy Rider is quite energetic. This armband is broken in several places, and has recently been repaired.

INSCRIPTION

Band: *He that dwells in the help of the Highest (will abide) under the protection of (God).*

Ὁ κατοικὸν ἐν βοηθία τοῦ ὑψίστου ἐν σκέπε τοῦ [Θεοῦ]

Medallions: *Holy, Holy, Holy, Lord (Sabaoth).*
Health.
Theotoke, help Anna. Grace.

Ἅγιος, ἅγιος, ἅγιος Κύριος.
Ὑγία.
Θεοτόκε βο(ήθει) Ἄννα, χάρις.

The letters are simple and lunate, and the *beta* takes the form of a Latin R with a bar across the bottom (compare no. 75). While "Grace" (or "Grace of God") appears on a variety of inscribed objects of the Early Byzantine period—as, of course, do invocations beginning *Theotoke, boethei*—Psalm 90 and *hygieia* (here in its simplified, typically Byzantine spelling) are specifically associated with amulets (see Bonner, 1950, 5, 294 ff.; and Vikan, 1984, 69 ff.)

COMMENTARY

This is one of more than a dozen surviving examples of a type of amuletic armband produced in the east Mediterranean (i.e., Syria-Palestine and/or Egypt) in the sixth and seventh centuries (see *ibid.,* 75ff., note 54). The group is distinguished by recurrent inscriptions and images, and by a ribbonlike design highlighted by incised, figurative medallions (numbering as many as eight); finer specimens, like this, are of silver. That the iconographic roots of these armbands lie in the pilgrim trade is clear from the fact that their version of the Women at the Tomb includes architectural elements of the Holy Sepulchre shrine (e.g., the "grills"; see Wilkinson, 1972, 83 ff.), and from the striking similarity that exists between the choice and configuration of their scenes and those that appear on the well-known Palestinian metal *ampullae* preserved in Monza and Bobbio (Grabar, 1958, *passim;* and Vikan, 1984, 75, figs. 8, 11). Similarly, that these armbands were intended to be at least generally amuletic is clear from their inclusion of Psalm 90 and such patently magical images as, here, the Holy Rider (on which, see Bonner, 1950, 5, nos. 294 ff.; and Vikan, 1984, 75, note 57). Moreover, that they were more specifically medicomagical is indicated by the word *hygieia,* and by the portrayal on some other examples of the Chnoubis, one of Antiquity's most popular "gem amulets"—and one long recognized to be especially effective in the cure of abdominal disorders (Bonner, 1950, 54 ff.; and Vikan, 1984, 75 ff.; figs. 8, 9, 12). There is, furthermore, a clear and close relationship between this armband amulet type and contemporary amuletic rings (like our no. 92) and pendants (like our no. 93)—and all three show a marked "preference" for silver (over bronze or gold) and a marked association with women, either through their inscribed uterine charms (no. 93) or through invocations (Entry no. 92, and this specimen).

Said to have come from eastern Anatolia.

BIBLIOGRAPHY

Vikan, 1984, 75 f.

Fig. 94.1

The Daphne Treasure (nos. 95–100)

This silver treasure, composed of four pieces—a plate, bowl, ewer, and (silver gilt) statuette; nos. 95–98—was excavated in April 1939 in a large villa, the "House of Menander" (House 1), at Daphne (modern Harbiye), the affluent suburb of Antioch (fig. II.1; Ross, 1953, 39). According to the excavation reports (*Antioch,* III, 25), the building phases (I–III) of the house extended from the second to the sixth century. Part of the Phase II construction, dated to the fourth century on the basis of the style of the pavements, and the lamp and potsherds sealed under them (Levi, 1947, 198), was the room (no. 3; a *triclinium*) in which the silver was found (see accompanying figure). The house of the Phase II construction contained some twenty rooms, with homogeneous and contemporary pavements (*ibid.,* 198 ff.; no. 101); it was richly decorated with marble revetments (no. 100), and at least three rooms had *nymphaea* backed by niches, undoubtedly intended to display marble statuary (no. 99).

This treasure was discovered under a limestone drain that was laid just above the Phase II level during the Phase III construction of the complex (Antioch excavation records, Princeton), which came as the result of an earthquake in either 485 or 526 (*Antioch,* III, 25). (The evidence of this last phase is ambiguous and is confusingly reported; *ibid.,* 25 f., 155, no. 49; Levi, 1947, 198.) It would appear that the family occupying the Phase II level (*ca.* 300–526?) of the "House of Menander" lost their four silver objects—left in a *triclinium,* where they might have been in use—when the building collapsed in an earthquake. The family was either unsuccessful or uninterested in retrieving the objects before they rebuilt their house as another "large villa" (*Antioch,* III, 155, no. 49).

95. Plate

Worcester, Worcester Art Museum, no. 1940.17

Daphne Treasure, Fourth Century

D 33.2 cm

This hammered plate is concave in profile with a flat outer rim having an edge which is square in profile. It rests on a footring, which is apparently a separate piece soldered into place (contrast no. 75). The plate is decorated with a twelve-petal rosette set within an eight-pointed star composed of two interlocking arcuated quadrangles. The rosette and star have gouged surfaces. Surrounding this motif is a circular border of a square notched moulding followed by a *cyma recta* profile ornamented by two types of oval punches; the mouldings are separated by heavy grooves. The flat outer rim is covered with a series of gouged flutes and flat darts. There are lathe turning points in the center of the rosette and the footring. On the reverse is a scratched quatrefoil and a graffito. When found, this plate was covered with lime deposit, bent, torn in half, and missing silver in several areas. It was restored by W. J. Young at the Museum of Fine Arts, Boston (1940–1951; report of L. Dresser, Worcester Art Museum [8/1/51]), and corrosion was removed in 1953 at the Worcester Art Museum (WAM files).

INSCRIPTION

Reverse *(graffito): (Plate) of MAKAR(IOS).*

Whereas it is thought that only great masterpieces of silver were signed by their craftsmen, owners often scratched their names on the reverse of the object (Strong, 1966, 20; Cahn *et al.,* 1984, 388 ff.). There is a proposed reading of the name *Makar* on a second-century altar in Syria (*IGLS,* no. 1872); as read here, however, the *graffito* may be the Greek form of Macarius, the name of a pupil of Libanius at Antioch, attested in 359/60 (*PLRE,* vol. 1, 525).

COMMENTARY

This plate shares characteristics with several fourth-century plates and bowls. Comparisons have been made with the Kaiseraugst treasure (Cahn *et al.,* 1984, 192), which contains three objects with gouged interlocking geometric forms in central medallions, one of which, a lobed bowl (*ibid.,* no. 41), has a fluted rim as on this object. A related lobed bowl in Budapest also has a gouged central geometric motif combined with a fluted rim (*ibid.,* 134, pl. 67). On this group of objects, which includes a bowl in the Mildenhall treasure, see the discussion which compares these geometric motifs with those in mosaic pavements, including some at Antioch and Seleucia Pieria, as well as with sixth- and seventh-century silver (*ibid.,* 136, 162; see also Entry no. 17). (On the fluting, see Cahn *et al.,* 1984, 161 f.; and on other types of domestic plates, see Entries nos. 102–106.)

BIBLIOGRAPHY

Ross, 1953, 40.; *idem,* 1962, 1; Strong, 1966, 166, 174; Cahn *et al.,* 1984, 192, 321.

96. BOWL

Baltimore, The Baltimore Museum of Art, no. 1940.33

Daphne Treasure, Fourth to Fifth Century

D	19.0 cm
H	4.5 cm

This hammered and lathe-turned bowl has a footring and a flat upper rim which turns straight down at its outer edge. At the center of the bowl is a medallion containing a five-leaved acanthus rosette from which spreads a calyx of overlapping spear-shaped leaves, which are repeated as a pattern on the upper

Fig. 95.1

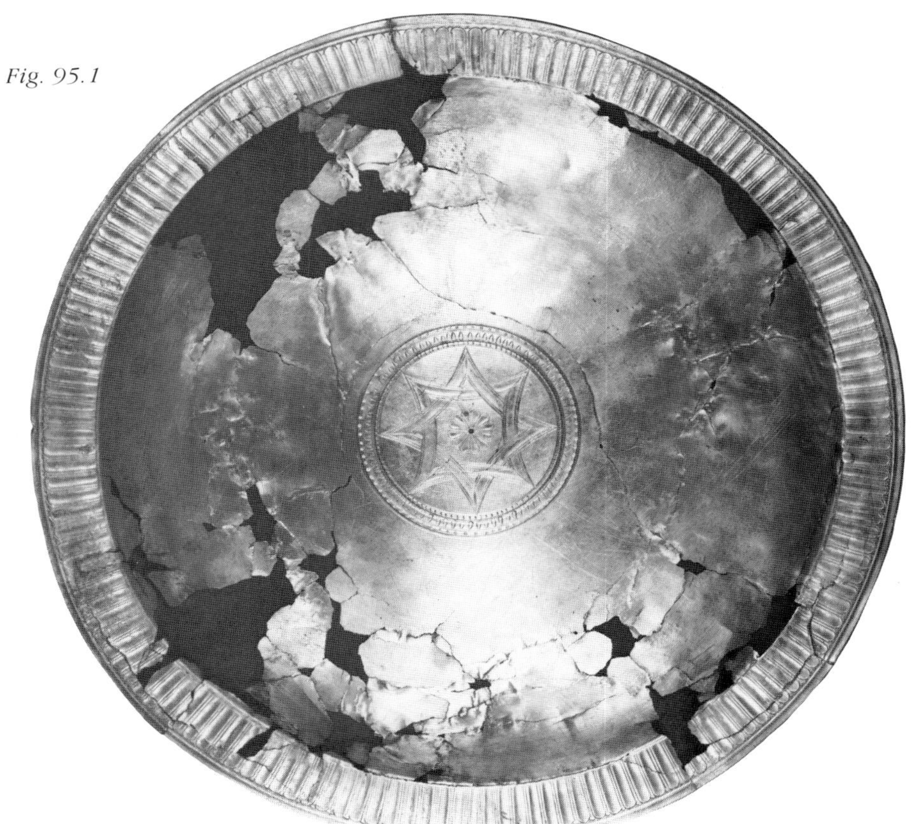

rim. Engraved turned lines frame the medallion and patterned rim, while turned burnishing lines are visible inside and outside the bowl. When found, the bowl was intact except for some losses of silver in the lower sides of the bowl; it was, however, damaged in transit to Baltimore, where it was repaired at The Walters Art Gallery (Ross, 1953, 40). At present, The Baltimore Museum of Art is unable to locate the piece.

Commentary

The shape of the bowl is typical for the fourth and fifth centuries (e.g., Cahn *et al.,* 1984, nos. 47–52), with its turned-down rim, where often beading is added to the outer edge (e.g., Dodd, 1961, nos. 81, 82, 85). In view of the rosette in the center, it seems likely that the accompanying decoration was meant to represent leaves (and not feathers; contrast Ross, 1953, 40). They resemble the overlapping leaves on the knobs of chalices nos. 3, 57, 59, and the raised border of the Antioch mirror (see no. 48). While all these comparisons are with sixth-century objects, a (presumably) contemporary example of the same motifs can be found on the dish from Mileham (Ross, 1953, 40; Kent and Painter, 1977, no. 103).

Bibliography

Ross, 1953, 40; *idem,* 1962, 1; Strong, 1966, 166, 174; Cahn *et al.,* 1984, 192, 321.

Fig. 96.1

97. Ewer

Washington, D.C., Dumbarton Oaks Collection, no. 40.24

Daphne Treasure, Fourth Century

H	20.0 cm
D (rim)	6.3 cm

This ewer has a hammered ovoid body on a flat, sightly flaring base; it tapers up to a narrow neck above which is a round mouth with a wide vertical rim, which slopes downward on the inside. Attached to the vessel is a cast handle, which extends horizontally from the rim and bends down at a right angle to the body. At the rim, the handle widens into a scalloped horizontal plate, to which a rolled thumb tab has been added, while at the bottom, it terminates in a leaf-shaped soldering plate. When found (see figure, above), the foot and back of the ewer under the handle were broken through; they have since been repaired.

Commentary

This ewer, attributed to the fourth century by Strong (1966, 166) and Ross (1962, no. 1), is of a kind that derives from a type popular in the first century (Strong, 1966, 140 f., 165 f.). Comparisons have been made with ewers from Chaourse, Trier, Syria, and Nubia (*ibid.,* 166, 190; Ross, 1962, no. 1), all of which, however, display differences in the shape of body or handle. Closer in both these elements is a bronze ewer found on the German *limes,* although the handle is heavier in appearance and terminates in a foot-shaped soldering plate (Kellner and Zahlhaas, 1984, no. 45, fig. 23). Also similar are two glass ewers, one found in a fourth-century tomb at el-Bassa (Iliffe, 1934, fig. 18), and another from Kertch (*Iskusstvo,* 1977, no. 94). On the various functions of ewers, see Entry no. 14.

BIBLIOGRAPHY

Ross, 1953, 40; *DO Handbook,* 1955, no. 123; Ross, 1962, no. 1; Strong, 1966, 166; *DO Handbook,* 1967, no. 53; Cahn *et al.,* 1984, 192, 321.

Fig. 97.1

98. STATUETTE

Antakya, Hatay Archaeological Museum

Daphne Treasure, Fourth Century

H	20.5 cm
D (top of base)	8.0 cm

This silver gilt statuette of Aphrodite is hollow cast. Her *chiton,* which slips from her left shouder, is fastened at the waist where her *himation* is tied. She stands with her right leg bent; in her left hand she holds a pomegranate while her right is raised in front of her breast. She wears a diadem; her hair is parted in the center with tresses falling over each shoulder. The base is composed of an octagonal plinth with two *torus* mouldings and a concave moulding between. Metal is missing from the back of the statuette, the right leg, and the base, from which the statuette had become separated.

COMMENTARY

This statuette has been compared with four others (three in bronze, one in silver) found in Syria (*Antioch,* III, 124, no. 367; de Ridder, 1905, vol. 3, nos. 101–104, pl. 20), which differ only in certain details—namely, in the position of the right arm (which held a scepter?) and in the arrangement of the *chiton,* which in the other cases is tied with a belt and leaves the left breast exposed. Moreover, the folds of their *himatia* are less full, and the fruit held is an apple.

These statuettes have been identified as deriving from the fifth-century (BC) Aphrodite created by the school of Phidias. The Daphne Aphrodite is closer to the prototype than the other examples cited in not leaning on a pier, but differs from all in having her left breast covered.

Fig. 98.1

The Venus *Genetrix* was a maternal or household goddess overseeing the birth and education of children. Aphrodite in all her forms was especially honored in Syria, where burial customs dictated that only gold jewelry, glass flacons, and her image, placed under the head of the deceased, be placed in a woman's tomb. A large number of bronze statuettes of Aphrodite have, consequently, been recovered in Syria, a good selection of which entered the de Clercq Collection, which was formed almost entirely in that region (*ibid.,* 3). Another fourth-century silver statuette of Venus, a combination of the Anadyomene and Thera types, is in the Kaiseraugst treasure, holding a mirror like no. 48 in this catalogue. (Cahn *et al.,* 1984, no. 64.)

BIBLIOGRAPHY

Antioch, III, 124, no. 367; Ross, 1953, 39 f.; *idem,* 1962, 1; Strong, 1966, 166; Cahn *et al.,* 1984, 192, 321.

99. Marble Statue

Worcester, Worcester Art Museum, no. 1940.9

Daphne, Fourth to Fifth Century

H (as fragment)	50 cm

Fig. 99.1

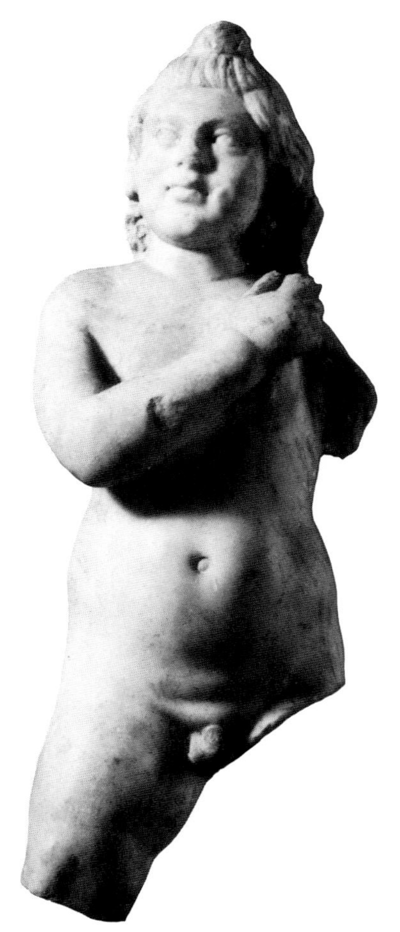

This naked child has his hair drawn into a knot on the top of his head. He stands with his right arm before his chest; in his right hand he holds the handle of an object now lost. His left arm, left leg, and the lower half of his right leg have broken off.

Commentary

This figure has been identified as Harpocrates (*Antioch,* III, 120, no. 288) who, however, normally holds the fingers of his right hand to his lips in an infantile or "silencing" gesture, and often carries a cornucopia on his left arm (*ibid.*). The deity Harpocrates—that is "the child Horus" in the Egyptian language (Lafaye, 1884, 18)—was worshipped together with his parents, Isis and Osiris, in Egypt and then throughout the Greco-Roman world (*ibid.,* 35 ff.). As he had represented the rising sun in Egypt, Harpocrates became identified with Apollo. Hellenistic artists gave him the appearance of Eros, and he was also associated with both Herakles and Dionysos; in the latter guise he carried the cornucopia (*ibid.,* 259 f.). This statue may have been associated with the marble quiver found in the same house (*Antioch,* III, 121, no. 297), as an attribute of Apollo.

This statue was found in the foundations of a "late pool" built on top of the fourth-century pavement (excavation notes, Princeton University) which featured in its *emblema* a portrait of Menander (Levi, 1947, 201 ff.), after whom the house is named. It is uncertain when this pool was built. This is one of twelve or thirteen fragmentary marble statues (of Hygieia, Tyche, Dionysos, Silenos, *etc.*) found in the house, each of which may have stood about sixty centimeters high (*Antioch,* III, 119 ff., nos. 285–297). The statue of Hygieia has been compared stylistically with the silver statuette of Aphrodite (no. 98). This silver statuette and the marble statues may have been displayed, until the late fifth or early sixth century, in some of the niches of the Daphne house, at least seven of which were found in *nymphaea* in rooms 1 and 17, and in the courtyard (Levi, 1947, 67). Another collection of statues, including imperial portrait busts, was found in the city of Antioch (Brinkerhoff, 1970).

Excavated in room 11, "House of Menander" (DH26–M/N), at Daphne (Harbiye; see fig. II.1).

Bibliography

Antioch, III, 120, no. 288.

100. Marble Slab

Baltimore, The Baltimore Museum of Art, no. 44.170A
(Antioch Project Fund)

Daphne, circa *500*

H	65.4 cm
W	69.8 cm
Th	8.9 cm

This slab is carved on the obverse, worked smooth on the reverse, and is rough along its top edge, where there is a hole for attachment. On the front at the top are two narrow decorative zones—the upper ornamented with a simple rinceau and projecting volutes, and the lower with a tight drilled acanthus scroll between plain fillets. The large lower field of the slab is densely covered with two rows of upright acanthus leaves, each composed of a central twisted stem sprouting long spiky tendrils with drilled contours which bend back on themselves. The lower row of acanthus leaves is larger and their tops project forward. There are rosettes between the leaves. The slab is broken off on three sides.

Commentary

The spiky acanthus leaves of this unusual plaque have been compared with fine-toothed acanthus capitals at Thessalonike (*Antioch,* III, 169) of the so-called Theodosian type, which has few other representatives at Antioch (*ibid.,* 170). This marble slab has recently been linked, as an "urban model," to a group of limestone capitals in the territory of Antioch—at Dehes, Me'ez, Banqusa, and Bafetin (Sodini *et al.,* 1980, 233 f.; Strube, 1983, 79 ff.). It is the most ornate piece of marble architectural sculpture recovered from the House of Menander, which otherwise contained another large ornamented slab (*Antioch,* III, 169, no. 230), as well as a series of champlevé marble plaques (*ibid.,* 155, no. 49; 169, nos. 222–229) of the type found at Seleucia Pieria; many of the latter were carved as pilaster capitals, indicating a rich wall revetment. (For other architectural sculpture, see *ibid.,* 154, nos. 45–48; 161, nos. 116–118; and for statues, see Entry no. 99). As mentioned above, the two later construction phases of this house were recorded in a confusing manner by the excavators. This marble slab was thought to have adorned a "fountain decorated with a fourth-century mosaic pavement" (*ibid.,* 170, no. 231), probably as part of the front parapet—but whether as a contemporary part or later addition is unclear, although its

Fig. 100.1

style would indicate a date *ca.* 500. In the House of Menander there were at least three fountains, or *nymphaea* (in rooms 1, 17, and the courts; Levi, 1947, 67), whose back niches may have been used to display statues like that of Harpocrates (no. 99).

Excavated in the "House of Menander" (DH 26–M/N), at Daphne (Harbiye; see fig. II.1).

Bibliography

Antioch, III, 169 f.; *Early Christian,* 1947, no. 61; *Age,* 1979, no. 594; Sodini *et al.,* 1980, 233 f.; Strube, 1983, 79 ff.

101. PLATE

Richmond, Virginia Museum of Fine Arts, no. 66.77 (The Williams Fund)

"North Syrian" Treasure, Fourth Century

D	41.0 cm

This hammered and lathe-turned plate has a convex inner surface, a flat outer rim with beading above a vertical edge, and a footring . At its center is a medallion with relief decoration showing a mounted hunter in short tunic and flying cloak facing right, spearing a lion from behind. Above them to the right is a twisted tree and below, to the left, a fallen shield. The scene was executed on several planes (from high relief to flat incision) entirely from the front, leaving only faint traces on the reverse. Circular and crescent punches were used on the shield and horse trappings. On the horse's front flank is a turning point, which is also visible on the reverse. A wide concave moulding between turned lines surrounds the hunting scene, and the flat beaded rim has five turned lines.

Commentary

This "display plate" continues the Hellenistic tradition of dishes with figural decoration restricted to a central medallion or emblem (Strong, 1966, 111)—which is eventually replaced by the Roman plate with overall decoration, in use from the first century AD (*ibid.,* 150; see Entry no. 102). Late *emblemata* include those on the stamped Euthenia, Nereid, and horse plates (Dodd, 1961, nos. 7, 26, 93), and on the sixth-century Erotes plates (Boyd, 1983). (On the technique used here, see Maryon, 1948; and Foltz, 1975.) Plates and bowls with beaded edges were very popular in the fourth and fifth centuries, and this Richmond plate has recently been compared to one in the Kaiseraugst treasure (Cahn *et al.,* 1984, 184, 186). As with the fourth-century Daphne plate and bowl (nos. 95, 96), comparisons for this plate are most easily made with contemporary silver found in the West (see Entry no. 17)—as, for example, a Mildenhall bowl with a similarly composed hunting scene (Painter, 1977[II], pl. 16). Animal scenes in general are among the most frequent subjects in Syrian pavements, with the hunt featuring on the highest quality floors (see, e.g., Balty, 1969, 22 f). This hunting plate was found together with what was described as a silver hunting horn (Ross, 1967/1968) in "North Syria," an area which included the *Kynegia chora,* or "hunting country," near Kaper Koraon (see Chapter I, above), and Dehes, where a lion's paw bone was found in a recently excavated house (Sodini *et al.,* 1980, 303).

Other silver objects in this treasure include a beaded bowl (Dodd, 1973, no. 9) and two spoons with swan-neck handles—one decorated with a goose (*ibid.,* no. 10) and the other with a Hermaphrodite(?) nude figure (Wixom, 1970). While these three objects are now divided between the Abegg Stiftung, Bern and The Cleveland Museum of Art, the present whereabouts of the two remaining silver objects of this treasure, a spoon and the hunting horn formerly in the Mallon Collection (Ross, 1967/1968), are unknown. This "North Syrian" treasure is contemporary with, and comparable to, the Daphne treasure (nos. 95–100) in its contents and, apparently, in its domestic context. But like the silver church treasures included in this catalogue, its precise provenance will probably never be ascertained (see Cahn *et al.,* 1984, 186).

Bibliography

Ross, 1967/1968, 59 f.; Wixom, 1970, 142; Cahn *et al.,* 1984, 88, note 104, 184, 186.

Fig. 101.1

102. Plate

Boston, Museum of Fine Arts, no. 69.1146 (Theodora Wilbour Fund in memory of Zoë Wilbour)

Eastern Mediterranean, Fifth Century(?)

D 20.5 cm

This plate has a flat surface with an edge rolled forward to form a raised rim. In the center of its footring is a turning point beside which is a stamp. It bears a relief composition of a tigress attacking an ibex; a lizard looks on from the lower right and a small tree bends from behind the tigress to fill the top of the composition. The coats of the animals are finely delineated in overall patterns. The decoration was worked from the front, leaving no impression on the burnished surface of the reverse side. There is some metal missing from the plate near the rear legs of the tigress.

Stamps

This plate's rectangular stamp, inscribed *Basiliou* in Greek, will be published by Dodd (forthcoming). It has been compared (*Age,* 1979, no. 72) to other single rectangular stamps attributed to the fourth and fifth centuries (Dodd, 1961, nos. 81–85). It is also similar to that on a small unpublished plate in the Ashmolean Museum, Oxford.

Commentary

This plate can be compared (*Age,* 1979, no. 72), from the point of view of its composition, style, and technique, with those portraying combat between men and animals (*ibid.,* nos. 139, 428, 429); indeed, this is the only known instance wherein fighting animals fill a Late Antique silver "display plate." Animals are featured alone elsewhere: in compositions on cups (Héron de Villefosse, 1899, 215 f.), spoons (Dalton, 1901, nos. 414–424), and plate rims (*Age,* 1979, no. 72). That the Boston plate belonged to an established type of plate decoration is documented by the fact that among the silver services given to his cathedral by Desiderius, bishop of Auxerre (603–623), is a set of six small plates, each decorated in relief (*anaclea;* see Colin, 1947, 94) with animals (including a lion seizing a goat; see Adhémar, 1934, 48 f., nos. 10–15).

The animal hunt was very popular in Late Antique art. Animals alone were also favored subjects, particularly in tessellated pavements in Syria during the fifth and sixth centuries. The significance of these compositions, which include animals running together, attacking each other, or in repose together, is obscure. C. Vermeule (1971) has suggested that the pair of animals on this plate represent an allegory of government. The royal connotations of the attacking lion are of ancient Near Eastern derivation and the motif appears in Byzantine and Umayyad palace pavements (Levi, 1947, 581; Ettinghausen, 1977, 38 f.). But even if it was once conceived as an expression of such great power struggles, the subject had filtered down the social strata, for it also appears in the pavement of a village bath at Serjilla (fig. II.1; see Butler, *AAES,* vol. 2B, 288 ff.; see also Balty, 1969, 22).

Fig. 102.1

This object belongs to that category of "display plate" wherein the subject came to emerge from the central *emblema* to fill the entire surface. These plates, occasionally made in pairs or sets, and decorated, basically, with three main subjects—imperial, pagan/mythological, and Christian (*Age,* 1979, nos. 64, 111, 482)—or a combination thereof (*ibid.,* nos. 425–432), continued to be produced into the seventh century (Dodd, 1961, no. 70). Although no examples that late may be attributed to Syria, the ewer from there now in The Cleveland Museum of Art (*Age,* 1979, no. 131), which is decorated with Dionysiac scenes, may attest to the flourishing of such themes in that region well into the sixth century.

Bibliography

BMFA, 1970, 30; Vermeule, 1971; *Boston,* 1976, no. 204; *Age,* 1979, no. 72; Dodd, forthcoming.

103. PLATE

Baltimore, The Walters Art Gallery, no. 57.652

Cyprus Treasure(?), 610–613

D 25.5 cm

This plate is the largest of a set of three (nos. 103–105). It is almost flat, with a vertical rim and a separate, soldered footring. At its center is a monogram set within a medallion formed by two sets of concave and raised mouldings banded by turned lines, between which runs an ivy scroll. The latter and the monogram were engraved and inlaid with niello. The mouldings, engraved lines, and burnishing of the surface were done on a lathe. Five stamps appear within the footring.

STAMPS

These stamps were dated by Dodd (1961, no. 38) to 610–613 because of the presence of an early monogram of Heraclius (610–641), and the name of an official (Sissinios), which also appears in stamps from the reign of Phocas (602–610).

INSCRIPTION

(Plate) of THEODORE A(?)

The letters, which are lunate (*theta*), square (*epsilon*), and angular (*omicron*), have large serifs. This monogram, considered by Dodd to be indecipherable (also Ross, 1962, no. 17), contains the letters of *Theodorou,* and an *alpha* (Dalton, 1906[II], 617). It may be of some relevance that the first Cyprus treasure contains a spoon which is engraved with the name Theodore and a set of spoons bearing the mysterious legend *AUAL* (Dalton, 1901, no. 400), the two elements perhaps combined in this plate's monogram.

Fig. 103.1

COMMENTARY

See Entry no. 105.

BIBLIOGRAPHY

Early Christian, 1947, no. 378; Dodd, 1961, no. 38; Ross, 1962, 23.

104. PLATE

New York, The Metropolitan Museum of Art, no. 52.25.2 (Fletcher Fund, 1952)

Cyprus Treasure(?), 610–613

D 13.4 cm

This plate may be described in the same terms as no. 103, except that its ivy wreath has a slightly different arrangement of leaves, due to its smaller size. It is an exact match to no. 105.

STAMPS

These stamps are virtually identical to those on plate no. 103, except for their condition.

INSCRIPTION

See Entry no. 103.

COMMENTARY

See Entry no. 105.

BIBLIOGRAPHY

Dodd, 1961, no. 37; Ross, 1962, 22.

Fig. 104.1

105. Plate

Washington, D.C., Dumbarton Oaks Collection, no. 60.60 (Gift of Mrs. Paul I. Fagan, San Francisco, 1960)

Cyprus Treasure(?), 610–613

D 13.5 cm

The form and decoration of this plate, which has corrosion marks on the back and on the upper part of the front, may be described in the same terms as nos. 103 and 104, with which it forms a set.

Stamps

These stamps are apparently identical to those on plate no. 104, (Dodd, 1961, no. 39).

Inscription

See Entry no. 103.

Commentary

The diameters of plates nos. 103–105 (*ca.* 13 and 26 cm) correspond to two of the three basic sizes in which plain, flat silver plates with a small central medallion were made between the fifth and seventh centuries (Mundell-Mango, 1984, 219). Examples have been found singly, and in sets in the Esquiline, Carthage, Canoscio, Mytilene, Smyrna, and Cyprus treasures. The medallions are decorated with a monogram, cross, or other symbol, often with niello inlay. Although often described as patens (e.g., by Dalton, 1901, no. 397; Giovagnoli, 1935, 314; Dodd, 1973, 27 f.; Kent and Painter, 1977, no. 174; *Age,* 1979, no. 548), these plates are clearly domestic (e.g., Ross, 1962, no. 17; Engemann, 1972, 157 ff.), and continue a type of Roman *missorium* having a swastika, rosette, or other emblem at the center (Strong, 1966, 174). Flatter than the explicitly dedicated church patens with large cross (nos. 4–6, 34–36, 39, *etc.*), none of these plates can be directly associated with a church, either by inscription or by provenance (Mundell-Mango, 1984, 219).

These three plates, which have, apparently, identical stamps and cross monogram, obviously formed part of a set containing, perhaps, at least five other plates—that is, four of each size. According to their weight inscription, one set of Esquiline *scutellae* (D 16 cm) numbered four (Shelton, 1981, no. 5). In publishing this Dumbarton Oaks plate, Dalton (1906[II]) was "practically certain" that its provenance was the vicinity of Kerynia, where the first and second Cyprus treasures were also found in the same period. Although not published with either of these finds (on which, see Stylianou, 1969), it may still have come from the same site, as other pieces from these treasures have "gone astray" since first reported (e.g., twelve spoons; Dalton, 1900, 159; *idem,* 1901, nos. 400–424). The first Cyprus treasure contains a plate with a cross in the center (Dodd, 1961, no. 28), while the second Cyprus treasure has, in addition to the set of nine David plates (*ibid.,* 178 ff.), a similar plate with a cross in the center (*ibid.,* no. 54), and a plate which resembles these present three, but which is larger (D 44 cm), has an acanthus rather than ivy scroll, and the monogram "of John" (*ibid.,* no. 33; AD 605). It is possible, then, that the latter person was a relative of "Theodore A(ual)(?)" who bought this set of plates around 610–613.

Fig. 105.1

Bibliography

Dalton, 1906[II]; Rosenberg, 1928, vol. 4, 678 f.; Dodd, 1961, no. 39; Ross, 1962, no. 17; *DO Handbook,* 1967, no. 76.

106. Plate

Washington, D.C., Dumbarton Oaks Collection, no. 51.24 (Gift of Mrs. Gilbert L. Steward, 1951)

Smyrna Treasure, 613–629/30

D 13.3 cm

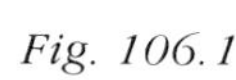

This plate has a raised rim ornamented by a concave moulding alternating with engraved lines, and a separate soldered footring. The plate was shaped by hammering, marks of which are visible on the reverse. To finish the surface and decorate it, the plate was turned on the lathe; a turning hole is in the center of the reverse and concentric burnishing lines are clearly visible on the obverse, in the middle of which is a circular area. There is a tiny hole in the rim and five stamps inside the footring.

Stamps

These stamps were dated by Dodd (1961, no. 44) to the years 613–629/30, because of the presence of the monogram and bust portrait of Heraclius (610–641), and the relation of the secondary monogram and names to those in other stamps of this period.

Commentary

This plate belongs to a set of four *pinakia* or *scutellae,* which have related stamps (Ross, 1962, no. 16.1, 2). Two of the other three are in the same collection. They have slightly different rims and a central medallion with niello-inlaid decoration consisting of a wreath encircling a cross, between whose flaring arms is inscribed a motto: "Honor of God" and "Hope of God," respectively. The third plate, which is now in Switzerland and as yet unpublished, bears a similar legend. These inscriptions differ from the dedications engraved on objects in the first part of the catalogue, which mention "vows," the names of donors or saints, and other phrases which indicate they were presented to a church. As Ross recognized (*ibid.*), these small plates were for domestic use, and their inscribed formulae correspond to those Christian "household wishes" discussed for an earlier period by Engemann (1972).

Said to have been found in or near Izmir (Smyrna).

Bibliography

DO Handbook, 1955, no. 133; Gettens and Waring, 1957, 89, no. 22; Dodd, 1961, no. 44; Ross, 1962, no. 16.3; Bruce-Mitford, 1983, vol. 3, no. 1.

Fig. 106.1

Bibliography, Index, and Concordances

BIBLIOGRAPHY

AAES	*Publications of an American Archaeological Expedition to Syria, 1899–1900,* 4 vols. (New York, 1903–1914).
Adhémar, 1934	J. Adhémar, "Le trésor d'argenterie donné par Saint Didier aux églises d'Auxerre (VIIe siècle)," *Revue archéologique,* ser. 6, no. 4, (1934), 44–54.
Age, 1979	*Age of Spirituality: Late Antique and Early Christian Art, Third to Seventh Century,* K. Weitzmann, ed., The Metropolitan Museum of Art, New York, 1977–1978 (New York, 1979) (exhibition catalogue).
Agnellus, *Liber*	*Agnellus, Liber pontificalis ecclesiae Ravennatis,* A. Testi Rasponi, ed., Rerum ital. scriptores, fasc. 196, 197, 200 (Bologna, 1924).
Ainalov, 1900	D. V. Ainalov, *The Hellenistic Origins of Byzantine Art,* E. and S. Sobolevitch, trans.; C. Mango, ed. (New Brunswick, N. J., 1961).
Alföldi and Cruikshank, 1957	A. Alföldi, "A Sassanian Silver Phalera at Dumbarton Oaks" with "A Contribution on the Stamps" by E. Cruikshank, *Dumbarton Oaks Papers,* 11 (1957), 237–245.
Alt, 1921	A. Alt, *Die griechischen Inschriften der Palaestina Tertia westlich der 'Araba* (Berlin/Leipzig, 1921).
Alt, 1923	A. Alt, "Die neuen Inschriften der *Palaestina Tertia," Zeitschrift des deutschen Palästina-Vereins,* 46 (1923), 51–64.
Anatolian, 1983	*The Anatolian Civilisations,* Istanbul, 1983, 2 vols. (Istanbul, 1983) (exhibition catalogue).
Anguili, 1977	*Puglia ex voto,* E. Anguili, Biblioteca provinciale de Gemmis, Bari, 1977 (Bari, 1977) (exhibition catalogue).
Antioch, I	*Antioch-on-the-Orontes, I. The Excavations 1932:* Publications of the Committee for the Excavation of Antioch and its Vicinity, G. W. Elderkin, ed. (Princeton/London/The Hague, 1934).
Antioch, II	*Antioch-on-the-Orontes, II. The Excavations 1933–1936:* Publications of the Committee for the Excavation of Antioch and its Vicinity, R. Stillwell, ed. (Princeton/London/The Hague, 1938).
Antioch, III	*Antioch-on-the-Orontes, III. The Excavations 1937–1939:* Publications of the Committee for the Excavation of Antioch and its Vicinity, R. Stillwell, ed. (Princeton/London/The Hague, 1941).
Apostolic Constitutions	*Didascalia et constitutiones apostolorum,* F.-X. Funk, ed., I (Paderborn, 1905).
Arnason, 1941	H. H. Arnason, "The History of the Chalice of Antioch," part 1, *The Biblical Archaeologist,* 4 (1941).
Arnason, 1942	H. H. Arnason, "The History of the Chalice of Antioch," part 2, *The Biblical Archaeologist,* 5 (1942).
Art Treasures, 1952	Metropolitan Museum of Art, *Art Treasures of the Metropolitan Museum of Art* (New York, 1952).
Avi-Yonah, 1948	M. Avi-Yonah, "Greek Christian Inscriptions from Rihab," *Quarterly of the Department of Antiquities of Palestine,* 13 (1948), 68–72.
Baccache and Tchalenko, 1979–1980	E. Baccache and G. Tchalenko, *Églises de village de la Syrie du Nord.* Documents d'archéologie: la Syrie à l'époque de l'empire romain d'Orient, I, 2 vols. (Paris, 1979–1980).
Balty, 1969	J. Balty, *La grande mosaïque de chasse du triclinos* (Brussels, 1969).
Balty, 1972	J. Balty, "Archéologie et témoinages littéraires," *Apamée de Syrie. Bilan des recherches archéologiques 1969–1971* (Brussels, 1972), 209–214.
Balty, 1977	J. Balty, *Mosaiques antiques de Syrie* (Brussels, 1977).
Balty, 1980	J. Balty, "Sur la date de création de la *Syria Secunda," Syria,* 57 (1980) 465–481.
Balty, 1984	J. C. Balty, "Monnaies Byzantines des maisons d'Apamée: Étude comparative," *Apamée de Syrie. Bilan des recherches archéologiques 1973–1979. Aspects de l'architecture domestique d'Apamée* (Brussels, 1984), 239–240.
Baratte, 1975 [I]	F. B. Baratte, "Les ateliers d'argenterie au bas-empire," *Journal des Savants,* (1975), 193–212.
Baratte, 1975 [II]	F. B. Baratte, "Apropos de l'argenterie romaine des provinces danubiennes," *Starinar,* 26 (1975), 33–41.
Baratte, 1977	F. B. Baratte, "Le plat d'argent du Château d'Albâtre à Soissons," *Revue du Louvre,* 27 (1977), 125–130.
Baratte, 1981	F. B. Baratte, *Le trésor d'argenterie gallo-romaine de Notre-Dame d'Alençon (Maine-et-Loire)* (Paris, 1981).
Barbarians, 1976	*Romans and Barbarians,* Museum of Fine Arts, Boston, 1976–1977 (Boston, 1976) (exhibition catalogue).
Bellinger, 1966	A. R. Bellinger, *Catalogue of the Byzantine Coins in the Dumbarton Oaks Collection, and in the Whittemore Collection, I: Anastasius I to Maurice (491–602)* (Washington, D.C., 1966).
Belting-Ihm, 1965	C. Belting-Ihm, "Das Justinuskreuz in der Schatzkammer der Peterskirche zu Rome," *Jahrbuch des Römisch-Germanischen Zentralmuseums, Mainz,* 12 (1965), 142–166.
Bendinelli, 1937	G. B. Bendinelli, *Il tesoro di argentaria di Marengo* (Turin, 1937).
Beyer, 1925	H. W. Beyer, *Der syrische Kirchenbau, Studien sur spätantiken Kunstgeschichte,* Auftrage des deutschen Archäologisches Instituts, 1 (Berlin, 1925).
BMFA, 1970	"Centennial Acquisitions," *Boston, Museum of Fine Arts Bulletin,* 68 (1970), 1–170.
Bonner, 1950	C. Bonner, *Studies in Magical Amulets, Chiefly Graeco-Egyptian* (Ann Arbor, 1950).
Book of Ceremonies	*Constantine Porphyrogenitus, De Cerimoniis,* J. J. Reiske, ed., 2 vols., Corpus scriptorum historiae byzantinae (Bonn, 1830).
Bookbinding, 1957/1958	*The History of Bookbinding,* The Walters Art Gallery, Baltimore, 1957–1958 (Baltimore, 1957) (exhibition catalogue).
Boreux, 1932	C. C. Boreux, *Musée national du Louvre. Département des antiquités egyptiennes. Guide-catalogue sommarie* (Paris, 1932).
Boston, 1976	see *Barbarians,* 1976.
Boucher, 1980	S. Boucher, G. Perdu, and M. Feugere, *Bronzes antiques du Musée de la Civilisation Gallo-romaine à Lyon, II: Instrumenta aegyptiaca* (Paris, 1980).
Boyd, 1979	S. Boyd, "The Sion Treasure: Status Report," *Fifth Annual Byzantine Studies Conference: Abstracts of Papers* (Washington, D.C., 1979), 6–8.
Boyd, 1983	S. Boyd, "A Sixth-Century Silver Plate in the British Museum," *Okeanos: A Tribute to I. Ševčenko, Harvard University Ukrainian Studies,* 7 (1983), 66–79.

Boyd, 1986 — S. Boyd, "A Bishop's Gift: Openwork Lamps from the Sion Treasure," *L'argenterie romaine et paléobyzantine.* Centre National de Recherche Scientifique. (Paris, in press).

Braun, 1932 — J. Braun, *Das christliche Altargerät in seinem Sein und in seiner Entwicklung* (Munich, 1932).

Breckenridge, 1959 — J. D. Breckenridge, *The Numismatic Iconography of Justinian II (685–695, 705–711 AD)* (New York, 1959).

Bréhier, 1919[I] — L. Bréhier, 20 juin 1919, *Académie des inscriptions et belles lettres. Comptes rendus* (1919), 256.

Bréhier, 1919[II] — L. Bréhier, 24 octobre 1919, *Académie des inscriptions et belles lettres. Comptes rendus* (1919), 420.

Bréhier, 1920 — L. Bréhier, "Les trésors d'argenterie syrienne et l'école artistique d'Antioche," *Gazette des beaux-arts,* 62 (1920), 173–196.

Bréhier, 1951 — L. Bréhier, "Un trésor d'argenterie ancienne au musée de Cleveland," *Syria,* 28 (1951), 256–264.

Brett, 1939 — G. L. Brett, "Formal Element on Late Roman and Early Byzantine Silver," *Papers of the British School at Rome,* 15 (1939), 33–41.

Brightman and Hammond, 1896 — F. E. Brightman and C. E. Hammond, *Liturgies, Eastern and Western, I: Eastern Liturgies* (Oxford, 1896).

Brinkerhoff, 1970 — D. M. Brinkerhoff, *A Collection of Sculpture in Classical and Early Christian Antioch* (New York, 1970).

Brock, 1977 — S. P. Brock, "Some Syriac Accounts of the Jewish Sects," *A Tribute to Arthur Vööbus: Studies in Early Christian Literature and Its Environment, Primarily in the Syrian East* (Chicago, 1977), 265–276.

Brock, 1983 — S. P. Brock, "A Syriac Collection of Prophecies of the Pagan Philosophers," *Orientalia lovaniensia perodica,* 14 (1983), 203–246.

Brock, 1984 — S. P. Brock, "Some Syriac Excerpts from Greek Collections of Pagan Prophesies," *Vigiliae christianae,* 38 (1984), 77–90.

Brock, 1985 — S. P. Brock, "The Thrice-holy Hymn in the Liturgy," *Sobornost/East Church Revue,* 7 (1985), 24–34.

Bruce-Mitford, 1983 — R. L. S. Bruce-Mitford, *The Sutton Hoo Ship-Burial,* vol. 3 (London, 1983).

Brünnow and Domaszewski, 1904–1909 — R. E. Brünnow and A. von Domaszewski, *Die Provincia Arabia,* 3 vols. (Strasbourg, 1904–1909).

Brummer, 1979 — *The Ernest Brummer Collection. Medieval, Renaissance and Baroque Art, I,* Galerie Koller, A. G., Zurich, October 16–19, 1979 (Zurich, 1979) (auction catalogue).

Buschhausen, 1967 — H. Buschhausen, "Ein byzantinisches Bronzekreuz in Kassandra," *Jahrbuch der österreichischen Byzantinischen Gesellschaft,* 16 (1967), 281–296.

Buschhausen, 1971 — H. Buschhausen, *Die spätrömischen Metallscrinia und früchristlichen Reliquiare, 1. Teil: Katalog,* Wiener Byzantinische Studien, 9 (Vienna, 1971).

Byzantine Art, 1964 — *Byzantine Art: An European Art,* Zappeion Exhibition Hall, Athens, 1964 (Athens, 1964) (exhibition catalogue).

Cahn *et al.,* 1984 — *Der spätrömische Silberschatz von Kaiseraugst,* H. A. Cahn and A. Kaufmann-Heinimann, eds. (Derendingen, 1984).

Caillet, 1985 — J.-P. Caillet, *L'antiquité classique, le haut moyen âge et Byzance au musée de Cluny* (Paris, 1985)

Candemir and Wagner, 1978 — H. Candemir and J. Wagner, "Christliche Mosaiken in der nördlichen *Euphratesia,*" *Studien zur Religion und Kultur Kleinasiens* (Leiden, 1978).

Canivet, 1973 — P. Canivet, "Un nouveau nom sur la liste épiscopale d'Apamée: l'archevêque Photius en 483," Centre de Recherches d'Histoire et Civilisation de Byzance, *Travaux et mémoires,* 5 (1973), 243–258.

Canivet, 1979 — P. Canivet, "Nouvelles inscriptions grecques chrétiennes à Huarte d'Apamène (Syrie)," Centre de Recherches d'Histoire et Civilisation de Byzance, *Travaux et mémoires,* 7 (1979), 349–362.

Carré, 1930 — L. Carré, *Guide de l'amateur d'orfévrerie française* (Paris, 1930).

Cavallo, 1967 — G. Cavallo, *Ricerche sulla maiuscola biblica* (Florence, 1967).

Cavallo *et al.,* 1982 — G. Cavallo, V. von Fralkenhausen, R. F. Campanati, M. Gigante, V. Pace, and F. P. Rosati, *I Bizantini in Italia* (Milan, 1982).

Cecchelli *et al.,* 1959 — C. Cecchelli, G. Furlani, and M. Salmi, *The Rabbula Gospels* (Olten/Lausanne, 1959).

Cedrenus — *Georgius Cedrenus,* I. Bekker, ed., Corpus scriptorum historiae byzantinae, 2 vols. (Bonn, 1838–1839).

Chéhab, 1957 — M. H. Chéhab, "Mosaïques du Liban," *Bulletin du Musée de Beyrouth,* 14–15 (1957–1959) 29–52.

Chronicle of Edessa — *Chronica minora,* I. Guidi, ed. and trans. Corpus scriptoum Christianorum orientalium, scr. syri 1 (1903).

Chron. Pasc. — *Chronicon Paschale,* L. Dindorf, ed., Corpus scriptorum historiae byzantinae, 2 vols., (Bonn, 1832).

Chron. 1234 — *Chronicon ad ann. Christi 1234 pertinenes,* J. B. Chabot and A. Abouna, eds. and trans., Corpus scriptorum christianorum orientalium, scr. syri 36, 56, 154 (1920, 1937, 1974).

Coche de la Ferté, 1956 — É. Coche de la Ferté, "Le verre de Lycurge," *Monuments et mémoires,* publiés par l'Académie des Inscriptions et Belles-Lettres, Fondation Eugène Piot 48/2 (1956), 131–162.

Coche de la Ferté, 1958 — É. Coche de la Ferté, *L'antiquité chrétienne au Musée du Louvre* (Paris, 1958).

Cohen, 1979 — R. Cohen, "A Byzantine Church and Mosaic Floor Near Kissufim," *Qadmoniot,* 12 (1979), 19–29.

Colin, 1947 — J. Colin, "La plastique 'gréco-romaine' dans l'empire carolingien," *Cahiers archéologiques,* 2 (1947), 87–114.

Colt, 1950–1962 — *Colt Archaeological Expedition 1936–1937. Excavations at Nessana,* 3 vols. (Princeton/London, 1950–1962).

Connolly and Codrington, 1913 — R. Connolly and H. Codrington, *Two Commentaries on the Jacobite Liturgy* (London, 1913).

Conway, 1924 — M. Conway, "The Antioch Chalice," *Burlington Magazine* 45 (1924), 106–110.

Cormack, 1985 — R. Cormack, *Writing in Gold* (London, 1985).

Creswell, 1958 — K. A. C. Creswell, *A Short Account of Early Muslim Architecture* (Harmondsworth, 1958).

Crum, 1909 — W. E. Crum, *Catalogue of the Coptic Manuscripts in the Collection of the John Rylands Library, Manchester* (Manchester, 1909).

CTh — *Codex Theodosianus,* T. Mommsen and P. M. Meyer, eds. (Berlin, 1905).

Curle, 1923 — A. O. Curle, *The Treasure of Traprain: A Scottish Hoard of Roman Silver Plate* (Glasgow, 1923).

Cyril of Skythopolis, *Life of Abraamios* — A.-J. Festugière, trans., *Les moines d'orient,* III (Paris, 1963), 69–79.

Cyril of Skythopolis, *Life of Kyriakos* — A.-J. Festugière, trans., *Les moines d'orient,* III (Paris, 1963), 35–52.

Cyril of Skythopolis, *Life of Theodore* — See Festugière, 1970.

DACL — F. Cabrol and H. Leclercq, *Dictionnaire d'archéologie chrétienne et de liturgie,* vols. 1–15 (Paris, 1924–1953).

Dagron, 1978 — G. Dagron, *Vie et miracles de Sainte Thècle,* Subsidia hagiographica, Société des Bollandistes, 62 (Brussels, 1978).

Dagron, 1985 — G. Dagron and D. Feissel, "Inscriptions inedits du Musée d'Antioche," Centre de Recherches d'Histoire et Civilisation de Byzance, *Travaux et mémoires,* 9 (1985), 421–461.

Dagron and Marcillet-Jaubert, 1978 — G. Dagron and J. Marcillet-Jaubert, "Inscriptions de Cilicie et d'Isaurie," *Belleten,* 42 (1978), 373–420.

Dalton, 1900 — O. M. Dalton, "A Byzantine Silver Treasure from the District of Kerynia, Cyprus, now Preserved in the British Museum," *Archaeologia,* 57 (1900), 1–16.

Dalton, 1901 — O. M. Dalton, *Catalogue of Early Christian Antiquities and Objects . . . in the British Museum* (London, 1901).

Dalton, 1906 — O. M. Dalton, "A Second Silver Treasure from Cyprus," *Archaeologia,* 60 (1906), 21–24.

Dalton, 1906[II] — O. M. Dalton, "Byzantine Silversmiths' Work from Cyprus," *Byzantinische Zeitschrift,* 15 (1906), 615–617.

Dalton, 1921 — *British Museum: A Guide to the Early Christian and Byzantine Antiquities in the Department of British and Mediaeval Antiquities,* 2nd ed. (London, 1921).

Daremberg and Saglio — C. Daremberg and E. Saglio, *Dictionnaire des antiquités grecques et romaines, d'après les textes et les monuments,* 5 vols. (Paris, 1877–1919).

Dark Ages, 1937 — *The Dark Ages,* Worcester Art Museum, Worcester, 1937 (Worcester, Mass., 1937) (exhibition catalogue).

Davidson, 1952 — G. R. Davidson, *Corinth: The Minor Objects,* American School of Classical Studies at Athens, 12 (Princeton, 1952).

de Francovich, 1951 — G. de Francovich, "L'arte siriaca e il suo influsso sulla pittura medievale nell'oriente e nell'occidente," *Commentari* (1951), 75–92.

de Ridder, 1905 — A. de Ridder, *Collection de Clercq Catalogue* (Paris, 1905).

de Ridder, 1924 — A. de Ridder, *Catalogue sommaire des bijoux antiques* (Paris, 1924).

Diehl, 1921 — C. Diehl, "L'école artistique d'Antioche et les trésors d'argenterie syrienne," *Syria,* 2 (1921), 81–95.

Diehl, 1926 — C. Diehl, "Un nouveau trésor d'argenterie syrienne," *Syria,* 7 (1926), 105–122.

Diehl, 1930 — C. Diehl, "Argenteries syriennes," *Syria,* 11 (1930), 209–215.

DO Handbook, 1955 — *The Dumbarton Oaks Collection . . . Handbook* (Washington, D.C., 1955).

DO Handbook, 1967 — *Handbook of the Byzantine Collection,* Dumbarton Oaks (Washington, D.C., 1967).

Dodd, 1961 — E. C. Dodd, *Byzantine Silver Stamps,* Dumbarton Oaks Studies, 7 (Washington, D.C., 1961).

Dodd, 1968 — E. C. Dodd, "Byzantine Silver Stamps, Supplement II: More Treasure from Syria," *Dumbarton Oaks Papers,* 22 (1968), 141–149.

Dodd, 1973 — E. C. Dodd, *Byzantine Silver Treasures,* Monographien der Abegg-Stiftung, Bern, 9 (Bern, 1973).

Dodd, 1980 — E. C. Dodd, "The Sion Treasure: Problems of Dating and Provenance," *Sixth Annual Byzantine Studies Conference: Abstracts of Papers* (Oberlin, Ohio, 1980), 3, 4.

Dodge, 1927 — B. Dodge, "A New Explanation for Ancient Treasures," *Al-Kulliya* (Journal of the American University of Beirut Alumnae Association) (November 1927), 34–44.

Dodge, 1950 — B. Dodge, "The Chalice of Antioch," *Bulletin of the Near East Society,* 3 (1950), no. 5, 3 f.; no. 6, 10.

Dothan, 1955 — M. F. Dothan, "Excavation of a Monastery near Sha'ar Ha-'Aliyah," *Israel Exploration Journal,* 5 (1955), 96–102.

Downey, 1948 — G. Downey, "The Art of New Rome at Baltimore," *Archaeology,* 1 (1948), 21–29.

Downey, 1951 — G. Downey, "The Inscription on the Silver Chalice from Syria in The Metropolitan Museum of Art," *American Journal of Archaeology,* 55 (1951), 349–353.

Downey, 1953 — G. Downey, "The Dating of the Syrian Liturgical Silver Treasure in the Cleveland Museum," *Art Bulletin,* 35 (1953), 143–145.

Downey, 1954 — G. Downey, "A Processional Cross," *Bulletin of The Metropolitan Museum of Art,* 12 (1954), 276–280.

Downey, 1961 — G. Downey, *A History of Antioch in Syria from Seleucus to the Arab Conquest* (Princeton, 1961).

Drew-Bear, 1979 — M. Drew-Bear, *Le nome Hermopolite: toponymes et sites* (Missoula, Montana, 1979).

Drexler, 1899 — W. Drexler, "Alte Beschwörungsformeln," *Philologus,* 58 (1899), 594 ff.

Duffy and Vikan, 1983 — J. Duffy and G. Vikan, "A Small Box in John Mochus," *Greek, Roman, and Byzantine Studies,* 24/1 (1983), 93–99.

Ebersolt, 1911 — J. Ebersolt, "Le trésor de Stûmâ au musée de Constantinople," *Revue archéologique,* ser. 4, 17 (1911), 407–419.

Ebla, 1985 — *Ebla to Damascus: Art and Archaeology of Ancient Syria.* H. Weiss, ed., The Walters Art Gallery, Baltimore, *etc.,* 1985 (Washington, D.C., 1985) (exhibition catalogue).

Early Christian, 1947 — *Early Christian and Byzantine Art,* The Baltimore Museum of Art, Baltimore, 1947 (Baltimore, 1947) (exhibition catalogue).

Eisen, 1916 — G. A. Eisen, "Preliminary Report on the Great Chalice of Antioch, Containing the Earliest Portraits of Christ and the Apostles," *American Journal of Archaeology,* ser. 2, 20 (1916), 426–437.

Eisen, 1923 — G. A. Eisen, *The Great Chalice of Antioch: Portraits of Christ, Apostles and Evangelists,* 2 vols. (New York, 1923).

Eisen, 1933 — G. A. Eisen, *The Great Chalice of Antioch* (New York, 1933).

Elbern, 1963 — V. H. Elbern, "Der eucharistische Kelch im frühen Mittelalter," *Zeitschrift des deutscher Verein für Kunstwissenschaft,* 17 (1963), 1–76, 117–188.

Elbern, 1965 — V. H. Elbern, "Eine frühbyzantinische Reliefdarstellung des älteren Symeon Stylites," *Jahrbuch des deutschen Archäologischen Instituts,* 80 (1965), 280–304.

Elbern, 1966 — V. H. Elbern, "Le pied de verre d'un vase liturgique (?) trouvé à Qâlât Semân," *Annales des journées internationales du verre. Congrès de Damas (1964)* (Liège, 1966), 99–103.

Emery, 1948 — W. B. Emery, *Nubian Treasure: An Account of the Discoveries of Ballana and Qustul,* (London, 1948).

Emery and Kirwan, 1938 — W. B. Emery and L. P. Kirwan, *The Royal Tombs at Ballana and Qustul* (London, 1938).

Engemann, 1972 — J. Engemann, "Anmerkungen zu spätantiken Geräten des Alltagslebens mit christlichen Bildern, Symbolen und Inschriften," *Jahrbuch für Antike und Christentum,* 15 (1972), 154–173.

Engemann, 1984 — J. Engemann, "Eine Spätantike Messingkanne mit zwei Darstellungen aus der Magiererzählung im F. J. Dölger-Institut in Bonn," *Jahrbuch für Antike und Christentum,* 27 (1984), 115–136.

Ettinghausen, 1977 — R. Ettinghausen, *Arab Painting,* 2nd. ed. (Geneva, 1977).

Euchologion — *Euchologion, sive rituale graecorum,* J. Goar, ed. (Paris, 1647).

Eusebius, *VC* — Eusebius, *De vita Constantini,* F. Winkelmann, ed. (Berlin, 1975).

Evagrius, *HE* — *Evagrius, Ecclesiastical History,* J. Bidez and L. Parmentier, eds. (London, 1898).

Exposition, 1931 — *Exposition internationale d'art byzantin,* Musée des Arts Décoratifs, Paris, 1931 (Paris, 1931) (exhibition catalogue).

Feissel, 1982 — D. Feissel, "Remarques de toponymie syrienne d'après des inscriptions grecques chrétiennes trouvées hors de Syrie," *Syria,* 59 (1982), 319–343.

Feissel, 1985 — D. Feissel, "Magnus, Mégas et les curateurs des 'Maisons divines' de Justin II à Maurice," Centre de Recherches d'Histoire et Civilisation de Byzance, *Travaux et Mémoires,* 9 (1985), 465–476.

Festugière, 1970 — *Vie de Théodore de Sykéôn,* A.-J. Festugière, ed. and trans. (Brussels, 1970).

Festugière and Rydén, 1974 — *Léontios de Néapolis: Vie de Syméon le Fou et Vie de Jean de Chyrpe,* A.-J. Festugière and L. Rydén, eds. and trans. (Paris, 1974).

Fiey, 1961 — J.-M. Fiey, "Les saints Serge de l'Iraq," *Analecta bollandiana,* 79 (1961), 102–114.

Firatlı, 1965 — N. Firatlı, "Un trésor du VIe siècle à Kumluça en Lycie," *Akten des VII. Internationalen Kongresses für Christliche Archäologie, Trier, 5–11 September 1965* (Vatican City, 1969) 524, 525.

Firatlı, 1969 — N. Firatlı, "Some Recent Acquisitions," *Istanbul Arkeoloji Müzeleri Yilliği,* 15/16 (1969), 180, ff.

Fitzgerald, 1939 — G. M. Fitzgerald, *A Sixth Century Monastery at Beth-Shan (Scythopolis),* Publications of the Palestine Section of the University Museum, University of Pennsylvania, 4 (Philadelphia, 1939).

Foltz, 1975 — E. Foltz, "Zur Herstellungstechnik der byzantinische Silberschalen aus dem Schatzfund von Lambousa," *Festschrift Hans-Jürgen Hundt zum 65. Geburtstag, Jahrbuch des Römisch-Germanischen Zentralmuseums, Mainz,* 22 (1975), 221–245.

Forsyth and Weitzmann, n.d. — G. H. Forsyth and K. Weitzmann, *The Monastery of Saint Catherine at Mount Sinai: The Church and Fortress of Justinian* (Ann Arbor [1973]).

Frey, 1936–1952 — J.-B. Frey, *Corpus inscriptionum Iudaicarum,* 2 vols. (Vatican City, 1936–1952).

Garsoïan, 1982 — N. G. Garsoïan, "The Iranian Substratum of the 'Agat'angelos' Cycle," *East of Byzantium: Syria and Armenia in the Formative Period,* N. G. Garsoaïn, T. F. Mathews and R. W. Thomson, eds. (Washington, D.C., 1982), 151–174.

Gerasimov, 1967 — T. Gerasimov, "Rannobizantijski srebürni sveshchnici ot Sudovec," *Izvestija na Arheologičeskija Institut,* 30 (1967), 200–205.

Gesta — *Gesta apud Zenophilum, S. Optati Milevitani libri VII,* C. Ziswa, ed., *Corpus scriptorum ecclesiasticorum latinorum,* 26 (1893), 185–197.

Gettens and Waring, 1957 — R. J. Gettens and C. L. Waring, "The Composition of Some Ancient Persian and other Near Eastern Silver Objects," *Ars Orientalis,* 2 (1957), 83–90.

Giovagnoli, 1935 — E. Giovagnoli, "Una collezione di vasi eucaristici scoperti a Conoscio," *Rivista di archeologia cristiana,* 12 (1935), 211 ff.

Giron, 1922 — N. Giron, "Notes épigraphiques," *Journal asiatique* (1922), 69.

Glenny *et al.,* 1985 — M. Glenny, C. Simpson, and J. Schaire, "The Holy Grail," *Arts and Antiques* (May 1985), 41–48.

Gough, 1965 — M. Gough, "A Thurible from Ďag Pazari," *Anadolu Arastirmalari, Jahrbuch für kleinasiatische Forschung,* 2 (1965), 231–235.

Grabar, 1954 — A. Grabar, "La 'Sedia di San Marco' à Venise," *Cahiers archéologiques,* 7 (1954), 19–34.

Grabar, 1958 — A. Grabar, *Ampoules de Terre Sainte (Monza, Bobbia)* (Paris, 1958).

Grabar, 1960 — A. Grabar, "Quel est le sens de l'offrande de Justinien et de Théodora sur les mosaïques de Saint-Vital?" *Felix Ravenna,* 30 (1960), 63–77.

Grabar, 1962 — A. Grabar, "Un reliquaire provenant d'Isaurie," *Cahiers archéologiques,* 13 (1962), 49–59.

Grenfell and Hunt, 1897 — B. P. Grenfell and A. S. Hunt, *New Classical Fragments and Other Greek and Latin Papyri* (Oxford, 1897).

Grierson, 1964 — P. Grierson, "Weight and Coinage," *The Numismatic Chronicle,* ser. 7, 4 (1964), iii–xvii.

Grierson, 1968 — P. Grierson, *Catalogue of the Byzantine Coins in the Dumbarton Oaks Collection, and in the Whittemore Collection, II: Phocas to Theodosius III (602–717)* (Washington, D.C., 1968).

Grumel, 1958 — V. Grumel, *La chronologie,* Traité d'études byzantines, 1 (Bibliothèque byzantine) (Paris, 1958).

Guillou, 1979 — A. Guillou, "Rome, centre transit des produits du luxe d'Orient au Haute Moyen Age," *Zograf,* 10 (1979), 17-21. *Quaderni medievali,* 8 (1979), 106–115.

Hanfmann, 1951 — G. M. A. Hanfmann, "Socrates and Christ," *Harvard Studies in Classical Philology,* 60 (1951), 205–233.

Hawkins and Mundell, 1973 — E. J. W. Hawkins and M. C. Mundell, "The Mosaics of the Monastery of Mâr Samuel, Mâr Simeon, and Mâr Gabriel near Kartmin," with "A Note on the Greek Inscription," by C. Mango, *Dumbarton Oaks Papers,* 27 (1973), 279–296.

Hayes, 1984 — J. W. Hayes, *Greek, Roman, and Related Metalware in the Royal Ontario Museum. A Catalogue* (Toronto, 1984).

Héron de Villefosse, 1892 — A. Héron de Villefosse, *Bulletin de la société nationale des antiquaires de France* (1892), 239–246.

Héron de Villefosse, 1899 — A. Héron de Villefosse, "La trésor de Boscoreale," *Monuments et mémoires,* publiés par l'Académie des Inscriptions et Belles-Lettres, Fondation Eugène Piot, 5 (1899).

Hitti, 1951 — P. K. Hitti, *History of Syria, Including Lebanon and Palestine* (London, 1951).

Holum, 1982 — K. G. Holum, *Theodosian Empresses: Women and Imperial Dominion in Late Antiquity,* The Transformation of the Classical Heritage, 3 (Berkeley/Los Angeles/London, 1982).

Hunt and Edgar, 1932–1934 — A. S. Hunt and C. C. Edgar, *Select Papyri* (London, 1932–1934).

IGLS — L. Jalabert, R. Mouterde *et al., Inscriptions grecques et latines de la Syrie,* Bibliothèque archéologique et historique, vols. 1–7, 13 (Paris, 1929–1982).

Ikusstvo, 1977 — *Iskusstvo Vizantii v Sobraniyax SSSR,* The Hermitage, Leningrad, 1976, Moscow, 1977 (Moscow, 1977) (exhibition catalogue).

Iliffe, 1934 — J. H. Iliffe, "A Tomb at El Bassa of c. A.D. 396," *Quarterly of the Department of Antiquities in Palestine,* 3 (1934), 81–91.

Islamic State — Al-Baladhuri, *The Origins of the Islamic State,* P. K. Hitti, trans. (New York, 1916).

Jerphanion, 1926 — G. de Jerphanion, "Le Calice d'Antioche. Les théories du Dr. Eisen et la date probable du calice," *Orientalia christiana,* 7/27 (Rome, 1926).

Jerphanion, 1930 — G. de Jerphanion, *La voix des monuments: notes et études d'archéologie chrétienne* (Paris/Brussels, 1930).

John Moschos, *PS* — Joannes Moschus, *Pratum spirituale,* J.-P. Migne, ed., *PG,* vol. 87/3, cols. 2851–3112.

John of Ephesos, *HE* — *Iohannis Ephesini Historiae ecclesiasticae par tertia,* E. W. Brooks, ed. and trans., *Corpus scriptorum christianorum orientalium,* scr. syri 55 (1936).

John of Ephesos, *Lives* — *John of Ephesus, Lives of the Eastern Saints,* E. W. Brooks, ed. and trans., *Patrologia orientalis,* 17–19 (1923–1925).

Johns and Potter, 1983 — C. Johns and T. Potter, *The Thetford Treasure: Roman Jewellry and Silver* (London, 1983).

Jones, 1960 — A. H. M. Jones, "Church Finance in the Fifth and Sixth Centuries," *Journal of Theological Studies,* 11 (1960), 84–94.

Jones, 1971 — A. H. M. Jones, *Cities of the Eastern Roman Provinces,* 2nd. ed. (Oxford, 1971).

Jones, 1973 — A. H. M. Jones, *The Later Roman Empire, 284–602: A Social, Economic, and Administrative Survey,* 2 vols. (Oxford, 1973).

Justinian, *Novels* — Justinian, *Novellae,* S. P. Scott, trans., *Justinian, The Civil Law* (Cincinnati, 1932).

Kellner and Zahlhaas, 1984 — H.-J. Kellner and G. Zahlhaas, *Der römische Schatzfund von Weissenburg* (Munich/Zurich, 1984).

Kent and Painter, 1977 — *Wealth of the Roman World, AD 300–700,* British Museum, London, 1977, J. P. C. Kent and K. S. Painter, eds. (London, 1977) (exhibition catalogue).

Kisa, 1908 — A. Kisa, *Das Glas im Altertum,* vol. 3 (Leipzig, 1908).

Kitzinger, 1958 — E. Kitzinger, "Byzantine Art in the Period between Justinian and Iconoclasm," *Berichte zum XI. Internationalen Byzantinisten-Kongress, München, 1958* (Munich, 1958), IV, 1–50.

Kitzinger, 1974 — E. Kitzinger, "A Pair of Silver Book Covers in the Sion Treasure," *Gatherings in Honor of Dorothy E. Miner* (Baltimore, 1974), 3–17.

Knögel, 1936 — E. Knögel, "Schriftquellen zur Kunstgeschichte der Merowingerzeit," *Bonner Jahrbücher,* 140/141 (1936), 1–258.

Kondoleon, 1979 — C. Kondoleon, "An Openwork Gold Cup," *Journal of Glass Studies,* 21 (1979), 39 ff.

Lafaye, 1884 — G. L. Lafaye, *Histoire du culte des divinités d'Alexandrie. Serapis, Isis, Harpocrate et Anubis, hors de l'Égypte depuis les origines jusqu'à la naissance de l'école neo-platonicienne* (Paris, 1884).

Lassus, 1935 — J. Lassus, *Inventaire archéologique de la région au nord-est de Hama,* Documents d'études orientales, Institut Français de Damas, 4 (Paris, 1935).

Lassus, 1947 — J. Lassus, *Sanctuaires chrétiens de Syrie: Essai sur la genèse, la forme, et l'usage liturgique des édifices du culte chrétien, en Syrie, du IIIe siècle à la conquète musulmane,* Institut Français d'Archéologie de Beyrouth. Bibliothèque archéologique et historique, 42 (Paris, 1947).

Lassus, 1960 — J. Lassus, "Une image de Saint Syméon le Jeune sur un fragment de reliquaire syrien du Musée du Louvre," *Monuments et mémoires,* publié par l'Académie des Inscriptions et Belles-Lettres, Fondation Eugène Piot, 51 (1960), 129–148.

Laurent, 1936 — V. Laurent, "Amulettes byzantines et formulaires magiques," *Byzantinische Zeitschrift,* 36 (1936), 303 ff.

Lawrence, 1954 — *The Home Letters of T. E. Lawrence and His Brothers,* M. R. Lawrence, ed. (Oxford, 1954).

Lawrence, 1964 — *The Letters of T. E. Lawrence,* D. Garnett, ed. (London, 1964).

Lazovic *et al.,* 1977 — M. Lazovic, N. Dürr, H. Durand, C. Houriet, and F. Schweizer, "Objets byzantins de la collection du Musée d'Art et d'Histoire," *Genava,* 25 (1977), 5–62.

Lechtman, 1971 — H. N. Lechtman, "Ancient Methods of Gilding Silver: Examples from the Old and the New Worlds," *Science and Archaeology,* R. H. Brill, ed. (Cambridge, Mass./London, 1971), 2–29.

Leroy, 1964 — J. Leroy, *Les manuscrits syriaques à peinture* (Paris, 1964).

LeStrange, 1965 — G. LeStrange, *Palestine under the Moslems: A Description of Syria and the Holy Land from AD 650–1500* (reprint of 1890 ed.) (Beirut, 1965).

Levi, 1947 — D. Levi, *Antioch Mosaic Pavements, I* (Princeton/London/The Hague, 1947).

Liber Pontificalis — *Liber Pontificalis.* L. Duchesne (Paris, 1886).

Life and Miracles of St. Thekla — see Dagron, 1978.

Lloyd-Morgan, 1981 — C. Lloyd-Morgan, *Description of the Collections in the Rijksmuseum G. M. Kam at Nijmegen, 9: The Mirrors* (Nijmegen, 1981).

Loerke, 1975 — W. Loerke, "The Monumental Minature," *The Place of Book Illumination in Byzantine Art* (Princeton, 1975), 61–97.

Malalas — *Ioannis Malalae Chronographia,* G. Dindorf, ed., Corpus scriptorum historiae byzantinae (Bonn, 1831).

MAMA — *Momumenta Asiae Minoris antiqua,* American Society for Archaeological Research, vols. 1–8 (London, 1928–1962).

Mango, 1950 — C. Mango, "Byzantine Brick Stamps," *American Journal of Archaeology,* 54/1 (1950), 19–27.

Mango, 1962 — C. Mango, *Materials for the Study of the Mosaics of St. Sophia at Istanbul,* Dumbarton Oaks Studies, 8 (Washington, D.C., 1962).

Mango, 1972 — C. Mango, *The Art of the Byzantine Empire: 312–1453,* Sources and Documents in the History of Art Series (Englewood Cliffs, N.J., 1972).

Maraval, 1985 — P. M. Maraval, *Lieux saints et pèlerinages d'Orient. Histoire et géographie. Des origines à la conquête arabe* (Paris, 1985).

Marrou, 1940 — H. I. Marrou, "L'origine orientale des diaconies romaines," *Mélanges d'archéologie et d'histoire,* 57 (1940), 95–141.

Martinelli, 1974 — P. A. Martinelli, "Le produzione argentea dei secoli IV–VII d. C. rinvenuta in Siria," *XXI Corso di cultura sull'arte ravennate e bizantina* (1974) 7–30.

Maryon, 1948 — H. Maryon, "The Mildenhall Treasure: Some Technical Problems," part 1, *Man* (March 1948), 25–27; part 2, *Man* (April 1948), 38–41.

Masterpieces, 1958 — *Masterpieces of Byzantine Art,* D. Talbot Rice, Royal Scottish Museum, Edinburgh; Victoria and Albert Museum, London, 1958 (Edinburgh, 1958) (exhibition catalogue).

Matheson, 1980 — S. B. Matheson, *Ancient Glass in the Yale University Art Gallery* (New Haven, 1980).

Mattingly *et al.*, 1937 — H. Mattingly, J. W. E. Pearce, and T. D. Kendrick, "The Coleraine Hoard," *Antiquity,* 9 (1937), 39–45.

Matzulevich, 1929 — L. Matzulewitsch, *Byzantinishe Antike,* Archäologishe Mitteilungen aus russischen Sammlungen, 2 (Belin/Leipzig, 1929).

McVey, 1983 — K. E. McVey, "The Domed Church as Microcosm: Literary Roots of an Archaeological Symbol," *Dumbarton Oaks Papers,* 37 (1983), 91–121.

Mécérian, 1964 — J. Mécérian, *Expédition archéologique dans l'Antiochène occidentale.* Recherches. L'institut de Lettres Orientales de Beyrouth, 27 (1964).

Mepisashvili and Tsintsadze, 1979 — R. Mepisashvili and V. Tsintsadze, *The Arts of Ancient Georgia* (London, 1979).

Metzger, 1972 — C. Metzger, "Croix à inscription votive," *Revue du Louvre,* 22 (1972), 32–34.

Michael the Syrian — *Chronique de Michel le Syrien,* J.-B. Chabot, ed. and trans., 3 vols. (Paris, 1899–1924).

Middle Ages, 1969 — *The Middle Ages: Treasures from The Cloisters and The Metropolitan Museum of Art,* V. K. Ostoia, The Los Angeles County Museum of Art, Los Angeles, 1969 (Los Angeles, 1969) (exhibition catalogue).

Milik, 1960 — J. T. Milik, "Notes d'épigraphie et de topographie palestiniennes," *Revue biblique,* 67 (1960), 354–367, 550–591.

Milliken, 1951 — W. M. Milliken, "The Cleveland Byzantine Silver Treasure," *Bulletin of The Cleveland Museum of Art,* 38 (1951), 142–145.

Milliken, 1958 — W. M. Milliken, "Early Byzantine Silver," *Bulletin of The Cleveland Museum of Art,* 45 (1958), 35–41.

Milojčić, 1970 — V. Milojčić, "Zu den spätkaiserzeitlichen und merowingischen Silberlöffeln," *Bericht der Römisch-Germanischen Kommission, 49, 1968* (Berlin, 1970) 111–147.

Miracles of St. Demetrios — *Les plus anciens recueils des Miracles de S. Démétrius,* P. Lemerle, ed. and trans., 2 vols. (Paris, 1979, 1981).

Mittmann, 1967 — S. Mittmann, "Die Mosaikinschrift der Menas-Kirche in Rihab," *Zeitschrift des deutschen Palästina-Vereins,* 83 (1967), 42–45.

Morrison, 1972 — C. Morrison, "Le trésor byzantin de Nikertai," *Revue belge de numismatique et de sigillographie,* 118 (1972), 29–91.

Mostra, 1981 — *Mostra di opere d'arte restaurate nelle province di Siena e Grosseto II* (Genoa, 1981) (exhibition catalogue).

Mouterde, 1922 — R. Mouterde, "Inscriptions grecques et latines de Syrie," *Mélange de l'Université Saint-Joseph, Beyrouth,* 8 (1922), 75–111.

Mouterde, 1926 — R. Mouterde, Review of G. de Jerphanion, "Le Calice d'Antioche. Les théories du Dr. Eisen et la date probable due calice" and C. Diehl, "Un nouveau trésor d'argenterie syrienne," in *Mélanges de l'Université Saint-Joseph, Beyrouth,* 11 (1926), 361–367.

Mouterde, 1932 — R. Mouterde, "Mission epigraphique et relevés archéologiques en Syrie (1931)," *Mélanges de l'Université Saint-Joseph, Beyrouth,* 16 (1932), 83–117.

Mouterde, 1934 — R. Mouterde, "Les découvertes intéressantes d'archéologie chrétienne, récemment effectuées en Syrie," *Atti del III congresso internazionale di archeologia cristiana, Ravenna, 25–30 settembre 1932* (Rome, 1934), 459–476.

Mundell, 1977 — M. Mundell (-Mango), "Monophysite Church Decoration," *Iconoclasm,* A. Bryer and J. Herrin, eds. (Birmingham, U.K., 1977), 59–74.

Mundell-Mango, 1981 — M. Mundell-Mango. "Patrons and Scribes Indicated in Syriac Manuscripts, 411–800 AD," *XVI. Internationaler Byzantinistenkongress, Akten, 2/4, Jahrbuch der österreichischen Byzantinistik,* 32/4 (1982), 3–12.

Mundell-Mango, 1983 — M. Mundell-Mango, "Where was Beth Zagba?," *Okeanos: A Tribute to I. Ševčenko, Harvard University Ukrainian Studies,* 7 (1983), 363–388.

Mundell-Mango, 1984 — M. Mundell-Mango, *Artistic Patronage in the Roman Diocese of Oriens, 313–641 AD,* unpub. diss. (Oxford, 1984).

Mundell-Mango, 1986 — M. Mundell-Mango, "The Origins of the Syrian Ecclesiastical Silver Treasures of the Sixth–Seventh Centuries," *L'argenterie romaine et paléobyzantine,* Centre National de Recherche Scientifique (Paris, in press).

Muñoz, 1907 — A. Muñoz, *Il codice purpureo di Rossano e il frammento Sinopense* (Rome, 1907).

Murray, 1898 — A. S. Murray, "The Mosaic with Armenian Inscription from near Damascus Gate, Jerusalem," *Palestine Exploration Fund Quarterly Statement,* (1898), 126, 127

Negev, 1981 — A. Negev, *The Greek Inscriptions from the Negev* (Jerusalem, 1981).

Oates, 1962 — D. Oates, "Qasr Serij—A Sixth-Century Basilica in Northern Iraq," *Iraq,* 24 (1962), 78–89.

Oliver, 1977 — A. Oliver, Jr., *Silver for the Gods: 800 Years of Greek and Roman Silver,* The Toledo Museum of Art, *etc.*, 1977 (Toledo, 1977) (exhibition catalogue).

Oliver, 1980 — A. Oliver, Jr., "A Set of Ancient Silverware in the Getty Museum," *The J. Paul Getty Museum Journal,* 8 (1980), 155–166.

Painter, 1977[I] — K. S. Painter, *The Water Newton Early Christian Silver* (London, 1977).

Painter, 1977[II] — K. S. Painter, *The Mildenhall Treasure: Roman Silver from East Anglia* (London, 1977).

Pal. Anth. — *The Greek Anthology,* W. R. Paton, ed. and trans., Loeb Classical Library, 5 vols. (Cambridge, 1968–1980).

Peirce and Tyler, 1934 — H. Peirce and R. Tyler, *L'art byzantin,* 2 vols. (Paris, 1932, 1934).

Perdrizet, 1922 — P. Perdrizet, *Negotium perambulans in tenebris,* Publication de la Faculté des Lettres de l'Université de Strasbourg, 6 (Strasbourg, 1922).

PG — *Patrologia cursus completus, series graeca,* vols. 1–161, J.-P. Migne, ed. (Paris, 1857–1866).

Photios, *Bibliotheca* — *Photios, Bibliotheca,* R. Henry, ed., 8 vols. (Paris, 1959–1977).

Piccirillo, 1982 — M. Piccirillo, "La chiesa della Virgine a Madaba," *Liber annuus,* 32 (1982), 373–403.

Platner and Ashby, 1929 — S. B. Platner and T. Ashby, *A Topographical Dictionary of Ancient Rome* (London, 1929).

PLRE — A. H. M. Jones, J. R. Martindale, and J. Morris, *The Prosopography of the Later Roman Empire, I, AD 260–395* (Cambridge, 1971). J. R. Martindale, *The Prosopography of the Later Roman Empire, II, AD 365–527* (Cambridge/London/New York, 1980).

Procopius, *Buildings* — Procopius, *Buildings,* H. B. Dewing, ed. and trans., Loeb Classical Library (Cambridge, Mass./London, 1940).

Procopius, *Wars* — Procopius, *Wars,* H. B. Dewing, ed. and trans., Loeb Classical Library, 5 vols. (London/New York/Cambridge, Mass., 1916–1954).

PUAES — *Princeton University Archaeological Expeditions to Syria in 1904–1905 and 1909.*

PW — A. Pauly and G. Wissowa, *Realencyclopädie der classischen Alterumswissenschaft,* (Stuttgart, 1893–).

Reinhold, 1970 — M. Reinhold, *History of Purple as a Status Symbol in Antiquity* (Brussels, 1970).

Rey-Coquais, 1977 — J.-P. Rey-Coquais, "Inscriptions grecques et latines découvertes dans les fouilles de Tyr (1963–1974)," *Bulletin du Musée de Beyrouth,* 29 (1977).

Rice, 1959 — D. Talbot Rice, *The Art of Byzantium* (London/New York, 1959).

Richter, 1959 — G. M. A. Richter, *A Handbook of Greek Art* (London/New York, 1959).

Richter, 1965 — G. M. A. Richter, *The Portraits of the Greeks* (London, 1965).

Robert, 1953 — L. Robert, "Bulletin épigraphique," *Revue des études grecques,* 66 (1953), 113–212.

Rorimer, 1951 — J. J. Rorimer, *The Cloisters,* 11th ed. New York, Metropolitan Museum of Art (New York, 1951).

Rorimer, 1954 — J. J. Rorimer, "The Authenticity of the Chalice of Antioch," *Studies in Art and Literature for Belle da Costa Greene* (Princeton, 1954), 161–168.

Rosenberg, 1928 — M. Rosenberg, *Der Goldschmiede Merkzeichen, vol. 4* (Berlin/Leipzig, 1928).

Ross, 1950 — M. C. Ross, "A Second Byzantine Treasure from Hamah," *Archaeology,* 3 (1950), 162, 163.

Ross, 1953 — M. C. Ross, "A Silver Treasure Found at Daphne-Harbié," *Archaeology,* 6 (1953), 39–41.

Ross, 1955 — M. C. Ross, "Notes on Byzantine Gold and Silversmiths' Work," *The Journal of The Walters Art Gallery,* 18 (1955), 59–67.

Ross, 1962 — M. C. Ross, *Catalogue of the Byzantine and Early Medieval Antiquities in the Dumbarton Oaks Collection, I: Metalwork, Ceramics, Glass, Glyptics, Painting* (Washington, D.C., 1962).

Ross, 1965 — M. C. Ross, *Catalogue of the Byzantine and Early Mediaeval Antiquities in the Dumbarton Oaks Collection, II: Jewelry, Enamels, and Art of the Migration Period* (Washington, D.C., 1965).

Ross, 1967/1968 — M. C. Ross, "Luxuries of the Eastern Empire," *Arts in Virginia,* 8 (1967/1968), 56–65.

Rouse, 1902 — W. H. D. Rouse, *Greek Votive Offerings: An Essay in the History of Greek Religion* (Cambridge, 1902).

Rufus — *Jean Rufus, Plérophories,* F. Nau, ed. and trans., *Patrologia orientalis,* 8 (1912), 1–20.

Rypins, 1956 — S. Rypins, "Two Inedited Leaves of Codex N," *Journal of Biblical Literature,* 75 (1956), 27–39.

Sachsen, 1912 — Johann Georg, Herzog zu Sachsen, *Tagebuchblätter aus Nordsyrien* (Leipzig, 1912).

Saller and Bagatti, 1949 — S. J. Saller and B. Bagatti, *The Town of Nebo (Khirbet el-Mekhayyat), with a Brief Survey of Other Ancient Christian Monuments in Trans-Jordan* (Jerusalem, 1949).

Sarre and Herzfeld, 1911 — F. P. T. Sarre and E. Herzfeld, *Archäologische Reise im Euphrat- und Tigrisgebiet,* 4 vols. (Berlin, 1911–1920).

Schrader, 1979 — J. L. Schrader, "Antique and Early Christian Sources for the Riha and Stuma Patens," *Gesta,* 18/1 (1979), 147–156.

Schwartz, 1935 — *Concilium universale chalcedonense, I,* E. Schwartz, ed. (Berlin/Leipzig, 1935).

SEG — *Supplementum epigraphicum graecum,* ed. P. Roussel *et al.*, vols. 1–32 (Leiden, 1923–1982).

Seibt and Sanikidze, 1981 — W. Seibt and T. Sanikidze, *Schatzkammer Georgien: Mittelalterliche Kunst aus dem Staatlichen Kunstmuseum Tbilisi,* Künstlerhaus, Vienna, 1981 (Vienna, 1981) (exhibition catalogue).

Ševčenko, 1966 — I. Ševčenko, "The Early Period of the Sinai Monastery in the Light of its Inscriptions," *Dumbarton Oaks Papers,* 20 (1966), 255–264.

Severus, *Homily* — *Les Homiliae Cathedrales de Sévère d'Antioche. Homélies XCIX à CIII,* I. Guidi, ed., *Patrologia orientalis,* 22 (1930), 201–311.

Severus, *Letters* — *The Sixth Book of the Select Letters of Severus, Patriarch of Antiochia,* E. W. Brooks, ed. and trans., 2 vols. (London, 1902–1904).

Seyrig, 1939 — H. Seyrig, "Antiquités syriennes, Séleucie de Pierie," *Syria,* 20 (1939), 306–309.

Seyrig, 1952 — H. Seyrig, "Antiquités syriennes. 53. Antiquités de la necropole d'Emèse," *Syria,* 29 (1952), 204–250.

Shelton, 1981 — J. K. Shelton, *The Esquiline Treasure* (London, 1981).

Sherlock, 1974 — D. Sherlock, "Zu einer Fundliste antiker Silberlöffel," *Bericht der Römisch-Germanischen Kommission,* 54, 1973 (Berlin, 1974), 203–211.

Sodini and Tate, 1984 — J.-P. Sodini and G. Tate, "Maisons d'époque romaine et byzantine (IIe-VIe siècles) du Massif Calcaire de Syrie du Nord: étude typologique," *Apamée de Syrie. Bilan des recherches archéologiques 1973–1979. Aspects de l'architecture domestique d'Apamée.* (Brussels, 1984), 377–430.

Sodini *et al.,* 1980 — J.-P. Sodini, G. Tate, B. and S. Bavant, J.-L. Biscop, and D. Orssaud, "Déhès (Syrie du Nord). Campagnes I–III (1976–1978). Recherches sur l'habitat rural," *Syria,* 57 (1980), 1–304.

Sotheby's 1973 — Sotheby & Co. *Catalogue of Egyptian, Western Asiatic, Greek, Etruscan and Roman Antiquities. Ancient Glass and Jewellery, Islamic and Isnik Pottery.* July 9, 1973 (sale catalogue).

Sourdel-Thomine, 1954 — J. Sourdel-Thomine, "Le peuplement de la région des 'villes mortes' (Syrie du nord) à l'époque ayyubide," *Arabica,* I (1954), 187–200.

Sourdel-Thomine, 1956 — J. Sourdel-Thomine, "Steles arabes anciennes de Syrie du nord," *Annales archéologiques Arabes Syriennes. Revue d'archéologie et d'histoire,* 6 (1956), 11–38

Spieser, 1984 — J.-M. Spieser, *Thessalonique et ses monuments du IVe au VIe siècle. Contribution à l'étude d'une ville paléo-chrétienne* (Paris, 1984).

Stein, 1949–1959 — E. Stein, *Histoire du Bas-Empire,* 2 vols. (Paris/Brussels/Amsterdam, 1949–1959).

Strong, 1966 — D. E. Strong, *Greek and Roman Gold and Silver Plate* (Ithaca, N.Y./London, 1966).

Strube, 1979 — C. Strube, "Tempel und Kirche in Me'ez," *Mitteilungen des deutschen Archäologischen Instituts, Abteilung Istanbul,* 29 (1979), 355–365.

Strube, 1983 — C. Strube, "Die Kapitelle von Qasr ibn Wardan," *Jahrbuch für Antike und Christentum,* 26 (1983), 59–106.

Strzygowski, 1904 — J. Strzygowski, *Koptische Kunst: Catalogue général du Musée du Caire* (Vienna, 1904).

Stylianou, 1969 — A. and J. Stylianou, *The Treasures of Lambousa* (Lapithos, 1969).

Sukenik, 1935 — E. L. Sukenik, "The Ancient Synagogue of el-Hammeh," *Journal of the Palestine Oriental Society,* 15 (1935), 101–180.

Syria, 1983 — "Chronique archéologique," *Syria,* 60 (1983), 271–333.

Tardy, 1984 — Tardy, *Les poinons de garantie internationaux pour l'argent, 15th ed.* (Paris, 1984).

Tchalenko, 1953–1958 — G. Tchalenko, *Villages antiques de la Syrie du nord,* 3 vols. (Paris, 1953–1958).

Theodoret, *Graec. affec. cur.* — *Theodoreti Graecorum affectionum curatio,* I. Raedner, ed. (Leipzig, 1904).

Topography, 1889–1900 — R. Garrett, *Topography and Itinerary,* AAES, I (New York, 1914).

Treasury, 1984 — *The Treasury of San Marco, Venice,* The Metropolitan Museum of Art, New York, *etc.,* 1985 (Milan, 1984) (exhibition catalogue).

Trempelas, 1940 — P. N. Trempelas, "He akolouthia ton mnestron kai tou gamou," *Theologia,* 18 (1940).

Trilling, 1982 — J. Trilling, "The Roman Heritage: Textiles from Egypt and the Eastern Mediterranean, 300 to 600 AD," *Textile Museum Journal,* 21 (1982).

Tsaferis and Bar-Lev, 1976 — V. Tsaferis and S. Bar-Lev, "A Byzantine Inscription from Khisfin," *Atiqot,* English series, 11 (1976), 114, f.

Ulbert, 1977 — T. Ulbert, "Eine neuentdeckte Inschrift aus Resafa (Syrien)," *Archäologischer Anzeiger,* (1977), 563–569.

Van den Ven, 1962/1970 — *La vie ancienne de S. Syméon Stylite le Jeune (521–592),* P. van den Ven, ed. and trans., 2 vols., Subsidia hagiographica, Société des Bollandistes, 32 (Brussels, 1962, 1970).

Vavritsas, 1957 — A. K. Vavritsas, "Anaskaphe Krategou Mytilenes," *Praktika tes en Athenais Archaiologikes Hetaireias* (1954/1957), 317–329.

Vermeule, 1971 — C. Vermeule, III, "Recent Museum Acquisitions. Greek, Etruscan, Roman Gold and Silver—II: Hellenistic to Late Antique Gold and Silver," *Burlington Magazine,* 113 (1971) 396–406.

Vikan, 1982 — G. Vikan, *Byzantine Pilgrimage Art,* Dumbarton Oaks Byzantine Collection Publications, 5 (Washington, D.C., 1982).

Vikan, 1984 — G. Vikan, "Art, Medicine, and Magic in Early Byzantium," *Dumbarton Oaks Papers,* 38 (1984), 65–86.

Vikan and Nesbitt, 1980 — G. Vikan and J. Nesbitt, *Security in Byzantium: Locking, Sealing, and Weighing,* Dumbarton Oaks Byzantine Collection Publications, 2 (Washington, D.C., 1980).

Vincent and Abel, 1926 — L. H. Vincent and F-M. Abel, *Jérusalem nouvelle* (Paris, 1926).

Volbach, 1921[I] — W. F. Volbach, *"Metallarbeiten des christlichen Kultes in der Spätantike und im frühen Mittelalter,"* Kataloge des Römisch-Germanischen Zentralmuseums, Mainz, 9 (Mainz, 1921).

Volbach, 1921[II] — W. F. Volbach, "Die Silberschatz von Antiochia," *Zeitschrift für bildende Kunst,* N. F. 32 (1921), 110–113.

Volbach 1931/1932 — W. F. Volbach, "Die byzantinische Ausstellung in Paris," *Zeitschrift für bildende Kunst,* 65 (1931/1932), 102–113.

Volbach, 1958 — W. F. Volbach, *Frühchristliche Kunst: Die Kunst der Spätantike in West- und Ostrom* (Munich, 1958).

Volbach, 1963/1964 — W. F. Volbach, "Silber-, Zinn- und Holzgegenstände aus der Kirche St. Lorenz bei Paspals," *Zeitschrift für schweizerische Archaeologie und Kunstgeschichte,* 23 (1963/1964), 75–82.

Volbach, 1976 — W. F. Volbach, *Elfenbeinarbeiten der Spätantike und des frühen Mittelalters,* Römisch-Germanisches Zentralmuseum zu Mainz, Katalog vor- und frühgeschichtlicher Altertümer, 7, 3rd ed. (Mainz, 1976).

Von Hessen *et al.,* 1977 — O. von Hessen, W. Kurze, and C. A. Mastrelli, *Il tesoro di Galognano* (Florence, 1977).

Walters, 1921 — H. B. Walters, *Catalogue of the Silver Plate (Greek, Etruscan, and Roman) in the British Museum* (London, 1921).

Watts, 1922 — W. W. Watts, *Catalogue of Chalices and Other Communion Vessels* (London, 1922).

Weigand, 1937 — E. Weigand, "Ein bisher verkanntes Diptychon Symmachorum," *Jahrbuch des deutschen Archäologischen Instituts,* 52 (1937), 121–138.

Weitzmann, 1947 — K. Weitzmann, "Byzantine Art and Scholarship in America," *American Journal of Archaeology,* 51 (1947), 394–418.

Weitzmann, 1976 — K. Weitzmann, *The Monastery of Saint Catherine at Mount Sinai. The Icons, I: From the Sixth to the Tenth Century* (Princeton, 1976).

Weitzmann, 1977 — K. Weitzmann, *Late Antique and Early Christian Book Illumination* (London, 1977).

Weitzmann and Ševčenko, 1963 — K. Weitzmann and I. Ševčenko, "The Moses Cross at Sinai," *Dumbarton Oaks Papers,* 17 (1963), 385–398.

Wessel, 1964 — K. Wessel, *Abendmahl und Apostelkommunion* (Recklinghausen, 1964).

Wessel, 1969 — K. Wessel, "Lo sviluppo stilistico della toreutica nell' epoca paleobizantina (da Giustiniano I ad Eraclio)," *XVI Corsi di cultura sull'arte ravennate e bizantina* (1969), 353–389.

Wessel, 1971 — K. Wessel, "Flabellum," *Reallexikon zur byzantinischen Kunst, II* (Stuttgart, 1971), cols. 550–555.

Wilkinson, 1972 — J. Wilkinson, "The Tomb of Christ: An Outline of its Structural History," *Levant,* 4 (1972), 83–97.

Wilkinson, 1977 — J. Wilkinson, *Jerusalum Pilgrims Before the Crusades* (Warminster, 1977).

Wilkinson, 1981 — J. Wilkinson, *Egeria's Travels to the Holy Land* (Jerusalem/Warminster, 1981).

Wilpert, 1926 — J. Wilpert, "Early Christian Sculpture: Its Restoration and Its Modern Manufacture," *Art Bulletin,* 9 (1926), 89–141.

Wilpert, 1927 — J. Wilpert, "Restauro di sculture cristiane antiche e antichitá moderne," *Rivista di archeologia cristiana,* 4 (1927), 59–101, 289–343.

Wixom, 1970 — W. D. Wixom, "A Mystery Spoon from the Fourth Century," *Bulletin of The Cleveland Museum of Art,* 57 (1970), 141–148.

Woolley, 1924 — L. Woolley, in "Proceedings of the Society for the Promotion of Roman Studies, 1924–1925," *Journal of Roman Studies,* 14 (1924), 281–287.

Wright, 1870–1872 — W. Wright, *Catalogue of the Syriac Manuscripts in the British Museum,* 3 vols. (London, 1870–1872).

Wulff, 1909 — O. Wulff, *Altchristliche Bildwerke,* Königliche Museen zu Berlin, Beschreibung der Bildwerke der christlichen Epochen, 3, 1 (Berlin, 1909).

Wulff, 1918 — O. Wulff, "Kriegszuwachs in der altchristlische-byzantinischen Skulpturensammlung," *Amtliche Berichte aus den Königlichen Kunstsammlungen,* 39 (1918), 238–256.

Zahn, 1921 — R. Zahn, *Galerie Bachstitz—S'Gravenhage. Antike, islamische Arbeiten der Kleinkunst und des Kunstgewerbes* (Berlin, 1921) (sale catalogue).

Zahn, 1928 — O. Lenel and R. Zahn, "Diatreta," *Archäologischer Anzeiger,* 1928, cols. 563–570.

Zalesskaja, 1982 — V. N. Zalesskaja, "Die byzantinische Toreutik des 6. Jahrhunderts: Einige Aspekte ihrer Erforschung," *Metallkunst von der Spätantike bis zum ausgehenden Mittelalter,* A. Effenberger, ed. (Berlin, 1982), 97–111.

Zwisa, 1893 — see *Gesta*.

INDEX

This index includes names, technical terms, and devotional formulae; silver treasures, well-known art objects; place names (ancient and modern); iconography; dealers, owners (present and former), and collections; terms relating to manufacture and conservation, *et cetera*.
CI = Chapter I; E1 = Entry no. 1; (E67-E72) = prefatory summary.

List of Catalogued Objects

(= Objects in the Exhibition)*

No.	Object	Location	Accession No.
*1	Chalice	Baltimore, The Walters Art Gallery	57.633
*2	Chalice	Baltimore, The Walters Art Gallery	57.642
*3	Chalice	Baltimore, The Walters Art Gallery	57.636
*4	Paten	Baltimore, The Walters Art Gallery	57.644
*5	Paten	Baltimore, The Walters Art Gallery	57.637
*6	Paten	Baltimore, The Walters Art Gallery	57.643
*7	Cross	Baltimore, The Walters Art Gallery	57.632
*8	Cross	Baltimore, The Walters Art Gallery	57.641
*9	Cross	Baltimore, The Walters Art Gallery	57.629
*10	Cross	Baltimore, The Walters Art Gallery	57.630
*11	Lampstand	Baltimore, The Walters Art Gallery	57.634
*12	Lampstand	Baltimore, The Walters Art Gallery	57.635
*13	Lamp	Baltimore, The Walters Art Gallery	57.640
*14	Ewer	Baltimore, The Walters Art Gallery	57.645
*15	Flask	Baltimore, The Walters Art Gallery	57.639
*16	Bowl	Baltimore, The Walters Art Gallery	57.631
*17	Box	Baltimore, The Walters Art Gallery	57.638
*18	Spoon	Baltimore, The Walters Art Gallery	57.651
*19	Spoon	Baltimore, The Walters Art Gallery	57.649
*20	Spoon	Baltimore, The Walters Art Gallery	57.647
21	Spoon	Present Location Unknown	
*22	Spoon	Baltimore, The Walters Art Gallery	57.648
*23	Ladle	Baltimore, The Walters Art Gallery	57.646
*24	Strainer	Baltimore, The Walters Art Gallery	57.650
25	Strainer	Present Location Unknown	
*26	Strainer	Jerusalem, Museum, Church of St. Anne	
*27	Chalice	Jerusalem, Museum, Church of St. Anne	
*28	Chalice	Washington, D.C., W. L. Eagleton Collection (on loan to Dumbarton Oaks)	
*29	Chalice	London, British Museum	1914.4–15.1
*30	Chalice	Washington, D.C., Dumbarton Oaks Collection	55.18
31	Fan	Istanbul, Archaeological Museum	3758
*32	Fan	Washington, D.C., Dumbarton Oaks Collection	36.23
33	Lamp	Bern, Abegg Stiftung	8.114.64
34	Paten	Istanbul, Archaeological Museum	3759
*35	Paten	Washington, D.C., Dumbarton Oaks Collection	24.5
36	Paten	Istanbul, Archaeological Museum	3761
37	Ewer	Bern, Abegg Stiftung	8.112.64
38	Ewer	Bern, Abegg Stiftung	8.113.64
39	Paten	Istanbul, Archaeological Museum	3760
*40	Lamp?	New York, The Metropolitan Museum of Art (The Cloisters Collection, 1950)	50.4
*41	Chalice	New York, The Metropolitan Museum of Art (Fletcher Fund, 1947)	47.100.34
*42a	Cross Revetment	New York, The Metropolitan Museum of Art (Fletcher Fund, 1950)	50.5.3
*42b, c	Revetment (Medallions)	Paris, Musée du Louvre, Département des Antiquités Grecques et Romaines	MNE 632 MNE 633
43	Cross	Present Location Unknown	
*44	Plaque	New York, The Metropolitan Museum of Art (Fletcher Fund, 1950)	50.5.1
*45	Plaque	New York, The Metropolitan Museum of Art (Fletcher Fund, 1950)	50.5.2
*46	Plaque	New York, The Metropolitan Museum of Art (Fletcher Fund, 1947)	47.100.36
*47	Plaque	Paris, Musée du Louvre, Département des Antiquités Grecques et Romaines	MNE 659
*48	Mirror	New York, The Metropolitan Museum of Art (Fletcher Fund, 1947; gift Fahim Kouchakji, 1952)	47.100.35 52.37
*49	Spoon	Washington, D.C., Dumbarton Oaks Collection	37.35
*50	Spoon	Washington, D.C., Dumbarton Oaks Collection	37.36
*51	Spoon	Washington, D.C., Dumbarton Oaks Collection	37.37
*52	Spoon	Washington, D.C., Dumbarton Oaks Collection	37.38
*53	Spoon	Washington, D.C., Dumbarton Oaks Collection	37.39
*54	Spoon	Washington, D.C., Dumbarton Oaks Collection	37.40
*55	Spoon	Washington, D.C., Dumbarton Oaks Collection	37.41
*56	Spoon	Washington, D.C., Dumbarton Oaks Collection	37.42
*57	Chalice	Cleveland, The Cleveland Museum of Art (Purchase from the J. H. Wade Fund)	50.378
*58	Chalice	Cleveland, The Cleveland Museum of Art (Purchase from the J. H. Wade Fund)	50.379
*59	Chalice	Cleveland, The Cleveland Museum of Art (Purchase from the J. H. Wade Fund)	50.380
*60	Paten	Cleveland, The Cleveland Museum of Art (Purchase from the J. H. Wade Fund)	50.381
61	Chalice	Bern, Abegg Stiftung	8.39.63
62	Chalice	Bern, Abegg Stiftung	8.38.63

63	Paten	Bern, Abegg Stiftung	8.37.63
64	Paten	Bern, Abegg Stiftung	8.36.63
*65	Cross	Washington, D.C., Dumbarton Oaks Collection	55.17
65a	Fragmentary Fitting for a Cross Staff	Present Location Unknown	
66	Seal	Bern, Abegg Stiftung	8.41.63
*67	Cross	Toledo, The Toledo Museum of Art (Gift of Edward Drummond Libbey)	53.48a
*68	Cross	Baltimore, The Walters Art Gallery	57.1827
*69	Spoon	Toledo, The Toledo Museum of Art (Gift of Edward Drummond Libbey)	53.48b
*70	Box	Baltimore, The Walters Art Gallery	57.1835
71	Plaque	Paris, Musée du Louvre, Département des Antiquités Grecques et Romaines	Bj 2180
*72a-n	Fourteen Plaquettes	Baltimore, The Walters Art Gallery	57.1865
*73	Chalice	Boston, Museum of Fine Arts (Edward J. and Mary S. Holmes Fund)	1971.633
74	Paten	Beirut, F. Alouf Collection	
*75	Paten	Switzerland, Private Collection	
76	Cross	Istanbul, Archaeological Museum	8051
*77	Chalice	Siena, Pinacoteca, Soprintendenza per i Beni Artistici e Storici di Siena	I.S.B. 22
*78	Chalice	Siena, Pinacoteca, Soprintendenza per i Beni Artistici e Storici di Siena	I.S.B. 23
*79	Chalice	Siena, Pinacoteca, Soprintendenza per i Beni Artistici e Storici di Siena	I.S.B. 24
*80	Chalice	Siena, Pinacoteca, Soprintendenza per i Beni Artistici e Storici di Siena	I.S.B. 25
*81	Paten	Siena, Pinacoteca, Soprintendenza per i Beni Artistici e Storici di Siena	I.S.B. 26
*82	Spoon	Siena, Pinacoteca, Soprintendenza per i Beni Artistici e Storici di Siena	I.S.B. 27
*83	Box	St. Louis, The St. Louis Art Museum	44.1924
*84	Ewer	Paris, Musée du Louvre, Département des Antiquités Grecques et Romaines	Bj 1895
*85	Censer	New York, The Metropolitan Museum of Art (Rogers Fund, 1985)	1985.123
*86	Flask	New York, The Metropolitan Museum of Art (purchase, Rogers Fund, and Schimmel Foundation, Inc. gift, 1984)	1984.196
*87	Vellum Leaf	New York, Pierpont Morgan Library	cod. M874
*88	Vellum Codex	London, British Library	cod. Add. 12156
*89	Vellum Codex	London, British Library	cod. Add. 14472
*90a, b	Two Silk Fragments	Washington, D.C., Textile Museum	11.21 11.26
91	Papyrus Inventory	Oxford, Bodleian Library	cod. gr. th. d.2[P]
*92	Ring	Houston, Menil Foundation Collection	R24
*93	Pendant	Houston, Menil Foundation Collection	824
*94	Armband	New York, Private Collection	
*95	Plate	Worcester, Worcester Art Museum	1940.17
96	Bowl	Baltimore, The Baltimore Museum of Art	1940.33
*97	Ewer	Washington, D.C., Dumbarton Oaks Collection	40.24
98	Statuette	Antakya, Hatay Archaeological Museum	
*99	Marble Statue	Worcester, Worcester Art Museum	1940.9
*100	Marble Relief	Baltimore, The Baltimore Museum of Art (Antioch Project Fund)	44.170A
*101	Plate	Richmond, Virginia Museum of Fine Arts (The Williams Fund)	66.77
*102	Plate	Boston, Museum of Fine Arts (Theodora Wilbour Fund in memory of Zoë Wilbour)	69.1146
*103	Plate	Baltimore, The Walters Art Gallery	57.652
*104	Plate	New York, The Metropolitan Museum of Art (Fletcher Fund, 1952)	52.25.2
*105	Plate	Washington, D.C., Dumbarton Oaks Collection	60.60
*106	Plate	Washington, D.C., Dumbarton Oaks Collection	51.24

LIST OF LENDERS TO THE EXHIBITION

Baltimore, The Baltimore Museum of Art
Baltimore, The Walters Art Gallery
Boston, Museum of Fine Arts
Cleveland, The Cleveland Museum of Art
Houston, Menil Foundation Collection
Jerusalem, Museum, Church of St. Anne
London, British Library
London, British Museum
New York, Pierpont Morgan Library
New York, Private Collection
New York, The Metropolitan Museum of Art
Paris, Musée du Louvre
Richmond, Virginia Museum of Fine Arts
Siena, Pinacoteca
St. Louis, The St. Louis Art Museum
Switzerland, Private Collection
Toledo, The Toledo Museum of Art
The Honorable W. L. Eagleton, United States Ambassador to Syria
Washington, D.C., Dumbarton Oaks
Washington, D.C., Textile Museum
Worcester, Worcester Art Museum

LIST OF CATALOGUED OBJECTS BY COLLECTION

(= Objects in Exhibition)*

Antakya, Hatay Archaeological Museum	No. 98
Baltimore, The Baltimore Museum of Art, no. 1940.33	No. 96
The Baltimore Museum of Art, no. 44.170A	No. 100*
Baltimore, The Walters Art Gallery, no. 57.629	No. 9*
The Walters Art Gallery, no. 57.630	No. 10*
The Walters Art Gallery, no. 57.631	No. 16*
The Walters Art Gallery, no. 57.632	No. 7*
The Walters Art Gallery, no. 57.633	No. 1*
The Walters Art Gallery, no. 57.634	No. 11*
The Walters Art Gallery, no. 57.635	No. 12*
The Walters Art Gallery, no. 57.636	No. 3*
The Walters Art Gallery, no. 57.637	No. 5*
The Walters Art Gallery, no. 57.638	No. 17*
The Walters Art Gallery, no. 57.639	No. 15*
The Walters Art Gallery, no. 57.640	No. 13*
The Walters Art Gallery, no. 57.641	No. 8*
The Walters Art Gallery, no. 57.642	No. 2*
The Walters Art Gallery, no. 57.643	No. 6*
The Walters Art Gallery, no. 57.644	No. 4*
The Walters Art Gallery, no. 57.645	No. 14*
The Walters Art Gallery, no. 57.646	No. 23*
The Walters Art Gallery, no. 57.647	No. 20*
The Walters Art Gallery, no. 57.648	No. 22*
The Walters Art Gallery, no. 57.649	No. 19*
The Walters Art Gallery, no. 57.650	No. 24*
The Walters Art Gallery, no. 57.651	No. 18*
The Walters Art Gallery, no. 57.652	No. 103*
The Walters Art Gallery, no. 57.1826; 57.1865	No. 72*
The Walters Art Gallery, no. 57.1827	No. 68*
The Walters Art Gallery, no. 57.1835	No. 70*
Beirut, The Alouf Collection	No. 74
Bern, Abegg Stiftung, no. 8.36.63	No. 64
Abegg Stiftung, no. 8.37.63	No. 63
Abegg Stiftung, no. 8.38.63	No. 62
Abegg Stiftung, no. 8.39.63	No. 61
Abegg Stiftung, no. 8.41.63	No. 66
Abegg Stiftung, no. 8.112.64	No. 37
Abegg Stiftung, no. 8.113.64	No. 38
Abegg Stiftung, no. 8.114.64	No. 33
Boston, Museum of Fine Arts, no. 69.1146	No. 102*
Museum of Fine Arts, no. 1971.633	No. 73*
Cleveland, The Cleveland Museum of Art, no. 50.378	No. 57*
The Cleveland Museum of Art, no. 50.379	No. 58*
The Cleveland Museum of Art, no. 50.380	No. 59*
The Cleveland Museum of Art, no. 50.381	No. 60*
Houston, The Menil Foundation Collection, no. R24	No. 92*
The Menil Foundation Collection, no. 824	No. 93*
Istanbul, Archaeological Museum, no. 3758	No. 31
Archaeological Museum, no. 3759	No. 34
Archaeological Museum, no. 3760	No. 39
Archaeological Museum, no. 3761	No. 36
Archaeological Museum, no. 8051	No. 76
Jerusalem, Museum, Church of St. Anne	No. 26*
Museum, Church of St. Anne	No. 27*
London, British Library, cod. Add. 12156	No. 88*
British Library, cod. Add. 14472	No. 89*
London, British Museum, no. 1914.4–15.1	No. 29*
New York, Pierpont Morgan Library, cod. M874	No. 87*
New York, Private Collection	No. 94*
New York, The Metropolitan Museum of Art, nos. 43.100.35; 52.37	No. 48*
The Metropolitan Museum of Art, no. 47.100.34	No. 41*
The Metropolitan Museum of Art, no. 47.100.36	No. 46*
The Metropolitan Museum of Art, no. 50.4	No. 40*
The Metropolitan Museum of Art, no. 50.5.1	No. 44*
The Metropolitan Museum of Art, no. 50.5.2	No. 45*
The Metropolitan Museum of Art, no. 50.5.3	No. 42a*
The Metropolitan Museum of Art, no. 52.25.2	No. 104*
The Metropolitan Museum of Art, no. 1984.196	No. 86*
The Metropolitan Museum of Art, no. 1985.123	No. 85*
Oxford, Bodleian Library, cod. gr. th. d.2[P]	No. 91
Paris, Musée du Louvre, no. Bj 1895	No. 84*
Musée du Louvre, no. Bj 2180	No. 71
Musée du Louvre, no. MNE 632	No. 42b*
Musée du Louvre, no. MNE 633	No. 42c*
Musée du Louvre, no. MNE 659	No. 47*
Present Location Unknown	No. 21
	No. 25
	No. 43
	No. 65a
Richmond, Virginia Museum of Fine Arts, no. 66.77	No. 101*
Siena, Pinacoteca, no. I.S.B. 22	No. 77*
Pinacoteca, no. I.S.B. 23	No. 78*
Pinacoteca, no. I.S.B. 24	No. 79*
Pinacoteca, no. I.S.B. 25	No. 80*
Pinacoteca, no. I.S.B. 26	No. 81*
Pinacoteca, no. I.S.B. 27	No. 82*
St. Louis, The St. Louis Art Museum, no. 44.1924	No. 83*
Switzerland, Private Collection	No. 75*
Toledo, The Toledo Museum of Art, no. 53.48a	No. 67*
The Toledo Museum of Art, no. 53.48b	No. 69*
Washington, D.C., Dumbarton Oaks, no. 24.5	No. 35*
Dumbarton Oaks, no. 36.23	No. 32*
Dumbarton Oaks, no. 37.35	No. 49*
Dumbarton Oaks, no. 37.36	No. 50*
Dumbarton Oaks, no. 37.37	No. 51*
Dumbarton Oaks, no. 37.38	No. 52*
Dumbarton Oaks, no. 37.39	No. 53*
Dumbarton Oaks, no. 37.40	No. 54*
Dumbarton Oaks, no. 37.41	No. 55*
Dumbarton Oaks, no. 37.42	No. 56*
Dumbarton Oaks, no. 40.24	No. 97*
Dumbarton Oaks, no. 51.24	No. 106*
Dumbarton Oaks, no. 55.17	No. 65*
Dumbarton Oaks, no. 55.18	No. 30*
Dumbarton Oaks, no. 60.60	No. 105*
Washington, D.C., Dumbarton Oaks, Eagleton Collection (on extended loan)	No. 28*
Washington, D.C., Textile Museum, nos. 11.21, 11.26	No. 90a,b*
Worcester, Worcester Art Museum, no. 1940.9	No. 99*
Worcester Art Museum, no. 1940.17	No. 95*

List of Catalogued Objects by Major Treasures

Reconstructed Kaper Koraon Treasure	Nos. 1–56
Hama Treasure	Nos. 1–29
Stuma Treasure	Nos. 31, 33, 34, 36, 39
Riha Treasure	Nos. 30, 32, 35, 37, 38
Antioch Treasure	Nos. 40–56
Beth Misona Treasure	Nos. 57–60
Phela Treasure	Nos. 61–66
Ma'aret en-Noman Treasure	Nos. 67–72
Marato tes Myrtes(?) Treasure	Nos. 73, 74
Sarabaon Treasure	No. 75
Čaginkom(?) Treasure	No. 76
Gallunianu Treasure	Nos. 77–82
Daphne Treasure	Nos. 95–100
Cyprus Treasure(?)	Nos. 103–105
Smyrna Treasure	No. 106

List of Catalogued Objects by Object Type

SILVER

Armband	No. 94
Boxes	Nos. 17, 70, 83
Bowls	Nos. 16, 96
Censer	No. 85
Chalices	Nos. 1–3, 27–30, 41, 57–59, 61, 62, 73, 77–80
Crosses	Nos. 7–10, 42, 43, 65, 67, 68, 76
Ewers	Nos. 14, 37, 38, 84, 97
Fans	Nos. 31, 32
Flasks	Nos. 15, 86
Ladle	No. 23
Lamps	Nos. 13, 33, 40(?)
Lampstands	Nos. 11, 12
Mirror	No. 48
Patens	Nos. 4–6, 34–36, 39, 60, 63, 64, 74, 75, 81
Pendant	No. 93
Plaques (bookcovers?)	Nos. 44–47
Plaques, plaquettes (votive)	Nos. 71, 72
Plates	Nos. 95, 101–106
Ring	No. 92
Seal	No. 66
Spoons	Nos. 18–22, 49–56, 69, 82
Statuette	No. 98
Strainers	Nos. 24–26

NON-SILVER

Manuscripts	Nos. 87–89
Marble sculpture	Nos. 99, 100
Papyrus	No. 91
Silk	No. 90

Photo Credits

Abegg Stiftung, 33, 37, 38, 61–64, 66
Bodleian Library, 91
Pierre Bonnet, W.F., 26
Boston Museum of Fine Arts, 73, 102
British Library, 88, 89
British Museum, 29
J.-P. Caillet, Musée de Cluny, 11
Department of Archaeology, University of Newcastle-upon-Tyne, 35
Department of Conservation and Technical Research, The Walters Art Gallery, 1–12, 14, 15, 18, 19, 20, 22, 23
Dumbarton Oaks, 28, 30, 32, 35, 49–56, 65, 65a, 97, 105, 106
Erica Dodd, 74
Fahim Kouchakji, CII, 21, 25
Menil Foundation, 92, 93
Marlia Mundell Mango, CII, 31, 34, 36–39, 48, 76, 98
Musée du Louvre, 42, 47, 71, 84
Pierpont Morgan Library, 87
Princeton University, 95, 96
Ihor Ševčenko, 27
Soprintendenza per i Beni Artistici e Storici di Siena, 77–82
Textile Museum, 90
The Cleveland Museum of Art, 57–60
The Metropolitan Museum of Art, CII, 40–42, 44–46, 48, 85, 86, 100, 104
The St. Louis Art Museum, 83
The Toledo Museum of Art, 67, 69
Virginia Museum of Fine Arts, 101
The Walters Art Gallery, CIII, 72, 103
The Walters Art Gallery, Susan Tobin, CIII, 1–20, 22–24, 68, 70, 72, 75
Worcester Art Museum, 95
David Wright, 35